# BABYN YAR
## HISTORY AND MEMORY

# BABYN YAR
## HISTORY AND MEMORY

*Edited by*

Vladyslav Hrynevych and Paul Robert Magocsi

Distributed by the University of Toronto Press
for the
Chair of Ukrainian Studies
University of Toronto
2023

Publication of this volume was made possible
by the generous support of the Ukrainian Jewish Encounter
Toronto, Canada
The editors appreciate the support of the sponsor and acknowledge
that the views expressed herein are not necessarily those of the
Ukrainian Jewish Encounter.

---

Library and Archives Canada Cataloguing in Publication

Title: Babyn Yar : history and memory / edited by Vladyslav Hrynevych and Paul Robert Magocsi.
Other titles: History and memory
Names: Hrynevych, Vladyslav, editor. | Magocsi, Paul R., editor. | University of Toronto. Chair of Ukrainian Studies, publisher.
Description: Includes bibliographical references and index. | Text in English; some chapters translated from the Russian and Ukrainian.
Identifiers: Canadiana 20230219624 | ISBN 9780772751164 (hardcover)
Subjects: LCSH: Jews—Ukraine—Kyïv—History. | LCSH: Babi Yar Massacre, Ukraine, 1941. | LCSH: Holocaust, Jewish (1939-1945)—Ukraine—Kyïv—History.
Classification: LCC DS135.U42 K544 2023 | DDC 940.53/18094777—dc23

Translation from Russian: Marco Carynnyk—Chapter 5
Translations from Ukrainian: Marta Olynyk—Chapters 1, 2, 6-9, and 11-13.
Design and layout by John Beadle


Printed in Canada


ISBN: 978-0-7727-5116-4

# Preface

*Norman M. Naimark*

Genocide has been part of human history from its very beginnings. Ancient empires subjected their own and conquered peoples to elimination, just as modern states destroyed minority peoples through programs of mass murder. Communist governments engaged in genocide, as have ostensibly democratic ones. Settler genocide—sometimes known as colonial genocide—condemned entire groups of indigenous peoples to death as a way to seize territory and resources. Recent history seems no more immune to genocide than the past. Rwanda, Bosnia, Darfur, Congo, and the Islamic State's attack against the Yazidi Kurds remind us that political leaders and their followers, motivated by ideology and immediate gains, are ready to isolate and murder alleged enemies both within their own states and in conquered territories.

Within this dark tableau of the history of genocide, the Holocaust stands out as a particularly beastly example of human evil. Hitler and the Nazis, along with their helpmates throughout Europe, designated the Jews for elimination and did everything they could to pursue their lethal aims. As World War II progressed and German victory became increasingly unlikely, the Third Reich only intensified its efforts to eliminate every man, woman, and child of Jewish origin, sometimes sacrificing its own military needs to implement the "Final Solution." Close to six million Jews fell to the voracious Moloch known as Nazi Germany. Genocide has a way of spreading to envelop other groups of victims, and the Holocaust was no exception. Millions of Roma and Sinti, Soviet POWs, Poles and Ukrainians, the disabled and handicapped were pursed and killed by the Nazi mass murderers.

In both a historical and symbolical sense, Babyn Yar is crucial to any account of the Holocaust. It was one of the first and largest massacres of the Jews in the Nazi campaign of mass killing. Already in mid-August 1941, the Germans had begun to murder indiscriminately men, women, and children. When they seized Kyiv on September 19, 1941, their intention was to eliminate the city's entire remaining Jewish population, which in and of itself constituted a significant escalation in their conception of eliminating the Jews from the European continent. There had been other massacres—the killing of 23,600 Jews in Kamianets-Podilskyi the most notable—but nothing with the genocidal fury of Babyn Yar. The Nazis used as a pretense for rounding up the Jews, if they needed any, the explosions and subsequent fires on the Khreshchatyk organized by Soviet sappers before the Red Army evacuated the city.

On September 28, the infamous Nazi order was issued for all the Jews of Kyiv to appear at 8 o'clock in the morning near the Lukianivka freight train station, according to rumor, for deportation. The images of the Babyn Yar massacre of nearly 34,000 Jews on September 29 and 30 that followed are etched in stone in the historical memory of the Holocaust: crowds of Jews of every age, carrying their possessions while wending their way to the unexpected rendezvous with death; increasingly frightened and suspicious victims entering a heavily guarded compound manned by Germans and Ukrainian auxiliary police with no escape; Nazi soldiers forcing them to strip and leave their possessions, passports, and clothes in piles behind them, sorted and carted off mostly by the Ukrainian police; then the beating, the screaming, the German firing squads, executions, and masses of naked bodies falling or thrown to the bottom of the ravine and buried; a few lucky survivors miraculously crawling out of the still undulating mass graves, surviving to tell the tale of horror afterwards.

According to Vitaliy Nakhmanovych, over the course of the next few months and years, another 30,000 or so Jews were murdered at Babyn Yar, along with an additional 30,000 Ukrainian, Roma and Sinti, and Soviet POWs of various nationalities. By the end, approximately 100,000 people were murdered and buried at Babyn Yar. The exact numbers are hard to know.

Few who encounter the history of Babyn Yar can forget the "denouement" of the destruction. In late August and September 1943, teams of prisoners from the Syrets concentration camp, mostly surviving Jews, were forced by the SS Special Commando 1005 to exhume the bodies at Babyn Yar and place them on huge pyres that were built from ransacked rail ties and from tombstones from the Jewish Cemetery. This was gruesome work, as many of the bodies were melded with others; children were hard to pry loose from their mothers' arms. Pouring incendiaries on the stacked rows of corpses and setting them on fire, the chained and starving participants in these ghastly details, who were themselves slated for extermination, finished the job by sifting through the ashes, separating out pieces of skeleton to be crushed, and scattering the ashes in the ravine. The idea was to destroy the evidence before the Soviet armies broke through to the city in early November 1943.

The shattering impact of Babyn Yar is most notable among Ukrainians and East European Jews and their progeny, who know the history of the Holocaust and of World War II on the eastern front. The Soviet intelligentsia was moved by the Babyn Yar story through the brilliant poem of Yevgeny Yevtushenko ("Babi Yar"), published in *Literaturnaia gazeta* in September 1961, and by the 13th Symphony (also named "Babi Yar," after its first movement) by Dmitrii Shostakovich (July 1962), which itself was inspired by Yevtushenko's work. Anatoly Kuznetsov's seminal work, *Babi Yar: A Document in the Form of a Novel*, first published in 1966, broke an important barrier of silence about detailing the events of September 1941.

Regretfully, Western representations of Holocaust memory often have only the vaguest understanding of the killing of Jews in the east, with the exception of the death camps, Auschwitz being most notable for the sheer power of its symbolism as a "site of memory." The mass shooting of Jews in German-occupied Soviet territory attracted less interest than the horrifying images of the gas chambers and the crematoria. One could say the same of scholarly examinations in the West of Babyn Yar, which have been strikingly few and relatively recent. Especially when thinking about reaching the broad Western educated public, Timothy Snyder's important contributions, *Bloodlands* (2010) and *Black Earth* (2015), are the exceptions that prove the rule. Part of the problem with coming to terms with the killing fields in the east, no doubt, had to do with the way

Soviet scholars and memory agents were forced to minimize the specific fate of Soviet Jews murdered by the Nazis in comparison to the suffering and heroism of the Soviet people. But part of the problem in the West was the sheer distance from and ignorance of the wartime suffering and death of Ukrainian Jews.

This important book, *Babyn Yar: History and Memory*, successfully shifts our focus to Kyiv, to the mass murder of Ukrainian Jews there seventy-five years ago, and to the former intersecting ravines—Babyn Yar—where the remains of the bodies of the victims are strewn over an extended mass grave, marked today by scattered monuments of varied provenance. In a series of "state-of-the-art" scholarly articles, complemented by two shorter "memory" pieces, the authors in this book explore the cultural, political, and historiographical dimensions of Babyn Yar, without sparing the reader the sometimes fierce arguments and unbecoming political tensions that lie behind the quest for memorialization. The well-written and expertly translated contributions also tell the uplifting stories of witnesses who insisted on speaking their minds despite the prohibitions of Soviet censors, and of artists—writers, musicians, painters, filmmakers, sculptors, and poets—who felt the overwhelming need to come to terms in their work with the human tragedy of Babyn Yar. The reader is provided with the most up-to-date historical knowledge about Babyn Yar, with the warning that there is still much to be learned about the causes of the mass murder of the Jews of Kyiv and the intersection of events that culminated in those horrible days at the end of September.

Even as it represents one of the most important historical and symbolic events in the history of the Holocaust, indeed in the history of genocide, Babyn Yar is in many ways still unfinished business. There is no consensus on how to memorialize the elimination of the Kyivan Jews that took place there. There is no agreement on how to represent the collaboration of Ukrainian police auxiliaries in the mass murder of the Jews. There is also considerable confusion about how to deal with the multiple interests of victim groups, in addition to the Jews, who lost substantial numbers of their people at Babyn Yar in the years before liberation from the Nazis.

One thing is certain: Babyn Yar will be remembered in Ukraine. In the wake of Ukrainian independence in 1991, the "Orange Revolution" of 2004, and the Euromaidan demonstrations of the winter 2013-14, Ukrainians and Jews have linked arms to honor those who perished at the hands of the Nazis during the war. Babyn Yar unites their common grief and inspires common hopes for amity, justice, and truth. An exemplary book like this one, a book that places scholarly understanding at the core of coming to terms with the many dimensions of Babyn Yar, will surely contribute to that goal.

# Contents

# Contributors

**Karel C. Berkhoff** is a Senior Research Fellow at the NIOD Institute for War, Holocaust and Genocide Studies in Amsterdam, The Netherlands.

**Gelinada Grinchenko** is Professor of Ukrainian Studies at V. N. Karazin Kharkiv National University, Ukraine.

**Vladyslav Hrynevych** is a Senior Research Fellow at the Institute of Political and Ethnic Studies, National Academy of Sciences of Ukraine.

**Mykhailo Kalnytskyi** is a researcher specializing in the history of Kyiv, Ukraine.

**Iryna Klimova** is Director of the Sholem Aleichem Museum branch of the Museum of Kyiv History, Ukraine.

**Asia Kovrigina** is a research fellow at CERILAC, University of Paris, France.

**Oleksandr Kruglov** is a specialist in the history of the Holocaust in the lands of the former Soviet Union.

**Paul Robert Magocsi** is Professor of History and Political Science, Chair of Ukrainian Studies at the University of Toronto, Canada.

**Norman Naimark** is Professor of History at Stanford University, USA.

**Vitaliy Nakhmanovych** is a Senior Research Fellow at the Museum of Kyiv History and Executive Secretary of the "Babyn Yar" Civic Committee, Kyiv, Ukraine.

**Igor Shchupak** is the Director of the Tkuma Ukrainian Institute for the Study of the Holocaust and of the Museum of the Jewish Memory and the Holocaust, Dnipro, Ukraine.

**Natalia Semenenko** is a Senior Research Fellow at the M. T. Rylskyi Institute of Art, Folklore Studies, and Ethnology, National Academy of Sciences of Ukraine.

**Iryna Zakharchuk** is Associate Professor of Ukrainian Literature at Rivne State University of Humanities, Ukraine.

**BABYN YAR**
circa 1940

**CEMETARY**

1 St. Cyril's Orthodox Christian
2 Lukianivka Jewish
3 Karaite
4 Muslim
5 Orthodox Brotherhood (Bratske)
6 Protestant Evangelical
7 Maronite
8 Military / War
9 Lukianivka Municipal
10 German Prisoner of War

**STRUCTURES**

A St. Cyril's-Holy Trinity Church
B St. Cyril's / Pavlov Psychiatric Hospital
C Jewish Cemetary Office (Kontora)
D Lukianivka Freight Station

- Area of mass shootings
- Area of Kurenivka mudslide
- Existing streets circa 1940
- Streets created after 1945
- Barbed wire enclosure

# Introduction

Babyn Yar is a place that has been populated since pre-historic times. During Kyiv's 1,500-year-long existence, Babyn Yar was always a suburb, which thanks to its picturesque landscape was dubbed the "Kyivan Switzerland."

During World War II Babyn Yar, like Auschwitz in present-day Poland, became a prominent symbol of the destruction of the European Jews during the Holocaust. This deadly process began in September 1941 with the murder of nearly 34,000 Jews and continued over the next several years with the shootings of tens of thousands more Jews as well as the Roma people, the mentally ill, Soviet prisoners of war, Ukrainian national activists, Communist party members, and ordinary residents of Kyiv taken as hostages. These people were stripped of their dignity as individuals, subjected to inhuman brutality, and then murdered. Babyn Yar became one of the most traumatic sites in the Ukrainian experience of World War II.

There are still many of mysteries surrounding the history of Babyn Yar. Questions connected with a scholarly understanding of the tragedy seem to be no less profound, obscured, and festering than the very ravines that were located in the suburbs of Kyiv before the war. To this day scholars do not have definite answers, and therefore a significant number of important questions are still under discussion. When the shootings began in Babyn Yar? Who were the first victims? Where were the sites of the mass shootings of the Jews on 29 and 30 September 1941? What was the total number of Jews killed, as well as the number of executed Roma, Soviet POWs, and civilians? Who were the executioners and participants of the crime? What role was played by "ordinary people" from among the local population? Did the "Ukrainian police," the "Bukovinian Battalion," and other Organization of Ukrainian Nationalist (OUN) formations take part in the shootings? The list of questions can be extended. Against this background, numerous myths, blatant falsifications, and even the utter denial of Babyn Yar as a symbol of the Holocaust are put forward not only in the media but also in popular and some scholarly literature.

This book initially took the form of a commemorative volume to mark the occasion of the seventy-fifth anniversary of Babyn Yar, 29-30 September 2016. It was the result of the collaborative effort of scholars working in various disciplines in Canada, France, Israel, the Netherlands, Ukraine, and the United States. All the contributors were united by a desire to inform the international community about the history of one of the twentieth century's most terrible human tragedies and by their realization of the importance of preserving its memory.

The original concept was a book of three sections: "Before Babyn Yar," "The Babyn Yar Tragedy," and "After Babyn Yar." At the center of the story lay the history of a Nazi crime, the politics of memory and forgetting from the Stalinist period to the present day, and the cultural memory of Babyn Yar. The contributions were designed to provoke questions for further discussion, especially since the various authors may have raised the same questions, but did not always arrive at the same answers.

Preparations for commemorating the 75$^{th}$ anniversary of the Babyn Yar tragedy showed us that the past is not some ossified construct, but rather a dynamic phenomenon open to new discoveries. Every generation contributes its own vision and interpretation of the Babyn Yar tragedy. These are expressed in a variety of dimensions: commemorative, mutual recognition, philosophical, and anthropological. Finally, there is a generational aspect to the reinterpretation of this tragedy, as every generation does this in its own way.

Persons who were born in an independent Ukraine are today posing the following questions: What is Babyn Yar in our memory, and how does this memory fit into our understanding of the past and the philosophical and ideological picture of the present and the future? In Babyn Yar Jews were killed only because they were Jews; the Roma people because they were Roma; the mentally ill because they were "defective and useless"; and Ukrainian nationalists and communists because of their political views. In the end, Babyn Yar as a Jewish memory was killed because someone deemed it "politically expedient." Behind all these crimes was a brutal disregard for the most important values: human dignity and the inherent right to life. To know and remember the Babyn Yar tragedy means not allowing such a crime to be repeated. In the Ukrainian experience, Babyn Yar is also a symbolic farewell to empire and its mythological legacy, a return to the work of sadness and the formation of a culture of mourning.

From the perspective of the third millennium, we realize somewhat in astonishment that the lessons of Babyn Yar have not lost their political, moral, or humanistic relevance. Today, the values that were ostensibly regarded as indispensable and inviolable in postwar Europe—respect for human life and ethnic and religious identify, the inadmissibility of using war as a way to change state borders—are once again under threat and being eroded by doubts and nihilism. Humanity's continuing existence, not just that of individuals or countries, depends today on whether the democratic world will be able to halt the manifestations of barbarism through solidarity-based efforts. Babyn Yar as a symbol of the Holocaust and other tragedies is reminding us of all this once again.

The commemorative 75th anniversary volume noted above served as the inspiration for this fully revised and expanded scholarly version of *Babyn Yar: History and Memory*. Each of the chapters has been revised and all the quotations, interpretive statements, and technical terms have been given footnote references to archival and secondary sources. An entirely new chapter (five) has been added as well as an afterword which surveys efforts at commemoration from 2016 to the present.

Transliteration from Cyrillic alphabets is always a challenge. Keeping in mind the English-language reader, we have opted to use in the text (but not in the source references) a simplified version of the Library of Congress transliteration system for Russian and Ukrainian no apostrophes for soft signs; no diacritical elisions; and the use of ***ya***, ***ye***, ***yu*** (instead of ***ia***, ***ie***, ***iu***) at the beginning of a word. Placenames are given in the state language of the country in which they are presently located (Ukrainian for Ukraine; Polish for Poland, etc.). Personal names are given in the forms used in major reference works such as the *Encyclopedia of Ukraine*, 5 vols (University of Toronto Press, 1984-93) and *The YIVO Encyclopedia of Jews in Eastern Europe*, 2 vols. (Yale University Press, 2008).

Finally, a collaborative volume of this kind could not be realised without the cooperation of supportive "staff," in particular our translator Marta D. Olynyk, scholarly editor Serhiy Bilenky, critical reader Marco Carynnyk, copy editor Peter Bejger, and page designer John Beadle. We are extremely grateful to the work of all these individuals, knowing full well that any errors and shortcomings that remain are the sole responsibility of the editors.

Vladyslav Hrynevych
Paul Robert Magocsi
June 2022

CHAPTER 1

# Babyn Yar in Space and Time

*Mykhailo Kalnytskyi*

The history of Kyiv, the capital of Ukraine, encompasses a multitude of diverse events that took place over many centuries. Kyiv is rightfully considered the cradle of spirituality, education, and culture of Eastern Slavdom. The city is home to magnificent monuments of the Kyivan Rus′ era, which are mentioned in the Rus′ *Primary Chronicle*, a seminal source in Ukrainian national historiography. The foundations of Ukrainian statehood were formed in Kyiv, and it was there that the inhabitants of several ethnic backgrounds helped the city develop and flourish.

Equally diverse and meaningful is the landscape of the contemporary city, which was created by wondrous nature and human intervention. Amidst the ancient towers and modern skyscrapers is the highest structure in Ukraine, the 380-meter television tower, which instantly catches the eye. In the minds of the residents of Kyiv the immense metal needle piercing the sky above the Ukrainian capital is not only associated with the achievements of engineers and builders. This is because right next to the tower is the infamous ravine, Babyn Yar.

The very name Babyn Yar evokes, first and foremost, the most horrific events of the World War II Nazi German occupation of Kyiv. Moreover, the past history of Babyn Yar and surrounding territory is not limited to the tragedies that took place in 1941–1943. Over an extended period of time the traces of wide-ranging human activities, embodied in documentary evidence and man-made monuments, were stratified here.

**Earliest reports about the area**

By its nature, Babyn Yar is part of a system of ravines (Ukrainian: yar)

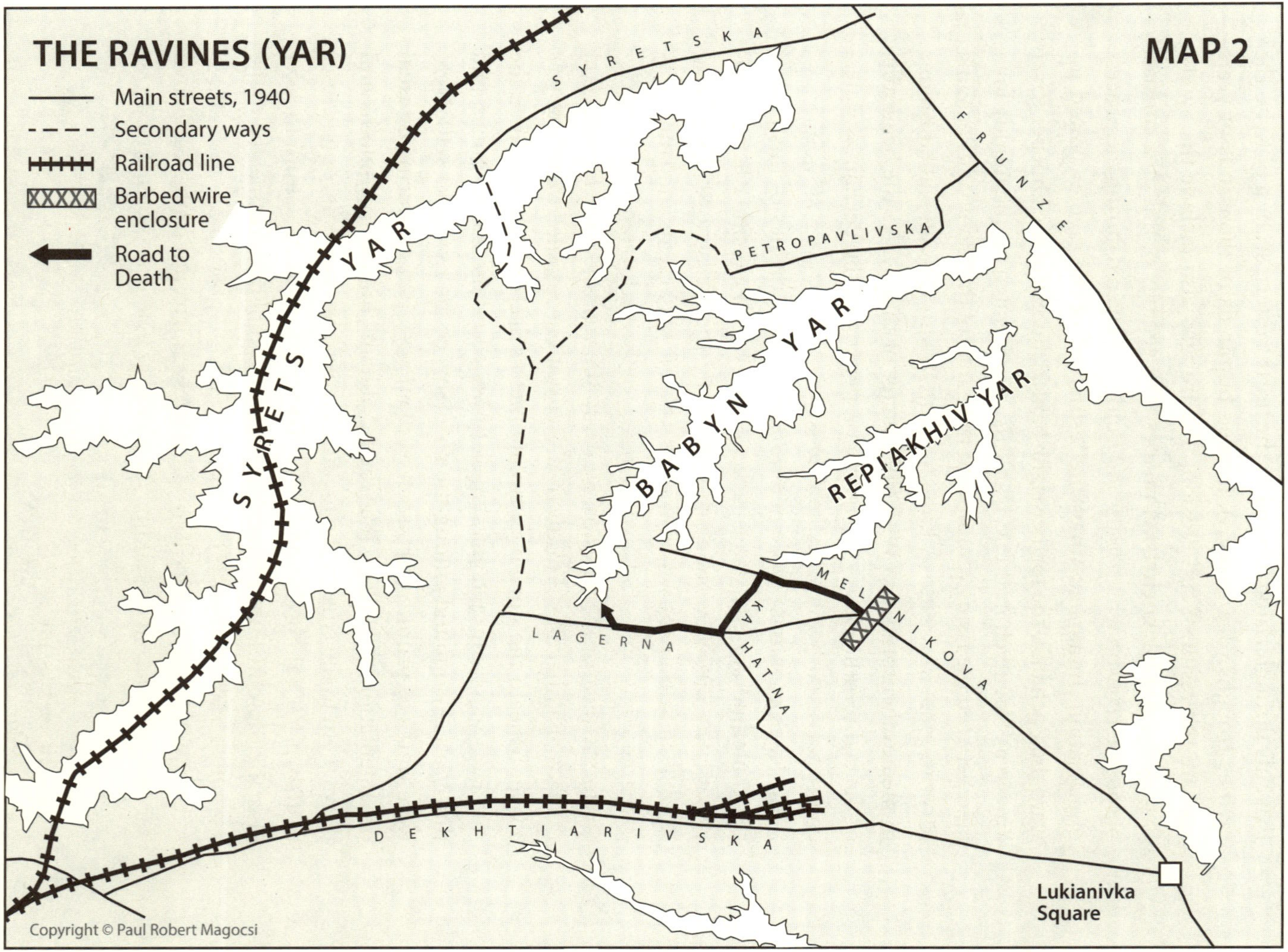
THE RAVINES (YAR)
MAP 2
Main streets, 1940
Secondary ways
Railroad line
Barbed wire enclosure
Road to Death
SYRETSKA
FRUNZE
PETROPAVLIVSKA
SYRETS YAR
BABYN YAR
REPIAKHIV YAR
MELNIKOVA
LAGERNA
KAHATNA
DEKHTIARIVSKA
Lukianivka Square
Copyright © Paul Robert Magocsi

that cuts through rising ground in the northwestern section of Kyiv. The ravine's troughs (depressions), formed hundreds of thousands of years ago, are the result of soil erosion. The troughs also include the Syrets, Repiakhiv, and Hlybochytskyi ravines. The geology of this area consists of speckled clay on which loam and sand were layered during the process of glaciation. In ancient times the "estuaries" of the ravines flowed toward the Pochaina, the former right-bank tributary of the Dnieper River known as Slavutych in the Kyivan Rus′ era. Situated on the muddy lowland between the rising ground and the banks of the Slavutych/Pochaina River were flood-meadows known as the Kyivan Obolon (called Bolone in medieval chronicles).[1] With the passage of time (since the beginning of the eighteenth century) a significant portion of the Pochaina's watercourse was absorbed by the Dnieper River.

Evidence of human settlement in the lowland ravines of this part of the contemporary city dates back to the Upper Paleolithic Period (approximately 20,000 years ago), specifically the well-known Kyrylivka/Kurenivka settlement which was discovered, excavated, and studied by the archeologist Vikentii Khvoika in the 1890s. It is located near Kyrylivska (former Frunze) Street, nos. 59-61, in the vicinity of the farmstead at the foot of a hill called Yurkovytsia. Excavations revealed that there was a layer beneath the slope over twenty meters deep, which contained the remnants of a bonfire, houses made of wood and mammoth bones, and flint tools. Also found among the remnants of the Kyrylivka settlement were works of primitive art, such as mammoth tusks featuring unusual ornamentation. It is likely that the inhabitants hunted mammoths and drove them to the edge of the ravine.[2] Traces of settlements found closer to Babyn Yar (along the odd side of Kyrylivka Street) date from later eras: the Mesolithic and Neolithic periods, and periods connected to the Trypillian and Zarubynets cultures.

During the Kyivan Rus′ period (ninth to thirteenth centuries) Babyn Yar and the adjacent Repiakhiv Yar served as a natural protective barrier

---

1 See Petro Tolochko, *Istorychna topohrafiia starodavnioho Kyieva* (Kyiv: Naukova dumka, 1972), p. 151.

2 P. Boryskovs'kyi, *Liudyna kam'ianoho viku na Ukraïni* (Kyiv: Vyd. AN URSR, 1940), pp. 78-88.

for ancient Kyiv. The two ravines became the site of frequent armed conflicts between the defenders of Kyiv and other Rus' princes who hoped to make this natural barrier a bridgehead along their way to capture the capital city. Such clashes are mentioned in *Rus' Primary Chronicle* entries for the years 980, 1146, 1150, 1161, and 1169–1171. In particular, the locality of Dorohozhych (also called Dorohozhychi, Dorozhych) is described as the site of major historical events. For example, Prince Ihor Olhovych suffered a catastrophic defeat in 1146 "in the Dorohozhych swamps," while resisting the forces of Prince Iziaslav Mstyslavych, who was vying for the Kyivan throne.[3]

Dorohozhych is comprised of hilly terrain near the Babyn, Repiakhiv, and Hlybochytskyi ravines.[4] The meaning of the toponym Dorohozhych is most often interpreted as an "intersection of roads" because of the junction of important roads leading to the towns of Vyshhorod, Chernihiv, and Bilohorodka to the north and west of Kyiv. Some scholars, however, suggest that the name was derived from a piece of property owned by an individual named Dorohozhyt.[5] The steep and long rising ground between Babyn Yar and Repiakhiv Yar, just northeast of the contemporary Menorah Monument may have been of artificial origin referring to the remnant of an old Kyivan defensive wall protecting the roads in Dorohozhych.[6] In the nineteenth century, the historian of Kyiv, Mykola Zakrevskyi, noted in magisterial tones: "Menacing hordes approached the walls of the ancient capital city; the armed force of the grand prince came out of Kyiv and a terrible slaughter commenced provoked by the princes' passions. It is surmised correctly that perhaps there is no place in all of Rus' that is so steeped in blood and bones as this locality has consumed for more than two centuries."[7]

---

3 *Litopys Rus'kyi za Ipats'kym spyskom*, translated by Leonid Makhnovets' (Kyiv: Dnipro, 1989), pp. 46, 200-202, 233, 281, 295.

4 Leonid Dobrovol'skii, *Letopisnyi Dorogozhich: k voprosu o davnikh kievskikh prigorodnykh ukrepleniiakh* (Kyiv: Izd. Kievskogo otdela Imperatorskogo russkogo voenno-istoricheskogo obshchestva, 1914).

5 Iryna Zhelezniak, *Kyïvs'kyi toponimikon* (Kyiv: Vydavnychyi dim "Kyi," 2014), pp. 37-38.

6 Dobrovol'skii, *Letopisnyi Dorogozhich*, pp. 21-22.

7 Nikolai Zakrevskii, *Opisanie Kieva*, Vol. 1 (Moscow, 1868), p. 342.

Some historians, particularly Petro Tolochko, basing themselves on their analyses of chronicle references, have argued that Dorohozhych was located elsewhere, closer to the Obolon meadows, on a lowland "beneath St. Cyril" and, perhaps, on the adjacent St. Cyril's Hill.[8] The latter name is derived from the Church of St. Cyril that was built on a promontory above Babyn Yar in the 1140s during the reign of Prince Vsevolod-Kyrylo Olhovych (r. 1139-1146). The builders embodied the traditions of ancient Rus' architecture creating a single-domed structure in brick. The church served as the family tomb of the princely Olhovych branch of Kyiv's founding Riuryk royal dynasty. A monastery was formed around the church. It is very likely that the first monks lived in the caves of St. Cyril's Hill, the partial remnants of which have been preserved to this day. Some scholars have speculated that the princely residence was located nearby. At any rate, in 1963, when a bulldozer was digging into the northern promontory of the hill on which the church stands, a dwelling dating to the twelfth–thirteenth centuries was discovered.[9]

Over the next several centuries St. Cyril's Church and its adjacent structures were practically the only urban elements in the vicinity of Babyn Yar. Following the Mongol invasion of 1240, the church, although falling into a state of decay, nevertheless remained operational. In the early seventeenth century restoration work was undertaken, and the church was reconsecrated in honor of the Holy Trinity, with St. Cyril retained as the name of the south chapel. In effect, the church continued to be called St. Cyril's or Holy Trinity-St. Cyril's, and by the seventeenth century it came to be headed by renowned ecclesiastical figures such as Inokentii Gizel and Lazar Baranovych. Another distinguished ecclesiastic, Dymytrii (Tuptalo) of Rostov, was from 1697 the hegumen (abbot) of the nearby St. Cyril Monastery. It was also at this time that the church's external appearance underwent conversion with the addition of four corner domes. Further Baroque features were added in the mid-eighteenth century, when the architect Ivan Hryhorovych-Barskyi designed a magnificent, undulating gable for the western façade. Then, in 1759, Barskyi was commissioned to build a stone, three-tiered bell tower for

8 Tolochko, *Istorychna topohrafiia starodavnioho Kyieva*, pp. 150-151.

9 Ibid., p.147.

the nearby St. Cyril's Monastery as well as for another church, that of the Annunciation, completed in the early 1770s. Together the new and restored structures comprised a distinct Ukrainian Baroque ensemble.[10]

In keeping with Empress Catherine II's policy of secularizing monastic lands in the Russian Empire, St. Cyril's Monastery was dissolved in 1786, and a refuge for invalids was founded on its premises. As a result of developments undertaken in the nineteenth and early twentieth centuries, there came into being in the area around the former monastic territory several "St. Cyril's charitable institutions" under secular governmental control, as well as numerous medical buildings and a hospice. In 1806, an insane asylum began operating, while plans were hatched to construct a water supply system. All the while, Holy Trinity-St. Cyril's Church was used as a hospital church.[11] [see Plate **II**]

During the second half of the nineteenth century the medical practices used at the psychiatric hospital in the Kyrylivka (today Kurenivka) district brought notoriety to the medical establishment, which became known as the "Kyivan Bedlam." At the same time, the restoration of ancient twelfth-century frescoes was undertaken in St. Cyril's Church under the direction of the St. Petersburg art professor Adriian Prakhov. Part of the work was carried out by the distinguished artist Mikhail Vrubel, who painted icons for the church iconostasis and new compositions on those sections of the walls, where there were no longer any traces of the original paintings.[12] Ever since that time, the church and the picturesque surroundings have attracted the attention of art lovers.

### Local toponyms

By the nineteenth-century Kyiv had significantly developed the northwestern district of the city well beyond the nucleus that had formed the medieval city. For example, in the second half of the nineteenth century the former suburban hamlet of Lukianivka (its name is traditionally associated

---

10 Iryna Marholina and Vasyl' Ul'ianovs'kyi, *Kyïvs'ka obytel' Sviatoho Kyryla* (Kyiv: Lybid', 2005), pp. 239-259.

11 See Pavel Nechai, *Kratkii ocherk Kirillovskikh bogougodnykh zavedenii v g. Kieve* (Kyiv, 1904).

12 Marholina and Ul'ianovs'kyi, *Kyïvs'ka obytel' Sviatoho Kyryla*, pp. 284-333.

with Lukian Oleksandrovych, a Kyivan guild master who lived in the late seventeenth century)[13] was incorporated into the city as the Lukianivka police district, whose territory expanded to the crest of Babyn Yar. The main Lukianivka thoroughfare was laid out as a suburban route, and in accordance with the 1837 general development plan for Kyiv it became the first leg of the Zhytomyrska Road. Then, in 1869, it was renamed Velyka Dorohozhytska Street.[14] Large brick buildings were constructed on several streets in the Lukianivka district. One of the residents in those buildings was, in the 1890s, an educated worker and Marxist named Yuvenalii Melnikov, who founded a workers' group. This took the form of a studio school for the propagation of social-democratic views in a one-storey building (no longer existing) at the top of Velyka Dorohozhytska Street.[15] In 1923, the street was again renamed. This time, in honor of the pre-revolutionary Marxist, it was called Melnikova Street (sometimes in the distorted form "Melnyk" Street), the name by which it was known during the tragic events of World War II.[16]

Just to the northwest of Lukianivka was the district of Syrets, already mentioned in documentary sources from the fourteenth and fifteenth centuries.[17] It owes its name to the small Syrets River, which to this day flows through the huge ravine of the same name. A settlement which sprang up along its banks eventually became the large village of Syrets. It was initally owned by a Dominican monastery, but it was acquired by the city of Kyiv in the second half of the seventeenth century.[18] In the late nineteenth and early twentieth cen-

---

13 Zakrevskii, *Opisanie Kieva*, Vol. 1, p. 435.

14 The descriptor Velyka (Great) was added to distinguish it from another street created at the time, Mala (Little) Dorozhytska. *Kievlianin* (Kyiv), 14 August 1869; N. Taranovskii, comp., *Kiev i ego okrestnosti: putevoditel' s topograficheskim planom i vidami Kieva* (Kyiv: Tipografiia Shtaba Kievskogo voennogo okruga, 1884), p. 97.

15 Ts. Fradkina, comp., *Putevoditel' po istoriko-revoliutsionnym pamiatnikam Kieva* (Kyiv: Politizdat pri TsK KP(b)U, 1940), pp. 7-9.

16 Derzhavnyi arkhiv Kyïvs'koï oblasti, Kyiv (hereafter: DAKO), Fond R-111, Opys1, Sprava 375, Arkuch 12, 20. In 2018, the street was renamed Yurii Iliyenko after the contempoprary Ukrainian film director.

17 *Sbornik materialov dlia istoricheskoi topografii Kieva i ego okrestnostei.* Part III (Kyiv: Izd. Vremennoi komissii dlia razbora drevnikh aktov pri Kievskom, Podol'skom i Volynskom General-Gubernatore, 1874), pp. 3-4.

18 Lidiia Ponomarenko and Oleksander Riznyk, *Kyïv: korotkyi toponimichnyi dovidnyk* (Kyiv: Pavlim, 2003), pp. 94-95.

turies a considerable part of the Syrets district consisted of privately owned hamlets that were used for a variety of purposes, ranging from suburban cottages to industrial enterprises, in particular mills and brickworks.

The neighboring district of Kurenivka was situated in an area that opens up into the lower part of Babyn Yar. Kurenivka is mentioned in the first half of the eighteenth century as a village located north of Kyiv, which belonged to the urban "suburb" also owned by the city of Kyiv. According to Mykola Zakrevskyi, in the wake of the Treaty of Andrusovo (1667) the battalions (*kureni*) of borderland guards that were stationed in Kurenivka gave rise to the name of this suburb.[19] During the nineteenth century Kurenivka was incorporated into Kyiv as part of the Ploska police district. The latter was located north of Nyzhnii Val Street, between the Obolon meadows and the slopes of the elongated hills of Shchekavytsia and Yurkovytsia. The main thoroughfare of the Ploska district was Kyrylivska Street.

The gradual clarification and specification of urban toponymics also led to the establishment of personal names for the ravines located in this vicinity. For a long time, the depressions on both sides of the former St. Cyril's Monastery were generally referred to as the St. Cyril's ravines. Streams flowed at the bottom of the two ravines, merging farther on with St. Cyril's stream, which flowed in the direction of the Pochaina. On the 1695 plan of Kyiv, prepared under the direction of colonel I. Ushakov, Babyn Yar was designated in the following way: "Behind St. Cyril's Monastery there is a large ravine, about 600 sazhens in size, which makes passage difficult for the mounted people."[20] In the opinion of Lidiia Ponomarenko and Oleksandr Riznyk, a view shared by many other authors, the name Babyn Yar is linked with the former land holdings that a female tavern keeper ("baba") sold to the Dominican monastery in 1401.[21] It is difficult to accept this interpretation, however. According to documents dating to the fifteenth–seventeenth centuries, there was a tract

19 Zakrevskii, *Opisanie Kieva*, Vol. 2, p. 724.

20 Galina Alferova and Viktor Kharlamov, *Kiev vo vtoroi polovine XVII veka: istoriko-arkhitekturnyi ocherk* (Kyiv: Naukova dumka, 1982), appendix.

21 Anatolii Kudryts'kyi, Lidiia Ponomarenko, and Oleksandr Riznyk, comps., *Vulytsi Kyieva: dovidnyk* (Kyiv: Ukraïns'ka entsyklopediia imeni M.P. Bazhana, 1995), p. 265; compare Ponomarenko and Riznyk, *Kyïv*, p. 8 which states that the tavern keeper did not "sell" but "bequeathed" the land.

known as Bisova Baba or Shalena Baba (Polish: Biesowa Baba—"Damn Woman"). The property, owned by Kyiv's Dominican Order, was indeed acquired from a female tavern keeper. But the document-based topographic reference to this tract (stretching from Syrets to the village of Bilohorodka, that is, in a westerly direction) does not correspond to the true location of Babyn Yar. As Zakrevskyi noted, the Shalena Baba tract was actually located in the village of Bilychi.[22]

The names of particular ravines in the area appeared on maps only in the middle of the nineteenth century. Professional cartographers under the direction of "the city's chief surveyor" Aleksandr Terskii prepared a collection of "plotting boards indicating pastures and developed land" of the city of Kyiv and its suburbs.[23] The plotting boards, on a scale of 1:4200, depict in detail the topography, water bodies, roads, and urban development in the area. It is here that the name "Babyn Yar" appears for the first time in sources. [see Plate **I**]

And yet, Babyn Yar is not the only name that appears on the mid-nineteenth century plotting boards. On one board titled, "A part of the suburb of Kurenivka that belongs to Kyiv" (1852), the upper part of the ravine is called Zmiinyi Yar or Snake Ravine, the middle and lower parts are called Vovchyi Yar or the Wolf's Ravine, while the upper reaches of the western branch are called the "Babyn Yar Tract (*urochyshche*)." [24] This branch no longer exists, and by its location it corresponds to the parts of the present-day neighborhoods of Syrets to the north from Olzhych Street. Similarly, the plotting board titled "Part of a pasture and the suburb of Lukianivka that belongs to Kyiv" (1852) depicts the upper reaches of Babyn Yar under the name Zmiinyi Yar. [25] Here one can also see the upper reaches of the Repiakhiv Yar which was then also called Kyrylivskyi Yar. It appears that when the land surveyors composed these plans, they questioned the local residents and landowners about the folk names of the places.

Subsequently, the names Vovchyi Yar and Zmiinyi Yar ceased to refer to Babyn Yar. Already in 1870 "A Copy from the General Plan of Kyiv"

---

22 Zakrevskii, *Opisanie Kieva*. Vol. 2, p. 560.

23 DAKO, Fond 1542, Opys 1, Sprava 27 and others.

24 DAKO, Fond 1542, Opys 1, Sprava 467, Arkush 1.

25 DAKO, Fond 1542, Opys 1, Sprava 163, Arkush 1.

showed the "Ravine Babyn Yar" extending to the upper reaches of the western branch, which in 1852 had been designated as the "summit of the Vovchyi Yar."[26] Perhaps the reason for this was that the folk name "Vovchyi Yar" was associated with other parts of the city.

On the Plan of the City of Kyiv of 1902, compiled by the city surveyor I. Tairov, the name the "Babyn Yar Tract" appears on the spot of the western branch and the name "Babyn Yar" refers to the ravine's upper reaches.[27] The same plan has an additional name for the lower part of Kyrylivskyi Yar– Repiakhiv Yar. Later plans show Babyn Yar and Repiakhiv Yar with their present-day meanings.[28]

It is widely accepted that the name *Repiakhiv* is derived from the thickets of brambles that grew there. As for the toponym *Babyn Yar*, one can assume the influence of the ancient microhydronym *Babyne Cherevo*, which according to Mykola Zakrevskyi was the name given in the nineteenth century to one of the muddy lakes located in the Obolon meadows.[29] In fact, Babyne Cherevo is a kind of generic name that applies to several bodies of water (lakes and swamps) in various parts of Ukraine. The most likely explanation of the name Babyne Cherevo (literally: Woman's Belly) is the external similarity between the contours of the basin and the swollen belly of a pregnant woman.

The principal landowner on the territory of Babyn Yar was the city of Kyiv, whose government leased parcels of land to private individuals. It was only in 1910 that for the first time municipal agencies defined the precise borders of city lands.[30] Erosion eventually led to the formation of gullies and clefts in the soil, forcing the city government to carry out in 1890-1891 comprehensive engineering works to strengthen the ravine's slopes.[31]

---

26 DAKO, Fond 1542, Opys 1, Sprava 165, Arkush 1.

27 I. Tairov, comp., *Plan goroda Kieva so vsemi zemliami, sostoiashchimi v vedenii onogo po Kievskoi gubernii* (Kyiv, 1902).

28 *Plan goroda Kieva i predmestii: sostavlen v 1914 godu po poslednim svedeniiam Kievskimi Gorodskimi Zemlemerami* (Kyiv, 1914).

29 Zakrevskii, *Opisanie Kieva*, Vol. 2, p. 587.

30 "K voprosu o nanesenii na plan goroda Kieva gorodskikh zemel'," *Kievlianin* (Kyiv), 9 September 1910.

31 "Kirillovskii ovrag," *Kievskoe slovo* (Kyiv), 29 March 1891.

Recently, the Jewish civic activist Ilya Levitas, head of the Memory of Babyn Yar Foundation, put forward an original view that "Babyn Yar itself was a small branch (up to 180-200 meters long) of St. Cyril's Ravine, which stretched nearly parallel to today's Olena Teliha Street (formerly Korotchenko Street). Babyn Yar angled off the ravine toward this street."[32] Yet, elsewhere, he states something completely different: "Babyn Yar is a huge ravine with a branch that led toward Kurenivka, to St. Cyril's Church, for nearly three and a half kilometers."[33] Despite this major discrepancy between Levitas's two versions that are based on a single source, historical plans (beginning at least in 1870) leave no doubt that the entire, deep, bifurcated depression on the northwest of the complex of the St. Cyril charitable institution complex was called the "Babyn Yar Tract."

**Reminiscence about the Jewish philanthropy**

A study of Kyiv's general condition in the latter years of the nineteenth and early twentieth centuries reveals that during this period the city, thanks to its unofficial status as the "sugar capital" of the Russian Empire among other factors, experienced extensive development. One result was the accelerated development of surrounding areas, which was sparked by comparatively low land prices. Important initiatives were undertaken by various civic and charitable associations, as well as the municipal government, which capitalized on the expansive plots of land to carry out various kinds of social projects.

In this context it is not surprising that a large number of charitable complexes were established in Kyiv's Lukianivka district. Among these were the Dehterov philanthropic institutions founded by the municipal authorities in the early 1900s, thanks to funds willed for this purpose by the millionaire businessman Mykhailo Dehterov/Mikhail Degtiarev. A 500-bed hospice for the elderly and infirm, an orphanage, elementary school, hospital, and other institutions were housed in specially built structures designed by the architect Vladimir Nikolaev. These in-

32 Ilia Levitas, comp., *Babii Iar: kniga pamiati* (Kyiv: Stal', 2005), p. 6.

33 Ibid., p. 7.

cluded St. Michael's Church, which occupied the largest building.[34] The Dehterov complex faced the former Staro-Zhytomyr Road, renamed as Dehtiarivska Street in 1908.

Even earlier an equally important philanthropic institution, the Jewish Hospital, began operating in a manor house on Bahhovutivska Street in direct proximity to Repiakhiv Yar. Founded in 1862 by the local Jewish community, it was originally housed in rented accommodations. The Jewish Hospital complex on Bahhovutivska Street, with a hundred beds, was built in 1884–1885 with funds donated by Jewish patrons, above all, by the founder of the leading national sugar trust, Izrail Brodsky. The complex consisted of one- and two-storey brick buildings designed by Vladimir Nikolaev, the largest of which housed the surgical and therapeutic departments. Subsequent expansions of the hospital in the 1880s–1910s were funded by various wealthy Jewish families in Kyiv, each of which had its "own" named building devoted to a certain specialization. For example, the Frenkel family donated funds for a neurology building; the Halperin family funded the pulmonary and urology buildings; the sugar factory owner Leon Brodsky (one of Izrail Brodsky's sons) honored the memory of his late wife by donating funds to build an obstetric-gynecological building; and Leon's descendants built an infectious diseases building in honor of his elder brother, the sugar magnate Lazar Brodsky. The ophthalmology building (which no longer exists) funded by the Zaks family, housed a hospital synagogue. The city's leading physicians as well as university professorial staff were invited to provide free medical care. The Jewish Hospital was especially popular among Kyivites of various nationalities and religions. No one was ever turned away. According to estimates compiled in 1921, 17 percent of visitors to the stationary clinics and 35 percent of visitors of the hospital's outpatient clinic were Christians.[35]

---

34 *Blagotvoritel'nye uchrezhdeniia kommertsii sovetnika, potomstvennogo pochetnogo grazhdanina i pochetnogo grazhdanina g. Kieva Mikhaila Parfentievicha Degtereva i Priiut potomstvennoi pochetnoi grazhdanki Elizavety Ivanovny Degterevoi za desiatiletie 1902-1912* (Kyiv, 1913).

35 Petr Neishtube, comp., *Istoricheskaia zapiska v pamiat' 50-tiletiia sushchestvovaniia Kievskoi Evreiskoi Bol'nitsy. 1862–1912 g.* (Kyiv, 1912).

It should be noted here that the centuries-long history of Kyiv is inextricably tied to the history of the local Jewish community, whose emergence dates to pre-Christian Rus′ lands. Scholars disagree about the exact place where the Jews of Kyiv came from, but the earliest period of Jewish settlement may date to the existence, simultaneously with Kyivan Rus′, of the Khazar Kaganate, whose official religion was for a time Judaism. According to the historians Norman Golb and Omeljan Pritsak, the so-called "Kyivan letter," written by the Jewish community of Kyiv to their coreligionists, dates to this very period (the first half of the tenth century).[36] Medieval Rus′ chronicles record the existence of a Jewish quarter in Kyiv called Zhydove, as well as a "Jewish gate" in the fortress wall near it.[37] Both the Jewish quarter and gate were located in the northwestern part of Kyiv—near present-day Lvivska Ploshcha/Lviv Square—during the reign of grand prince Yaroslav I ("the Wise," r. 1036-1054).[38]

The Mongol invasion caused heavy casualties in Kyiv, including among Jewish residents. But in the late thirteenth century the Jewish community revived, and during the period of Lithuanian and Polish rule from the fourteenth to mid-seventeenth centuries, Kyiv became an important cultural and religious center for Jews throughout eastern Europe. This was eloquently attested by a Jewish proverb from those times: "It is from Kyiv that knowledge and enlightenment derive."[39]

During the second half of the seventeenth century, Kyiv's Jewish community practically came to an end in large part because Jews were not allowed to reside in the Tsardom of Muscovy, which after 1654 ruled the city.[40] It was only in the late eighteenth century after Poland was partitioned that the large Jewish communities living in numerous cities and towns of Right-Bank Ukraine, Belarus, and Lithuania now found them-

36 The letter subsequently turned up in the Genizah (manuscript repository) of the Cairo synagogue, and in the late nineteenth century it was transferred to the Cambridge University library. Norman Golb and Omeljan Pritsak, *Khazarian Hebrew Documents of the Tenth Century* (Ithaca, NY: Cornell University Press, 1982).

37 *Litopys Rus'kyi*, pp. 171, 180, 200, and 243.

38 Tolochko, *Istorychna topohrafiia starodavnioho Kyieva*, p. 93.

39 Cited in Izrail' Darevskii, *K istorii evreev v Kieve ot poloviny VIII v. do kontsa XIX v.* (Kyiv, 1907), pp. 9-12.

40 Ibid., pp. 87-93.

selves in the Russian Empire. Consequently, Empress Catherine II was forced to create a territory open to Jewish settlement, which came to be known as the "Pale of Settlement." Kyiv and the surrounding region ended up in the Pale, where the Jewish community was soon revitalized with the arrival of Jewish artisans and traders who began constructing residential and religious buildings.[41]

The Jewish revival was interrupted, however, by the restrictive policies of Tsar Nicholas I (r. 1825-1855), whose government forcibly expelled many Jews from Kyiv. Nicholas's successor, Alexander II (r. 1855-1881), introduced a series of reforms, some of which allowed Jews to return to Kyiv. Consequently, a wide range of entrepreneurs and businessmen, engineers and scholars, lawyers and physicians, and writers and artists of Jewish background functioned productively in Kyiv during the second half of the nineteenth–early twentieth centuries. Nevertheless, discriminatory antisemitic legislation remained on the books in the Russian Empire until the February Revolution of 1917, so that Kyivan Jewry suffered from periodic acts of violence. For example, in 1911–1913 Kyiv was rocked by the events connected with the infamous "Beilis trial," whose organizers sought to accuse the Jewish people of committing blasphemous, bloody rituals. The main actors in this case, the modest Jewish civil servant Menahem Beilis and the key witnesses, all lived in the Lukianivka district. It was there where the body of the Christian boy Andrii Yushchynskyi, of whose ritual murder Beilis was accused, was discovered in the spring of 1911 in a clay cave on the Yurkovytsia hill near Kyrylivska (Kurenivska) Street.[42]

## Zone of burials and military exercises

In 1891 the City Duma allocated a large plot of land (5 dessiatin or 5.5 hectares) to the members of the Jewish community for a new Jewish cemetery situated close to the Jewish Hospital.[43] Planning for the new

41 Ibid., pp. 94-103.

42 See Aleksandr Tager, *Tsarskaia Rossiia i delo Beilisa*. 2nd ed. (Moscow: OGIZ, 1934); Ezekiel Leikin, *The Beilis Transcripts: The Anti-Semitic Trial that Shook the World* (London, 1993).

43 DAKO, Fond 1, Opys 132, Sprava 279, Arkush 8. Earlier, the community had used a cemetery founded in the late eighteenth century, which was located in the Zvirynets district (no longer existing) close to Pechersk.

burial complex known as the Lukianivka Jewish Cemetery commenced in 1892–1893, when Vladimir Nikolaev made architectural drawings and drew up estimates that were approved by the gubernial administration.[44] But the project was reviewed in due course, and Nikolaev finally built a one-storey building for washing (it no longer exists) opposite the main entrance, and to its left, a two-storey brick building to house the office, the guard, and other services.[45] [see Plate II] Enlarged during the Soviet era, presently this building is located at 44 Iliyenko Street. The cemetery, which began operations in 1894, was maintained by a portion of the funds that Kyiv's Jews paid to the city treasury in the form of an integrated tax on the use of kosher meat (known as *korobochnyi zbir*). Other funds came from donors, who were found by a specially created board that oversaw the cemetery.

The Lukianivka Jewish Cemetery was situated in a vacant spot bounded by Melnikova Street, the slopes of the Repiakhiv Yar and Babyn Yar, and the boundary of the much older St. Cyril's Orthodox Cemetery (attached to St. Cyril's Church and the hospital). A brick wall, featuring two large, arched gates designed by Nikolaev, extended along a significant portion of the perimeter of the Jewish Cemetery. According to data compiled in 1929, the cemetery covered 23.3 hectares.[46] Tens of thousands of people were buried here, including a considerable number of well-known Jewish entrepreneurs and civic and religious figures. Among them was the famous sugar magnate and multimillionaire Lazar Brodsky.[47]

In 1888, Kyiv's municipal government allocated another plot of land measuring 1,670 *sazhens* (approximately 7,250 meters) near the western edge of the Jewish Cemetery, not far from Babyn Yar. This allotment was for the Karaite community, whose religious beliefs, while based on Judaism, reject the rabbinical-Talmudist tradition. Kyiv's Karaite community

---

44 See DAKO, Fond 1, Opys 228, Sprava 232.

45 The architect planned to build three one-story brick structures on the cemetery premises. These included quarters for the cemetery caretaker and the guard; a building for washing the bodies of the deceased; and a building for performing ritual songs (the latter structure was supposed to stand opposite the main entrance, flanked on both sides by the other two buildings).

46 Mykola Stel'mashenko, *Kladovyshcha mista Kyieva* (Kyiv: Vyd. VUAN, 1929), p. 12.

47 *Kievskaia gazeta* (Kyiv), 22 September 1904.

dated only from the mid-nineteenth century. Their cemetery in the city's Lukianivka district was expanded in 1902 and 1910 eventually fronting Melnikova Street.[48]

In 1902 land was allocated (1926 sq. sazhen/8765 sq. m) for a Muslim cemetery. It was situated just to the west of the Karaite Cemetery.[49] The location of this plot corresponded to a narrow parcel of land overlooking the slope of a spur of Babyn Yar. Because of its inconvenient location, the Muslim community used it only on a limited basis.

The choice of the Lukianivka district and the area of Babyn Yar for Kyivan cemetaries had a long tradition. As noted earlier, the Jewish Cemetery was adjacent to the much older St. Cyril Orthodox Christian Cemetery. At first the Orthodox Christian cemetery was directly adjacent to the former St. Cyril Monastery, but in 1871 its territory was expanded considerably in a southwesterly direction,[50] by 1929 growing to 9.7 hectares.[51] The graves in St. Cyril's Cemetery were not laid out close to one another. Prominent among them was a concrete crypt in the modern style (damaged but still standing), built in 1912 for a famous Kyiv physician named P. E. Kachkovskyi and his younger brother, A. E. Kachkovskyi.[52] From the late nineteenth century the small Kopylivskyi Cemetery began functioning on the opposite slope of Babyn Yar, where residents of the Kurenivka and Syrets districts were buried. This cemetery was destroyed in 1961 as a result of the Kurenivka mudslide catastrophe.

In 1878 the municipal cemetery for Orthodox Christians was established on the northwestern periphery of the Lukianivka district. Known as the Lukianivka Municipal Cemetery, it was on the site of former public pastureland (between today's Dorohozhytska, Oranzhereina, and Dehtiarivska streets).[53] In 1887 a cemetery chapel was consecrated and

---

48 The 1902 addition measured 278 sq. sazhens/1,265 sq. meters; the 1910 addition 313 sq. sazhens/1,426 sq. meters. DAKO, Fond 163, Opys 38, Sprava 665, Arkush 8, 13, and Opus 41, Sprava 644.

49 Ibid., Arkush 8 and 10.

50 DAKO, Fond 163, Opys 7, Sprava 40, Arkush 7 and 8.

51 Stel'mashenko, *Kladovyshcha mista Kyieva*, p.13.

52 *Kievlianin* (Kyiv), 27 April 1912.

53 Initially, the Kyiv City Council (Duma) allotted three *desiatynas* (nearly 3.3 hectares) of land to the Lukianivka Cemetery. Subsequently, it expanded

subsequently was known as St. Catherine's Church (no longer existing). A significant number of distinguished Kyivites—civic activists, businessmen, engineers, scientists, writers, artists—are buried there. Today the Lukianivka Municipal Cemetery is recognized as a state historical and commemorative preserve.[54]

Another former vacant city plot, located between Melnikova (today's Iliyenko) and Dorohozhytska streets, also became a burial zone. In 1910, land was allocated there for the future expansion of the Orthodox Lukianivka Municipal Cemetery and for cemeteries designated for other religions: Protestant Evangelicals and Maronites (Lebanese Eastern Catholics).[55] Even earlier, in the late nineteenth century, there was for soldiers an Orthodox Brotherhood/Bratske Cemetery sometimes called Military Cemetery (the graves have not been preserved).[56] After World War II this cemetery formed the basis of the current War Cemetery.

The presence of a military cemetery next to Babyn Yar is explained by the following. In the spring of 1869, the city allocated a huge plot of land (several hundred desiatynas) in the Syrets district, specifically at the summit of Babyn Yar and the old Zhytomyrska Road, to the military for housing the Kyiv garrison's summer camps. Numerous, lightly constructed residential buildings, a hospital, parade grounds, firing ranges, and a training field were built there.[57] In 1895, a divisional church for the Syrets camps was built for soldiers attending religious services, as well as for holding solemn liturgies. This took the form of a wooden building with a tent-like dome and bell tower that was constructed cost-free by the builder Andrei Krauss. The church did not have a name because it was, in fact, only a shell of a building.[58] A moveable field altar and the

---

considerably, so that by the early twentieth century it measured 17 desiatynas (over 18.5 hectares).

54 See Liudmyla Protsenko and Iurii Protsenko, *Luk'ianivs'ke tsyvil'ne kladovyshche: putivnyk*, 2nd ed. (Kyiv: Interhrafik, 2001).

55 DAKO, Fond 163, Opys 7, Sprava 1794, Arkush 17.

56 Ibid., Arkush 4 reverse.

57 See *Osobennosti sluzhby v lagere na Syrtse (pri gorode Kieve)* (Kyiv, 1914).

58 *Kievlianin* (Kyiv), 7 May 1895. The church, situated within a block between today's Olena Teliha, Ivan Gonta, Tymofii Shamrylo, and Dorohozhytska streets, has not been preserved.

antimins of the division that was based in the camp were placed inside. Kyiv's municipal administration also took into account the location of the camps when it earmarked parcels of land and the premises for the garrison's winter barracks. In the early twentieth century a set of buildings designated for military purposes was constructed in the Lukianivka district for the personnel of the 131st Tyraspil Infantry Regiment on Velyka Dorohozhytska Street and the 165th Lutsk Infantry Regiment on Dehtiarivska Street.

The impression of the area occupied by the Syrets camps is described in the memoirs of the distinguished Ukrainian scholar and government official Serhii Yefremov who completed his military service here in 1901:

> A line of trees stretched endlessly in an even line along both sides, among which gleamed a whitely soldiers' canvas, sharp-peaked tents, packed at the bottom with earth and sod. In front of the line was a clean, empty field on which stood a small wooden structure, the camp church, at a distance of some two *hony*. Farther away, behind the Lukianivka camp, fog-bound Kyiv was visible with its solid buildings, golden church domes, spires, and orchards still enveloped in the early morning blue-gray mist that was already starting to fluctuate and dissolve beneath the sun. The officers' 'ruler'—a path planted on both sides with trees on which only officers could walk and under no circumstances the 'lower ranks' (as I found out right away)—stretched behind the four rows of soldiers' tents in an even string, from edge to edge of the endless camp. Behind that ruler, small buildings and pavilions were scattered in even rows, the architecture of some which was rather quaint; they served as officers' quarters. Even farther back amidst the green thickets of acacias, hornbeams, and elms rose the domes of the buildings of the officers' assemblies.[59]

The military's use of those lands was constrained by adjacent city farmsteads that had been granted to private individuals for their long-term use. Hence, the Syrets camps was territorially defined and it did not expand past the summit of Babyn Yar.

---

59 Serhii Iefremov, *Shchodennyk: pro dni mynuli (spohady)* (Kyiv: Tempora, 2011), pp. 496-497.

### Transportation routes in the northern outskirts

The activities at the huge military camp complex and the gradual urban development of the Lukianivka district prompted an improvement in transport links. A network of roads was created in the late nineteenth and early twentieth centuries. Lagerna Street (today an extension of Dorohozhytska Street) passed right next to the summit of Babyn Yar along the eastern side of the military camps. The Syrets and Kurenivka districts were linked by a meandering road that bypassed the spur of Babyn Yar and the Syrets ravine. Today's Syretska Street was gradually created at the rear of the camps. Initially it was an inconvenient road that began behind the Jewish Cemetery and led to the St. Cyril Hospital complex from the upland side. In 1910 the director of St. Cyril's Hospital sought to have a new main entrance built for his institution, for which purpose the summit of the spur of Repiakhiv Yar was crossed by levees and a roadway was built.[60]

The introduction of Kyiv's streetcar system in the early 1890s left its mark on the transport situation near Babyn Yar. By 1896 a streetcar line was created to connect the Lukianivka and Syrets districts, although in contrast to the great majority of urban streetcar lines powered by electricity, here steam cars were used. The route operated only in the warm seasons and according to the schedule of operations of the military camp. The line started at Lukianivka's St. Fedir Church (at the intersection of Bahhovutivska/Sichneva and Ovrutska streets), and from there it headed to Lagerna Street.[61]

In 1904, the route between the Lukianivka and Kurenivka districts was shortened with the help of the streetcar. The new, now electric, Lukianivka line went from St. Fedir's Church to Makarivska Street and continued along the slope of Repiakhiv Yar to Kyrylivska Street. Passengers could admire the extraordinarily picturesque panorama of Repiakhiv Yar and Babyn Yar, beyond which were the slender silhouettes of St. Cyril's Church and its bell tower. This landscape gave rise to the popular name "Kyiv's Switzerland."[62] [see Plate **III**]

---

60 Zinov'iev-Ikonnikov, "Kyrylivs'kyi haiok," *Hlobus* 19 (Kyiv, 1929), p. 301.

61 Serhii Tarkhov and Kost' Kozlov, Olander Aare, *elektrotransport Ukraïny: Entsyklopedychnyi putivnyk* (Kyiv: VARTO, 2010), p. 282.

62 Ibid., p. 284.

Railroads also helped resolve the area's transportation problems. During the first decade of the twentieth century, the question of building a railway loop around the historic part of the city was raised. The idea was to extend railway tracks to the Dnieper River and construct a new bridge to the other side. Consequently, large-scale work began on a railway near Syrets Yar through the Kurenivka and Obolon meadows. Improvements to Kyiv's logistical system became especially important following the outbreak of World War I in 1914. By 1917–1918 sections of the railway and a stop near the present-day Pochaina Station in the Kurenivka district were already in operation. It is interesting to note that as of 1918 Babyn Yar was one of the orientation landmarks featured in the plans for various segments of Kyiv's railway system.[63]

Even with the creation of the railway loop, urgent needs fueled by the war forced the municipal and railway administrations to build an additional freight station in order to supply Kyiv more conveniently with firewood and food. The chosen site was located near Dehtiarivska Street, to which the Lukianivka district branch line was connected from the main railway line. At the junction of this branch and the Brest-Litovsk Road (today: Peremoha Avenue), a transport solution known as a crossing had to be organized. Necessary work was completed in 1915, so that the Lukianivka freight station began functioning the following year.[64] Food storage facilities (*kahaty*) were established nearby, on the site of a former zoo and animal nursery, the so-called Society for Correct Hunting which was near the southeastern edge of Lukianivka Cemetery. Initially, the Lukianivka freight station was planned as a temporary, auxiliary measure during wartime. But, as the saying goes, there is nothing so permanent as a temporary solution, and the station remained in use until the 1960s.

Meanwhile, a considerable part of the land on the periphery of the Lukianivka district and the Kyryliv ravines remained for all intents and

---

63 Tsentral'nyi derzhavnyi istorychnyi arkhiv Ukraïny u Kyievi (hereafter: TsDIAK), Fond 693, Opys 2, Sprava 337, Arkush 2 and 3.

64 "K sooruzheniiu novoi tovarnoi stantsii Kiev-Lukianovka", *Kievlianin* (Kyiv), 11 June 1915; "Osmotr tovarnoi stantsii Kiev-Lukianovka," *Kievlianin* (Kyiv), 1 December 1915.

purposes as vacant spaces dotted here and there with small houses, gardens, and pastureland for goats. The "original" appearance of this area with its now convenient link to the city center led to the rise of educational nature excursions. The natural scientist Mykola Sharleman wrote at the time: "These places are not well known to sightseers. Nevertheless, there are amazing corners here, and you cannot believe that you are right near the city, separated from a streetcar by only a 15- to 20-minute walk."[65] Another researcher of Kyiv's suburbs, the pedagogue V. Kistiakovskii, wrote a lengthy description of the natural features of Repiakhiv Yar and Babyn Yar, which create a wonderful sense of immediacy.

> The ridge on which the Jewish Cemetery is situated divides a space that by its form resembles a square with a side of over two *versts* [3.4 kilometers] on two sloping depressions of gullies that descend swiftly as one approaches the steep cliff in the valley of the Dnieper River. At the present time both of them are covered with an abundant network of ravines that are expanding rapidly. . . . Skirting the fence of the Jewish Cemetery, which necessitates getting across a whole number of small but deep potholes that break into the last branch of the system situated to the left, we approach the steep (50-degree) slope of a very deep ravine that splits off from the last branch. The opposite slope, created by weakly cemented sandstone and dense loam, is higher and steeper. In flatter areas, rocky outcrops are covered with a layer of scree on which one cannot gain access. Here and there the steep walls reach 3–5 sazhens. For this reason, they have no vegetation. . . . We are moving along the somewhat bulging spine that rises in a northeasterly direction to its highest point. This elevation, sloping from the southwest, ends abruptly to the northeast. Its dominant position allows one to take in at a glance the entire system of northern ravines; the view from here of the Dnieper valley is partly obscured by the hill of St. Cyril's Hospital and the elevated rim of the plateau. Later, when you descend the terrace-like slope . . . to the bottom of the left branch with which we are already familiar, it is very interesting to explore both toward the summits and depressions. The bottom narrows toward the upper reaches, becoming step-like and steeper; the side

65 Mykola Sharleman', *Po Kyievu i ioho okolytsiakh* (Kyiv: Derzhavne vydavnytstvo, 1921), p. 20.

slopes also become more precipitous, the scree on them disappears and bedrock appears; the valley turns into a canyon. Moving in the opposite direction, the same phenomena are repeated in reverse order. Farther away or closer, depending on the place of descent, the sand that covers the bottom of the ravine becomes more moist; it moves beneath one's feet, and water splashes through an opening made with a cane. A bit farther and we reach the spot where the ravine cuts into the aquifer: Water comes to the surface, and within a few dozen paces you can see the weak current of a brook.[66]

**On the eve of World War II**

The tumultuous events of the Revolutionary and the Civil War era (1917-1920) brought few changes to the area around Babyn Yar. The first noticeable innovations were the appurtenances connected with the plots of and buildings that were placed at the disposal of the state organs under Bolshevik rule. The former Jewish Hospital was turned into the First Workers' Hospital (today the Regional Hospital). All of the St. Cyril's charitable institutions were re-profiled, becoming a psychoneurological hospital (for some reason bearing the name of Ukraine's national poet Taras Shevchenko until 1936 when it was renamed the Pavlov Psychiatric Hospital).[67] In 1929, the former monastic farm lands were reconfigured as the Kyiv-St Cyril State Preserve, while St. Cyril's Church was deconsecrated. The bell tower was dismantled in 1937, and that significantly impoverished the architectural ensemble of which only a small fragment and one tower was left.

Some of the old cemeteries in the Lukianivka district began to be closed to further burials. Thus, St. Cyril's Orthodox Christian Cemetery ceased operations in 1929 allegedly because of disorder,[68] while the Lukianivka Jewish Cemetery was forced to close in 1937 because of a shortage

66 V. Kistiakovskii, "Fiziko-geograficheskie ekskursii v okrestnostiakh Kieva," *Pedagogicheskaia mysl': izdanie Kollegii Pavla Galagana* II (Kyiv, 1905), pp. 72-75.

67 *Ves' Kiev. Spravochnaia kniga na 1926 god* (Kyiv: Izd-vo. Kievskogo gubkoma KP(b)U, 1926), pp. 89-90.

68 Liudmyla Protsenko, *Istoriia Kyïvs'koho nekropolia* (Kyiv: Ukrblankvydav, 1995), pp. 195-197.

of space.[69] Documents from that time reveal that in 1932 a new plant obtained permission from the Kyiv municipal council to dismantle the brick wall surrounding the Jewish Cemetery and to use the bricks for its own building needs. In return, the factory managers promised to install a fence made of another type of material, but they were in no hurry to fulfill their promise. As a result, after part of the wall fronting on Melnikova Street was dismantled, it proved impossible to prevent the cemetery from being overrun by cattle and vandals. When the presidium of Kyiv's municipal council learned of this outrageous situation, it put a stop to the further destruction of the wall and issued a resolution ordering the plant director "in the next ten days to erect a new enclosure in the place of the old one."[70] Finally, the brick wall of the cemetery facing Melnikova Street was replaced by a wooden fence. These details need to be considered when analyzing the recollections of the participants of the tragic events that took place on 29–30 September 1941.

The cemeteries in the Lukianivka district were struck by horrific events that took place in the 1930s. Archival testimonies reveal that in 1933 the Orthodox Brotherhood/Military Cemetery was the site of mass burials of nameless victims. They were the "homeless declassed element," that is, refugees from the Ukrainian countryside, who perished during the Great Famine/Holodomor. Their corpses were found on the city streets, brought to Zhovtnevyi Hospital to be autopsied, and then transported in batches to the Brotherhood/Military Cemetery near Babyn Yar.[71] The Lukianivka Municipal Cemetery was for executed "enemies of the people" who had been brought from the torture chambers of the NKVD in Lukianivka Prison on Dehtiarivska Street and buried secretly at night.[72]

The camps at Syrets remained at the disposal of the defense ministry, and the military presence continued to grow in Lukianivka district. In the 1930s the former Dehtiariv charitable institutions were transformed,

69 Derzhavnyi arkhiv mista Kyieva, Kyiv (hereafter: DAK), Fond R-1, Opys 8, Sprava 149, Arkush 99.

70 DAK, Fond R-1, Opys 1, Sprava 4105, Arkush 1, 2, 3, and 6.

71 DAK, Fond R-3, Opys 1, Sprava 187, Arkush 57.

72 Leontii Forostivs'kyi, *Kyïv pid vorozhymy okupatsiiamy* (Buenos Aires: Vyd-vo. Mykoly Denysiuka, 1952), pp. 72-73.

creating a garrison town where a tank brigade was stationed. A tank training technical school was also established there.[73] Nearby, on both sides of the first segment of Lagerna (Dorohozhytska) Street, there was a repair shop servicing automobiles and armored vehicles. Some of the buildings that are still standing today housed a motorcycle factory and garages. After the Soviet regime abolished the private use of land, the territory of the Syrets camps expanded significantly. In the years leading up to World War II armored tank units trained there, and a testing site was also based there.

Municipal improvements in the Lukianivka district took place gradually, especially after capital-city status was restored to Kyiv in 1934. Large-scale construction work was carried out on Melnikova Street. In the 1930s the city built a residential building and a physician's dormitory (today Iliyenko Street, no. 12), another residential building for NKVD employees (no. 75), and yet a third residential building for the command personnel of the Dnieper navy flotilla (no. 32).

Nevertheless, the natural environment still defined the area's character. Although the streetcar route that ran through "Kyiv's Switzerland" was scrapped after 1920, many Kyivites still loved to visit the Kyryliv ravines. In an article about "the little Kyivan grove" published in the local magazine *Hlobus* (1929), the author calls the space around the ravines "a comprehensive monument of nature," and he lists the variety of popular names for the area's most distinctive corners: "Great Caucasus," "Small Caucasus," "Zhiguli Mountains," and "Happy Valley," among others.[74] In his novel *Babi Yar*, the writer Anatoly Kuznetsov mentions a brook with clear water at the bottom of Babyn Yar, where he swam as a child.[75] A nursery to acclimatize plants, founded by the Academician Mykola Kashchenko, was established not far from the ravines (the site of today's Institute of International Relations on Iliyenko Street).

---

73 V. Ablesimov et al, *Kievskoe vysshee tankovoe inzhenernoe ordena Krasnoi zvezdy uchilishche imeni Marshala Sovetskogo Soiuza Iakubovskogo I.I. Istoricheskii ocherk.* 1930-1990 (Kyiv, 1990), pp. 20-21.

74 Zinov'iev-Ikonnikov, "Kyrylivs'kyi haiok," pp. 301-302.

75 Anatolii Kuznetsov, *Babii Iar: roman-dokument* (Zaporozhia: Interbook, 1991), pp. 14-15.

Several recent articles claim that in the 1930s Babyn Yar was used as a place of execution by the NKVD. Such claims are not backed up by any real facts or dates. On the contrary, documentary sources reveal that during the 1920s and 1930s the ravine functioned as an open pit for extracting high-quality sand for use in cement works.[76] At the same time Kyiv's municipal authorities considered Babyn Yar as a possible site for a sports complex. For instance, on the initiative of Tsoaviakhim (the Society for the Facilitation of Defense, Aviation, and Chemical Construction), Babyn Yar was for some time a site for marksmanship training. In 1935, Tsoaviakhim used explosives to create in the middle and widest part of the ravine "a model shooting range."[77] Two years later a report announced plans to build a shooting complex that would include stands for 1,500 to 2,000 spectators and a sharpshooter's school equipped with a dormitory and dining room.[78] That plan was never realized, and in 1940 a new plan called for a ski resort and ski jump.[79] Work actually began, but was interrupted because of the outbreak of war with Nazi Germany. Then, in September 1941, Babyn Yar was put to an entirely different—and tragic—use.

---

76 "Zabezpechennia kyïvs'kykh budivnytstv dobroiakisnymy piskamy," *Sotsialistychnyi Kyïv*, 6 (Kyiv, 1937), p. 40.

77 "Hora zletila u povitria: vybukh amonalu v Babynim Iaru," *Bil'shovyk* (Kyiv), 29 July 1935.

78 "Strilets'kyi stadion v Babynim iaru," *Bil'shovyk* (Kyiv), 21 March 1937.

79 DAK, Fond R-330, Opys 1, Sprava 2356.

CHAPTER 2

# On the Eve of Babyn Yar

*Igor Shchupak*

The roots of World War II and the tragedy of Babyn Yar lay in the preceding decades. Some historians call the period from the beginning of World War I to the end of World War II—1914 to 1945—the twentieth century's Thirty Years' War.[1] Ukraine was at the very center of these events, a part of what Timothy Snyder has termed the "bloodlands." On an expanse of territory stretching from central Poland to western Russia, the Nazi and Soviet regimes destroyed millions of people between 1933 and 1945.[2] The majority of Europe's Jews lived in these very "bloodlands"; it was here that both Hitler's and Stalin's imperialistic plans intersected and where the Soviet NKVD and the German SS concentrated their forces.[3]

## The roots of Nazi ideology

Nazi Germany, the aggressor country that was responsible for starting World War II, differed little from the other aggressor, the Soviet Union. However, the specific feature of Nazi ideology, concocted on a foundation of radical antisemitism, led to the emergence of one of the greatest crimes in the history of mankind, the Holocaust.

The historical precondition of the birth of Nazism was Germany's defeat in World War I. This defeat was regarded as the failure of the "German idea." The acknowledgement of Germany as the country responsible for

1 Iaroslav Hrytsak, "Nezrozumila viina," *Ukraïna Moderna*, No. 23 (Kyiv, 2016), p. 209.

2 Timothy Snyder, *Bloodlands: Europe between Hitler and Stalin* (New York: Basic Books, 2010), p. 4.

3 Ibid., pp. 9-10.

starting the war, together with the payment of immense reparations, as required by the Treaty of Versailles, led to changes in the German public's attitude toward its postwar "Weimar" republic and its experiment with democracy. Moreover, antisemitism, which was prevalent among certain strata of the German population, held "international Jewish financiers"[4] and Jewry in general responsible for the war and Germany's defeat.

Revanchism, antisemitism, and xenophobia constituted the ideological foundation of National Socialism. In the formation of the Nazi doctrine,[5] a varied and contradictory spectrum of philosophical, historical, and sociological concepts were utilized, especially the racial theories of Paul de Lagarde, Arthur de Gobineau, Houston Stewart Chamberlain, and Social Darwinism. In 1919, the National Socialist German Workers' party (Nazi party) was founded in Munich, and two years later was headed by Adolf Hitler. The party program, known as the Twenty-Five Points, was adopted in 1920. It called for the unification of all ethnic Germans into a Greater Germany, the abolition of the conditions set by the Versailles peace treaty, the creation of a strong and centralized state, the expansion of German "living space" (*Lebensraum*), the restriction of the activities of trusts and monopolies, and the creation of a "robust middle class." It also included a whole array of antisemitic clauses and demands.[6]

The two key texts that outlined the ideology of National Socialism were Adolf Hitler's *Mein Kampf* (1925) and Alfred Rosenberg's *The Myth of the Twentieth Century* (1929). These works featured pseudohistorical concepts on the special historical mission of the Aryan race mixed with antisemitic slogans, a critique of liberal democracy and communism, and propaganda calling for revenge and external expansion.[7] The ideological currents that existed within the Nazi party until 1934 differed from each other only in regard to the vision of future social reforms and attitudes to great capital.

The components of Nazi ideology were a racial credo and the theory

4 Myroslav Popovych, *Krovavyi vek* (Kharkiv: Folio, 2015), p. 362.

5 See K. Iu. Halushko, "Natsyzm," in *Entsyklopediia istorii Ukraïny*, Vol. VII (Kyïv: Naukova dumka/Instytut istorii Ukraïny NANU, 2010), pp. 234-235.

6 Ibid.

7 Ibid.

of an expanding *Lebensraum*. At the heart of Nazi teachings about the biological and spiritual differences among various nationalities lay the "basic principle of the blood," according to which only the Aryan-Nordic race could be the bearer of the finest human qualities. The Nazis put forward the postulate that the purer the blood the greater the qualities it has; hence, the Aryan-Nordic race should not mix with others.[8] Thus, the entire history of humanity was proclaimed as a struggle for the purity of the "master" race, the segregation from it of "other racial" elements, and the consolidation of the Aryans' ruling position in the world.[9]

According to Nazi racial theories, humankind was divided into "superior" and "inferior" races. The Aryan-Nordic race was proclaimed the "master" race; a rung lower was the Mediterranean race; below that was the Slavic race. Jews were not even included in this hierarchy.

A radical and militant antisemitism occupied a distinctive place in Nazi ideology. The dehumanization of Jews turned them into non-persons, literally parasites. [see Plate **IV**] The Nazis emphasized that Jews were the direct opposite of Aryans.[10] According to a leading Holocaust scholar Yehuda Bauer, the Nazis viewed Jews not only as a different race but also as an anti-race, the personification of Satan, the defilers of culture, and the mortal enemies of the Aryan peoples.[11] This ideology subsequently became the main justification for Nazi genocidal practices and the Holocaust, one symbol of which was Babyn Yar.

Nazi racial ideology, which emphasized the special characteristics of the German race and the inferiority of other races and peoples, became the justification for Germany's right to *Lebensraum*. Hitler declared that after World War I the world's territory was divided unfairly and that

---

8 Valentyna Shaikan, *Ideolohichna borot'ba v Ukraïni period Druhoï svitovoï viiny* 1939-1945 rr. (Kryvyi Rih, 2010), p. 51.

9 Vol'fram Vette, "Obraz vraga: rasistskie elementy v nemetskoi propaganda protiv Sovetskogo Soiuza," in *Vtoraia mirovaia voina—Vzgliad iz Germanii: sbornik statei* (Moscow: Iauza-EKSMO, 2005), p. 94.

10 Sergei Artamoshin, "Obraz vraga v natsistskoi ideologii Veimarskogo perioda," *Vestnik Tambovskogo universiteta; Seriia: Gumanitarnye nauki*, No. 8 (Tambov, 2008), pp. 225-231.

11 Iehuda Bauer, "Mistse Holokostu v suchasnii istorii," in *Poza mezhamy rozuminnia: bohoslovy ta filosofy pro Holokost* (Kyiv: Dukh i Litera, 2005), p. 68.

there was a disproportion among various states with regard to the size of their populations and the amount of land that was capable of feeding them.[12] In the words of Hitler, Germany had been "unjustly deprived," and therefore it had to struggle for the restoration of justice: "The foreign policy of the folkish state must safeguard the existence on this planet of the race embodied in the state, by creating a healthy, viable natural relation between the nation's population and growth on the one hand and the quantity and quality of its soil on the other."[13]

The struggle against the enemies of Germany's Third Reich, who allegedly were united around the "Jew, Our Archenemy," was one of the motives behind the Nazi decision to start World War II. According to Yehuda Bauer: "The anti-Jewish campaign was a decisive component of Nazi eschatology, the cornerstone of their universe, not just one of the parts of their program. The future of mankind depended on their victory over Jewry."[14]

Unlike the Bolsheviks, the Nazis held Jewish conspirators responsible for the world order, not capitalists and imperialists. Nazi views focused in particular on Jewish control of both capitalism and communism; hence, control over the United States, Great Britain, and the Soviet Union. For Hitler and his fellow thinkers, communism was a Jewish "fairy tale" about unachievable equality, which was invented in order to place naive Europeans in the Jewish yoke. Thus, the response to "ruthless Jewish capitalism and communism" could only be National Socialism, signifying the "restoration of justice for the German at others' cost."[15]

In addition to its historical and racial foundations, radical antisemitism was based on a religious and popular antisemitism that was reinforced by ideas about "Jewish Masons and revolutionaries" as enemies of the German people and the "culprits" responsible for Germany's defeat in World War I. All this was further nourished by myths about the

12 See the discussion in Iurii Levchenko, "Evoliutsiia ideolohii national-sotsializmu shchodo Ukraïny protiahom 1933-1942 rr.," *Naukovi zapysky Natsional'noho universytetu "Kyievo-Mohylians'ka akademiia": istorychni nauky*, Vol. 156 (Kyïv, 2014), pp. 42-47.

13 Adolf Hitler, *Mein Kampf* (Boston: Houghton Mifflin, 1943), pp. 642-643.

14 Bauer, "Mistse Holokostu v suchasnii istoriï," p. 57.

15 Cited in Snyder, *Bloodlands*, p. 17.

*Zhydokomuna*, the alleged Communist-Jewish conspiracy in the Soviet Union.

**The Nazi rise to power**

Nazism became the state ideology in Germany when the Nazis came to power in 1933. This was facilitated by the revanchist mood in the country after its defeat in World War I and the humiliating conditions imposed on it by the Treaty of Versailles. The social vulnerability of the majority of the population living under conditions of a profound socioeconomic crisis and the government's inability to overcome these problems only increased tensions among German populace. The effective use of propaganda as well as the acute struggle between the Nazis' opponents, the communists and social democrats, played an important role in the Nazi rise to power.

On 30 January 1933, Germany's President Paul von Hindenburg issued a decree appointing Adolf Hitler as chancellor and head of the government. This move foreshadowed Germany's transformation into a totalitarian state. Events unfolded quickly during the first three weeks of February: The German parliament Reichstag was dissolved and new elections were called; the president issued the "Ordinance for the Protection of the German People," banning any publications that might pose a threat to public order; police gained the right to use firearms against the political opposition; and the Auxiliary Police (*Hilfspolizei*, or Hipo) was created. The culmination came on 27 February, when the Reichstag building burned down, providing the government with a convenient pretext for arresting communists and banning the communist press.

Elections took place under conditions of terror on 5 March, in which the Nazi party won a plurality of the vote (43.9 percent). Having failed to win an absolute majority, the Nazis decided to drop any semblance of democracy and respect for the constitution. On 23 March Hitler introduced a law granting the government extraordinary powers. It passed easily in parliament, with only the social democrats voting against it. Three months later the Social Democratic party was outlawed, and on 14 July all political parties were declared illegal except for the Nazi party, which merged with the state. Starting in 1933, concentration camps for "enemies of the Reich" were established throughout the country. Basic political rights, including freedom of expression, freedom of assembly, the inviolability of the home, and the right to conduct private correspondence, were abolished.

In effect, the consolidation of Nazi rule in Germany took place with the tacit approval of German citizens. At the close of the war in 1945, the Lutheran pastor Martin Niemöller, an opponent of Nazism, recalled:

> They came first for the Communists,
> and I did not speak up because I wasn't a Communist.
> Then they came for the Jews,
> and I did not speak up because I wasn't a Jew.
> Then they came for the trade unionists,
> and I did not speak up because I wasn't a trade unionist.
> Then they came for the Catholics,
> and I did not speak up because I was a Protestant.
> Then they came for me,
> and by that time no one was left to speak up.[16]

Another aspect of strengthening Hitler's rule was the liquidation of political opponents within the Nazi party itself. In the early morning hours of 30 June 1934 (known as the Night of the Long Knives) the SS, acting on Hitler's orders, murdered Ernst Röhm and other leaders of the *Sturmabteilung* (SA), the paramilitary Brownshirts. These events were closely followed by another dictator, Joseph Stalin. According to the memoirs of the prominent Soviet statesman Anastas Mikoian, Stalin was thrilled by Hitler's audacity and perseverance on the path to consolidating his power. "Attaboy," Stalin said. "[Hitler] knows how to do it [treat his political opponents]!"[17] Further transformations within Germany involved the unification of the economy and other spheres of life, preparations for war, and mass violence and repressions against real and suspected opponents of Nazi rule.

---

16 Niemöller's text is cited in Clinton Bennett, *In Search of Jesus* (London and New York: Continuum, 2001), p. 256.

17 See Evgenii Gusliarov, *Stalin v zhizni: sistematizirovannyi svod vospominanii sovremennikov, dokumentov epokhi, versii istorikov* (Moscow: OLMA-PRESS Zvezdnyi mir, 2003), p. 542.

## Nazi repressions and state antisemitism

A signal of future violence was the burning of books whose authors were liberals, socialists, pacifists, and Jews. On 10 May 1933 book burning campaigns took place in numerous German cities to the accompaniment of "patriotic" music and "fire incantations" (*Feuersprüche*). [see Plate **IV**] Among the many authors, German and foreign, whose books were singled out for burning included: Isaac Babel, Bertolt Brecht, Jaroslav Hašek, Mikhail Zoshchenko, Erich Kästner, Heinrich Mann, Karl Marx, Lion Feuchtwanger, and Sigmund Freud.[18]

Books were not the only victims of the Nazi regime. During the course of repressions that took place before the beginning of 1935 alone, more than 4,200 "enemies of the Reich" were liquidated and 515,000 people were arrested. By 1939, more than 300,000 people had been imprisoned, while hundreds of thousands of Germans emigrated abroad.

Jews were the main target of repressions. As of 1933, there were nearly 500,000 Jews living in Germany (accounting for less than one percent of the total population). Most were highly assimilated, spoke German, and had an excellent knowledge of German history and culture. They were proud of their country. At times it seemed as though they were more German than Jewish. Nevertheless, official state antisemitism continued to intensify. The spring of 1933 marked the start of a government boycott of all Jewish-owned institutions, businesses, and shops, even though at this time the majority of the German population did not support the boycott. The Nuremberg Race Laws, adopted in 1935, stripped Jews of German citizenship and banned them from holding government offices, owning businesses, marrying German women, and studying at state educational institutions. Their property and businesses were registered and subject to confiscation.[19]

In the early morning hours of 10 November 1938, the Nazi authorities carried out an anti-Jewish pogrom known as *Kristallnacht* (the "Night of Broken Glass"), during which Jewish-owned shops, pharmacies, and other businesses were smashed and looted. The pogrom claimed tens of

---

18 Hagen Shul'tse [Hagen Schulze], *Istoriia Nimechchyny* (Kyiv: Nauka, 2010), p. 180.

19 Iryna Vyrtosu, "Uroky natsysts'koï Nimechchyny," *Dzerkalo tyzhnia* (Kyiv), 9 October 2015.

thousands of victims. Jews were forbidden to appear in public places and engage in various types of activities, and they were obliged to wear a yellow, six-pointed star sewn on their clothing.

The practice of mass killings was first used not against Jews, but against "incorrect" or "mentally defective" Germans. Nazi racial theories about "superior" and "inferior" races echoed other ideas, such as the social philosophy of eugenics. A considerable number of German physicians who were in favor of eugenics collaborated with the Nazis on a program of forced sterilization. In order for "racial hygiene" to take its proper place in medical practice, this policy was turned into an academic discipline, and in 1936 it was introduced as an exam subject. Those Germans found to suffer from genetic diseases were subject to surgical sterilization or irradiation.[20]

Also at risk of forced sterilization were people designated as "asocial psychopaths," that is, "mentally retarded" people as well as individuals without regular employment or people with a criminal record. The Roma and Sinti peoples were also victims of this policy because a pathological "commitment to crime" was ascribed to them. Up to two percent of all women died as a result of surgical interventions. According to some estimates, as of 1939, the number of victims of forced sterilization in Germany and Austria reached half a million people.

After Germany's attack on Poland on 1 September 1939 and the beginning of World War II, Hitler launched a secret war against his own German people. In October 1939 he wrote the following on a sheet of his private correspondence (backdated to 1 September 1939): "*Reichsleiter* Bouhler and Dr. Brandt are charged with the responsibility of expanding the authority of certain officially appointed doctors, so that after a critical diagnosis incurable persons may be granted a mercy death."[21] Hitler thus launched the transition from the prevention of so-called "defective life" to its destruction, and to a policy of killings masked by the euphemisms "death with pity" (mercy killing) and euthanasia.

A special meeting attended by twenty physicians and directors of psy-

---

20 Lecture by Uta Gerlant, "Evtanaziia – prestuplenie natsional-sotsialistov," cited in *Vestnik Assotsiatsii psikhiatrov Ukrainy*, No. 2 (2013), in http://www.mif-ua.com/archive/article/36252

21 Cited in ibid.

chiatric hospitals convened in Berlin in July 1939. Little is known about this "euthanasia conference," which took place two and half years before the Wannsee Conference addressed the "final solution of the Jewish question." Some data does exist, however, on the "practical results" of the criminal program of mercy killing, which claimed the lives of thousands of patients housed in psychiatric wards in Poland after Germany invaded that country. Already in the fall of 1939 SS units shot and gassed thousands of mentally ill Pomeranian Germans.

The murders of "mentally defective" Germans on the territory of the Third Reich were organized by a subdivision of Hitler's Reich Chancellery, which in 1940 was located on Tiergartenstrasse 4 in Berlin. The "death with pity" program was therefore called *Aktion T4*. Once all medical and care facilities as well as shelters for invalids that housed mentally ill people were registered, systematic killings began. Six psychiatric clinics in Germany were refitted as execution sites, which were equipped with gas chambers that operated without interruption. Concurrently with *Aktion T4*, German children with intellectual and physical handicaps were killed in thirty "children's wards" specially equipped for this purpose.

Despite the secrecy behind these killings, news trickled out as early as 1940. In August 1941, Bishop Von Galen of Münster made the following courageous declaration during one of his sermons: "If one is allowed forcibly to remove one's unproductive fellow human beings, then woe betide loyal soldiers who return to the homeland seriously disabled, as cripples, as invalids."[22] In order to prevent public disturbances, *Aktion T4* was suspended in August 1941. Nevertheless, people continued to lose their lives. German doctors simply carried on as before, starving patients to death and depriving them of medication in hospitals, clinics, and shelters. These murders were known as "wild euthanasia."

According to current scholarly research, as a result of the implementation of the euthanasia program, between 250,00 and 300,000 Germans suffering from psychological, intellectual, and physical handicaps were killed on the territory of the Third Reich alone. Later, a substantial number of sick people were killed by the Nazis on occupied Soviet territory:

22 Cited in ibid.

in Mahilioŭ (Belarus), in Zaporizhzhia and Dnipropetrovsk (Ukraine), and in Kursk and Stavropol (Russia). If the Germans were killing "defective Germans," citizens of their own state, then it is clear what fate awaited the residents of the countries that were occupied by the Nazis over the course of their continuing aggressions. Lands that had belonged to the Soviet Union before the start of the German-Soviet war were subjected to the totalitarian Stalinist regime whose characteristics to a large degree defined the events of World War II.

**The nationality question in an internationalist state**

On the one hand, the communists who ruled the Soviet Union and the Nazis who ruled Germany always emphasized the "fundamental difference" between each other. The chief distinction between the two lay in the fact that the communists championed the idea of a "class struggle," while the Nazis proclaimed the need to preserve "racial purity." In the socioeconomic sphere, the Nazis supported the inviolability of private property, whereas the communists abolished it, nationalized industry, collectivized agriculture, and introduced central command planning. According to Norman Davies, these very measures give grounds for regarding communism as the supreme form of totalitarianism.[23] In principle, the totalitarian essence of both communism and fascism was similar. Those people who had experienced both manifestations of totalitarianism called the communists "red fascists" and called the fascists "brown communists."[24]

The main features of Bolshevik nationality policy are worth recalling.[25] In the words of the historian Vladyslav Hrynevych:

> After destroying, with the help of the Red Army (comprised predominantly of ethnic Russians), the national governments that in 1918-1920 emerged in the "national borderlands" of the former Russian Empire, the Bolsheviks continued their practice in the sphere of state building in

23 Norman Davies, *Europe: A History* (Oxford and New York: Oxford University Press, 1996), p. 948

24 Ibid., p. 945.

25 Roman Szporluk, *Imperiia ta natsiï: z istorychnoho dosvidu Ukraïny, Rosiï, Pol'shchi ta Bilorusi* (Kyiv: Dukh i Litera, 2000), p. 10.

> the national republics. By granting the formerly oppressed nations some rights in the realm of language, culture, education, and in the training of national cadres, the Bolshevik government sought to extinguish all manifestations of nationalism that had emerged during the period of the Revolution and the Civil War, thereby strengthening the internal integrity of the Soviet Union. At the same time, Soviet political figures tried to combine nationalistic demands concerning national territory, culture, language, and elites with the socialist need for the economic and political unity of the Soviet state.[26]

In the early 1920s the Soviet government announced the policy of indigenization, which in Ukraine took the form of Ukrainianization. "Hence, when Ukrainianization was implemented," writes Paul Robert Magocsi, "policies with similar goals were introduced among some of the national minorities – Moldovanization, Yiddishization, Polonization, Tatarization, Hellenization."[27] Nationality districts and village and town councils, including Jewish ones, were formed throughout Ukraine.[28] The print runs of books, newspapers, and magazines in the languages of national minorities continued to increase, and technical institutes, scientific institutions, and theaters in minority languages were established. The main goal of indigenization was not, however, the development of the national life of Ukrainians, Jews, and other nationalities, but rather their Sovietization. The introduction in the late 1920s of Stalin's "revolution from above" marked the beginning of the destruction of Ukrainian and Jewish cultural achievements.[29]

The process of Jewish nationality and cultural building went on until the mid-1930s. Then, with the consolidation of the Soviet totalitarian

---

26 Vladyslav Hrynevych, *Nepryborkane riznoholossia: Druha Svitova viina i suspil'no-politychni nastroï v Ukraïni, 1939-cherven' 1941 rr.* (Kyiv and Dnipropetrovsk: Lira, 2012), p. 355.

27 Paul Robert Magocsi, *A History of Ukraine: The Land and Its Peoples*, 2nd ed. (Toronto, Buffalo, London: University of Toronto Press, 2010), p. 613.

28 Iurii Korohods'kyi, "Holod u ievreis'kykh zemlerobs'kykh koloniiakh Ukraïny (1932-1933 rr.): istoriohrafiia problemy," *Storinky istoriiï: zbirnyk naukovykh prats' Natsional'noho tekhnichnoho universytet "Ukraïny Kyïvs'kyi politekhnichnyi instytut,"* No. 36 (Kyïv, 2013), p. 118.

29 Magocsi, *History of Ukraine*, p. 615.

system, nationality institutions of education and culture were declared to be centers of "bourgeois-nationalist" influence whose activity was deemed "harmful" and a "national perversion." The suicide on 7 July 1933 of Mykola Skrypnyk, perhaps one of the most outstanding proponents of the policy of Ukrainianization as well as of the national and cultural development of minorities in Ukraine, signaled what might be called a "great breakthrough" in the nationality policy of Stalinism.[30]

Consequently, what in the words of the historian Roman Szporluk was the real revolution,[31] took place in the 1930s, during which the national republics of the Soviet Union were stripped of what little autonomy they had, and their inhabitants reduced to communities that were subordinated to the Russians. The Soviet authorities sought to reinforce their legitimacy and, simultaneously, to strengthen the loyalty of the population through the accelerated formation of a new Soviet identity. This required:

> essential correctives and changes to Soviet ideology and propaganda—above all a rejection of the utopian Marxist principle of proletarian internationalism that had begun to inhibit the mobilization of Soviet society with regard to modernization and war preparations. The result of this quest for a more pragmatic and unifying concept was the partial return to the model of Russocentric statism, which was supposed to foster state building and guarantee the population's loyalty to the existing Soviet regime.[32]

In essence, the Soviet regime recreated the imperialistic nature of its predecessor, the tsarist Russian Empire, even if the imperialism was presented in new ideological packaging. At its heart lay the Stalinist theory of the Russian people as the "elder brother" of the other Soviet peoples.[33] The Russian people were assigned a state-building and consolidation role

---

30 The phrases cited in the paragraph are taken from Oleksandr Rubliov, "Represiï proty poliakiv v Ukraïni u 1930-ti roky," *Z arkhiviv VUChK-HPU-NKVD-KHB*, No. 1/2 [2/3] (Kyiv, 1995), p. 117.

31 Szporluk, *Imperiia ta natsiï*, p. 10.

32 Hrynevych, *Nepryborkane riznoholossia*, p. 353.

33 Serhii Kal'ian, "Realizatsiia bil'shovyts'koï natsional'noï polityky v URSR (1920-1939)," *Naukovi zapysky Instytutu politychnykh i etnonatsional'nykh doslidzhen' im. I.F. Kurasa NAN Ukraïny* (Kyiv, 2011), No. 6 (56), pp. 456-457.

similar to the great-power principle from tsarist times that viewed the Russians as the ultimate pillar of the state.

Soviet society was informed in no uncertain terms of the new imperialism when, in the winter of 1936, the main ideological mouthpiece of the Bolshevik regime, *Pravda*, introduced the formula known as "the first among equals." That formula thereby emphasized the special place accorded to the Russians among the other peoples of the Soviet Union. The *Pravda* article noted the "exceptional role" of the Russian people in the struggle for the proletarian state and the importance of Russian culture to the development of all the other nationalities in the Soviet Union. Thereafter began the practice of identifying everything Russian as Soviet from the standpoint of its significant influence.[34] At this time a definite hierarchy of Soviet peoples was formed, at the top of which was the Great Russian people.

Henceforth, the rights of the non-Russian republics were reduced to a nominal status, while the declared principle of proletarian internationalism was a mask for russification. The special role of the Russian people within the so-called brotherly union of peoples became increasingly tangible. Russian patriotism was revived against the background of the struggle against "nationalistic perversions" of national minorities, and the process of rehabilitating traditional Russian historical, military, and political values got underway. In official historical scholarship some tsars were now treated as progressive historical figures, while the various peoples of Russia, which in the past had been presented as victims of colonial conquests, were transformed into recipients of fraternal assistance, whom the Russians had rescued from their own and Western enslavers.[35]

Particularly harsh criticism of Russophobia was directed at the so-called "Pokrovskii School" of historians, and even more brutal attacks were aimed at the conceptual views of the distinguished Ukrainian historian Mykhailo Hrushevskyi, whose writings allegedly created a rift be-

---

34 See the discussion in Iuliia Kysla, "Ukraïns'ka istorychna pam'iat': konstruiuvannia zahal'noradians'koï identychnosti v URSR u stalins'kyi period," *Naukovi zapysky Natsional'noho univ. 'Kyievo-Mohylians'ka Akademiia'*, Vol. 78 (Kyiv, 2008), pp. 34-39.

35 Szporluk, *Imperiia ta natsiï*, p. 10.

tween the Russian and Ukrainian peoples.[36] The Soviet population was now categorized according to the level of its loyalty to the Bolshevik regime. The categorization had both a social class and a national dimension, and in this context the Ukrainian peasantry was deemed especially unreliable.

### Famine as government policy

The building of a powerful military-industrial complex with a state-run economy and dictatorial system of government determined the radical transformation of Soviet agriculture. Industrious and self-sufficient Ukrainian peasants, who frequently championed a democratic approach in the functioning of their society's economic and political order, were unable to fit into the Soviet system. Consequently, they were viewed as a grave threat to the ever-growing might of the totalitarian Bolshevik system.[37] This was the main premise behind the implementation of collectivization, which gained momentum after 1928.

Collectivization and the destruction of agricultural farms, the forcible confiscation of grain from the peasants, and the accompanying repressions led to a horrific catastrophe, the genocidal Great Famine/Holodomor of 1932–1933. It should be noted that the Ukraine's peasantry suffered from famine both before and after Holodomor. Liudmyla Hrynevych actually speaks of a two-decade-long history of semi-starvation imposed upon Ukraine's population, which included the famines of 1921-1922, 1924-1925, 1928-1929, 1932-1933, and 1935-1936, and 1946-1947.[38] The famine of 1928-1929, which preceded the Holodomor, is un-

---

36 See the discussion in Dmitrii Churakov, "Stalinskaia natsional'naia politika i reshenie 'russkogo voprosa' v SSSR v 1920-1930-e gg.," *Dialog*, No. 10 (Moscow 1999), accessed in https://portal-slovo.ru/history/39063.php

37 L. Frei, "Sotsial'no-ekonomichni protsesy v ukrains'komu seli v konteksti polityky radians'koi derzhavy shchodo zamozhnoho selianstva (20-ti-seredyna 30-kh rokiv XX st.)," in *Istorychnyi arkhiv: naukovi studiï—Zbirnyk naukovykh prats' Chornomors'koho Derzhavnoho universtytetu im. Petra Mohyly*, No. 5 (Mykolaïv, 2010), pp. 67-70.

38 Lecture by Liudmyla Hrynevych, "Nevidomyi holod v Ukraïni 1928-1929 rr.," accessed at http://tkuma.dp.ua/index.php/ua/prosvescheniye/istoricheskiy-klub/123-nevidomij-golod-v-ukrajini-1928-1929-rr

known to many historians let alone Ukrainian society in general. It, too, was caused by the criminal policy of the country's Bolshevik leadership. According to Hrynevych, the famine of 1928-1929 was caused "not by a bad harvest but by the confiscation policy of the Soviet authorities, above all the introduction of a system of extraordinary measures as a result of which peasants were deprived of reserve food stocks."[39] This famine had a particularly horrible impact on Ukraine's Jewish agricultural colonies.[40]

Undoubtedly, the biggest losses were those suffered by ethnic Ukrainian peasants during the Great Famine/Holodomor. Its apogee occurred in the spring-summer of 1933. Among Ukraine's regions which sustained the biggest losses (52 percent of all who perished) were the former Kharkiv and Kyiv oblasts (today's Poltava, Sumy, Kharkiv, Cherkasy, Kyiv, and Zhytomyr oblasts). The death rate in those regions was 8 to 9 times more than the average for the rest of the country. In the Vinnytsia, Odesa, and Dnipropetrovsk oblasts the death rate was 5-6 times above the average, while in the Donbas it was 3 times.

Researchers offer varying mortality rates that resulted from the Holodomor, ranging from 3 to 10 million people. What is clear, however, is that millions perished regardless of their ethnic background.

Practically every recollection by Jews of life in small towns mentions the various horrors connected with the Holodomor.[41] The worst famine among Jews of southern Ukraine occurred in the northern districts of Mykolaiv oblast[42] and in the Stalindorf Jewish nationality district in the Dnipropetrovsk oblast.[43] The situation was particularly grave in those towns that had

---

39 Liudmyla Hrynevych, *Holod 1928-1929 rr. u radians'kii Ukraïni* (Kyiv: Instytut istoriï Ukraïny NAN Ukraïny, 2013), p. 330.

40 Liliia Menashevna Grinbaum-Sadovskaia, "Vospominaniia detstva," in *Vidrodzhennia pam'iati: spohady svidkiv ta zhertv Holokostu*, Vol. 2 (Dnipropetrovsk: Tsentr "Tkuma," 2009), pp. 49–53.

41 See the discussion in Viktoriia Vengerskaia, "Shtetl v istorii i politike imperii XIX-XX vv. (na primere mestechek Ukrainy i Moldovy)," in *Mezhdunarodnaia nauchno-prakticheskaia konferentsiia . . . Komratskogo gosudarstvennogo universitata*, No. 2 (Komrat, 2015), p. 134.

42 Korohods'kyi, "Holod u ievreis'kykh zemlerobs'kykh koloniiakh Ukraïny," p. 119.

43 Iurii Kotliar, "Trahediia ievreis'koho etnosu pid chas holodomoru-henotsydu," in *Holodomory 1921-1923 rr. ta 1932-1933 rr. na Pivdni Ukraïny: etnichnyi ta mizhnarodnyi aspekty*, Vol. 2 (Kyiv and Mykolaiv: Vyd. MDHU im. Petra Mohyly, 2008),

been struck off the list of centralized state food deliveries. Consequently, in the winter and spring of 1933 Jews and ethnic Ukrainians starved to death in Berdychiv, Zhytomyr, Uman, Bila Tserkva, Fastiv, and Proskuriv.

Desperate to avoid starvation, people fled to large cities, but, even there, implacable fate caught up with them. In January and February 1933 alone, the bodies of 918 Jews who had starved to death were retrieved from the streets of Kyiv, followed by another 249 bodies collected during the first ten days of March.[44] Jewish workers employed in one enterprise in Berdychiv sadly noted: "more than 100 dead bodies that perished from hunger are buried in the Russian [Orthodox] cemetery and another 40 in the Jewish cemetery."[45] International organizations—among them the Jewish Aid Committee created in [Polish-ruled] Lviv to help the starving Jews and non-Jews of [Soviet] Ukraine—were unable to do anything substantial due to the opposition on the part of Soviet authorities. Representatives of the Jewish Agro-Joint were also prevented from visiting Ukrainian villages.

The Great Famine was only one aspect of Soviet repression. In his discussion of the criminal nature of the Soviet and Nazi regimes, Timothy Snyder has noted that under Stalin in 1933 millions of Ukrainians died of starvation in the largest artificially engineered famine in the history of mankind, while less than a decade later, in 1941:

> Hitler took Ukraine from Stalin and tried to carry out his own colonial project, starting off by killing Jews and establishing camps for Soviet prisoners of war. The Stalinists colonized their own country, while the Nazis colonized a German-occupied Soviet Ukraine. During the years that both Stalin and Hitler were in power, more people were killed in Ukraine than anywhere else in the bloodlands, or in Europe, or in the world.[46]

---

pp. 90-98.

44 Iakiv Khonihsman, "Kolektyvizatsiia, holodomor i zanepad ievreis'koho zemlerobstva v Ukraïni," *Ukraïns'kyi istorychnyi zhurnal*, XXXVII, No. 2 (Kyiv, 1994), p. 73.

45 Cited in Vladyslav Hrynevych and Liudmyla Hrynevych, "Ievreï URSR u mizhvoiennyi period," in *Narysy z istoriï ta kul'tury ievreïv Ukraïny* (Kyiv: Dukh i Litera, 2005), p. 160.

46 Snyder, *Bloodlands*, p. 20.

**Nationality repressions**

The mass repressions in the Soviet Union had their own specific features compared to the terror that was subsequently organized by the Nazis. As Robert Conquest's research has shown, the Stalinist purges reached an unprecedented scale, victimizing millions of people and forcing all of society to live in a state of perpetual fear.[47] Another feature pertains to the methods by which the repressions were carried out, including the extraordinary public shows trials, during which the main opponents of Stalin were forced to accuse themselves publicly of state treason. Yet another feature was the impenetrable curtain of secrecy that surrounded the crimes of the Soviet government.[48]

Among the key targets were the country's national minorities.[49] Repression against them occurred in the wake of the further consolidation of the totalitarian regime, the crushing of all opposition, and the strengthening of Soviet Russian great-power chauvinism, which continued to be camouflaged by slogans of internationalism. The intensification of repressive policies was also influenced by external political factors and the difficulties affecting the Soviet Union's position in the international arena, particularly the Nazis' rise to power. On the one hand, Stalin was so impressed by the radicalism and decisiveness of the Brownshirts that he advised his colleagues in the Politburo to learn how Hitler dealt with his political opponents and how he managed to unite the German nation around himself. An important tool in the Nazi propaganda arsenal was to promote the image of the "blood-sucking Jew" as the ultimate enemy.[50] On the other hand, in the early 1930s a German-Polish rapprochement

---

47 Robert Conquest, *The Great Terror: Stalin's Purge of the Thirties* (London: Macmillan, 1968), p. xi.

48 Aside from the discussion in Conquest, ibid., see also Nicholas P. Vakar, *Belorussia: The Making of a Nation* (Cambridge, MA.: Harvard University Press, 1956); and Hryhory Kostiuk, *Stalinist Rule in the Ukraine: A Study of the Decade of Mass Terror, 1929–1939* (New York: Praeger, 1960). For the Soviet version of the same period see Mykola Bazhan, ed., Radians'ka Ukraïna (Kyiv: Akademiia nauk URSR, 1970).

49 Lecture by Valerii V. Engel', "Natsional'naia politika SSSR v 1930-e gg.—novye tendentsii," in his *Kurs lektsii po istorii evreev v Rossii* (Moscow, 2000-2001), accessed at http://jhist.org/russ/russ001-15.htm

50 Rubliov and Reprintsev, "Represiï proty poliakiv vv Ukraïni," p. 117.

based on anti-Sovietism emerged, and this influenced the escalation of repressions against the Polish and German minorities in Ukraine.

For example, in 1932–33 the NKVD fabricated the case of the so-called Polish Military Organization.[51] Repressions reached their peak during the "Polish Operation," and by mid-1938 nearly 135,000 Poles were arrested (roughly half of whom were from Ukraine and Belarus). About 67,000 were executed, the rest imprisoned in the Gulag or deported to Kazakhstan.[52] The mid-1930s also marked the intensification of repression against Ukraine's ethnic German population. The Soviet secret police exposed conspiratorial nests of German fascist spies, who were liquidated with all the severity of proletarian law. From the mid-1930s, there were further repressions against ethnic Germans. Soviet security police discovered "fascist German spy rings," which were liquidated with the full severity of proletarian law (that at the time also involved the execution of children from the age of 12).[53]

Other victims included 264,000 Jews who were imprisoned on various changes, 87,000 Jews accused of criminal offenses, and tens of thousands of family members of the above "enemies of the people" (including children) who were deported from Ukraine to other parts of the Soviet Union.

The Bolsheviks' nationality policy was not limited to repressions and deportations. The policy of militant atheism was intended to destroy the national and religious traditions of all minorities in the Soviet Union. The Jews and their religion were a special challenge. Judaism by its very existence was a barrier that impeded the assimilation of Jews and therefore it needed to be destroyed. Soviet efforts to transform Jewish traditional life did provoke resistance which took the form of attempts to emigrate abroad. No longer able to function legally, Zionist political parties and youth organizations in Ukraine could only operate clandestinely.

It should also be noted that a considerable number of revolutionaries and political and civic activists of Jewish background played an active role in the state's anti-people and anti-national experiments. For these

---

51 Ibid, p. 119.

52 Magocsi, *A History of Ukraine*, p. 620.

53 Ibid., p. 621.

Jews internationalism and world revolution were of paramount importance. Of the many who were drawn into the new Soviet political elite, several were natives of Ukraine, including Lev Trotsky (Bronshtein) from the Mykolaiv area, Grigorii Zinovev (Appelbaum-Radomyslsky) from the northern Kyiv region, and Moisei Uritsky from Cherkasy.[54] Jewish Communists changed their names and adopted Russian pseudonyms according to the pendulum principle ("we were persecuted, now we will take revenge on others"), and they joined in large numbers units of the Cheka punishments brigades fighting peasants.

Many scholars have attempted to determine the percentage of Jews as well as Latvians, Poles, Georgians, and other minorities in the leadership of the Communist party, in the all-Russian and Ukrainian state organs, and in the repressive organs such as Cheka-OGPU-NKVD. In making such calculations one must take into account not only the social but also national character of the 1917 Bolshevik coup and the subsequent Civil War throughout the vast territory of the former multiethnic Russian Empire. Furthermore, the origins of people born into ethnically mixed marriages are hard to define. Also, in order to determine changes in the nationality composition of the institutions mentioned above, one must differentiate and between the Ukrainian republic and all-Soviet structures and between members of the leadership class and the rank-and-file operatives on the peripheries. More importantly still, it is imperative to understand that many Jews who decided to serve the new Soviet state and become an integral part of the system rejected their national identity and transformed themselves into the bearers of a *homo sovieticus* mentality. In this context, the connection to the Jewish people of someone like Lazar Kaganovich was as meaningless as the alleged Polish "patriotism" of Felix Dzerzhinsky or the pro-Georgian "sentiments" of Sergo Ordzhonikidze.

Another important factor was the pace of change among the political elite. Immediately after the 1917 Bolshevik coup and continuing into the following two decades several non-Russian individuals adapted fully to

54 Ihor Hyrych, "Stavka na syl'nishoho: chomu ukraïntsiam ta ievreiam ne vdalosia dosiahnuty konstruktyvnoho dialohu v XIX – na pochatku XX stolittia," *Ukraïns'kyi tyzhden', No. 14 [231], 15 April 2012.*

the new system and were part of the overall policy of Russification that affected Soviet personnel policy. In Soviet Ukraine, the political elites, whether the pre-revolutionary intelligentsia, Communist opponents of Stalin, and even Stalinist cadres were replaced by Russian or Russified elements. For instance, of the 102 members and candidates for membership in the Central Committee of the Communist party (Bolshevik) of Ukraine, only three persons survived the purges of 1937.

As a consequence, the composition of Soviet Ukraine's government changed completely, as did the heads (secretaries) of oblast party committees.[55] By the summer of 1938 the Communist party Central Committee apparatus stopped appointing functionaries of Jewish origin, and the following year, at the beginning of the Soviet-German rapprochement, Jews who had survived the Great Terror began to be dismissed from government posts.[56]

If one seeks to clarify the question of the Bolshevik attitude to Jews, it becomes clear that Stalin's antisemitism stemmed not from ethnic sympathies or antipathies, but rather was determined by his political objectives. Having rejected in the mid-1930s the "principle of proletarian internationalism as the basis of revolutionary patriotism, Stalin henceforth consistently implemented national patriotism as the underlying principle of his ideology and propaganda in ethnic matters. Thus, Jews, who from the very beginning had been actively recruited for the dissemination of the propaganda of internationalism, turned out to be superfluous in the new Russian imperial project.

**Vinnytsia, Bykivnia, and Katyn: Soviet crimes on the eve of Babyn Yar**

Terror, the disregard for human life, and mass killings for the sake of realizing a certain idea were traits shared by communism and Nazism. "The bureaucracies of Nazi Germany and the Soviet Union turned individual lives into mass death," to quote Timothy Snyder. "The Soviets hid

55 Conquest, *The Great Terror, pp. 255-258;* Vakar, *Belorussia*, pp. 145–154; Kostiuk, *Stalinist Rule in the Ukraine*, pp. 76-78.

56 S. Ie. Kal'ian, "Realizatsiia bil'shovyts'koï natsional'noï polityky v URSR (1920-1939), in *Naukovi zapysky Instytut politychnykh i etnonatsional'nykh doslidzhen' im. I.F. Kurasa NAN Ukraïny*, No. 6 (Kyiv, 2011), p. 458.

their mass shootings in dark woods and falsified the records of regions in which they had starved people to death; the Germans had slave laborers dig up the bodies of their Jewish victims and burn them on giant grates."[57] The wave of large-scale Soviet mass repressions encompassed specifically Ukraine, where in the early 1930s the Ukrainian peasantry resisted collectivization.[58] It is perhaps not surprising that by 1938 the percentage of death sentences was especially high in Ukraine in comparison with other types of punishment. Regular mass shootings ended with bodies dumped in mass graves, the precursors of Babyn Yar during the Nazi occupation. Present–day historians have captured some of the horrors of those days.

> In Vinnytsia, people sentenced to death were tied, gagged, and driven to a car wash. There a truck awaited, its engine running to cover the sound of the gunshots. The bodies were then placed in the truck and driven to a site in the city: an orchard, perhaps, or a park, or a cemetery. Before their work was done, the NKVD men had dug no fewer than eighty-seven mass graves in and around Vinnytsia.[59]

Another example was Bykivnia, where the remains of Soviet citizens were found. They were victims shot by the NKVD between 1937 and 1941.[60] Local residents recall intense activity taking place at a special site located in the Bykivnia woods, where the NKVD arranged for pits to be prepared in advance.

> Every night closed trucks delivered something from Kyiv and would return before morning. There were two or three vehicles, and sometimes an entire column of five or six trucks, and always accompanied by a car carrying soldiers. After the war broke out in June 1941, the traffic heading to this zone increased. A few days before the Germans arrived, Soviet

57 Timothy Snyder, "Holocaust: The Ignored Reality," *The New York Review of Books*, LVI, 12 (New York, 2009).

58 Snyder, *Bloodlands*, p. 84.

59 Ibid.

60 Tamara Vrons'ka, "Bykivnia," in *Entsyklopediia istoriï Ukraïny*, Vol. 1 (Kyiv: Naukova dumka, 2003), pp. 251-252.

> NKVD officers herded a large column of arrested people from prisons in Kyiv across Bykivnia into the "green fence" zone. The column was an entire day's walk long. Shots rang out the whole night in the zone behind the 'green fence'; you could hear the awful cries of people. Soldiers, so-called deserters, were also brought to the woods. They dug a pit for themselves; they were ordered to lie face down, and they got a bullet in the back of the head.[61]

The total number of victims found in Bykivnia has not been established, with the figures ranging from 6,323 to tens of thousands.[62]

Perhaps the most notorious site of crimes perpetrated by the Soviet totalitarian regime was Katyn, where Polish soldiers and officers were shot en masse. In the wake of the Soviet Union's participation with Nazi Germany in the destruction of Poland, tens of thousands of Polish military officers were taken as prisoners of war by the Soviet forces. Most of them were ethnic Poles, although considering the multinational character of the Polish armed forces, there were also Ukrainians, Belarusans, and Jews among them.[63]

On the territory the "liberated" by the Red Army, the new Soviet authorities of Western Belarus and Western Ukraine also organized massive arrests of so-called class enemies, including political and civic activists of different nationalities and former soldiers. In early March 1940, over 18,000 prisoners, of whom more than 10,000 were Poles, were apprehended and held in NKVD prisons, mostly in oblast-based NKVD solitary confinement cells in Lviv, Rivne, Lutsk, Ternopil, Drohobych, Stanyslaviv, Berestia, Pinsk, and Baranovychi.[64] On 5 March 1940, Lavrentii Beria, the Soviet Union's Commissar of Internal Affairs, sent Stalin the draft of a decree to liquidate Polish citizens. It projected the shooting of 14,700 captives held in Kozelsk, Starobilsk, and Ostashkiv, as well as

---

61 Cited in Dmytro Kravchenko, "Rol' usnoï istoriï u rozkrytti istorychnoï pravdy pro Bykivniu," in *Storinky istoriiï: zbirnyk naukovykh prats'*, Natsional'nyi tekhnichnyi universytet Ukraïny "Kyïvs'kyi politekhnichnyi instytut," No. 40 (Kyïv, 2015), p. 93.

62 Vrons'ka, "Bykivnia," p. 252.

63 Snyder, *Bloodlands*, p. 151.

64 *Zagłada polskich elit: Akcja AB – Katyń*, 2nd revised ed. (Warsaw: IPN, Komisja Ścigania Zbrodni przeciwko Narodowi Polskiemu, 2009), p. 25.

11,000 people who were imprisoned in Western Belarus and Western Ukraine. As a result of the decision handed down by the Bolshevik leadership, nearly 26,000 Polish citizens were condemned to death.[65]

On 2 April 1940, the head of the NKVDs Department for POWs instructed the commandant of a camp in Kozelsk to prepare the first "death transport" which left the following day. At the station of Gnezdovo, located just west of Smolensk, POWs were transferred to buses and transported to the site of execution, just a few kilometers away. This hilly terrain, the Katyn forest, was a recreational zone of the NKVD and, therefore, inaccessible to the local civilian population. NKVD operatives killed the Polish officers with a shot at the temple from a short range. According to one version, the executions took place inside a zone fenced off with barbed wire directly over open pits. According to another version, the mass executions took place in the NKVD mansion in Smolensk after which the bodies were transported to the Katyn forest. The "operation" ended on 21 May 1940.[66] The term "Katyn executions" subsequently referred to all mass executions of Polish citizens (largely officers) carried out in the Soviet Union in April-May 1940.

It was the invading Nazi German forces who first discovered the mass graves at Katyn. A special international commission was created whose investigation concluded that the executions were carried out by NKVD operatives.[67] The Soviet leadership categorically rejected any involvement. Later, when the Soviets retook Smolensk from the Nazis, a special commission declared that the executions were carried out by the Nazi German occupying forces in 1941. Not until 1990 did the Soviet leadership admit the guilt of the NKVD.[68]

Among the other crimes of Soviet totalitarianism were the mass shootings in the summer of 1941 of prisoners held in NKVD prisons as German armies were pushing ever farther eastward into the Soviet

65 Ibid., p. 33.

66 Ibid, p. 36.

67 Snyder, *Bloodlands*, p. 375.

68 "Stalinskie deportatsii 1928-1953: Deportatsii byvshikh pol'skikh grazhdan iz anneksirovannykh raionov Vostochnoi Pol'shi (fevral'-iiun' 1940)," cited in Fond Arkhiv Aleksandra N. Iakovleva, accessed at http://www.alexanderyakovlev.org/fond/issues-dok/102128

Union. Many people remained in prisons in western Ukraine, having been imprisoned after the Soviet annexation of formerly Polish-ruled Galicia and western Volhynia (1939) and of formerly Romanian-ruled northern Bukovina (1940). In July 1941, within the first week of the Nazi German invasion of the Soviet Union, prisons in western Ukraine were filled to 1.5 -2 times their capacity. The Soviet security organs planned to transport the captives deeper eastward into Soviet territory. But the rapid advance of the German forces, problems with transport, and the increased attacks by the Ukrainian nationalist underground intent on freeing the prisoners thwarted their plans. After repeated requests from Soviet Ukraine's NKVD to Moscow for guidelines, a telegram arrived which stated: "according to the decision of Lavrentii Beria and based on the list approved by the [state] prosecutor, all persons under investigation sentenced for counterrevolutionary crimes by the article 170 of Criminal code are to be executed. Persons who committed embezzlement and who are not indicted on those charges are to be freed."[69]

In practice, not only those sentenced to capital punishment were executed but also those sentenced to various prison terms and even those who were only under investigation.[70] From the very outset of World War II political prisoners were eliminated in Przemyśl/Peremyshl and Dobromyl prisons just beyond the German front. The inmates were executed without trials, following the orders from the local prison authorities. The Soviet murder techniques varied depending on the concrete circumstances. In the last days before the Soviet troops retreated, prisoners were executed without death lists, sometimes right inside the cells, with machine guns and grenades. In order to prevent the screams of the dying prisoners from reaching the city residents, car or tractor engines were run during the executions. Prisoners tried to mount resistance, but their efforts usually failed.[71] During the first weeks of the war approxi-

69 Cited in Oleksandr Pahiria, "Masovi roztrily v'iazniv u tiurmakh NKVS URSR vlitku 1941 roku," accessed in http://territoryterror.org.ua/uk/publications/details/?newsid=248

70 Lesia Bondaruk, "Znyshchennia v'iazniv u Luts'kii tiurmi. 70 rokiv biini NKVD," *Istorychna pravda* (Kyiv, 20 July 2011), accessed at http://www.istpravda.com.ua/articles/2011/07/20/46167/

71 Ibid.

mately twenty thousand people were executed in the prisons of Western Ukraine. Most of them were Ukrainians, a certain percentage was comprised of Poles, and nearly ten percent were Jewish Zionists.[72]

Hence, Vinnytsia, Bykivnia, Katyn, and other places of mass executions became symbols of the crimes of the Soviet regime, just like Babyn Yar and numerous other "babyn yars," where subsequently Jews and other "enemies of the Reich" were executed en masse became symbols of crimes of the Nazi German regime.

### Nazi Germany and the Soviet Union on the eve of the Holocaust

In 1939–1941 Nazi Germany continued along a course marked by the conquest of much of Europe and the consistent intensification of its anti-Jewish policies, especially after the occupation of Poland with its several million strong Jewish population. During this period Stalin tried not so much to preserve peace in Europe as to whip up the military conflict. As the situation in Europe escalated, he got the chance to realize imperialistic ambitions that he identified with his country's security. Stalin expected that Germany's conflict with the Anglo-French bloc would allow him to intervene at an opportune moment, after having already ensured the expansion of the socialist front into Poland.[73]

During negotiations with Great Britain and France in the summer of 1939, the Soviets demanded conditions that were unacceptable to their potential Western partners, and the talks were suspended. Meanwhile, both Stalin and Hitler were interested in a Soviet-German rapprochement. Stalin hoped to obtain spheres of influence in Europe, while Hitler sought to open up better opportunities for launching an attack on Poland.

After the requisite diplomatic preparations were completed, the Soviet-German Non-Aggression Pact (the Molotov-Ribbentrop Pact) was signed in the early morning hours of 24 August 1939. [see Plate V] An additional—secret—protocol was also signed between the two states that divided eastern Europe into Soviet and German "spheres of influence." The Pact not only allowed Germany and the Soviet Union to destroy

72 Pahiria, "Masovi roztrily."

73 Hrynevych, *Nepryborkane riznoholossia*, p. 67.

Poland and to capture a number of other small European states located between the two aggressor states, it also provided Hitler with an opportunity to attack the West, now that he had Stalin's support and encouragement.

Such an abrupt reorientation of the Soviet politics from confrontation to friendship with Germany could not but disrupt and disorient the Soviet public. Nevertheless, Stalin and his ideologists moved forward and actively promoted the thesis about "friendship with Germany." The Soviet government's leading organ, *Pravda*, ran an editorial the day after the pact's signing which noted that a difference in the ideology and political system of both countries should not be a hindrance to the establishment of good neighborly relations.[74] Speaking at the extraordinary session of the Supreme Soviet of the USSR, Molotov alluded to the need to curtail "antifascist" and anti-German propaganda so common until then in the Soviet media. He also emphasized that "in our country there used to be some shortsighted people so carried away by simplified antifascist agitation" that they forgot about the "provocative work of our enemies." The head of the Soviet government stressed:

> The Soviet-German non-aggression agreement means a turnabout in the development of Europe... This agreement gives us not only the elimination of a threat of war with Germany... and thus serves the cause of universal peace, – it should [also] guarantee us new opportunities to grow forces, strengthen our positions, and further increase an influence of the Soviet Union on international development.[75]

This turnabout in "the development of Europe" gave rise to what the Ukrainian historian Vladyslav Hrynevych has called "unbridled dissonance" in Soviet society.[76] Such social discord attested to the reaction to the changes in the Bolshevik ideological orientation and in political life both in the "land of the soviets" and outside its borders. The discord was

---

74 "O ratifikatsii sovetsko-germanskogo dogovora o nenapadenii: soobshchenie tov. Molotova na zasedanii Verkhovnogo Soveta Soiuza SSR 31-go avgusta 1939 goda," *Pravda*, 1 September 1939.

75 Ibid.

76 Hrynevych, *Nepryborkane riznoholossia*, pp. 71-79.

also revealed in the population's reaction to the start of the German-Soviet war and the founding of the "new order" by the Nazis, Nazi antisemitic propaganda, and the beginning of the Holocaust in the Ukrainian lands.

The biggest confusion in the social consciousness of the late 1930s was caused by the change of Soviet goals from the "opposition to fascism" toward an alliance with Hitler's Germany. In one of his numerous reports, Soviet Ukraine's Commissar of Internal Affairs, Ivan Serov, touched upon the opinions of Soviet citizens regarding the conclusion of the Soviet-German pact. "What's going on?," referring to the words of Soviet scientist P. Pustokhod, "Fascists have become friends, while the so-called democratic countries have found themselves almost among the enemies."[77] Pustokhod's colleague, A. Iaroshevych, also expressed concerns about ideological and moral aspects of a Soviet-German conspiracy: "It is a bit shameful in the eyes of the world democracy. It looks like we handed it over to fascists for plunder ... One hears talk of 'Red fascism' and the Hitlerite one. And it appears to be true."[78]

It is important to note that the August 1939 Soviet-German pact generated antisemitic moods in society and a variety of myths about the "Jewish" character of the Bolshevik regime. In the words of one Ukrainian nationalist named Streletskyi: "Hitler concluded this pact as a distraction; meanwhile, he will conspire with the capitalist countries; together they will attack the USSR and destroy the Jews' power."[79] On the other hand, the Soviet secret police, especially in the days immediately following the signing of the Molotov-Ribbentrop Pact, recorded people's positive reactions to the Soviet-German pact, along the lines of "Germany is forced to recognize the USSR's might" and the pact "will decrease

---

77 "Special report of the people's commissar of the internal affairs of the Ukrainian RSR I. Serov to the secretary of the Central Committee of RKP(b)U N. Khrushchev regarding the population's reaction to the conclusion of the Soviet-German Non-Aggression Pact. 5 September 1939," cited in *Kyïv: viina, vlada, suspil'stvo. 1939-1945 rr. za dokumentamy radians'kykh spetssluzhb ta natsysts'koï okupatsiinoï administratsiï* (Kyiv: Tempora, 2014), p. 220.

78 Ibid.

79 Ibid., p. 222.

the threat of war."[80]

Subsequent events proved fateful for both Europe and Soviet-ruled Ukraine. On 1 September 1939 Germany attacked Poland, and almost immediately Wehrmacht troops began executing both Polish prisoners of war and civilians, including Jews.[81] On 17 September 1939 Soviet troops crossed the Polish border and, in keeping with the terms of the Molotov-Ribbentrop Pact, occupied the territories that were reserved for the Soviet Union. In the words of Timothy Snyder:

> By opening half of Poland to the Soviet Union, Hitler would allow Stalin's Terror, so murderous in the Polish operation, to recommence within Poland itself. Thanks to Stalin, Hitler was able, in occupied Poland, to undertake his first policies of mass killing. In the twenty-one months that followed the joint German-Soviet invasion of Poland, the Germans and the Soviets would kill Polish civilians in comparable numbers . . .[82]

Thus, another step towards Babyn Yar was made.

The Soviet-Polish war was no less a shock for the Soviet people than the non-Aggression Pact with Nazi Germany. After all, the war contradicted all slogans connected with Stalin's "politics of peace." The gradual realization that the Soviet Union had suddenly turned from a "peace-loving country" into an actual aggressor proved to be a very unpleasant "surprise" for Soviet citizens.[83]

In 1939–1941 Soviet propagandists and news reporters applied considerable efforts to present every military campaign in the context of the "further development of Stalin's policy of peace." The first victim of the Soviets' "peace policy" was Finland, followed by Romania.[84]

What were the results of this expansionist policy? The Soviet Union's aggression toward other countries and peoples, the scale of its annexa-

---

80 Report from Soviet Ukraine's Commissar for Internal Affairs, I. Serov, to the Central Committee Secretary of the All-Russian Communist party Nikita Khrushchev, 5 September 1939, cited in ibid, pp. 220-222.

81 Snyder, *Bloodlands,* pp. 115-117.

82 Ibid., pp. 117-118.

83 Hrynevych, *Nepryborkane riznoholossia,* pp. 84–86.

84 Ibid., p. 89.

tions, and the ease with which they took place gave rise to the phenomenon of "Red imperialism." This brand of imperialism was a bizarre blend of imperialistic, chauvinistic, communist, great-power, and revanchist ideas that coexisted in the public mind.[85] Advocates of "Red imperialism" comprised, however, a rather insignificant proportion of Soviet society. Far more widespread were anti-Soviet attitudes of citizens who expected the collapse of Stalin's rule in the context of the approaching war.[86]

The next shock to society was the German-Soviet Treaty of Friendship, Cooperation, and Demarcation that was signed in Moscow on 28 September 1939. The Soviet Union had until recently proclaimed itself the sole fighter against fascism. Now all anti-fascist rhetoric transmitted via the mass media was suspended. Instead, Soviet newspapers began printing the speeches of Nazi leaders, which were discussed widely and even studied in Red Army political indoctrination classes. Somewhat parallel to anti-Soviet attitudes were antisemitic attitudes. As relations improved between the Soviet Union and Nazi Germany, there was no longer any criticism of the Reich's official policy of antisemitism. In fact, a number of Soviet military officers expressed a positive attitude toward Germany's antisemitic policies.[87] These policies were well known through a wide range of Soviet Union official sources (newspapers, the cinema), private letters written by Jews living outside the Soviet Union, and the internal documentation known to the Soviet state security organs.[88]

Military operations and repressions led to a huge wave of refugees moving from the west to the east and in the reverse direction. Those who fled sought to escape either the Nazi and Soviet totalitarian regimes. Among such people were very many Jews seeking to escape either Bolshevik or Nazi rule. The Israeli scholar Aaron Weiss, who was living at the time in Boryslav, recalled how Jewish refugees, encountering each other on the border in a kind of "collision course," argued about and were astonished by the incorrect direction of flight taken by their coreligionists, who were heading either "into the paws" of the NKVD or the Nazis.

85 Ibid., p. 103.

86 Ibid., p. 108.

87 Ibid., p. 204.

88 Ibid., p. 290.

A considerable number of Jews choose the "lesser evil": Stalin's "land of the soviets" over openly antisemitic Nazi Germany.

The situation in the world and the one that existed in Soviet society changed fundamentally after Germany's attack on the Soviet Union. Soviet territory, where the second-largest (after Poland) community of European Jews lived, ended up under Nazi control. Thus, Hitler's dream of eliminating European Jews could now be possibly realized.[89]

The fate of the Jews depended not only on the Nazi invaders but also on the attitude of the local inhabitants to the occupiers and their policies. The first days of the German-Soviet war in late June and early July 1941 saw a rise in patriotic fervor among a certain proportion of Soviet citizens, as well as anti-Soviet and antisemitic moods. Interestingly enough, a substantial number of Jews breathed a sigh of relief when the war broke out because this meant the end of the "strange friendship" between the Soviet government and the antisemitic Nazi regime. A report of Soviet Ukraine's Commissar of Internal Affairs, Pavlo Meshyk, cites a comment expressed by a citizen named Kammershtein: "I am certain that from now on Jews in all countries will feel good; they know that we will destroy Hitler."[90] Similar thoughts were expressed by the writer Lurie in the first days of the war: "Of course, in any war there can be victims, but ultimately Hitler will be destroyed. I say this not just because I am a Jew."[91]

The remarks of Professor Belov serve as an illustration of similar views that were held by the non-Jewish population: "I am relieved, finally. Never before have had I felt so devoted to the Soviet government as I do now. For two whole years I was depressed by our friendship with Hitler, with the bearer of obscurantism and fascist fanaticism and antisemitism."[92] Meanwhile, others anticipated a normal life under German occupation: "The Germans are not at all the barbarians they are made out to be in the press."[93]

---

89 Snyder, Bloodlands, pp. 9-10.

90 "Special report of the people's commissar of internal affairs of the Ukrainian RSR P. Meshyk to the secretary of Central Committee of RKP(b)U Nikita Khrushchev about the reaction of population of Kyiv to the start of the hostilities between Germany and the USSR, 23 June 1941," cited in *Kyïv: viina, vlada, suspil'stvo*, p. 244.

91 Cited in ibid., p. 246.

92 Cited in ibid., p. 250.

93 Cited in ibid., p. 251.

As the Red Army continued to suffer defeat after defeat and the Wehrmacht forces approached Kyiv, the interconnected anti-Soviet and antisemitic moods among the Soviet population intensified. A report written in late July 1941 cites the remarks of one Klepfer-Chumak, a female resident of Kyiv: "Hitler will come soon and . . . . he will kill all the Jews. Then all of us will be better off."[94] A lecturer named P. M. Korbut expressed similar thoughts on 6 August 1941: "No one wants to fight . . . The Soviet regime is coming to an end. Devastation, panic, and the collapse on the home front are everywhere evident. The Jews have derailed the war. They were the first to sow panic and devastation. They brought the country to a catastrophe."[95]

A few days before the tragic events that took place at Babyn Yar in September 1941, part of Ukraine's population was ready to defend its homeland from the German invaders. At the same time, there were also a considerable number of Ukraine's inhabitants who were waiting for the German troops to arrive, thinking that the new rulers would pose a threat only to communists and Jews. Reflective of such attitudes is a special report written in August–September 1941 by the head of the NKVD for the Kyiv oblast, which cites the remarks of several individuals, including a woman named S. F. Zelinska: "The Germans are a cultured people, and only Jews and communists must fear them; others must await calmly"[96]; an unnamed citizen who "is waiting impatiently for the Germans' arrival . . . [and who] will then go and carry out a pogrom; I will kill Jews"[97]; and

94 "Report of the people's commissar of internal affairs of the Ukrainian RSR V. Serhiienko to the secretary of Central Committee of RKP(b)U Nikita Khrushchev on the actions regarding the "elimination of anti-Soviet expressions" in Kyiv and other districts and cities of the republic, 30 July 1941," cited in ibid., p. 301.

95 "Special report of the head of the UNKVS in Kyiv oblast O. Chermnykh to the people's commissar of internal affairs of the Ukrainian RSR V. Serhiienko about the attitudes of the population of Kyiv, 6 August 1941," cited in ibid., p. 308.

96 "Special report of the head of the UNKVS in Kyiv oblast O. Chermnykh to the people's commissar of internal affairs of the Ukrainian RSR V. Serhiienko about the attitudes of the population of Kyiv, 13 August 1941," cited in ibid., p. 326.

97 "Special report of the acting head of the UNKVS in Kyiv oblast M. Cherevatenko to the people's commissar of internal affairs of the Ukrainian RSR V. Serhiienko about the reaction of the population of Kyiv to the war, 6 September 1941," cited in ibid., p. 348.

a female citizen named S: "It is necessary to beat everyone: communists, and Jews, and everyone who ingratiated themselves with them."[98]

Hence, the internal division within Ukrainian society—the "unbridled dissonance"—influenced the conditions in which the Soviet and Nazi totalitarian regimes perpetrated their crimes in Ukraine on the eve of the Babyn Yar tragedy.

98 Cited in ibid.

CHAPTER 3

# Ukraine under Nazi Rule

*Karel C. Berkhoff*

Ukraine was very important in Nazi plans, for it belonged to the *Lebensraum* (living space) that the Germans supposedly needed in order to survive. Ukraine's fertile lands would enable them to revitalize their agrarian roots and thus regenerate themselves as a Germanic "race". Moreover, the produce from there would foster the Third Reich's economic independence. Except for the ethnic Germans, not just Jews but the entire native population, sooner or later, would have to be removed from an "East" where ultimately only people of "pure German blood" would live. What was the result of an invasion driven by such an ideology?

At the time of the German invasion that began on 22, June 1941, the Soviet Union had recently expanded the Ukrainian Soviet Socialist Republic through annexation from Poland and Romania of western Volhynia, eastern Galicia, northern Bukovina, and southern Bessarabia. After an initial period of military rule, the largest German territorial unit became the Reichskommissariat Ukraine, headquartered in Rivne and led by Reich Commissar Erich Koch. It had five large districts: Volhynia-Podolia, Zhytomyr, Kyiv, Mykolaiv, Dnipropetrovsk, and a "partial district" called Taurida. In the north, the Reichskommissariat included regions that today are part of Belarus. Meanwhile, the city of Lviv and the rest of eastern Galicia was made part of the Galicia District within a German territory called the Generalgouvernement Polen (Government General). The Galicia District was subdivided into counties and under Governor Karl Lasch and then Otto Wächter. Germany's Rear Army Area South, in the far eastern military zone of occupation, was ruled by Karl von Roques and Erich Friderici. Finally, Subcarpathian Rus', or

Transcarpathia, continued to be ruled by Hungary, which had annexed it in 1939.

Life and death under Nazi rule were brutal and full of fear. Terror took many forms: plunder; evictions from homes; deportations; and above all, the mass murder of Jews, Roma, psychiatric patients, prisoners of war, communists, Soviet activists, and other suspects. The killings were often carried out for everyone to see. A wide range of German "security" units amply used their unbridled license to kill. These units included commandos of two large task forces of the Security Police and Security Service, the *Einsatzgruppe C* and *Einsatzgruppe D*. But besides these mobile killing squads, later turned into local offices of the Security Police and Security Service, there were also nine battalions of the regular German Order Police, the 1st SS Infantry Brigade of the Waffen-SS, and three army security divisions. Numerous camps were created, such as Syrets in Kyiv and Janowska in Lviv.

Never before in the history of Ukraine, with the time of the Great Famine of 1933 as a possible exception, did so many social and ethnic groups suffer so much during one period. For most of inhabitants of the new Reichskommissariat Ukraine, conditions were far worse than anywhere in western Europe, and also far worse than in the Generalgouvernement. That said, Galicia was also littered with new corpses and mass graves. So was Rear Army Area South, to which the Donbas (Donets Basin) and Crimea belonged, and which did not have a German civilian administration. In fact, no military occupation regime in European history had ever been as brutal as this one. The German armed forces in the military zone of occupation were responsible for mass crimes, mainly because the Wehrmacht had become thoroughly nazified and its leaders largely shared Hitler's views on Jews and Slavs.

Two southern Ukrainian regions were fully rejoined with the Romanian state: northern Bukovina (with Chernivtsi) and the southwestern corner of the current Odessa oblast. Other southwestern Ukrainian regions between the Southern Buh and Dniester rivers, including the city of Odessa, became part of Transnistria. Formally separate from the Romanian state, this entity had thirteen districts or counties and a governor, Gheorghe Alexianu. Transnistria had about two hundred ghettos, concentration camps, and penal labor camps. The most lethal of these, where Romanians and Ukrainian and ethnic German policemen carried out mass shootings of Jews, were in the Holta district at Akhmechetka, Bohdanivka, and Domanivka.

### Jews, Roma, and psychiatric patients

The victims of Nazi murder were mainly Jews, Roma, psychiatric patients, and prisoners of war. On the eve of the Second World War, about five percent of Soviet Ukraine's population was of Jewish descent. By the middle of 1941, there were about 2.7 million Jews within present-day Ukraine's borders (those internationally recognized as of 2016). During the German-led war against the Soviet Union, a stunning proportion of them, some 1.5 million, died at the hands of Germans as well as Romanians, Hungarians, Ukrainians, and others. About 60 percent of the pre-war Jewish population was murdered. Some 900,000 Jews had fled or were evacuated to the east in time, mostly from the industrialized eastern Dnieper bend and the Donbas. But in Ukraine's western regions, the Jewish communities of Galicia, Volhynia, and Podolia were exterminated almost in full. In eastern Galicia, just a few percent of the Jews survived; in Volhynia, even less. Overall, only about 100,000 Jews survived in Ukraine while it was under Nazi rule.

Soon after the invasion that began in late June 1941, ever greater proportions of Jews were murdered. This process included able-bodied men (early July); Jews among the prisoners of war (middle of July); and then also women and children (late August). Although some individual SS officers had begun shooting Jewish women and children, the expansion of the shootings was driven from the top, mainly by the Higher SS and Police Leader Russia South, Friedrich Jeckeln. It is a little-known fact that Romania initially acted even more radically. Hence, from the very start, while Germans were focusing on Jewish men, in little-known Bukovinian and Bessarabian places the Romanian invaders shot not only Jewish men but also women and children.

Pogroms may be defined as spontaneous or seemingly spontaneous acts of anti-Jewish violence by locals. They erupted in June and July 1941, soon after the start of the German invasion, in regions of western Ukraine that less than two years before had recently been occupied by the Soviet Union. Thousands of Jews were killed in pogroms in numerous localities, including the cities of Lviv and Ternopil. Principal responsibility remained with the invaders, who wanted and encouraged such pogroms. Nevertheless, radical Ukrainian nationalists were involved, if only because of their own propaganda. For instance, when Germans occupied Lviv on June 30, 1941, supporters of Stepan Bandera's Organization of Ukrainian Nationalists told the people in a proclamation that "Moscow, Poland, the Hungarians, the Jews are your enemies. Destroy them."[1] The next day, a pogrom by all kinds of perpetrators began and climaxed in the German shooting of hundreds of Jews.

After the pogroms, there were in Ukraine some two thousand German murder actions that took the form of shootings of large and small groups of Jews. The transition toward mass shootings took place at a breathtaking speed. An important watershed event, which established that Germans would murder entire Jewish communities, was the mass shooting of 23,600 Jews in Kamianets-Podilskyi, a town near the pre-1939 border between Poland and Romania.

Kyiv became the first large city anywhere in Europe where virtually all its Jewish inhabitants were murdered in one stroke, mainly on 29 and 30 September 1941. Less than a week later, mines that were deliberately placed by the departing NKVD and Red Army engineers exploded, setting off a fire that demolished most of the city center. Analogously, the Romanian occupiers killed about 25,000 of the about 90,000 Jews in Odessa in two days in October 1941, after a Soviet mine there killed a Romanian general and sixty officers and soldiers.

In the second half of 1942, a second and final wave of mass shootings began and moved from eastern to western Ukraine, murdering the remaining Jews. Here eastern Galicia stood out in the sense that mass shootings also occurred there late in the war and that its Jews were also deported and gassed in the death camp of Bełżec.

Ukraine had Jewish ghettos, places where Jews were concentrated with

1 "Ukraïns'kyi Narode!," poster, available in fascimile and in English translation at https://training.ehri-project.eu/a04-nationalist-placard-posted-lviv-30-june-1941-incites-pogroms [last accessed June 3, 2021].

restrictions on entry and departure. Mostly existing in eastern Galicia and Volhynia, and mostly set up by the German Army, they were meant to fully isolate and then kill the inmates. Besides the ghettos there were numerous forced labor camps; those around Transit Highway 4 first held local Jews and then Jewish deportees from Transnistria.

Growing international awareness of the shootings and the diminishing prospects for a German victory in the war prompted a Nazi effort to destroy the evidence; that is the corpses of the dead. A Special Commando 1005 forced prisoners to unearth the mass graves with the Jewish (and non-Jewish) victims.

Ukraine's Roma were also exterminated for racist reasons. Little is known about that history, which largely remains to be written. In southern Ukraine, including Crimea, sedentary Roma were shot already from the fall of 1941, without differentiating them from the so-called itinerant Gypsies being killed by the Nazis in other regions. Merging of the treatment of all Roma with that of the Jews was the personal initiative of Otto Ohlendorf, the leader of *Einsatzgruppe D*.

Psychiatric patients were also systematically murdered. In Kyiv, for instance, starting with the Jews among them, almost eight hundred were shot or gassed in four waves, and buried in or near Babyn Yar.

**Prisoners of war**

The other large group killed in the German massacres were the Soviet prisoners of war, a term which can be misleading. Some of these prisoners did not consider themselves "Soviet," and they actually included many who were not formally soldiers but NKVD troops, the People's Levy, railroad workers, and civilians building fortifications.

French, British, American, and Canadian military men in German captivity, even if they were of Jewish descent, were very likely to survive World War II. In stark contrast, between 2.8 and 3 million persons considered to be Soviet POWs died in German captivity in Ukraine and beyond, and about a third did so while near the frontline. (The number specifically for Ukraine is difficult to establish.)

Almost always, Jews among the prisoners were immediately shot. Meanwhile, from the Nazi perspective, the inferior Slavs could be useful. That was why POWs identified as Ukrainian often were released, especially in 1941. Unofficial Ukrainian Red Cross societies played an important role in these releases. But many soldiers in the Wehrmacht evidently assumed that Bolshevism, the vicious ideology and political party supposedly created by "Jewry," had irreversibly "infected" all soldiers whom they called Russian, regardless of their actual ethnic background. In this nazified frame of mind, such "Russians" were either superfluous or positively dangerous.

Therefore, not only guidelines and orders—such as the "Commissar Order," a death verdict on military commissars issued even before the invasion—but also racism created an unmistakable scenario: the deliberate destruction of most of the POWs. The starvation, abuse, and shooting of the "Russian" POWs was not solely due to racism. But that factor did make it possible to embark on the abuse and murder in the first place.

After initial shootings, the prisoners were marched westward via transit camps toward permanent camps, often for very long distances. These are best described as death marches, for German (and Hungarian) army escorts shot on sight fugitives and stragglers, and mostly prevented locals from giving the prisoners food or water. Because the harvest of 1941 was excellent, the German authorities and the native population had plenty of food to spare. The latter tried hard to pass some of it on, but German policy makers wanted most of the prisoners to die, and so they deliberately starved the numerous POWs who could not work. Feeding non-working POWs was even proclaimed "wrongheaded humanity."[2] Camp guards often shot at civilians who tried to save lives. Had those civilians not been obstructed, and had the escorts and camp guards behaved in a more humane fashion, hundreds of thousands of lives could and would have been saved. Unless prisoners got out through release or escape, their only chance for survival was to be selected for daytime work outside the camp. Flight attempts by Soviet POWs were a daily event, whether during the marches, in the camps, and at the work sites. The escapes were often facilitated by outsiders.

---

2 Karel C. Berkhoff, *Harvest of Despair: Life and Death in Ukraine under Nazi Rule* (Cambridge, Mass.: The Belknap Press of Harvard University Press, 2004), p. 100.

### Peasants and city dwellers

Peasants who had not been members of a Soviet collective farm had to join its German successor, the "communal" farm, and all members had to actually work there, even – unlike before 1941 – the women with small children. Regulations on the duration of that labor became more and more strict. Machine-Tractor Stations often became bases for supervision of the farms. The supervisors—Germans, Dutch, and apparently also natives—tended to be ruthless and to force peasants to work even on important holidays. Worst of all, Germans abused the peasants for the smallest things, such as not saying a proper greeting, failing to do so at once, or having one's hands in one's pockets.

Many peasants had on average more food at their disposal in the two to three years of German rule than they used to have under Soviet rule, mainly because they worked their gardens well and because for a long time the German system of supervision and requisition was less efficient than its Soviet predecessor. But the main problem for the peasants was that collective farming remained and eventually became what they considered full-blown serfdom. The ever-increasing abuse and violence were why, eventually, most peasants feared for their lives whenever a German was around. Moreover, girls and women knew they could be arrested and locked up somewhere in an army brothel.

Terror and food shortages were the key elements of everyday city life. In the cities, passers-by could be forced to watch public hangings of those labeled saboteurs or Jews. [see Plate **XII**] Inhabitants of large cities also saw gas vans speeding by. They called them mobile gas-chambers, each of which could hold fifty prisoners. They were the *dushehubka*—destroyers of the soul. Shots resounded from many killing sites down to the very end of Nazi rule. And that included Babyn Yar. City dwellers also constantly encountered overt racism. Germans never stood in line and always could claim a seat in trams. There came insults ("Russian pig!") and widespread and official physical abuse, even for misunderstanding something. Making ends meet was hard, particularly for intellectuals. For instance, in early 1942, all institutes of higher education in the Reichskommissariat were closed.

In the winter of 1941–1942, there was a major famine in Crimea, in which hundreds, if not thousands, of civilians and prisoners of war starved to death. In Kyiv and Kharkiv, meanwhile, large numbers starved to death in *artificial* famines deliberately created by the German authorities in order to get rid of human beings considered useless or dangerous. There was plenty of food around these cities, even late in 1941; consequently, peasants were eager to barter with the proceeds of their rich harvest. But police cordons were set up with the express purpose of confiscating "surplus" food. Everything was confiscated unless a large bribe was paid. If not, peasants and city dwellers were blocked from venturing into or out of urban centers. In July 1942, for instance, General Commissar Waldemar Magunia banned "free" or "illicit" food trade in Kyiv.[3] Although the blockades were not total, they nonetheless cost many lives.

Ten thousand may approach the number of famine deaths in Kyiv. But famine was not the only reason for the drop in the city's population in less than two years, from an estimated 400,000 in October to 300,000 in 1943. Flight, deportation to Germany, and Nazi shootings also played their part in the precipitous drop of numbers.

For a long time, the frontline remained only fifty kilometers away from the eastern city of Kharkiv. Although it was the largest Soviet city ever occupied by the Germans, the number of inhabitants was less than 500,000. While the Germans ruled Kharkiv from October 1941 to August 1943 (except for four weeks early in 1943), the city commander demanded "extreme harshness" toward the locals and he had, as he wrote to other Germans, "no interest whatsoever" in feeding them.[4]

At least 30,000 Kharkivans starved to death. This figure is the minimum because of unclarity about the famine deaths far beyond the city: emaciated Kharkivans who were deported and died from exhaustion on their way to the Reich, or soon after arriving there. It is clear, however, that in no other city in Europe occupied by the German armed forces did so many who were not Jewish suffer and die from famine.

---

3 Karel C. Berkhoff, "'Wir sollen verhungern, damit Platz für die Deutschen geschaffen wird': Hungersnöte in den ukrainischen Städten im Zweiten Weltkrieg," in Jörg Morré and Babette Quinkert, eds., *Deutsche Besatzung in der Sowjetunion. Vernichtungskrieg. Reaktionen. Erinnerung* (Paderbron: Vlg. Ferdinand Schöningh), p. 61.

4 Berkhoff, "'Wir sollen verhungeren,'" p. 58.

**Deportations to Germany**

Early in 1942, in the wake of many mass shootings of Ukraine's Jews and Roma and a winter of hunger for prisoners and city-dwellers, the German authorities launched a campaign to obtain laborers for factories and farms in the Reich. They had not anticipated such a campaign before the war, but now felt the need to alleviate the unexpected labor shortages in Greater Germany. Some financial assistance was provided to the family members of the Ostarbeiter (Eastern Workers), as they were called in the Reich. [see Plate **XII**] After news about the bad working conditions in Germany spread, many Ukrainians became terrified of being sent there. In order to be disqualified, many people in Ukraine mutilated themselves. Some were convinced that they would die in Germany, whether from famine or Allied bombs. They also started to doubt that Germans were only murdering Jews and Roma. Contemporary songs and sayings about the deportations expressed profound sadness.

When there were no more volunteers, the Germans sent out commissions to carry out the deportations. Local administrators in Ukraine were threatened with death if they could not supply the assigned total of "recruits." Sometime in late 1942, native officials no longer had to supply a certain number of people, but simply all people of a certain age. Hence, it was not just German policemen, but raion leaders, city mayors, and auxiliary policemen who started to arrest people for deportation. Roundups became a frequent phenomenon at city markets. Those who tried to escape were shot at. In the countryside, the police simply went from house to house.

Still frustrated, the regime took even harsher action, ordering for instance, in the Volhynia-Podolia General District, the burning of the homes of those who refused to go, and confining relatives to labor camps as hostages. Entire villages went up in flames. The boarding of the deportation trains also produced highly violent and emotional scenes. Soon more and more auxiliary policemen, realizing that Germany was losing the war, began issuing warnings of upcoming roundups, and sometimes helping people to escape.

One in every forty inhabitants of the Reichskommissariat and Rear Army Area South combined was deported by August 1943. Ultimately,

1,500,000 people from these two Ukrainian regions ended up in Germany's Third Reich. They were mostly from villages, but the deportations affected almost every family in Ukraine.

**Auxiliaries**

Particularly in the Reichskommissariat, the "Ukrainian auxiliary administration," as it was collectively called, consisted of city administrations each headed by a mayor, raion administrations each headed by a raion chief, and village administrations each headed by a village elder (starosta). These figures played an important role in Nazi rule, if only because the invader initially lacked detailed knowledge of local affairs. But there was no one body representing the Ukrainian populace as a whole. In that sense, Ukrainians in Galicia were better off, having a local branch of the Cracow-based Ukrainian Central Committee, led by Volodymyr Kubijovyč.

The earliest local police formations, particularly in western Ukraine, appeared as militias with little or no German involvement right after the invasion started. After a while the *Einsatzgruppen* or the German military reduced the size of these militias, not least by expelling many OUN members. In the Reichskommissariat alone, there were eventually about 80,000 police auxiliaries—four times as many as German policemen.

The police auxiliaries played a key role in intimidating, abusing, robbing, arresting, guarding, and sometimes even personally murdering Jews. They also transported Jews from the countryside to major cities for questioning, which was generally followed by murder. Wherever ghettos were formed, these policemen tended to plunder and guard them. The sad climax of their participation in the Holocaust came during the second half of 1942, when they drove the victims and stood guard at the shooting pits.

The level of involvement in these actions of the Organization of Ukrainian Nationalists, be it the faction led by Stepan Bandera (OUN-B) or the faction led by Andrii Melnyk (OUN-M), remains problematic and is far from a "case closed." A good example is the large Bukovinian Battalion. This unit was comprised of thousands of Ukrainians of the OUN Melnyk faction, which in early August 1941 left Bukovina for Kyiv and elsewhere in Ukraine. Some writers say that they have established beyond doubt that the men and women of the Bukovinian Battalion were not in Kyiv during the Babyn Yar massacre—and therefore could have been involved in it in any way. On the other hand, some Ukrainian emigrés (among them Yaroslav Haivas) have recalled that thousands of nationalists[5] were in nearby Zhytomyr for an important funeral in late August 1941, and that "as soon as Kyiv was liberated from the Bolsheviks, everyone wanted to be there and at once. They were unstoppable."[6] Indeed, Bukovinians did arrive in Kyiv while the Khreshchatyk "was burning,"[7] and one Jewish survivor (Viktor Stadnik) recalled seeing them in the city center in September. The question, then, is whether one can rule out the arrival of all of the Bukovinians in that month.

The relationship between the Germans and the Ukrainian nationalist activists deteriorated quickly. First, in the summer of 1941, the OUN-B began to be persecuted, mainly because that faction refused to annul its declaration of Ukrainian statehood made in Lviv on the day (June 30, 1941) that the German Army arrived in the city. The OUN-M, which was particularly active in Kyiv, was suppressed as well. Nevertheless, it generally remained open to the possibility of collaboration with Germany.

**Partisans**

The OUN-B mostly broke with Germany in early 1943, in particular after it set up in central and southern Volhynia a large Ukrainian Insurgent Army (UPA). Historians generally agree that, like so many other partisan forces in Europe during World War II, the UPA perpetrated massacres of innocent civilians, in this case mainly Poles. The Soviet partisans also made a big impact on everyday life. They engaged in sabotage, distributed leaflets and newspapers, but at least as high on their agenda was killing, and not just of Germans. Ukraine's NKVD had as its official goal

5 Iaroslav Haivas, "V roky nadii i beznadiï (Zustrichi i rozmovy z O. Ol'zhychem v rokakh 1939–1944)," in *Kalendar-al'manakh Novoho Shliakhu 1977* (Toronto, Ontario: Drukom i nakladom "Novoho Shliakhu," [n.d.]), p. 108.

6 Iaroslav Haivas, *Koly kinchalasia epokha* (Chicago: Українсько-Американська Видавнича Спілка, 1964), p. 59.

7 Petro Voinovs'kyi, *Moie naivyshche shchastia* (Kyiv: Vyd-vo im. Oleny Telihy, 1999), p. 254.

systematically to "exterminate" the "fascist" regime that was set up in Ukraine. The Soviet partisans seemingly paid little or no attention to the consequences of their actions for locals.

The predominant German reaction to partisan activity was to kill and burn, with careful planning and horrible precision, some 50,000 people. This often happened in the wake of village burnings, especially in northern Ukraine, where sustained partisan activity was made possible by protection from the abundance of forests. Nevertheless, the Germans destroyed over three hundred villages fully or in part. One of the earliest casualties of these assaults in the Reichskommissariat became the village of Kortelisy near Ratne in the Polissia region. On 23 September 1943, auxiliary policemen and a German police company based in Brest-Litovsk (with mainly policemen from Nuremberg) surrounded the village. After ordering everyone, including all the children, to assemble, they shot nearly 2,900 inhabitants with submachine guns and pistols, or drowned them, or bayonetted them to death.

In February 1943, Soviet partisans led by Oleksii Fedorov attacked the garrison in the small town of Koriukivka in the Chernihiv region, in an attempt to liberate hostages. The garrison consisted of German soldiers, Hungarians, and auxiliary policemen. In the terrible revenge that followed, on 1 and 2 March, the entire town was annihilated. Survivors were finished off on 9 March. Koriukivka had become an ash heap filled with the remains of thousands of people. This was just one group among the many who lost their lives as direct or indirect result of the Nazi occupation of Ukraine.

CHAPTER 4

# Babyn Yar: The Holocaust and Other Tragedies

*Vitaliy Nakhmanovych*

On 28 September 1941 announcements in three languages—Russian, Ukrainian, and German—appeared on various buildings in German-occupied Kyiv. "All Jews in the city of Kyiv and vicinities are ordered to assemble on Monday, 29 September 1941, by 8:00 a.m. on Melnikova and Dokterivska [Dehtiarivska] streets (near the cemeteries). Everyone must take documents, money, underclothing, and other items with them. Those who do not comply with this directive will be shot. Those who occupy a Jewish residence or loot items from those residences will be shot."[1] (See Map 1, page xiv)

On 29 September 1941 columns of Jews from every district of the city, mainly women, children, and elderly people carrying suitcases and bundles, streamed into Lukianivka Square and headed toward Babyn Yar. The majority of the victims did not suspect what was happening until it was too late. Moreover, the occupiers had circulated rumors that plans were afoot to transport the Jews from Kyiv. After passing through a barbed-wire enclosure before the intersection of Melnikova and Lagerna (today Dorohozhytska) streets, there was no turning back. Near the Orthodox Brotherhood (Bratske) Cemetery, arriving people were divested of their belongings, documents, and valuables, and led in columns to the ravine. On a small square right next to the ravine the people were forced to undress completely, descend into the ravine, and lie face-down; then they were shot in the back of the head. That day 22,000 people were executed. Those whom the Germans did not manage to shoot were locked overnight in the garages of a tank repair plant located on the corner of

---

1 Tsentralnyi derzhavnyi arkhiv hromads'kykh ob'iednan' Ukraïny, Kyiv (hereafter: TsDAHOU), Fond 1, Opys 23, Sprava 121, Arkush 2.

Melnikova and Lagerna streets. The shootings resumed the next day. According to a report of *Einsatzgruppe C*, 33,771 people were killed in the space of two days, 29–30 September 1941.

It is these two very days, 29-30 September, which eventually turned Babyn Yar into an international symbol of the Holocaust, even though in the fall of 1941 no one in Kyiv was aware of the Holocaust or the Genocide, as those two words were not in use yet. For many years after the war—until the very end of Soviet rule—people visited this place to pay their respects to the tens of thousands of Kyivan Jews who were shot there, because, as the writer and dissident Viktor Nekrasov once remarked, "only Jews were shot here because they were Jews."[2]

All this is true. But it is not the whole truth because executions took place in Babyn Yar during the subsequent two years of the Nazi occupation of Kyiv. Not only Jews were shot there (or were buried after being killed elsewhere), but anyone whom the Nazis regarded as their enemies: Ukrainian nationalists and Roma (Gypsies), Soviet commissars and mentally ill people, underground members and hostages. Close to a hundred thousand bodies lay here until the summer of 1943, when the Germans began exhuming corpses from this sinister mass grave and burning them. That is precisely why we will never be able to arrive at an exact number of victims.

### Chronology of the tragedy

In order to create an honest record of the past, on the one hand, and to preserve a sense of the symbolic relationship among various tragedies, on the other, we should identify the key event and the historical background of Babyn Yar during the Nazi occupation. That event was the execution of Kyiv's Jews, or specifically 29 September 1941, the first day of the mass shootings. Clearly, this particular day is a certain culmination that was preceded and followed by a number of events:

BEFORE 29 SEPTEMBER 1941

– the Wehrmacht captures Kyiv on 19 September; [see Plate **VI**]

---

2 Viktor Nekrasov, "Babii Iar," *Novoe russkoe slovo* (New York), 28 September 1986.

– Soviet saboteurs blow up the Kyiv Citadel and the Khreshchatyk thoroughfare; the deaths of a significant number of German officers; fires that continue to burn in downtown Kyiv; [see Plate **VII**]
– the decision to carry out a demonstrative "reprisal operation";
– the arrest and shooting of 1,600 Jewish hostages;
– the appearance of announcements on the streets of Kyiv on 28 September: "All Jews in the city of Kyiv and vicinities are ordered to assemble on Monday, 29 September 1941, by 8:00 a.m." [see Plate **VIII**]

It should be noted that by this time the fate of Kyiv's Jews, like that of all the Jews in Ukraine and the rest of the Soviet Union as well as Europe, was already sealed. At the same time, the Germans used the sabotage actions targeting the Khreshchatyk as a handy pretext for organizing a *Gross-Aktion* (large operation) in Kyiv in close collaboration with the military occupation authorities, with full support from the Wehrmacht, and with some sympathy on the part of the non-Jewish population.

29 SEPTEMBER 1941
– columns of Jews, mostly women, children, and elderly people from various districts of Kyiv assemble at Lukianivka Square. The announcements ordering the Jews to assemble are written by people unfamiliar with the topography of the Ukrainian capital. Owing to this, two assembly points are indicated in the announcements: the place where Melnikova and Dehtiarivska (the Ukrainian- and Russian-language announcements mistakenly state "Dokterivska") streets merge at Lukianivka Square; and "near the cemeteries" just beyond the Melnikova-Lagerna corner. The distance between these two points is approximately two kilometers;
– the movement of densely packed columns of Jews who at 8:00 a.m. move continuously along Melnikova Street in the direction of Babyn Yar; the people are convinced that they are going to be transported somewhere because of the proximity of the Lukianivka freight station (the Nazis had purposefully spread such rumors);
– the patrolling of streets by German policemen and Military Police

(Feldgendarmerie) who check to see if any Jews have remained in their homes;
– the first wire enclosure (near the intersection of Melnikova and Lagerna streets) through which groups of 500 to 600 people are sent, this area being the point of no return;
– a convoluted street with three turnings, along which the Jews are being led so that the people walking in the back cannot see what is happening to the ones in front;
– a dense police cordon along the Jews' entire route and around Babyn Yar;
– crowds of Kyivites who are silently observing this procession of thousands of condemned people;
– a "registration" table near the Orthodox Brotherhood Cemetery, where the Jews are stripped of their money, valuables, and documents, and they are ordered to leave their belongings and outer clothing. It is sorted right then and there by members of the Ukrainian auxiliary police;
– the further route between the Lukianivka Municipal and Orthodox Brotherhood cemeteries to the top of Babyn Yar. Here, of course, one can hear shots being fired and people screaming;
– a double row of SS men with dogs are clubbing people, depriving them of any will to resist;
– the small square at the edge of the ravine, on which the beaten, confused people are forced to strip naked and descend into the ravine;
– finally, the ravine itself, where people are laid face-down, layer on top of layer; between the rows walk German policemen methodically shooting them in the back of the head. This lasts until 6:00 p.m., when the remaining people are locked inside the garages of a tank repair plant. That day 22,000 people are killed.

### AFTER 29 SEPTEMBER 1941

The mass shootings of Jews did not end that day, and neither did their mournful procession to Babyn Yar. The only difference was that over the next few days they were taken out of the garages and transported to the place of execution by truck. The composition of the executioners also changed. On 30 September approximately 12,000 more people were shot by the members of the same *Sonderkommando 4a* team. Later, German police battalions of Regiment South carried out executions until 15 October. By early October they were joined by *Einsatzkommando* 5, which had remained in Kyiv and formed the nucleus of the local Security Police and the SD. By mid-November, up to 65,000 Jews from Kyiv and surrounding towns and villages were shot. The pace of these operations slowed gradually, and their impact on the non-Jewish population lessened.

Naturally, the concentration of these dramatic events, whose apogee was the mass shooting that took place on 29 September, brings them into the foreground of the history of Babyn Yar during the German occupation. But this should not cause us to overlook the tragedy that befell other Nazi victims, such as Soviet war prisoners (above all, commissars, communists, and Jews), Roma, ordinary communists and Ukrainian nationalists, members of the Soviet and Ukrainian underground movements, mentally ill patients from the Ivan Pavlov Psychiatric Hospital (former St. Cyril's Hospital), and ordinary Kyivites who were seized as hostages. These victims comprised approximately one-third (between 90,000 and 100,000) of the victims of who lost their lives in Babyn Yar. Short of providing a detailed description of those events here, I will divide them into three blocs: (1) systematic executions beginning the day after the Wehrmacht captures Kyiv and ending on the eve of the city's liberation by the Red Army on 6 November 1943; (2) the liquidation of prisoners in the Syrets concentration camp located next to Babyn Yar, starting in the spring of 1942; and (3) the burning of corpses in Babyn Yar by prisoners of the Syrets concentration camp in August–September 1943.

In order to create a more complete picture of the history of Babyn Yar during the Nazi occupation of Kyiv, the following three questions must be addressed: Who did the shooting? Who was shot there? How many people were shot? Some other questions related to topography need to be considered. Where specifically was Babyn Yar, the Syrets concentration camp, and the adjacent cemeteries located (during the Soviet period all these areas were almost completely destroyed). In which specific places did the executions and burials take place?

### Myths about Babyn Yar

Because these questions are objects of both scholarly interest and public discussions, they have become the topics of considerable speculation and falsification. At the same time, scholarly studies have no impact on people who, for extra-scholarly or pseudo-scholarly reasons, prefer to cling to a certain myth. Historians are also hostages to their convictions, which influence the choice of research topic, selection of historical facts, treatment of historical events, and, as a result, formation of ideologemes.

For example, the classical Soviet myth that is advanced in the volume on Kyiv in the Russian-language *History of Towns and Villages of the Ukrainian SSR (1982)*, states:

> After the occupation of Ukraine the authorities of fascist Germany assigned all Nazi troops the task of mercilessly destroying its population in order to liberate the territory of Ukraine for the future resettlement of Germans here. To this end, the mass destruction of the Soviet people was carried out.... The direct participants in the crimes of the German-fascist invaders, their henchmen, were Ukrainian bourgeois nationalists.... The nationalists took part in punitive actions against partisans and underground members, carried out bloody reprisals against party, Soviet, [and] Komsomol workers, civilians.... The fascist occupiers were given all kinds of assistance from anti-Soviet elements that were crawling out of every cranny.[3]

A somewhat modified version of this myth appears in a three-volume history of Kyiv published in the mid-1980s:

> On 19 September 1941 a horde of Nazi killers and looters broke into Kyiv.... Terrorist activity was unleashed by the fascist punitive organs: the Secret State Police (Gestapo), secret military police (GFP), operational formations created for the mass extermination of the Soviet population (*Einsatzgruppen*, *Sonderkommando*), subunits of SS troops.... To

3 *Istoriia gorodov i sel Ukrainskoï SSR: Kiev*, 3rd edition, edited by Petr T. Tron'ko et al. (Kyïv: Institut istorii Akademii nauk USSR, 1982), p. 355.

> assist the occupation apparatus and the Gestapo, they [the fascists—V.N.] created the so-called 'Ukrainian Protective Police' [*Schutzpolizei*] made up of criminal elements and a few traitors of the Fatherland.[4]

A contemporary Jewish myth, also formulated thirty years ago by the publicist and amateur historian Aleksandr Shlaen, is in fact merely another version of the Soviet myth.

> There were many executioners of Babyn Yar.... At the very least, 1,200 people took part in the first mass execution alone. First and foremost, the main perpetrator was *Einsatzkommando 4a* [*sic*; read: *Sonderkommando 4a*—V.N.]. Approximately 150 people. The 45th and 303rd Police Battalions were assigned to provide assistance. In addition, cutthroats from the 'Bukovynian Battalion' [and] 'volunteers' from among the nationalist bastards who were selected in advance by the Nazis, were rampaging. They included both locals and imported ones.[5]

Shlaen continues: "Babyn Yar was the unique prerogative of the SD. Only those who had previously experienced 'purgatory' in the Security Police, in the SD, were sent there for liquidation."[6] But this myth is focused mainly on the Nazis' henchmen: "The 'Bukovinian Battalion'... even later, for 725 days, dragged off to Babyn Yar all those who were not to the Nazi regime's liking. Such glory also accrued to their 'morally unblemished' brothers in arms...from the 23rd Battalion of the SD security police [*sic*; read: 23rd SD Police Battalion—V.N.], from the 114th, 115th, 117th police battalions, from a heavy weapons company...from the police school..."[7] The composition of these subunits is described in the following terms: "People with an 'unblemished past' joined the Ukrainian police: former criminals and deserters, former Petliurites and Makhnovists, current robbers and killers, all of whom from the first days sensed all the

4 *Istoriia Kieva*, Vol. 3, Book 1, edited by Iurii Kondufor et al. (Kyïv: Naukova dumka, 1986), pp. 326-327.

5 Aleksandr Shlaen, *Babii Iar: khudozhestvennaia publitsistika* (Kyïv: Abris, 1985), p. 324.

6 Ibid.

7 Ibid., p. 160.

attractions of pogromist outlaw life and extortion. Henceforth they were legally permitted to engage in robberies, murders, [and] violence."[8]

Ukrainian mythology surrounding the topic under discussion is, first and foremost, a reaction to Soviet or Jewish mythologies. Its main goal, as noted by one of the authors of a collected volume published in the diaspora, *V borotbi za ukrainsku derzhavnist* (In the Struggle for Ukrainian Statehood), is to refute the "incorrect Jewish treatment of Ukrainians who were supposedly German collaborators."[9] In its most radical version, formulated by a Ukrainian-American activist hiding under the pseudonym "Tetiana Tur," this myth utterly denies the mass shootings of Jews during the occupation of Kyiv, claiming that they had been shipped out of Ukraine and liquidated outside its borders.

According to another version of the Ukrainian myth, which was advanced by a pair of otherwise disreputable journalists, Valerii and Natalia Lapikura, 100,000 Kyiv residents were killed, including 40,000 Jews (both figures are controversial). The Lapikuras declare that "a former NKVD major, the ethnic Jew Vadym Maikovskyi, has at least 7,000 of these 40,000 on his conscience. In the first hours of the occupation of Kyiv he offered his services to the Germans and was appointed chief of the 'native [*tubilna*] police.'"[10]

Here is how a more traditional version of the Ukrainian myth—again, originating in the diaspora—treats these historical events:

> In the first days of the military occupation the Gestapo carried out mass shootings and burials of Ukrainian hostages, together with the Jewish segment of the population there [in Babyn Yar—V.N.], and for nearly three years of the occupation it exterminated leading Ukrainian activists in Kyiv en masse.... Bolshevik agents sneaked into the Gestapo and with the Germans' hands massacred Ukrainians.... This work of 'Cain' was spurred by the '*Volksdeutscher*' and the 'Black Hundreds,' Russians who until recently

8 Ibid., p. 183.

9 Ivan Omel'chenko, "U spil'nii mohyli Babynoho Iaru," in Mykhailo Marunchak, ed., *V borot'bi za ukraïns'ku derzhavnist'* (Winnipeg, 1990), p. 901.

10 Valerii and Natalia Lapikura, "Babyn Iar: trahediia iak tovar dlia gesheftu," *Personal-Plius* (Kyïv), No. 38, 22-28 September 2006.

had been disguising themselves as friends of the Ukrainians.[11]

As we can see, the principal difference between Soviet and Jewish myths lies in the question of victims. Whereas Soviet mythology describes them as *Soviet people*, essentially omitting even the very word *Jews*, Jewish mythology insists conversely that Jews were the main target of Nazi terror both by the nature of the persecutions and numbers.

In turn, the Jewish and Ukrainian myths share one feature. Both focus the utmost attention on the punishers who came from ranks of local residents. In Jewish mythology they are Ukrainians, while in Ukrainian mythology they are Russians, *Volksdeutscher*, or even Jews. In this way these two sets of myths are distinguished from Soviet mythology, which above all seeks political enemies: German Nazis and Ukrainian nationalists.

It must be emphasized that defining a mythology either as "Jewish" or "Ukrainian" does not mean that its promoters are exclusively people of a certain ethnic background; it means only that this mythology exists mostly within a corresponding ethnic or ethnocentric milieu. In similar fashion, Soviet mythology did not disappear along with the USSR, but has remained prominent in the contemporary neo-Soviet Russian reality, as well as among significant strata of the population in post-Soviet countries and in the emigration, where a corresponding system of values is cultivated.

**The German Third Reich's punitive system**

In order to answer the question, "Who did the shooting?," which is of primary concern in public discussions surrounding responsibility for the Holocaust and other Nazi crimes, it is necessary to understand the composition of the punitive system of the Third Reich, especially in occupied Ukraine.

The formation of Nazi Germany's Jewish policy on the whole, that is, the development of the general methods and directions of the "final solution of the Jewish question," was the responsibility of Hermann Göring. As head of the Reichstag and minister-president of Prussia who was

11 T. Koval's'kyi, "Kyïv pid vorozhymy okupatsiiamy," in Maruchak, *V borot'bi*, p. 838.

responsible for carrying out the four-year plan, Göring was the second most important person in the Third Reich. As Hitler's deputy, he was responsible for dealing with this issue from 1938 until the very end of the Nazi regime. But as the commander in chief of the Luftwaffe, Göring did not have any practical instruments for exterminating millions of people. Hence, the leading institutions that were tasked with the practical implementation of the "historic mission" involving the total extermination of European Jewry and other "enemies of the Reich" were the SS and the Ministry of the Interior. Not unexpectedly, disputes over jurisdiction would soon emerge between the SS, the paramilitary units of the Nazi party, and the Ministry of the Interior, a government institution. In order to prevent this, a bureaucratic device, known in medieval times as "personal union," was introduced. In keeping with this mechanism, in 1936 *Reichsführer-SS* Heinrich Himmler was appointed chief of the German police with the status of state secretary of the Ministry of the Interior, and in August 1943 he became the head of this ministry.

But this was just the first step. Personal union was followed by institutional union, that is, the unification of the leadership of party and police structures into one department: the Reich Main Security Office (*Reichssicherheitshauptamt*—RSHA). Although formally it was one of the main SS administrations, the RSHA was established in September 1939 through the amalgamation under one roof of the Main Administration of the Security Police (*Hauptamt der Sicherheitspolizei —Sipo*), to which were subordinated the Secret State Police (*Geheime Staatspolizei* —Gestapo), the Criminal Police (*Kriminalpolizei* —"Kripo"), and the Reichsfuhrer SS Security Service (*Sicherheitsdienst des Reichsführers*—SS/SD), which was the intelligence agency of the Nazi party. The dual character of the RSHA was also reflected in the position of its head, who was officially called the chief of the Security Police and the SD (and not the chief of the main administration of the SS). This position was held by three figures: Reinhard Heydrich (from the inception of the RSHA until he was wounded in an assassination attempt in May 1942); Himmler (until the end of 1942); and Ernst Kaltenbrunner (from late January 1943 until the end of the war).

Within the RSHA—specifically the IV office, or Gestapo[12], headed by Heinrich Müller, and Department B, which oversaw confessional questions[13]—there existed a small "Jewish" sub-department called *Referat IV B 4*,[14] headed by Adolf Eichmann. The subsequent kidnapping of Eichmann by Israeli intelligence agents in Argentina in 1961 and his well-publicized trial made it seem to the general public that he was the chief architect of the "Final Solution." Although Eichmann was indeed responsible for an important link in this process, especially for organizing the deportations of Jews to the death camps, he was in fact only one of a number of individuals who carried out criminal orders. One may say that Eichmann occupied one of the key places in the Nazi machinery for destroying the Jews en masse, but his was more like a driver who chooses the most convenient route, not a chief who decides where to go. While the foregoing in no way absolves Eichmann of responsibility, it is nonetheless useful to state this more realistic assessment of his role in the Holocaust.

One should keep in mind that the "technologies" used to liquidate the Jews of Europe varied from territory to territory. In the occupied European countries, with the exception of Poland and part of Yugoslavia (that is, from the Protectorate of Bohemia and Moravia, France, Belgium, the Netherlands, Luxembourg, Norway, and Greece; from Italy, starting in 1943; and from Hungary, starting in 1944), Jews were deported to death camps located in Polish lands or to ghettos situated on former Soviet territory, where extermination, together with local Jews, awaited them. In the Generalgouvernement and the Warthegau Jews were sent immediately to ghettos and later transported to death camps located in those territories. In former Soviet-ruled lands (within the 1941 borders) and

12 The formal name was: Amt IV—Gegner-Erforschung und Bekämpfung/Office for Research and Combat Against the Enemy.

13 The formal name was: Gruppe IV B—Weltanschauliche Gegner/Department IV B—Opponents of Our World view.

14 The formal name was: Referat IV B4—Judenangelegenheiten, Räumungsangelegenheiten/Sub-department IV B4—The Jewish Question and Evacuation Matters. This name is one of many examples of Nazi euphemisms. Aside from "evacuation," Räumung can also mean "liberation" or "cleansing" which was used by the Nazis in documents to describe their anti-Jewish policies.

in the German occupation zone of Yugoslavia (Serbia and Banat), Jews were shot from the very beginning by *Einsatzkommando* squads. Afterwards, survivors were sent to ghettos or camps. When the ghettos and camps were liquidated, in Distrikt Galizien and Bezirk Bialystok[15] they were transported to the death camps, while in other territories they were summarily executed.

Available documents do not offer researchers the possibility to give an unambiguous answer to the question of why the Nazis used various technologies in different lands. It is possible, however, to consider the Nazis' general racial views of one nationality or another and, accordingly, the plans for their future in keeping with Germany's "New Order."

Thus, we see two fundamentally different methods of extermination, which were carried out through two different systems of punitive institutions and structures. First there were the *Vernichtungslager* (death camps) that were subordinated to the following structures: Kulmhof (in the village of Chełmno on the Ner)—to the RSHA through the Security Police and *SD Warthegau*[16]; Auschwitz-Birkenau (just outside the city of Oświęcim) and Lublin (located on the outskirts of Majdanek)—to the *SS-Wirtschafts- und Verwaltungshauptamt* (SS Main Economic and Administrative Office) headed by Oswald Pohl through the *Inspektion der Konzentrationslager* (Inspection of Concentration Camps, Richard Glucks); and the camps of *Aktion Reinhardt* (Belzec, Sobibor, and Treblinka under the direct control of Adolf Hitler's personal chancellery), which they were managed by Himmler himself through Odilo Globocnik, commander of the SS and the police in Distrikt Lublin.

The camps were protected by subunits of the *SS-Division Totenkopf* (Skull and Crossbones SS Division). Like the SS troops, they were subordinated to the *SS-Führungshauptamt*, the operational headquarters of

15 This separate administrative unit, subordinated to the Third Reich, was created in June 1941 in the eastern Polish lands between the Generalgouvernement, East Prussia, and Reichskommisariat Ostland. In the fall of 1939, this territory was annexed to the Soviet Union in accordance with the Treaty of Moscow, and by the beginning of the German-Soviet war it was part of the Belarussian SSR.

16 Reichsgau Wartheland was an administrative unit of the Third Reich; its center was the city of Posen (Pol.: Poznań), which was created in October 1939 in the annexed western lands of Poland.

the SS. It was under Himmler's direct control until it was taken over by Hans Jüttner, former chief of the headquarters of SS troops.

The RSHA played a significant role in carrying out mass shootings and other forms of exterminating Jews in their areas of residence. It was responsible for the creation and activities of the *Einsatzgruppen*, mobile squads formed mostly out of former policemen and members of the SD. The *Einsatzgruppen* were temporary formations whose initial task was to seize archives as well as to uncover and isolate all those whom the Nazi regime considered its political enemies. In 1938–1939, *Einsatzgruppen* operated in Austria, Czechoslovakia, and Poland. Later, these formations were used in the anti-partisan struggle in Yugoslavia and Slovakia and in punitive actions in Norway, Tunisia, France, Luxembourg, and Belgium.

The most notorious *Einsatzgruppen* were the four that operated on the occupied territories of the USSR. Their composition ranged from 600 (*Einsatzgruppe D*) to 900 (*Einsatzgruppe* A) members who were divided into several *Sonderkommando* (Special Forces) and *Einsatzkommando* (task forces). Each *Einsatzgruppe* operated in the frontline zone of an army group: *Einsatzgruppe* A—Army Group North; *Einsatzgruppe B*—Army Group Center. The territory of Ukraine was the base of operations of *Einsatzgruppe C* (part of *Sonderkommando 4a* and *4b*, *Einsatzkommando 5* and *6*)—in the zone of Army Group South, and *Einsatzgruppe D* (part of *Sonderkommando 10a*, *10b* and *Einsatzkommando 11a*, *11b*, and *12*)—in the zone of the 11th Army. *Einsatzgruppe C* was commanded by Otto Rasch (until late September 1941) and Max Thomas; *Einsatzgruppe D*—by Otto Ohlendorf (until July 1941 ) and Walther Bierkamp.

As the front moved eastward, these formations were turned into stationary structures of the Security Police and the SD. Thus, the Territorial Command of the Security Police and the SD (*Befehlshaber der Sicherheitspolizei und des SD, BdS*) was created on the basis of *Einsatzgruppe C* within the Reichskommissariat Ukraine, while *Einsatzkommando 5* formed the nucleus of the Regional Command of the Security Police and the SD (*Kommandeur der Sicherheitspolizei und des SD, KdS*) for the Kyiv general district. It is worthwhile mentioning that, like the *Einsatzgruppen*, whose operational activities were independent of military leaders, the Security Police and SD structures were independent of civil administration agencies in the occupied territories.

The *Einsatzgruppen* played a leading role in the mass shootings of Jews in the occupied territories. But they were not the only subunits that carried out punitive functions, including those targeting Jews. Others that operated together with the *Einsatzgruppen* included:

(1) In the military administration zone: security divisions (*Sicherungs-Division*), military police (*Feldgendarmerie*), and Secret military police (*Geheime Feldpolizei*—GFP), who were subordinated to the Territorial Command of Army Group Rear Area (*Befehlshaber rückwärtiges Heeresgebiet*). In the Ukrainian lands this position was held at various times by Karl von Roques, Erich Friderici, and Joachim Witthöft. They were also responsible for prisoner-of-war camps, where Jewish combatants were singled out for summary execution. Therefore, these structures were subordinated to the Wehrmacht, which required additional coordination in the event that it was necessary to carry out joint operations.

(2) In the civilian administration zone: units of the Protective Police (*Schutzpolizei—Schupo*) in cities, and the *Gendarmerie* in rural areas, which came under the purview of the Order Police (*Ordnungspolizei—Orpo*). The latter was subordinated to Himmler as the chief of the German police through the Main Administration of the Order Police (*Hauptamt Ordnungspolizei*), headed by Kurt Daluege (until late August 1943) and Alfred Wünnenberg. The regional structure of the *Orpo* was identical to that of the Security Police and the SD. In the Reichskommissariat Ukraine it was headed by the Territorial Command of the Order Police (*Befehlshaber der Ordnungspolizei, BdO*), to which regional *Orpo* commanders (*Kommandeur der Ordnungspolizei, KdO*) in separate general districts were subordinated. In various years the position of territorial commander was held by Otto von Ölhafen, Adolf von Bomhard, Werner Lorge, and Karl Brenner.

(3) Police and SS units were subordinated to the heads of the SS and the police (*SS- und Polizeiführer*), who were personally appointed by Himmler. In the Ukrainian lands, in particular, these were the senior heads of the SS and the Police in the South of Russia (*Höhere SS- und Polizeiführer Rußland-Süd*): Friedrich Jeckeln (until October 1941) and his successor, Hans-Adolf Prützmann, who was appointed supreme com-

mander of the SS and the police in Ukraine (*Höchste SS- und Polizeiführer Ukraine*) in October 1943.[17] The Police Regiment South (consisting of three battalions), two separate police battalions, and SS infantry and cavalry formations were subordinated to them.

Functioning on a lower rung were commanders of the SS and the police in general districts and the District Galizien. The latter was subordinated to the Senior Head of the SS and the Police in the East (*Höhere SS- und Polizeiführer Ost*), that is, in the Generalgouvernement. In addition, at the end of October 1943 the Senior Head of the SS and Police in the Black Sea Region (*Höhere SS- und Polizeiführer Schwarzes Meer*), who was operating in the rear of Army Group A, was appointed. It must be noted that the commanders of the SS and the police were simultaneously senior commanders for heads of corresponding territorial subunits of the Security Police and SD as well as the Order Police, which enabled Himmler to maintain direct control over their activities and, if necessary, to intervene in them.

In addition to German formations, the punitive system included subunits composed of local residents and prisoners of war. These included: subunits protecting the death camps and concentration camps, particularly the so-called *Trawniki*[18]; stationary structures of the auxiliary police (*Hilfspolizei*); mobile subunits of Auxiliary Police (*Schutzmannschaft*); and Jewish police (*Judischer Ordnungsdienst*) based in ghettos, which were composed of ghetto residents.

All these formations were under overall German control; therefore, participation in punitive measures of any kind took place only on German orders. As regards the local "Ukrainian" police, very precise directives were issued in the fall of 1941 by the head of the rear area of Group

---

17 This was the second and last appointment of a "supreme" commander in chief of the SS and the police. The first to obtain this rank was Karl Wolff, the head of Himmler's personal headquarters and an SS communications officer under Hitler, when he was appointed to the same position in Italy in September 1943.

18 This word is derived from the Trawniki concentration camp near Lublin, where a center for training camp guards culled from the ranks of Soviet POW volunteers operated in 1941–1944, and from the fall of 1942, from the ranks of the civilian population in Distrikt Galizien, Distrikt Lublin, and Generalbezirk Wolhynien und Podolien.

Army South, Infantry General Erich Friderici: "Auxiliary subunits that are being created out of the local population can in no way have the hallmarks of any future Ukrainian formation; they serve German [emphasis in the original document—V.N.] goals exclusively.... It is necessary to prevent the penetration of Banderite propaganda or other political aspirations into such auxiliary commands."[19] The degree of responsibility was spelled out clearly: "Local residents who have been accepted into German service must be vetted most thoroughly by the secret military police or the SD and always be under control. For treason, only the death penalty by hanging is to be handed down."[20] The organizational assurance of upholding these directives was based on the clear-cut requirement that "the command must always remain in German hands."[21]

### The executioners

It is in this context that the events in occupied Kyiv can be examined. There were two main, chronologically overlapping, periods of executions that took place in the vicinity of Babyn Yar. The first period lasted from September to mid-November 1941, during which executions were carried out mostly by German mobile subunits. The following operated in Kyiv.

(1) Units of *Einsatzgruppe C* (commander: *SS-Brigadeführer* and Major-General of the Police Dr. Otto Rasch): group headquarters; *Sonderkommando 4a* (commander: *SS-Standartenführer* Paul Blobel); *Einsatzkommando 5* (commander: *SS-Sturmbannführer* August Meier); 3rd Company of the 9th Reserve Police Battalion (commander: Police Captain Walter Krumme); and 3rd Company of a special battalion of SS troops (commander: *SS-Obersturmführer* Bernhard Grafhorst).

(2) Units subordinated to the commander in chief of the SS and the Police in the South of Russia (*SS-Obergruppenführer* Friedrich Jeckeln): Police Regiment South (commander: Police Colonel Rene Rosenbauer); regimental headquarters; "headquarters company" (volunteer firing

19 Tsentral'nyi derzhavnyi arkhiv vyshchykh orhaniv vlady ta upravlinnia Ukraïny, Kyïv (hereafter: TsDAVOU), Fond KMF–8, T–501, Rolyk 6, Kadr 545.

20 Ibid.

21 Ibid.

squad); 45th Reserve Battalion (commander: Major of Police and *SS Sturmbannführer* Martin Besser); and the 303rd Battalion (commander: Major of Police and *SS Sturmbannführer* Heinrich Hannibal).

(3) Various units recruited as firing squads: uniformed military police; and the Wehrmacht, specifically the 454th Security Division, 75th and 299th infantry divisions.

From mid-October 1941 to late September 1943 Babyn Yar was the site of regular executions carried out by the Security Police and the SD in close cooperation with the military and civil authorities of Kyiv. [see Plates **X** and **XI**] This period can be divided into three main stages. The first lasted from mid-October 1941 until the spring of 1942. It began against the background of continuous mass operations, at which time local military authorities actively enlisted the services of subunits of the *Einsatzkommando 5* stationed in Kyiv to carry out the executions.

The second stage lasted from the late winter of 1942 to mid-August 1943 and was characterized by the independent activities of the Security Police and the SD. Initially, subunits of the Order Police were used to carry out the shootings and later, a specially created SD company. The Syrets concentration camp, which was established in April–May 1943, operated during this period in the vicinity of Babyn Yar.

The third and final stage, which was also the most intensive period of regular executions in Babyn Yar, took place at the same time of concerted efforts to destroy the bodies. [see Plate **XV**] This work was done by prisoners of the Syrets camp, who were transferred to dugouts located in the ravine itself. During this period, the Syrets concentration camp was steadily evacuated, while the work was undertaken between 18 August and 28 September 1943. Guard duty was performed by a Kommando 1005A team composed exclusively of officers and corporals. In October and early November 1943, the military authorities of Kyiv carried out executions once again in the vicinity of Babyn Yar.

What is most controversial from the standpoint of subsequent public discussions is the degree to which the local ("Ukrainian") police participated in punitive operations, as well as the description of its personnel. This pertains especially to the mass executions of Jews, which took place in late September–early October 1941.

There is no doubt that the local police took part in these events. The daily report of the 454th Security Division, dated 29 September 1941, notes: "In response to the desire of the local commandant's office in Kyiv, 300 Ukrainian auxiliary policemen who have completed on-site training and are very familiar with the conditions in Kyiv have been placed at the disposal of the 195th Feldcommandant's Office."[22] Clearly, these 300 policemen were supposed to be used in the *Gross-Aktion* that was launched that very day, and in which the military commandant of the city, Major-General Kurt Eberhard, who had once headed this same 195th Feldcommandant's Office, was most actively involved. But who were these policemen?

According to a sketch of the history of the Ukrainian Security Police in Kyiv drafted by its heads in 1942: "on 21 September Mr. Bohdan Konyk arrived in Kyiv with a unit of 18 Cossacks who were in the service of the Ukrainian Police from the Zhytomyr oblast. This small group formed the nucleus of the UOP [Ukrainian Security Police—V.N.]. On 23 September a Cossack company led by Lieutenant Ivan Kediulych arrived in Kyiv to carry out service on the orders of the German military command."[23] A similar document provides clarification: "From the very first days our police force was composed of 45 ordinary policemen and 5 investigators.... Sometime around 1 October two transports of policemen numbering around 150 men arrived from Zhytomyr.... Within a short period of time this garrison expanded to 300 men."[24]

Bohdan Konyk, Ivan Kediulych, and the "Cossacks" under their authority who formed the nucleus of the local police, were members of one of the so-called "expeditionary groups" created by the Melnykite faction of the Organization of Ukrainian Nationalists, the OUN-M. The same cannot be said of the rest of the police force, however. Another OUN member, Yurii Tarkovych, the former editor of the newspaper *Karpatska*

---

22 Ibid., Rolyk 5, Kadr 1279.

23 Derzhavnyi arkhiv Kyïvs'koï oblasty, Kyïv (hereafter: DAKO), Fond R–2412, Opys 2, Sprava 227, Arkush 2.

24 Oleksandr Kucheruk, "Pochatkovyi period diial'nosti ukraïns'koï politsiï Kyieva v chas nimets'koï okupatsiï," in *Kyïv i kyiany: materialy . . . naukovo-praktychnoï konferentsiï Muzeiu istoriï m. Kieva*, Vyp. 5 (Kyïv, 2005), p. 82.

*Ukraina* (Carpathian Ukraine), left very detailed recollections of the circumstances surrounding the formation of this police force in Zhytomyr. He writes:

> The number of policemen increased constantly. We were accepting new ones, selecting [men] above all from the camp...that was not far from Zhytomyr, . . . where there were 8,000–10,000 prisoners. . . . This was no easy matter. We come to the camp, and before us are thousands of gray overcoats, from which only thin, yellow faces with overgrown beards can be seen. A multitude of human misfortune. . . . [It was necessary to] recruit a police force from this.
>
> – 'Who wants to serve in the Ukrainian police?'
>
> A minute's silence, after which several thousand hands are raised. Everyone wants to [join] the police. I see that nothing will come of this. And again:
>
> – I yell, 'Only Ukrainians should raise their hands.'
>
> And again, everyone to a man raises his hand. And all sorts of Caucasus and Siberian peoples, Kalmyks, Tatars, Ossetians, Chuvashes, and who knows what kinds of other nationalities. All of them now consider themselves Ukrainians. Each one wants to get out of the prisoner-of-war camp. . . .
>
> It was very difficult for us to choose, and a prisoner's better boots were often the deciding factor. We had little footwear, and the police force could not be shoeless. Difficulties also lay in the fact that many Ukrainians did not know the Ukrainian language. Before the liberation of Kyiv my unit already had 700 policemen; in addition, I still had to choose 300 for the police in Kyiv.[25]

Therefore, the 300 "Ukrainian" policemen who were in Kyiv during the mass shootings of the Jews were mostly not conscious Ukrainian nationalists but average Soviet prisoners of war, who tried at any cost to get out of the POW camp.

We also learn about how roles were assigned during the mass shootings that took place on 29–30 September from postwar documents, such as materials from the German trials of war criminals and the memoirs of

25 TsDAVOU, Fond 3833, Opys 3, Sprava 14, Arkush 41 zv, 42 zv, 43 zv.

people who escaped Babyn Yar.

The sentence handed down in the 1968 Darmstadt trial of the members of *Sonderkommando 4a* notes:

> Since there were supposed to be approximately 150,000 Jews in the city, and the execution of no fewer than 50,000 Jews was anticipated, accurate planning, thorough-going preparation, and special organization, in which the headquarters of *Einsatzgruppe C* also took part, were indispensable. Negotiations took place between the commander of *Einsatzgruppe C* Dr. Rasch and Blobel, on the one side, and the commandant of the city . . . Major-General Eberhard and the 29th Army Corps that was in Kyiv [the commander of the Corps was Infantry General Hans von Obstfelder—V.N.], on the other. During them the planned killing in connection with the 'resettlement' was outlined in general terms. . . . Since the forces of *Sonderkommando 4a* and additional units of 3rd Company of the SS battalion and the 3rd Platoon of the 9th Reserve Police Battalion turned out to be inadequate for the anticipated scale of execution, they also turned to *SS Obergruppenführer* Jeckeln, who provided the 45th and 303rd police battalions from the Russia-South Police Regiment to assist *Sonderkommando 4a*.
>
> ...On the morning of 29 September 1941 columns of Jewish families began proceeding along the streets of Kyiv to the assembly point, the district of Lukianivka. From the early morning the assembly point and city streets were guarded by the 303rd [Major Hannibal refused to take part in the shootings because his battalion was used only for patrolling the city and the vicinity of the place of execution—V.N.] and 45th police battalions, which were stationed within earshot of each other.
>
> At the assembly point was a cordon manned, in addition to soldiers of *Sonderkommando 4a*, by Ukrainian militia, the SS, and policemen.[26]

Witnesses corroborated the presence of Ukrainian policemen in the outer circle. For example, Dina Pronicheva, who on two occasions avoided being shot on those days, testified in 1946 before a Soviet commission formed to compile a chronicle of the Great Patriotic War: "Once we

26 *Justiz und NS-Verbrechen: Die deutschen Strafverfahren wegen nationalsozialistischer Tötungsverbrechen 1945-1999*, Vol. XXXI (Amsterdam and Munich, 2004), p. 181-182.

nearly reached the gates of the Jewish cemetery, there was a wire barrier; anti-tank hedgehogs were standing there. Near the entrance stood Germans and Ukrainians, who were letting [people] pass through the roadblock."[27] Other witnesses add that there were also German military policemen in this area. Genia Batashova, who was also saved from death, recalled: "Germans were standing on both sides at the approach to Dorohozhytska Street. [They wore] light-green uniforms with white badges on their chests. This was the military police. They looked at us sullenly. Among them, Gestapo men in black uniforms were issuing some kinds of orders."[28]

Additional testimonies appear in the materials from the 1968 Darmstadt trial:

> Here those of non-Jewish nationality who were accompanying [the Jews] were sent back. Jews had to go through the barrier, after which no one was allowed back. Past the barrier was a dense cordon of well-armed guards who herded the Jews forward [From Genia Batashova's memoirs: "Along Dorohozhytska, between the two cemeteries, the entrance was narrowing. Here we saw something like a barrier. On both sides were black anti-tank 'hedgehogs.' Barbed wire stretched from them. Beyond the barrier stood Germans close to each other; they were holding wide-open sacks. This was the cordon"—V.N.]. At first, the Jews were supposed to walk farther along the road between the two cemeteries to an alleyway that led in the direction of Babyn Yar. The Jews were also registered, their passports and valuables were taken, and a little farther on they deposited their baggage [From the memoirs of G. Batashova: "Passports had to be thrown into the sacks; valuables, into others; a few steps away, belongings were being taken away"—V.N.][29]

It was in this place that the Ukrainian police reappeared. Fritz Höfer, a driver for *Sonderkommando 4a*, testified: "One day I was given an assignment to drive my truck out of the city. A Ukrainian acting as a navigator

27 TsDAHOU, Fond 166, Opys 3, Sprava 245, Arkush 116–117.

28 Iurii Petrashevych, "Tini Babynoho Iaru: novi fakty i svidchennia ochevydtsiv," *Kyïv*, No. 1 (Kyiv, 1994), pp. 97-98.

29 *Justiz*, Vol. XXXI, p. 182.

was with me. It was around 10 o'clock. En route we passed Jews who were moving in a column with luggage in the same direction. . . . On a large, open meadow lay piles of clothing; I drove right over them. I pulled up alongside, and Ukrainians who were in the meadow began loading the things onto the truck."[30]

In 1946, the Ministry of State Security arrested a resident of Kyiv named Oleh Stasiuk. He was captured during the German encirclement of Kyiv and then sent to a POW camp in Zhytomyr, where he, along with others, enlisted in the Kyiv police. They were brought to Kyiv immediately after the Germans occupied the city. Under interrogation Stasiuk recounted in detail that on the first or second day of the shootings forty policemen from their subunit were brought in two vehicles to a street near Babyn Yar. Eventually a German led them "to a place where the Jewish population was being stripped of clothing. . . . All of us policemen were forced to bring all those things to one spot and put it in order. . . . Once the things were gathered together, trucks arrived. We were ordered to load those things onto the truck, and when the loaded trucks left . . . for the city . . . we guarded the remaining things."[31]

Returning to Höfer's testimony: "From that spot I saw that the Jews who were arriving . . . were also met by Ukrainians and led to the place where, one by one, they were supposed to deposit their grain, coats, footwear, outer clothing, and even underwear. In a designated spot the Jews were also supposed to deposit their valuables."[32] Additional information is provided by the materials from the Darmstadt trial:

> Along that cordon, which stood like a tight chain along the road, they were driven with blows to an open area located at the end of the alleyway [From G. Batashova's memoirs: ". . . there was no road other than the passage to Babyn Yar. Trees grew alongside it, and standing in between them in a tight corridor were German gunners. After the surrender of documents and belongings, the Germans pounced on the people, beating

30 *"Schöne Zeiten": Judenmord aus der Sicht der Täter und Gaffner*, edited by Ernst Klee, Willi Dressen, and Volker Ries (Frankfurt am Main, 1988), pp. 66-67.

31 Haluzevyi derzhavnyi arkhiv Sluzhby bezpeky Ukraïny (hereafter: HDA SBU), Fond 5, Sprava 26 304, Arkush 15–17.

32 *"Shöne Zeiten"*, p. 67.

them with clubs.... The Germans set the dogs on those who fell"—V.N.]. . . . Those who came into the open space were forced to undress. For the sake of persuasiveness, the order was accompanied by blows. If the matter was proceeding slowly, clothing was torn off. Then the victims, naked or partially dressed in underwear, and, once again, with beatings to speed up the shooting, were herded to the ravine.[33]

Ukrainians appear once again, as Höfer testified: "There was a terrible din going on while some people undressed and most waited for their turn. The Ukrainians did not pay any attention to it. They continued to herd people quickly through the passages toward the ravine."[34]

The presence of Ukrainian policemen right next to the ravine is indicated unquestionably by the circumstances surrounding the rescue of at least three people. The first was Genia Batashova:

> We ended up in a glade with trampled grass. . . . On the opposite side of the meadow, surrounded on all sides by Germans, there was a mound of earth. Behind it machine guns clattered away relentlessly. Passageways in the mound were dug out at an acute angle, so that no one could see what was going on past that point. Here on the green square, people's clothing and underwear were torn off and, beaten with clubs, they were driven toward the passageways. Children and adults dashed in all directions, screaming in horror. An infant lay on the ground. . . . A German came up and smashed its head with a club. . . .
>
> I rushed toward a policeman, begged him to protect Grisha [Batashova's younger brother—V.N.]. He shouted something and pushed us so hard that we fell. . . .
>
> Nearby stood a policeman. We [Batashova and her neighbor Mariia Palti—V.N.] ran up to him, asked him for help, explained that we are Russians, we had come here by accident, out of curiosity.
>
> 'I see that you are not Jewesses,' he said. And suddenly, as though becoming frightened of someone, he shouted: 'Jews or not Jews, march to the ravine!'
>
> . . . I peered into the policemen's eyes, looked for sympathy. I had no

33 *Justiz*, Vol. XXXI, pp. 182-183.

34 *"Shöne Zeiten"*, p. 69.

hope for the Germans. Finally I noticed a policeman. I felt something human in him. We rushed over to him.

'I don't care who you are,' he said quietly. 'I will help you.'

He led us to a group of Germans who were standing on the other side of the enclosure, near a passenger car. There were mountains of things here. The Germans were dragging them from the place where people were undressing, they threw the clothing on the grass and turned back quickly.

The policeman began explaining to the Germans that we were sisters (I too had light eyes and a braid) and had ended up here by accident.

The Germans asked for [our] address and surname.

I gave my real name, Batashova. Mania identified herself as Chornetsky (the name of the woman who lived with her family). . . . The German yelled that we were lying: we're sisters but our surnames are different! With words [and] hands we began explaining that we were cousins. The policeman confirmed.

We were pushed into a car and driven away. And a few minutes later we were shoved out at the corner of Melnikova and Pugacheva streets.[35]

The second person saved was Dina Pronicheva:

I had thrown out my passport, leaving only some documents, like my trade union membership card, labor book in which only my surname was recorded but not and my nationality. After I ended up in the policemen's hands, I told the first policeman in pure Ukrainian that I was not a Jewess, that I was Ukrainian and had ended up here by accident; at the same time I showed him my documents. He suggested that I sit near the spot where the Jewish population was being undressed and told me to wait until evening, and in the evening I could go home. I joined a small group of people who had ended up here by accident. That's how I was not stripped of my clothing. I sat there until evening.

Throughout that day I saw horrifying scenes. Before my very eyes people were losing their sanity, their hair had turned gray, all around were frantic cries and groans. I saw the Germans taking children away from their mothers and throwing them from the precipice down into the ravine. Towards evening a car drove up to our group, a German officer

35 Cited in Petrashevych, "Tini Babynoho Iaru," pp. 98-99.

> came out of it. After inquiring about this group, he gave an order to shoot us all, explaining that people, even though they are not Jews, cannot be let go from here because they had seen everything that had taken place here.[36]

The third person to be saved was Viktor Alperin, who recalled how, as a five-year-old boy together with his mother and grandmother, he was led away practically from the muzzle of a machine gun past Babyn Yar by a Ukrainian policeman "with sad eyes," named "Mr. Gordon." The next day, the policeman gave them a certificate stating that they were a Ukrainian family; he even helped them obtain a residence permit for another apartment, because it was dangerous to live in their former apartment. This "Mr. Gordon" was Roman Bida, a member of the OUN-M and head of the investigation department of the Ukrainian auxiliary police, who was executed in Babyn Yar in the winter of 1941.

Why did the Germans need Ukrainian policemen, armed only with clubs, almost at the very site of the shootings? The unexpected answer to this question is found in a report that Dr. Rasch sent to Berlin in early September 1941:

> Nearly everywhere we have failed to persuade the population to take active steps against the Jews. This should be attributed to the fear that the Reds might still return, which is still felt among broader circles. . . . In order to overcome this fear psychosis and to dispel the fascination that the Jews, as the bearers of political authority, have held for the Ukrainians, *Einsatzkommando 6* repeatedly ordered that the Jews be led through the city under guard before execution. Weight was also given to the presence at the executions of militia men (Ukrainian service to maintain order).[37]

It was not enough to involve the Ukrainian police in the executions. Rather, it was the educational and psychological aspect that mattered to the Germans. Moreover, these policemen were not assigned the most important work. In this connection, the materials of the Darmstadt trial

36 HDA SBU, Fond 7, Opys 8, Sprava 1, Arkush 75–77.

37 *Sbornik dokumentov i materialov ob unichtozhenii natsistami evreev Ukrainy v 1941-1944 godakh*, compiled by Aleksander Kruglov (Kyiv, 1985), p. 72.

provide additional information:

> In one of those ravines that stretched several hundreds of meters and had numerous twists and turns, there were a few firing squads of the *Sonderkommando 4a*, additional units of the 3rd Company of the SS battalion [according to other documents, *Obersturmführer* Bernhard Grafhorst refused to take part in the executions, as his company has been assigned to patrol the city—V.N.], and the 3rd Platoon of the 9th Reserve Police Battalion [squads of the 45th Reserve Police Battalion were directly involved in the shootings, which fact was established during the trial of its heads in Regensburg in 1971—V.N.], which were deployed equidistantly from each other. The firing squads consisted of one gunner with a submachine gun, two people who loaded ammunition, and several people who were herding the victims to the ravine. The victims were pushed down to the bottom of the ravine toward the execution squads. They were made to lie face-down on the bloodied corpses of victims who had already been shot. If they did not do this willingly, they were beaten and knocked down. Then the gunners climbed over the wobbly mounds toward the victims and shot them in the back of the neck. The ravine thus filled up with many victims in an end-to-front direction and from side to side.[38]

Information about the role of the Ukrainian police in the subsequent mass executions that took place in Babyn Yar appears in the police force's own documents as well as the materials from Soviet postwar trials. The above-mentioned historical sketch notes the following: "On 29 September the Headquarters (later called the Ukrainian Police Command) begins to function. Lieutenant Orlyk is appointed commandant of the city. He begins to organize the first districts: Podil, Sofiivka [called Molotov district before the war—V.N.], Bohdaniv [called Lenin district before the war—V.N.], and Kurenivka. As of 1 October, these districts set about carrying out police service."[39]

From other information we learn that the Protective Police of Kyiv's Sviatoshyn district was created "in early October"; Pechersk district, "in the first half of October"; Zaliznychnyi, on 10 October; Yaroslav (called

38 *Justiz*, Vol. XXI, p. 183.

39 DAKO, Fond R–2412, Opys 2, Sprava 227, Arkush 2.

Kaganovich before the war), on 15 October, Shevchenko (called Stalin before the war), on 20 October; and Darnytsia, on 23 October. The report of the Volodymyr district (called Zhovtnevyi before the war) is not extant.

Thus, most of the district branches of the Ukrainian police apparently began functioning when, as noted in a report prepared by the Sviatoshyn district police, "there were practically no elements, such as Jews, NKVD men, and communists, left in the district, except for individuals who were exposed in due time."[40] But not everyone was so "lucky." According to a report drafted by the Yaroslav district police:

> there was a lot of work. Jews were retaliating against the German and Ukrainian peoples, burning down buildings, and cutting telephone wires; it was necessary to catch and destroy the vipers. We had to work day and night. . . . The period from 15 October to 1 January 1942 was a period of intensive work, both organizational and practical, on the struggle against Judaeo-Bolshevik agents and remnants of Jews, who throughout the whole time of our work actively wreaked damage and tried to disrupt our work.[41]

The policemen conscientiously carried out Commandant Orlyk's "Order No. 5":

> Within 24 hours all managers of buildings in the city of Kyiv are to report all Jews, NKVD employees, and Communist party members residing in their buildings to the nearest district Commissariats and Ukrainian Police Commands in the city of Kyiv, on 15 Korolenko Street, second floor.
>
> Concealing these people will result in the death sentence.
>
> The managers and caretakers of these buildings have the right personally to deliver Jews to the Jewish camp that is located at the prisoner of war camp on Kerosynna Street.[42]

40 Ibid., Sprava 221, Arkush 1.

41 Ibid., Sprava 224, Arkush 3–4.

42 TsDAHOU, Fond 1, Opys 23, Sprava 121, Arkush 7.

There were enough matters to deal with apart from this task. For example,

> The [Zaliznychnyi] Police District all this time has been carrying out the following work: It is helping the German Command, Municipal Administration, district administration, and other organizations to execute and carry out various resolutions and orders, and to guard various facilities, such as the freight station, the airfield, the Volhynian Station, the TETs [combined heat and power plant], the Kyiv train station, and other temporary facilities. Constant patrols of the district [are necessary], especially at night, so as to maintain order in the district and monitor compliance with blackout orders.
>
> Important work has been carried out in the matter of sending a workforce to Germany by helping the Dis[trict] Administration and the Labor Exchange in the forcible dispatching and by uncovering, by means of roundups and dispatching to Germany, of various elements that it is not desirable to leave in the city of Kyiv: speculators, idlers.[43]

In the Pechersk district,

> the police force, in addition to security is carrying out the following duties: 1. capturing hostile elements; 2. confiscating looted mismanaged property; 3. investigating the causes of fires in the district; 4. overseeing the cleanup of the district and care for its sanitary condition; and 5. organizing the security of buildings by residents with the help of the District Administration, through building managers. . . .
>
> Starting on 7 April [1942—V.N.], the Commandant's Office of the district is helping the District Administration to carry out work of great importance: the recruitment of a workforce for Greater Germany.[44]

Despite the fact that the Darnytsia police was the last to be organized, "from its first steps the following important measures were carried out: 1. An order was issued and the surrender of weapons from the population was organized, which were then handed over to the City Commandant's

43 DAKO, Fond R–2412, Opys 2, Sprava 223, Arkush 2.

44 Ibid., Sprava 226, Arkush 1.

Office; 2. In keeping with an order, the registration of communists and former personnel of the NKVD and militia was carried out (140 communists were registered); and 3. In keeping with an order, mismanaged and looted property was confiscated from the population."[45]

And "thanks to the circumstance that in due course and entirely correctly and in a timely fashion Soviet activists and all suspicious elements were handed over to the organs of the SD, terrorist acts and sabotage, which were not occurring and have not occurred to this day in any event, were thus prevented."[46]

For information on the participation of the Ukrainian police in the shootings that continued to take place without interruption, we can refer to the materials of Soviet postwar trials. For example, Vasyl Pokotylo, who began serving in the Ukrainian Protective Police in early October 1941, offered extensive testimony in which he admitted that he had taken part not only in the efforts to expose Jews and communists but also in the numerous executions of Jews, partisans, NKVD personnel, prisoners of war, parachutists, and communists, among whom were women and children. He and other policemen were recruited to carry out these shootings by the SD. And although Pokotylo eventually recanted his testimony, the court ignored this.

In another case, the Kyivan *Volksdeutscher* (ethnic German) Fedir Krul, who began working for the SD in the spring of 1942, stated that even though he had traveled to the shootings several times as part of an SD team, he himself never took part in them but was merely in the vicinity. Kyiv resident Mykola Fokyn, who through his wife had become acquainted with OUN members arriving in Kyiv, particularly Roman Gordon (Bida). From September 1941 until the latter's arrest, Fokyn had worked under Gordon's direction in the investigative department of the municipal Ukrainian police. Fokyn testified that during this period the staff of the investigative department "exposed Jewish families that remained in the city, drove them to the Lukianivka Cemetery, and shot [them],"[47] although he himself had not participated in this. In another

45 Ibid., Sprava 225, Arkush 4–5.

46 Ibid., Arkush 7.

47 HDA SBU, Fond 6, Sprava 69 330 FP, Arkush 33.

case, Serhii Orlov, a candidate for membership in the Communist party, who in early November was in the prisoner-of-war camp located on Kerosynna Street in Kyiv, volunteered to serve in a security squad (later, a battalion). He stated that on several occasions, servicemen from his battalion—not including him, of course—escorted Jews to Babyn Yar, but they did not take part in the shootings. Later, Orlov categorically emphasized again that even though the battalion took part in arresting Jews, "only the Germans did the shooting."[48]

Then there is the testimony of Lieutenant-General of Police Paul Scheer, who in November 1941 was appointed chief of the Order Police—that is, the commander of the Protective Police—*Schutzpolizei* and the Gendarmerie—in the Kyiv General District. Working under Scheer were a thousand members of the German *Schutzpolizei* and an equal number of policemen in two Ukrainian police battalions, as well as 200 *Volksdeutscher* from Estonia in two separate police companies. During the Kyiv trial of 1946 he testified that every night the policemen under his command shot between eight and ten people for violating the curfew. He also recounted that throughout 1942 he provided the SD with the necessary forces to carry out mass arrests of communists, as well as special firing squads to carry out executions. Therefore, it is entirely likely that there could have been Ukrainian policemen among General Scheer's subordinates whom the SD had recruited to carry out the shootings.

As for the sphere of authority of the municipal police force, which, following the creation of the German Order Police was also under Scheer's command, its personnel (as mentioned in Order No. 3 issued to the Volodymyr district police on 28 October 1941) were only supposed "to detain Jews, speculators, and other criminal offenders and suspicious individuals and direct them to the police."[49] Subsequently, Jews and those who hid them, as well as former NKVD personnel, partisans, and other "enemies of the Reich," were handed over (as we can see from the journal in which detainees were registered) either to the municipal investigation department at 15 Korolenko Street, the SD located at 33 Korolenko Street, or the Syrets concentration camp.

---

48 Ibid., Fond 5, Sprava 66 434, Arkush 30.

49 DAKO, Fond R–4437, Opys 1, Sprava 1, Arkush 321.

Summarizing the above, we can concur with the conclusions that were reached shortly after the described events by the leaders of at least the Banderite faction of the OUN. For example, one OUN-B document intended for explanatory work put forward the presumption that "a Ukrainian police force can only exist in a Ukrainian State" and proposed "explaining the following issues to the people":

1. There is no Ukrainian police anywhere.
2. There is only the German police, and Ukrainians, as so-called *shutsmany* [German: *Schutzmänner*], serve in it. . . .
4. The *shutsmany* are not just Ukrainians, they are also Muscovites (in the eastern oblasts), Poles (Polissia), and *Volksdeutscher* (everywhere).
5. People are being beaten and robbed not by the Ukrainian police but by the German [police] with the assistance of the *shutsmany*.
6. Among the Ukrainians who are serving as *shutsmany* are honest people and shady types, just like in all departments where Ukrainians work.
7. The excesses of shady types are to be laid at their feet, not at the feet of all Ukrainians who are serving as *shutsmany*.[50]

### The Syrets concentration camp

The Syrets concentration or forced labor camp, which was a branch of the Sachsenhausen concentration camp, is a separate page in the history of Babyn Yar. It was located right at the top of the ravine (between today's Ryzka, Olena Teliha, and Shamryla streets), and it occupied part of the territory of the Kyiv garrison's summer military camps that had existed on that spot since the mid-nineteenth century. The camp owed its name to Syrets, the historical district of Kyiv in which it was located. It should be noted that on the territory of Ukraine there were only two "classic-type" concentration camps: the Janowska concentration camp in Lviv, located on the territory of Distrikt Galizien within the Generalgouvernement; and the Syrets concentration camp in Kyiv, located on the territory of the General District of Kyiv within the Reichskommissariat Ukraine.

The Syrets concentration camp was created on the directive of the

50 TsDAVOU, Fond 3833, Opys 2, Sprava 1, Arkush 246–247.

German authorities in the spring of 1942. Before that time there was no forced labor camp in Kyiv. In September 1941 a transit camp for prisoners of war began operating on Kerosynna Street (near Lukianivka Square), which included a separate area for the temporary lodging before execution of Soviet commissars and Jews. In late April the residents of this camp, together with convicted criminals and other prisoners held in the Security Police and SD prison at 33 Korolenko Street were sent to build the Syrets camp. Security for the camp was provided by SS troops and members of the Ukrainian auxiliary police. The head of the Syrets camp was *SS-Sturmbannführer* Paul Otto Radomski. The camp held over 3,000 inmates, including convicted criminals and administrative offenders, saboteurs, Jews, underground members, communists, Ukrainian nationalists, and (from the spring of 1943, when the front began approaching Kyiv once again), Soviet prisoners of war.

The size of the Syrets camp was approximately three square kilometers. It was enclosed by two walls of barbed wire from which stretched between eight and ten rows of electrically charged, high-voltage lines. [see Plate **XIV**] In the corners of the camp stood towers manned by policemen armed with machine guns. The inmates lived in earthen huts, between 70 and 80 people in each. The camp originally had 16 such huts; by the spring of 1943 that number grew to 32. The earthen huts were trenches covered with logs and grass; grated doors and steps led inside. The living area was also enclosed by a barbed wire fence. In September 1942, a women's camp was created inside Syrets. The entire area was lit throughout the night.

The prisoners were subjected to acts of unbridled arbitrariness. While they were still able-bodied, they performed physical labor; later they were liquidated. The inmates were divided into brigades forming part of a company. Brigadiers and captains were selected by the commandant from among the criminal population, who were regarded as the "elite" among the inmates. The senior person in the men's division was a *Volksdeutscher* from Czechoslovakia named Anton Prokupek. He was a former machinist, who had been arrested for sabotage. The senior person in the women's division was Yelyzaveta Lohynova, who had been arrested in connection with her involvement in the Kyiv-based clandestine oblast committee of the Komsomol.

On the grounds of the concentration camp the inmates uprooted trees, produced lumber, built and repaired the barracks, made charcoal out of wood, and did carpentry, excavation work, saddle work, etc. The labor was exhausting, and the food issued to the inmates was meagre and disgusting. After the war surviving prisoners recalled that "usually the work was backbreaking, the abuse was pointless, people were forced to carry soil from place to place, 8 to 10 poods of earth were dumped on stretchers, and we were forced to carry them while running, and we were hit with shovels and shot at. [People] were instantly killed or buried alive in the earth."[51]

Captains, egged on by the commandant, devised various kinds of abuses that targeted Jews, first and foremost. For example, during the production of lumber Jews were forced to climb a tree. The partially sawed tree would be pulled down with a rope, it would fall on the ground, the prisoner along with it. Another captain would invent special "calisthenics". After work, before lights-out, prisoners were placed in a circle and ordered to hold hands. A man was placed on each of their shoulders, and they had to dance to the accompaniment of Jewish songs. The camp regimen was brutal: wake-up call at 4:00 a.m.; breakfast at 4:30; departure for work in formation at 5:00 a.m. Lunch was at 12:00; at 1:00 p.m. we went back to work and labored until 9:00 in the evening. In the morning we were given a ladleful of so-called coffee, which in fact was boiling water with an aftertaste of some kind of herb. For lunch prisoners were given a liter of *balanda*, simply unsalted water with a few grains of millet. They were issued 200 grams of bread made of millet flour per day. There was no supper. The prisoners ate rats, dogs, cats, and various herbs. Those who swelled up from starvation were taken to the so-called hospital, where no care was given, and people died or the commandant himself shot them. The bodies were buried in pits right on the camp or brought to Babyn Yar.

In September 1943, when it appeared that Kyiv would be captured by Soviet troops, the Syrets camp inmates were evacuated to Germany. Some escaped by road, and some returned after the war.

---

51 DAKO, Fond P–4, Opys 2, Sprava 85, Arkush 186.

Already in the summer of 1943 the Nazis had begun destroying the traces of the mass shootings in Babyn Yar. A year before, Paul Blobel, former commander of *Sonderkommando 4a*, which had carried out the mass murders of Jews in Babyn Yar on 29–30 September 1941, received an order from the Gestapo chief Heinrich Müller to identify the mass Jewish graves, exhume the bodies, and burn them. Two *Sonderkommando* consisting exclusively of SS officers and corporals were formed to carry out this task, which was called "Sonderaktion/Special Operation 1005." In August 1943 one of the *Sonderkommando* units arrived in Kyiv.

The inmates of the Syrets camp were forced to exhume and burn the corpses. Around the entire perimeter of the ravine a cloaking shield was erected and trees were planted, and the surrounding area was proclaimed a forbidden zone. A hundred prisoners were taken from the men's camp, and thirteen Jewish women were brought from the women's camp; they were housed in earthen huts on the territory of Babyn Yar. Eventually the number of inmates assigned to burn the corpses rose to 330. The prisoners worked in leg irons that allowed them only to move around and work, but not to escape.

In the ravine, ovens for burning the bodies were built. They were made of gravestones taken from the Jewish cemetery. On top of them were laid grates from the Lukianivka Cemetery, and the bodies were layered on top of them. The ovens were doused with petrol and then lit. Bone remnants were pulverized, and the ashes were scattered throughout the ravine.

In the early morning hours of 29 September 1943, two years to the day of the initial shootings at Babyn Yar, the Syrets inmates staged an escape attempt. Unlocking one of the two earthen huts, they rushed straight into the guards. Most of them were killed or caught and then shot. Only some twenty people escaped.

### The victims

The question of who, besides Jews, were shot in Babyn Yar, is inextricably linked to another question: the absolute figures and the ratio between the numbers of various victims. It should also be kept in mind that throughout the Soviet era, both communist officials and all those scholars dependent on them, deliberately distorted the statistics. The legacy of distortion has not been overcome to the present day and is still often used in the service of one contemporary historical mythology or another.

The propagandist aspect of Soviet mythology emerged from the need to overcome contradictions between the declarations of prewar propaganda ("with little blood on foreign soil") and the real results of the war. A solution was found. The Soviet authorities simply refused to carry out a population census until 1959 and they reduced the declared numbers of war losses, with Stalin proclaiming a figure of only seven million war dead.

The ideological aspect was supposed to overcome the contradictions between the heroic and the sacrificial-victim concepts of history. Two methods were employed. The first was to increase the number of losses among the civilian population at the preliminary count stage. This was the work of the NDK—the Extraordinary State Commission to Establish and Investigate the Crimes of the German-Fascist Invaders and Their Associates and the Damage Caused to Citizens, Collective Farms, Civic Organizations, State Enterprises, and Institutions of the USSR. The second method was to reduce the scope of military losses by increasing civilian losses, as in Nikita Khrushchev's announcement of 20 million dead, including 12 million civilians.

The civilizational aspect was marked by the contradiction between the fundamental disregard for individual human life ("man as a cog in a wheel") and the declaration about preserving the memory of war heroes ("No one is forgotten, nothing is forgotten"). In practice, this resulted in the refusal to search for and intern dead soldiers. Instead, cenotaphs were erected marking pseudo-mass graves, which indicated the total or estimated number of war dead, such as the many monuments dedicated to an "Unknown Soldier."

The general political aspect was supposed to overcome contradictions between the thesis concerning the leading role of the Communist party and the real and quite insignificant role of communists on occupied territory. Later, it became necessary to focus attention on communists who were victims of the Nazi punitive agencies and to inflate artificially the number of clandestine communist organizations. Such falsifications were particularly widespread in the 1960s.

The ethno-national aspect was supposed to take into account two factors: the real scope of civilian losses of various national groups, first and foremost Jews; and the official thesis concerning the leading wartime role of the Russian people and the "fraternal Slavic peoples," as well as the antisemitic policies of the postwar Soviet Union. The solution to this problem was simple. The Soviet leaders suppressed data on the ethnic composition of civilians and military personnel who were killed in the war, and instead focused attention on the destruction of the Slavic population, which was supposedly perpetrated in keeping with the Nazi Ostplan (Eastern Policy), whose implementation, in fact, was never approved.

As a result, to this day there are no reliable statistics on war losses, whether throughout the territory of the former Soviet Union and, in particular, Ukrainian lands including Kyiv and Babyn Yar. Nor is there a coherent set of sources that could help establish the exact scale of these losses. Therefore, historians are forced to rely on indirect data of wildly varying reliability and provenance. For example, according to the official data of the above-mentioned Extraordinary State Commission:

> in Kyiv more than 195,000 Soviet citizens were tortured to death, shot, and poisoned in 'gas vans'. 1. In Babyn Yar: over 100,000 men, women, children, and elderly people. 2. In Darnytsia [that is, in the Darnytsia POW camp located in left-bank Kyiv—V.N.]: over 68,000 prisoners of war and civilians. 3. In the anti-tank trench [next to Babyn Yar—V.N.], in the Syrets camp, and on the territory of the camp itself: over 25,000 Soviet civilians and prisoners of war. 4. On the territory of St. Cyril's Hospital [next to Babyn Yar—V.N.]: 800 mentally ill people. 5. On the territory of the Kyivan Cave Monastery [in downtown Kyiv—V.N.]: nearly 500 civilians. 6. At Lukianivka Cemetery [next to Babyn Yar—V.N.]: 400 civilians.[52]

It is not difficult to notice that the word "Jew" is not once mentioned here. Instead, we see the euphemism "civilians." This term would hence-

52 "Soobshchenie Chrezvychainoi Gosudarstvennoi Komissii o razrusheniiakh i zverstvakh, sovershennykh nemetsko-fashistskimi zakhvatchikami v g. Kieve," *Izvestiia* (Moscow), 29 February 1944.

forth accompany the entire body of historical writings about Babyn Yar and appear from time to time on monuments and in official texts.

At my disposal are reports on the interrogations of former inmates of the Syrets concentration camp who took part in burning corpses in the fall of 1943 and who managed to escape before they were shot. [see Plate **XVI**] It is their testimony that formed the basis of the findings of the Extraordinary State Commission. To a large degree, however, the estimates they provide on the number of victims do not coincide. For example, Yakiv Steiuk stated that 45,000–50,000 corpses were burned in Babyn Yar (beyond the anti-tank trench), and 500 bodies near St. Cyril's Hospital. Semen Berliant, Isak Brodsky, and Volodymyr Davydov estimated the number of bodies burned in Babyn Yar and in the anti-tank trench at 70,000; Leonid Ostrovskii, between 65,000 and 90,000; Vladyslav Kuklia and Yosyf Doliner, between 95,000 and 100,000. Thus, it appears from these testimonies that 70,000 is the lowest figure and 100,000, the highest figure of all victims, including those who were shot in Babyn Yar and in the anti-tank trench. Moreover, some of the interrogated former prisoners believed that not all the corpses from Babyn Yar were burned.

Another way to establish the number of victims of Babyn Yar is to do so by estimates according to separate categories. This method is actually quite common given the ongoing debates around this question.

Let us begin with the Jews. The demographic data is clearly difficult to navigate. For example, on the eve of the war Jews comprised 25 percent of Kyiv's population of 930,000. As of the beginning of the occupation in September 1941, and following mobilization (nearly 200,000) and evacuation (325,000), only about 400,000 people remained in the city. The Germans estimated the number of Jews the city they occupied at 150,000. This figure seems unrealistically high, because it is unclear why the proportion of Jews would have increased so much. Like other residents of Kyiv, Jews were subject to mobilization, and even larger numbers of them left the city during the evacuation operation. A census carried out by the municipal administration on 1 April 1942 revealed a population of 352,000. It may be stated unequivocally that the 50,000 missing people were executed Jews. But it was not just Kyiv-based Jews who perished in Babyn Yar. Even the announcement of 28 September

1941 ordered the Jews not only of Kyiv but also from surrounding areas vicinities to assemble. Moreover, it should be kept in mind that some of the Jews who were shot were Soviet POWs.

According to a report of *Einsatzgruppe C*, "on 29 and 30 September 1941 *Sonderkommando 4a*, in collaboration with the group headquarters and two squads from Police Battalion South executed 33,771 Jews in Kyiv."[53] But these victims were killed only in the space of two days.

The Germans entered Kyiv on 19 September 1941, and the very next day they began executing Soviet POWs in Babyn Yar. "I personally did not watch," recalled Ivan Yanovych, whose house stood about 800–1,000 meters away on a street that was then called Babyn Yar.[54] "There were guards, and they were not letting [anyone] come close; you could only hear the lamentation of people and submachine gunfire."[55]

Raisa Shvartsman, who escaped from Babyn Yar during the shootings on 29 September, recalled the first days of the German occupation:

> I saw a German convoy herding prisoners of war along the Brest-Litovsk Highway. There were thousands of them, half-naked and barefoot, with shovels in their hands. There were Ukrainians, Russians, and many young Jewish boys. They were being herded toward Lukianivka Cemetery. People were throwing pieces of bread to the exhausted, starving captives, but whoever picked some up was killed. Teenagers who were running behind the prisoners of war recounted that they dug pits, after which the German soldiers shot them and pushed them into these pits.[56]

Next, as indicated earlier, a transit camp for prisoners of war (called a Durchgangslager—Dulag) was set up on Kerosynna Street, in the former barracks of the Benderskyi Regiment. A special section for Jews and army commissars was created within the camp, which was based at Zenit (today Start) Stadium. Immediately following the explosions on the Khreshchatyk, which began on 24 September, 1,600 Jewish civilian

---

53 *Sbornik dokumentov i materialov*, p. 72.

54 HDA SBU, Fond 65, Sprava 937, Tom 1, Arkush 2.

55 Ibid.

56 *Zhivimi ostalis' tol'ko my: svidetel'stva i dokumenty*, edited by Borys Zabarko (Kyiv, 1999), pp. 486-487.

hostages were taken and very likely sent to the camp housed in Zenit Stadium. The execution in Babyn Yar of inmates from this camp began no later than 27 September 1941.

The continuous shootings in Babyn Yar of the Jewish civilian population and inmates from the camp at the Zenit Stadium lasted beyond 30 September, roughly until mid-November 1941. During this period (1 October–15 November 1941) *Einsatzkommando 5*, which was based in Kyiv, shot 29,835 people, of whom 96.5 percent (28,796) were Jews. It is highly likely that the killing squad carried out executions in other places besides Kyiv. By 14 October Police Battalion South was already in Kyiv, and it definitely took part in the operations of 1–3, 8, and 11 October or even carried them out on its own. On 13 October 1941, 308 mentally ill Jewish patients from the Pavlov Psychiatric Hospital were shot.

In the end, one must conclude that it is not possible to determine the number of Jews who remained alive after the shootings that took place in the fall of 1941 and who were subsequently captured and executed. Nor do we know how many perished in the Syrets concentration camp, especially since Jews from other settled areas were also brought there.

According to eyewitness testimonies, regular shootings began in Kyiv in November 1941. Every week one or two trucks arrived at Babyn Yar from the Security Police and SD prison, bringing people to be shot. If the arriving vehicles were gas vans (*Gaswagen*), they came already packed with corpses. Between August and late September 1943 (according to other testimonies into October as well) the trucks arrived every day. Furthermore, between October 1941 and the end of the occupation some eight to ten people arrested by the *Schutzpolizei* were shot here every day. The last shooting took place on 4 November 1943, and on 6 November the Red Army entered Kyiv. If all these figures are added together, it would appear that in a period of two years the local punitive agencies shot between 14,000 and 22,000 people.

What were the various categories of these Nazi victims? The first were the Roma/Gypsies. The amateur historian Ilia Levitas writes (without indicating his sources): the "gypsies were shot in the first days of the occupation [at] three Kurenivka-based campsites. They were shot behind St. Cyril's Church." But a contemporary of these events, Liudmyla Zavorotna, recalled that the Roma were shot in Babyn Yar, and she herself saw gypsy wagons driving past her house, although this was a long time after the mass shootings of the Jews. Volodymyr Nabaranchuk, whose family escaped death, also recalls that the Germans began shooting the Roma in late October 1941. It was not just the Roma living in their encampments who were shot but also those who lived conventional lives in the city. Nabaranchuk states that, in addition to Babyn Yar, Roma encampments were destroyed in what then were the Kyivan suburbs of Sviatoshyn and Berezniaky. In any case, we can confirm that at least 150 Roma were killed in Babyn Yar because nearly 50 people usually lived in the Roma encampment.

Starting in mid-October, the Germans began executing patients of the Pavlov Psychiatric Hospital. As an *Einsatzgruppe* report noted, "especially severe mental stress among the authorized members of *Einsatzkommando 5* was caused by the liquidation on 13 October 1941 of mentally ill Jews from the psychiatric hospital in Kyiv."[57] As revealed during the trial of the members of this squad, which took place in West Germany after the war, the execution took place following way:

> Around 25 SS troops, including two *Unterscharführer* [sergeants], left on one truck. Riding in the second truck were policemen from the Order Police.... They left at around 9:00 in the morning. After the journey, which took nearly an hour, the trucks stopped at the red-brick hospital that was located in a park. . . . The sick were led out one by one [by people from among] the Ukrainian support staff through the back door of the hospital. These were men and a few women.... The defendant [Karl] Jäger and his comrades stripped some switches from bushes. With them they indicated the route to the place of execution to the victims, so that they would not touch each other with their hands. . . . On rising ground was a pit 5 meters long, 2 meters wide, and 1.2 meters deep. Behind the pit stood Commander Maier of the *Einsatzkommando*. Next to the pit was a police official. He received the sick people and ordered them to undress. After the undressing, he told the victims to lie face-down in the pit. Then other policemen at the edge of the pit killed the sick people with shots from submachine guns set to single fire. . . . The operation lasted around an hour.[58]

57 *Sbornik dokumentiv i materialiv*, p. 98.

58 Ibid., pp. 158-159.

In early 1942 the Germans returned to the Pavlov Psychiatric Hospital. This time they were interested not only in Jews, as revealed in the testimony of the head doctor Musii Tantsiura at a trial in Kyiv in1946:

> On 8 January 1942 a detachment of armed Germans and a van arrived at the hospital. The van drove up to a ward, mentally ill people were shoved into it, the truck was closed, some kind of motor was switched on, and the patients died. It was explained that when the van starts, CO [carbon oxide] gas is pumped out, and it poisons the people who are inside it. . . .
>
> The poisoned corpses from this truck were dumped into the [hospital] club like firewood. The next day a truck came; the corpses were taken away and driven to a mass pit in the woods. Three hundred patients were destroyed this way.[59]

The gas van came to the psychiatric hospital two more times, on 27 March and 17 October 1942. According to Dr. Musii Tantsiura, approximately 800–820 patients were killed. As mentioned earlier, the first hostages taken in Kyiv were 1,600 Jews, who were arrested around 26 September in connection with the explosions on the Khreshchatyk and then shot in Babyn Yar, starting on 27 September. By the end of October everyone was being rounded up.

On 22 October 1941 Major-General Kurt Eberhard, the commandant of Kyiv, issued the following announcement: "By way of reprisal for the act of sabotage, 100 residents of Kyiv were shot today. Let this be a warning. Every resident of Kyiv is responsible for the act of sabotage."[60] This was by another announcement on 2 November: "Incidents of arson and sabotage, which have become more frequent in Kyiv, compel me to resort to the harshest measures. Therefore, 300 residents of Kyiv were shot today. For every new incident of arson and sabotage, a considerably larger number of Kyiv residents will be shot."[61] On 29 November the commandant issued yet a third announcement: "In Kyiv the means of communication (telephone, telegraph, cable) have been deliberated damaged.

59 HDA SBU, Fond 5, Sprava 55 663, Tom 20, Arkush 92–93.

60 TsDAHOU, Fond 1, Opys 23, Sprava 121, Arkush 4.

61 Ibid., Arkush 8.

Since it is not possible to tolerate [these] saboteurs, 400 men will be shot in the city, which should serve as a warning to the population."[62] These documents alone prove conclusively that of the 2,400 hostages who were executed in Kyiv, 800 were probably not Jews.

Direct German repressions against members of the OUN(M) commenced in late November 1941 in the Zhytomyr region, following commemorations of the Heroes of Bazar.[63] The twentieth anniversary of this tragedy was marked by a solemn gathering. Reluctant to disperse it immediately, the German authorities put off arresting the event's organizers and participants until a few days later. A total of 721 people who had attended the commemoration were arrested, 120 of whom were executed by the Nazis on 30 November 1941 in a suburb of the city of Zhytomyr.

The first wave of mass arrests of OUN members in Kyiv began in mid-December 1941. Most contemporaries of those events, as well as historians, mention the date of 13 December, when the Gestapo arrested numerous members of the editorial board of the newspaper *Ukrainske slovo* (Ukrainian Word), as well as 27 members of the municipal administration.

Arrests continued in the new year. In January 1942 approximately 60 young Kyiv residents with links to the OUN were arrested. Of the 100 members of the Bukovinian Battalion serving in the Darnytsia branch of the Ukrainian Protective Police, around 70 people were arrested and shot. On 7 February 1942 over 200 members of the OUN and their sympathizers, mostly members of the Kyivan intelligentsia, were arrested. The first to be captured by the Gestapo were "westerners" (that is, people from western Ukraine) who had arrived in Kyiv in the fall of 1941. In September, two OUN members were arrested in Kyiv; in early October, nine more were arrested, including Vasyl Kuzmyk, the head of the Propaganda Section of the Main OUN Leadership in the Eastern Ukrainian Lands (OUN SUZ).

---

62 Ibid., Arkush 9.

63 On 17 November 1921, near the village of Bazar in Zhytomyr oblast, the Red Army, specifically a division led by Grigorii Kotovskii, smashed the Volhynian Army Group of the Ukrainian National Republic (UNR) commanded by Brigadier-General Yurii Tiutiunnyk. The following day several hundred captured Ukrainian soldiers were shot in Bazar.

The arrests of members of the Ukrainian nationalist underground in Kyiv continued into 1943 and lasted virtually until the final days of the German occupation. According to a report prepared by the German Security Police and the SD dated 19 March 1943, over forty people, mostly intellectuals, were arrested in Kyiv for their involvement in the OUN. Among them was Zynovii Domazar (Dibrova), the Krai (Territorial) Leader of the OUN SUZ, who was captured by the Gestapo.

According to OUN data, during the German occupation of Ukraine, between 1941 and 1944 the Organization of Ukrainian Nationalists lost 4,756 members, including 197 leading staff members, 6 Krai leaders, and 5 members of the OUN Leadership. Of all the Ukrainian lands where OUN structures operated, the organization suffered the greatest losses in occupied Kyiv, where 621 Ukrainian patriots were killed. Among the victims were the poet Olena Teliha, head of the Union of Ukrainian Writers; Volodymyr Bahazii, mayor of Kyiv; and Roman Bida (Gordon), one of the organizers and leading members of the Kyiv police. Losses among the members of the Bukovinian Battalion who arrived in Kyiv are estimated at nearly 400.

With regard to Soviet prisoners of war, the Germans began shooting them the day after they entered Kyiv. A week later the Germans began bringing Jews and political commissars from the camp on Kerosynna Street to Babyn Yar. Filtration measures continued. During an inquiry held after the war Vasyl Pokotylo, who was one of Volodymyr Bahazii's personal bodyguards, recounted that on several occasions in October–November 1941 he traveled with the mayor to Babyn Yar in connection with executions. "There were three such trips. The first time, 100 people, including Jews, prisoners of war, and partisans, were shot."[64] Pokotylo also mentioned the shooting in July 1942 of 75 people, including Jews, partisans, parachutists, prisoners of war, and women, in which he personally took part.

Numerous witnesses recalled the shooting in January 1942 of several dozen captured sailors of the Soviet fleet. In the words of one eyewitness, Nadiia Horbachova:

---

64 HDA SBU, Fond 5, Sprava 43 555, Arkush 49.

> In the winter of 1942...German soldiers brought 65 captive Soviet sailors. Their arms and legs were so heavily chained that they could barely move. The completely undressed and barefoot prisoners were driven through the snow during a severe frost. Local residents threw shirts and boots at the column of prisoners, but the prisoners refused to take them, and I remember one of them said: 'We will perish for the Fatherland, for the Soviet Union, for Stalin.' After this declaration the captive sailors broke into the 'Internationale,' for which the German soldiers began beating them with their sticks. You could tell they were sailors by their sailors' caps. After they were brought to Babyn Yar, the sailors were shot by the Germans.[65]

It is difficult to estimate the total number of prisoners of war. Soviet documents and historiography usually state that 20,000 POWs were shot. Volodymyr Davydov cites this figure in his testimony: "20,000 commanders were shot in an anti-tank trench."[66] But Yakiv Steiuk gives a figure that is ten times smaller: "In one spot 2,000 [men] in the uniforms of commanders of the RKKA [Red Army]."[67] Obviously, both witnesses were referring to one and the same place, but it has yet to be determined which witness made a mistake, deliberately or not.

After the liberation of Kyiv, Sergei Matveev, a former warehouseman at the Pavlov Psychiatric Hospital, testified at an inquiry that, in addition to the graves of the murdered patients, "in St. Cyril's meadow there [were] also mass graves of prisoners of war who died in German captivity in 1941–1943, when they were in hospital, at this very hospital. The number of those who died from starvation and cold [and] typhus and prisoners of war who were shot and buried in the meadow reaches several thousand."[68] As we know, these graves were not exhumed during the corpse-burning operation, and thus were not included in official statistics.

The first setbacks experienced by the clandestine raion committees of the Communist party (Bolshevik) of Ukraine (CP(b)U) and arrests

65 Ibid., Fond 7, Opys 8, Sprava 1, Tom 1, Arkush 179.
66 Ibid., Arkush 90–91.
67 Ibid., Arkush 206.
68 Ibid., Fond 5, Sprava 74 159 FP, Tom 2, Arkush 290.

of remaining members of the communist underground commenced in October 1941. The main causes of these failures then (and in all future cases) were lack of professionalism and numerous betrayals. For example, on 22 October Ivan Romanchenko, who before the occupation was secretary of the Lenin raion party committee, went of his own free will to the investigative group of *Sonderkommando 4a*. He provided accurate information about the structure of clandestine party organizations and then traveled with German policemen around Kyiv, pointing out the apartments of former communists and Soviet functionaries. As a result, the following individuals were arrested: the secretaries of the clandestine Lenin raion committee and the Lenin backup raion committee Oleksii Fedorov and Mykola Tychyna, respectively; the secretaries of the clandestine Stalin raion committee and the backup Stalin raion committee Lev Linnyk and Prokip Komarov, respectively; the secretary of the clandestine Molotov raion committee Petro Karkots; and the secretary of the clandestine Kaganovich raion committee Ivan Skliar.

In the first days of October 1941 eighteen communists were arrested and shot in Darnytsia district alone, including Kostiantyn Dukhanin, secretary of the clandestine raion committee. Before the end of the year, over fifty leading figures of the remaining communist underground in the city were arrested or had disappeared without a trace. The Lenin, Kirov, Darnytsia, Stalin, Molotov, and Kaganovich municipal committees of the CP(b)U stopped functioning or were liquidaed as well as all raion committees of the Komsomol, with the exception of the Stalin raion committee of this communist organization. Their members were arrested, or they left Kyiv or refused to fight against the German occupiers.

Arrests of individual underground members Kyiv also took place in the winter of 1942. For example, Ivan Sykorskyi, member of the bureau of the Zaliznychnyi raion committee, and Volodymyr Kudriashov, a member of a terrorist group, were arrested on 5 January. Six days later two members of the backup, clandestine municipal party committee, Yakiv Khandei and Vasyl Viktorov, underground member Melaniia Horkovenko, and courier of the Petrovskyi raion committee Yelyzaveta Kachanivska were arrested.

Between April and July 1942 another wave of repressions swept through Kyiv. Among the leaders of the communist underground arrested in April were Ivan Kucherenko, the secretary of the municipal committee of the Komsomol (he turned traitor); the secretaries of the Kaganovich and Zhovtnevyi raion committees Volodymyr Artamonov and Ivan Dudinov, respectively; Mykola Ukho, the secretary of the Molotov raion committee, was killed while under arrest. In May the Gestapo captured Heorhii Levytskyi, member of the bureau of the Zaliznychnyi raion committee.

On 2–9 June the members of the main municipal committee (bureau members Kuzma Ivkyn, Volodymyr Kudriashov, Fedir Revutskyi, and Serhii Pashenko; the couriers Tamara Rohozynska and Oleksandra Khokhlova); and the backup municipal committee (bureau members Halyna Podshyvalova, the courier Mariia Vasylieva, and Denys Yakymenko, the owner of a safe house) were arrested; Semen Bruz was killed while being placed under arrest. Also arrested were the secretaries of the Stalin, Molotov, Kaganovich, and Zhovtnevyi raion committees of the CP(b)U, and the raion organizations were smashed.

As a result of the treachery of Ivan Kucherenko and other underground members, both the Communist party and Komsomol underground movements in Kyiv were nearly destroyed. In May 1942 alone, 69 members of the Komsomol were arrested, and in June, over 300 communists and Komsomol members. All clandestine raion committees of the Komsomol as well as the main Komsomol organizations suspended their activities because all their leaders had been arrested; some of them became traitors (for example, Yurii Pustovoitov, secretary of the Lenin raion committee of the Komsomol and Valyntyna Chaika, secretary of the Kaganovich raion committee).

In late October 1943, the third wave of repressions began. Mykhailo Dzhaharkava, secretary of the Molotov raion party committee, was arrested on 28 October, and the following day nineteen heads, couriers, and owners of safe houses in Zaliznychnyi district and other city districts were captured. Among these were Oleksandr Pyrohovskyi, secretary of the municipal party committee Bronislava Petrushko; couriers of the municipal committee Olha Svetlychna and Hanna Salan; and a member of the bureau of the Kirov raion committee Mykola Artiushenko, were imprisoned by the Germans. Also arrested were the members of the municipal headquarters in charge of organizing an armed action: Volodymyr Chernyshov, commander of armed detachments of the municipal committee; Ivan Kostenko, chief of the headquarters of the municipal committee's armed detachments; and Abram Nesviezhynskyi, head of intelligence of the municipal committee's armed detachments (the latter two became traitors). The Abwehr alone arrested nearly thirty people.

According to the publication, *Tsyfrovi dani pro osobovyi sklad pidpilnykh bilshovytskykh orhanizatsii m. Kyieva* (Digital Data on the Personnel of Clandestine Bolshevik Organizations in the City of Kyiv) compiled in 1946, 176 clandestine workers were killed. A total of 617 surnames appear in a list of underground members in Kyiv killed by the Gestapo in 1941–1943, which was compiled by the staff members of the Kyiv History Museum and activists of the Poshuk (Search) Club in 1980. The difference between the two figures is explained by the fact that the 1946 report listed only members of clandestine organizations recognized as such by the results of official verifications, whereas the museum employees arrived at their number by considering all reports on clandestine work, which became available after the war.

It should be noted that the foregoing refers only to those members of the Communist party underground about whom some kind of information has been preserved. No data exist on members of the NKVD and the Intelligence Directorate of Red Army illegal organizations, nor on members of the many organizations that operated at various enterprises but were not formally subordinated to clandestine party structures. Many clandestine party organizations, including nearly all the ones that were left behind when the Soviets retreated from Kyiv, were utterly destroyed, and no statistical data on their composition, activities, and losses have survived. Lastly, no information exists on the members of clandestine organizations operating in other populated areas who were executed in Kyiv.

The events of 29 September 1941 at Babyn Yar became an international symbol of the Holocaust. The subsequent two-year German occupation turned Babyn Yar into a symbol of all Nazi terror. Twenty years later, on 13 March 1961, a different kind of tragedy transformed Babyn Yar into yet another symbol, that of Soviet totalitarianism.

CHAPTER 5

# Babyn Yar: Executioners and Rescuers

*Oleksandr Kruglov*

The mass killing of Kyiv's Jews in late September–early October 1941 was a genocidal crime and a crime against humanity. As in all such crimes, several elements were involved: Nazi Germany's highest leaders (Hitler, Himmler), organizers (Higher SS and Police Führer in Russia-South Obergruppenführer Friedrich Jeckeln), executors (German punitive organs—the SD, SS, police), instigators (the Wehrmacht), and accomplices (the Ukrainian Auxiliary Police). All these elements can be considered to various degrees as the executioners of Babyn Yar.

## The role of the Wehrmacht in organizing the destruction of the Jews

Units of the Seventy-first and Seventy-fifth infantry divisions and the Ninety-ninth Light Infantry Division, which were part of the Twenty-ninth Army Corps, entered Kyiv at about noon on 19 September 1941.[1] At this time about 400,000 residents were still in the city; out of some 930,000 inhabitants in mid-1941, about 200,000 were called up for military service after 22 June 1941, and 325,000 were evacuated.[2] Before the war about one in four residents of the city was a Jew, and as will become clear below one in ten of the remaining 400,000 was a Jew.[3]

1 In addition to these divisions, the Ninety-fifth and 299th infantry divisions were part of the Twenty-ninth Army Corps.

2 Tatiana Evstafeva, "Tragediia Babego Yara (1941–1945)," in *Druha svitova viina i dolia narodiv Ukraïny: materialy 2-ï Vseukraïnskoï naukovoï konferentsiï, m. Kyïv, 30–31 zhovtnia 2006* (Kyiv, 2007), 278. Von Vroreich, councillor of military administration from the 454th Guard Division, also estimated the number of remaining inhabitants as 400,000. Bundesarchiv-Militärarchiv, Freiburg (subsequently BA-MA), RH-26-454/28.

3 Before the war about one in four residents of the city was a Jew.

Fifty-three SS-men commanded by Obersturmführers August Häfner and Adolf Janssen and a part of the staff of *Einsatzgruppe C* arrived in the city in eight trucks together with the advanced Wehrmacht units.[4] The bulk of the *Sonderkommando*, which was carrying out an "action" in Zhytomyr (on 19 September 3,145 Jews were executed) only arrived in Kyiv on 25 September together with most of the staff of *Einsatzgruppe C* and the attached Third Company of the SS Special Assignment Battalion (commander SS Obersturmführer Bernhard Grafhorst).[5] The following day, 26 September, a unit of *Sonderkommando 4a* began action in the city with permission of the Sixth Army.[6] The police regiment Süd arrived in Kyiv the same day. It was composed of the Forty-fifth Reserve Police Battalion (commander Police Major and SS Sturmbannführer Heinrich Hannibal), as well as part of the staff of SS and Police Führer and of Obergruppenführer Friedrich Jeckeln.[7] Finally, on 20 September two companies of the Eighty-second Reserve Police Battalion (commander Rudolf Ebert), which at that time was subordinated to the 454$^{th}$ Guard Division, arrived from Zhytomyr.[8] All in all, by the end of September more than two thousand German policemen and SS members had assembled in Kyiv.

---

4 Bundesarchiv Außenstelle Ludwigsburg (subsequently BArch), B162/17958, Bl. 7591, Fernschreiben des AOK 6 an XXIX AK v. 14.9.1941, Betr.: Einsatzkommandos für Kiew. The vanguard included a platoon of SS troops commanded by SS Oberscharführer Jaeger and several officials. Hefner's testimony from 31 May 1965 in BArch B 162/5652, Bl. 2906.

5 BArch, B 162/439, "Ereignismeldung UdSSR" No. 106, 7 October 1941.

6 BA-MA, RH 26-29/9, Tätigkeitsbericht des XXIX AK, 4 September–19 November 1941; BArch, B162/17958 Bl. 7595).

7 Vojenský historický archiv, Prague, KdoS RF SS, box 1, inv. č. 2, Radiogram by Higher SS and Police Führer, No. 136/37, 26 September 1941,10:00. According to another source (BArch, B 162/6670, Bl. 1981ff, final indictment by the Regensburg Procurator's Office 2 February 1970. in the case of Rosenbauer, Besser, and Kreutzer), the Forty-fifth Battalion arrived in Kyiv on 22 September 1941 and was located at first at the university and then at a savings bank. The 303d Battalion arrived in Kyiv on 23 September. See the entry in the police service passport of Oberwachtmeister Erich Karrasch: "23.9.–14.10.41: tasks concerning the guarding and cleansing of Kyiv."

8 Yad Vashem Archives, Jerusalem, MfS HA XII 11 ZUV 64 – Ermittlungsverfahren gegen Piehl, Johannes; NARA T 315, roll 2216, TR. 10. The battalion remained in the city until 8 October 1941.

Immediately after the Nazi German authorities seized Kyiv, they began to take repressive measures against the Jews who remained in the city. The first anti-Jewish measures were conducted not by the SD or by police, but by the Wehrmacht.[9] Each Wehrmacht division was stationed in a particular city district: the Ninety-fifth in Kyiv east; the Ninety-ninth in the Kyiv cantonment; the Seventy-fifth in Kyiv center, southern part; the 299th in Kyiv southwest; the 296th in Kyiv north and northwest.[10]

On 20 September, the Seventy-fifth Infantry Division issued an order "to recruit Jews to work uncovering and removing landmines, obstructions, and so forth."[11] The following day, the Ninety-fifth Infantry Division issued an order about "control of the male population of Kyiv," according to which early in the morning on 22 September a sudden action was to be taken to seize men of draft age. They were to be placed in an "investigation camp" where Abwehr officers, assisted by "reliable" Ukrainians, would check them. "Soldiers in civilian clothing, partisans or released criminals and… Jews" were sent to Dulag 201, a transit camp for prisoners of war.[12]

The 299th Infantry Division issued a similar order on 21 September. According to this directive, a purge of the district where the division was

---

9 The Wehrmacht forces were comprised of the Twenty-ninth Army Corps (commander General Hans von Obstfelder), which included five divisions: the Seventy-first (Artillery General Alexander von Hartman), the Seventy-fifth (commander Generalleutnant Ernst Hammer), the Ninety-fifth (commander Generalleutnant Hans-Heinrich Sixt von Arnim), the Ninety-ninth Light Infantry Division (commander Infantry General Kurt von der Chevallerie), and the 299th Infantry Division (commander Artillery General Moser), as well as the temporarily subordinated 296th Infantry Division (commander Generalleutnant Wilhelm Stemmermann).Von Hartman was killed at Stalingrad on 25 January 1943. Hammer was captured by American troops in April 1945, released in 1947, and died in 1957. Von Arnim was taken prisoner at Stalingrad on 20 January 1943 and died in captivity in 1952. Chevallerie went missing in action in Poland in April 1945. Moser died in Soviet captivity in 1946. Stemmermann was killed near Cherkasy on 18 February 1944.

10 BA-MA, RH 26-29/9.

11 BA-MA, RH 26-75/42.

12 BA-MA, RH 26-95/15; K. J. Arnold, "Die Eroberung und Behandlung der Stadt Kiew durch die Wehrmacht im September 1941: zur Radikalisierung der Besatzungspolitik," *Militärgeschichtliche Mitteilungen*, vol. 58 (Munich, 1999), p. 50.

stationed was to begin at 6:00 a.m. the following day. All men between the ages of sixteen and fifty were to be arrested; an investigation camp was to be set up; and soldiers in civilian clothing, commissars, released criminals, and partisans were to be sent to Dulag 201. All arrested Jews without exception were to be sent there as well.[13] The division notified its subordinated units that the planned action was being postponed for twenty-four hours and would begin at 6:00 a.m. on 23 September.[14]

In an order issued that same day about the "cleansing of Kyiv," the Seventy-fifth Infantry Division also ordered a cleansing action in the districts where it was stationed. During the action all men between the ages of sixteen and fifty were to be arrested and sent to investigation camps on the city outskirts that were capable of holding ten thousand inmates. Here, "Ukrainian elements worthy of trust" would separate the inmates into two groups: "A. redressed Russian soldiers, [Communist party] commissars, released criminals, partisans, Jews, and others; B. men who did not arouse suspicion." Soldiers and Jews in group A were to be sent to Dulag 201, while "all others are to be held under guard until they are taken in by the security service."[15] In an order issued on 23 September 1941, the division announced that the cleansing action was being postponed "until a municipal administration and a Ukrainian committee have been established." Reinforced street patrols were to be conducted day and night in the course of which "all persons suspected of being Red Army soldiers who had changed out of uniform," "all male Jews," "all persons who were out on the streets during the curfew ordered by the commandant's office" (from 20:00 p.m. to 6:00 a.m.) were to be arrested. Those arrested were to be delivered without investigation to Dulag 201 on Taborna Street. "Before being delivered to the camp, arrested Jews can be employed to remove street barricades and so on."[16]

Citing the Sixth Army's directive of 19 September concerning the arrest of men of draft age,[17] three days later the commander of the corps

13 BA-MA, RH 26-299/43.

14 Ibid.

15 BA-MA, RH 26-75/42.

16 Ibid.

17 BA-MA, RH 26-299/122, Armee-Oberkommando 6, O.Qu / Qu 2, A.H.Qu., den 19.9.1941, Betr.: Gefangennahme von Zivilisten.

ordered the arrest of both Red Army soldiers dressed in civilian clothing and male Jews. They should immediately be sent without investigation to Dulag 201. "The arrested Jews should first be employed to remove the numerous street obstacles."[18]

On 23 September, Hans von Obstfelder held a conference with six subordinated division commanders.[19] It was decided that patrols should arrest Jewish men first and that Jews and prisoners should be assigned to work.[20] The following day explosions and fires broke out in the city, including in the field command, killing a large number of German soldiers and officers.[21] The buildings occupied by *Sonderkommando 4a* and the staff of *Einsatzgruppe C* were also partly destroyed. Seventy-five Molotov cocktails were discovered and rendered harmless in the *Einsatzgruppe* building.[22] In response, either Major General Kurt Eberhard[23] or von Obstfelder demanded that the SD take revenge by shooting all the Jews in the city.[24]

It is very likely that Field Marshall Walther von Reichenau, who was then commanding the Sixth Army, approved the order to carry out mass punishment in Kyiv as a reprisal for the explosions.[25] Von Obstfelder had

---

18 Ibid.

19 In addition to his five divisions von Obstfelder was temporarily in command of the 296th Infantry Division from the Seventeenth Army Corps.

20 Arnold, "Die Eroberung und Behandlung," p. 51.

21 An exploding mine at the Kyiv Monastery (Lavra) had killed sixty-two-year-old Colonel Hans-Heinrich Freiherr von Seidlitz und Gohlau, Artillery Commander of the Ninety-fifth Artillery Division.

22 BArch B, 162/439, Ereignismeldung UdSSR No. 106, 7 October 1941.

23 Eberhard, commander of Field Command 195, was appointed city commander by orders from the Sixth Army on 24 September 1941 and subordinated to the commander of the Twenty-ninth Army Corps, who was the chief of the city garrison. On 27 September the garrison chief became Major General Friedrich Zickwolff, commander of the 113th Infantry Division. Arnold, "Die Eroberung und Behandlung," p. 43.

24 BArch, B 162/5653, Bl. 3092-95, testimony by former SS Obersturmbannführer August Hefner, 16 June 1965; BArch, B 162/5653, Bl. 3176–77, testimony by former SS Obersturmbannführer Adolf Janssen, 24 June 1965.

25 H. Rüß, "Wer war verantwortlich für das Massaker von Babij Jar?" *Militärgeschichtliche Mitteilungen*, vol. 57 (Munich, 1998), p. 489. Rüß cites a statement in 1963 by Erich Erlinger, who in 1942–1943 was commander of the Security Police and SD in Kyiv.

met him at the city's Boryspil airport on 25 September.[26] During the encounter he certainly told von Reichenau about the explosions and the fires and who he thought was involved in them. The same day there is an entry an entry in the military journal of the Twenty-ninth Corps: "Great fire continues to rage in Kyiv. It has been established that partisans and Jews are engaged in strengthening the fire as much as they can."[27] Also on that day the Ninety-fifth Division ordered its anti-tank battalion to prevent escape by Jews from the city.[28]

On 26 September, after the main SD and police forces arrived in the city, Eberhard conferred with Jeckeln, SS Brigadeführer Dr. Otto Emil Rasch, chief of *Einsatzgruppe C*, and SS Standartenführer Paul Blobel, commander of *Sonderkommando 4a*.[29] The details of the coming "reprisal action" were discussed. It was to be conducted by *Sonderkommando 4a*.[30] To support round-ups of victims, delivery of them to the execution site, and internal and external cordoning, Jeckeln called on the Forty-fifth and 303rd police battalions and the First Platoon of the Third Company of the Ninth Reserve Police Battalion.[31] The Wehrmacht allotted ammunition for the mass killings. Außenstelle Süd of the General

---

26 BA-MA, RH 26-29/9, Kriegstagebuch No. 2, Korpskommando XXIX. A.K, 20 September 1941–19 November 1941.

27 Ibid.

28 BA-MA, RH 26-95/11; Arnold, "Die Eroberung und Behandlung," p. 53.

29 Dieter Pohl, "Die Einsatzgruppe C 1941/42," in Peter Klein, ed., *Die Einsatzgruppen in der besetzten Sowjetunion 1941/42: Die Tätigkeits-und Lageberichte des Chefs der Sicherheitspolizei und des SD* (Berlin, 1997), p. 75; Dieter Pohl, *Die Herrschaft der Wehrmacht: Deutsche Militärbesatzung und einheimische Bevölkerung in der Sowjetunion 1941–1944* (Munich, 2008), p. 260; Rüß, "Wer war erantwortlich," p. 495, cites Blobel's testimony at the Nuremberg trials in 1948. See also BA-MA, B 162/4699, Bl. 319, the bill of indictment (12 January 1967) by the General Prosecutor's Office, Frankfurt am Main, in the case of Kallsen and others.

30 At that time the *Sonderkommando* had about 120 men. Urteil LG Darmstadt Ks1/67 (GStA), 29 November 1968, against Callsen and others, in *Justiz und NS-Verbrechen*, vol. XXXI (Amsterdam and Munich, 2004), p. 248. In addition to security police officials, drivers, and administrative and technical personnel the *Sonderkommando* included a platoon of reserve SS troops and a platoon of police guards.

31 Testimony by Rene Rosenbauer from 5 September 1963, in BArch, B 162/17927, Bl. 1187.

Quartermaster of the ground forces reported on 27 September that a hundred thousand cartridges had been delivered to the Higher SS and Police Führer.[32]

Thus, it is quite clear that the Wehrmacht played an essential part in preparing the destruction of Kyiv's Jews. Since it held power in the city in late September–early October 1941, its officers—von Reichenau, von Obstfelder, and Eberhard—could have prevented the killings. But instead of hindering them, the Wehrmacht directly contributed to the killing spree.

**The role of German punitive organs (SD, SS, Police)**

The first executions of Jews began on 27 September, when, as can be seen from an account by the intelligence section (1c) of the 113th Infantry Division, "a Jewish action conducted by the Police Regiment Süd" started in Kyiv.[33] This action is also mentioned in radiogram no. 142/143 at 10:15 a.m. on 28 September 1941, from Higher SS and Police Führer Russia South about the previous day's activities: "action in cleansing and cordoning Kyiv."[34] The victims were Jews arrested by *Sonderkommando 4a* and Wehrmacht patrols on the orders issued by the Twenty-ninth Army Corps on 22 September. The scale of the action is evident from Ereignismeldung UdSSR No. 97, dated 28 September 1941: "1,600 arrests in Kyiv in the course of the first action."[35]

The arrested Jews were confined at Dulag 201, which was located just south of Lukianivka Square in barracks on Kazarmenna and Kerosynna Streets (present-day Andriushchenko and Sholudenko Streets). The special "Jewish camp" set up in barracks on Kerosynna Street held both arrested Jewish civilians and Jewish prisoners of war who had been selected for Dulag 201.[36] Leonid Ostrovskii, a former prisoner of war, testified after the liberation of the city:

---

32 Pohl, *Die Herrschaft der Wehrmacht*, p. 260.

33 BA-MA, RH 26-113.

34 Vojenský historický archiv, Prague, KdoS RF SS, karton 1, inv. č. 2.

35 BArch, B 162/439.

36 Gosudarstvennyi Arkhiv Rossiiskoi Federatsii, Moscow, Fond 7021, Opis 148, Delo 60, Arkush 10, order of early October 1941 by Andrii Orlyk, commander of the Ukrainian police in Kyiv.

I spent about eight days at the camp on Kerosynna Street, at first with prisoners of war of various nationalities—Ukrainians, Russians, and others, about eight thousand in all. After two days I was transferred to a section of the camp where there were about three thousand prisoners of war and civilians, all of them from the Jewish population. From 28 September until I left all the Jews in the camp, younger than sixteen and older than thirty-five, were loaded into trucks every day and taken away. These trucks would soon return to the camp without the people and carrying only clothing, which was stored in separate rooms. This is why everyone in the camp realized that all those driven away by truck were not being taken to work, as the Germans tried to explain at first, but were being shot. Later these assumptions were confirmed by new arrivals at the camp who stated that all the Jews were being taken from the camp to Babyn Yar and were being executed there.

From 28 September until 3 October 1941, the Germans took away ten to fifteen truckloads of people every day. During my stay at the camp, more and more people arrived every day in groups of several hundred, but by the end of the day the total number of prisoners of war remained almost unchanged because just as many were being taken away to be executed.[37]

### The executions on 29–30 September 1941

On 27 September, as the journal of the Sixth Army's 1c/AO shows, "two thousand notices for Jews to appear at a specified place were prepared at the printing press of the Eastern Front for Kyiv."[38] The next day "members of the Ukrainian militia" posted these notices, while at the same time rumors spread that Jews were being assembled for resettlement.

On 29 September Kyiv's Jews began gathering at the Jewish cemetery on the northwest city outskirts. Anyone who would not leave their homes voluntarily was driven out by policemen from the Wehrmacht's Forty-fifth Battalion. Ferdinand Walsch, the former Oberwachtmeister of the Second Platoon who took part in removing Jews from their dwellings, recalled after the war:

---

37 Ostrovskii's testimony from 12 November 1943 in ibid., Fond 7021, Opis 65, Delo 6, Arkush 3 ob. 1943.

38 Bernd Boll and Hans Safrian, "Auf dem Weg nach Stalingrad: die 6. Armee 1941/42," in Hannes Heer and Klaus Naumann, eds., *Vernichtungskrieg: Verbrechen der Wehrmacht 1941 bis 1944* (Hamburg, 1995), p. 278.

> We members of the platoon were posted along the streets to search the houses for Jews and take them to a collection point. I can note that the doors of Jewish houses were marked with red crosses. I also remember the following incident: Meister Nöhring (a regular policeman from Reichenberg) and I were assigned to search houses. In one flat we found a woman lying on a bed with a five- or six-year-old child beside her. It was a girl. The woman said that she was the child's grandmother and that the girl was ill. Then Nöhring seized the child by the hair, went over to the flat's third-floor window, and holding the child by the hair leaned out the window. I will never forget that sight. I was certain, and still am certain, that Nöhring would have thrown the child to the street. I therefore ran over to him, grabbed the child by the torso, pulled it back in, and shouted at Nöhring: what, didn't he have children? Nöhring looked perplexed, even frightened, and gave me the child. We immediately went out of the flat and left the child with her grandmother. Nöhring never mentioned the incident again, and I am almost certain that he was ashamed.[39]

There were some local antisemitic types who helped German policemen cleanse the city of Jews. In some cases, they simply killed the Jews they had discovered on the spot. The following are testimonies from a "voluntary" assistant killer and two eyewitnesses[40], all of whom were questioned on 12 December 1943. In the words of the "volunteer" Ustinov:

> I was carrying a pail of wine to my flat in the evening… On the way I turned toward a noise I heard in the garden. When I came closer, I saw people were burying Jews whom they had caught. A housepainter by the name of Sergei… later took from these Jews a warm quilt and groceries for himself. Seeing this, I left the pail of wine with my son Nikolai, ran for a spade, and started to help with the burial. In all we buried six or seven people. Some were still alive and were crying out and begging us not to bury them, but we hit them over the head with spades and buried them.

---

39 Walsch's testimony from 16 February 1967, in BArch, B 162/6662, Bl. 205–206.

40 The three testimonies by Ustinov, Yushkov, and Herasymova are all cited in Evstafeva, "Tragediia Babego Iara," pp. 269-270. At the court-martial of the Eighth Guards' Tank Corps held on 21 January 1944, Ustinov, Yushkov, and Baranov were sentenced to death. They were hanged two days later at the place where they had killed people

> A girl of about twenty and an old woman with a fractured head particularly cried and pleaded. A German officer who was present wounded her with a pistol, and when she was in the pit a soldier finished her off with a submachine gun.

According to witness Yushkov:

> Late in the evening in late September 1941 I was coming home from Oleksandrivska Street. As I approached the garden near my building, I saw a crowd of people and heard noise. When I came closer, I saw that Jews were being beaten and buried. I found a pit that been half filled. Next to it a girl of about twenty who was being finished off was screaming and begging for mercy. The girl was not finished off that evening, and a German shot her the next morning. Yegor Denisovich Ustinov and Grigorii (I don't know his surname) were the most active in this work... Finally, women whose surnames I don't know took the spades away from Ustinov and Grigorii and kept them from burying the half dead girl. The next morning Aleksei, the janitor from 37 Nyzhnii Val Street, dragged down beaten up half dead Jews whom Germans shot in the pit.

According to witness Herasymova, she was passing by the garden in the evening, when she noticed "a crowd of children, armed Germans, and men working with spades." Coming closer, she saw that:

> the men were filling in a pit with live people, I think, about six or seven. They were mostly old women, and with them was one sturdy man. The pit had been dug out like a trench. When I came up, some soil had been thrown in, and the people could still move about. They were running about the grave, embracing each other, and crying. The men who were filling in the pit were telling the children to throw stones into the pit, so that the people would be killed and not be buried alive. I saw one of the men. who was busy burying, hit a half-buried man over the head with a spade because he was struggling to get out. The man in the grave fell down from the blow and immediately sank.

Probably thinking that they would obtain Jewish property, some inhabitants had detained Jews even before the mass shootings. They assembled them at one location and then handed them over to the German police. On the day of the mass shootings, they even delivered Jews to Babyn Yar of their volition. These local residents included a certain Syrosh and Muzyria (later convicted in 1947), who on 29 September, together with three other persons, among them a certain Hryhoriiv, first tried to hand over to the Ukrainian police at 15 Korolenko Street about fifteen Jews whom they had found in a cellar. When the police did not take in the Jews, Syrosh and Muzyria led them to Babyn Yar. There, according to Muzyria's testimony, they first stripped their victims and directly loaded their belongings into a car.[41]

German policemen directed the Jews who arrived at the cemetery along Melnikova Street to the turn at Kahatna Street (now known as Simï-Khokhlovykh Street), where their warm clothes, valuables, and papers were confiscated, then went along Kahatna Street and turned onto Lagerna (now Dorohozhytska) Street. On Lagerna Street the Jews walked pass the southern end of Babyn Yar to the turn to the right to the Lukianivka Highway (now approximately Olena Teliha Street), which at that time passed between the pre-war Syrets military camps and Babyn Yar itself. Along this road the Jews reached a broad even area (formerly a shooting range) that abutted upon the southern side of the large western spur. Here the Jews were forced to undress and then driven into the ravine and shot.

A large number of the Jews (up to ten thousand) on Dehtiarivska Street immediately set off to the Lukianivka freight station, thinking no doubt that a train was waiting to transport them to their new place of residence. The station, one of the main freight stations in the city, was located in those days at the juncture of Kahatna and Dehtiarivska Streets. But police and SS forces met the Jews at the station, forced them to put down their belongings, and led them to Babyn Yar.[42]

---

41 Vitalii Nakhmanovych, "Do pytannia pro sklad uchasnykiv karalnykh aktsii v okupovanomu Kyievi (1941–1943)," in *Druha svitova viina i dolia narodiv Ukraïny*, pp. 257–258.

42 BArch, B 162/5648, Bl. 1596–97, testimony on 1 November 1963 by Hinrich Kron, the former Wachtmeister of the Second Platoon, Third Company, 303d Police Battalion.

The killings were carried out at different places in the ravine along a distance of at least one and a half kilometers.[43] The execution squads consisted of several riflemen armed with submachine guns or pistols, two men who loaded the magazines, and several men who led the victims from the brink of the ravine down to the execution site.[44] By order of Standartenführer Paul Blobel, commander of *Sonderkommando 4a*, SS Obersturmbannführer August Hefner supervised the killings for two days. At the postwar trial in Darmstadt, Germany of former members of *Sonderkommando 4a*, one of the accused (Hefner) described the role of the SD, SS, and police:

> The following morning, 29 September, an order to officers was announced. We were informed that a battalion of Order Police and all of *Sonderkommando 4a*, including Grafhorst's company [special assignment SS troops] were to carry out executions of Kyiv's Jews. One officer was assigned to a place where belongings were assembled. I was ordered to go first to the ravine. . . . I was stunned to learn that I was the only one who had been appointed for this task. Then I learned that a formation had been drawn up, and everyone left. I do not know the details.
>
> We arrived at this place, the ravine Babyn Yar. It was located northwest of Kyiv. I cannot recall any buildings north of this execution site. I remember that on the way we saw a large number of Jews who were moving in this direction. This was a large area, small orchard plots on one side. It was slightly hilly. I also learned by chance that a place to register and a place to collect belongings were to be set up. When I arrived, the protection police and a detachment were already there. Many people were walking about. Blobel was giving instructions. He said that I should go with him.
>
> We began to argue. I defended myself because I was supposed to go to the execution site. He said, there's the ravine, the *Schutzpolizei* would shoot from the left, the SS from the right. I said that I knew perfectly well that the SS troops were using their own discretion and that Grafhorst would do the job, but he had openly forbidden interference in his actions. He ordered me to act, but not show myself to the police battalion.

43 BArch, B 162/5654, Bl. 3575, testimony by August Hefner on 4 August 1965: "The length of the ravine where the executions took place was about five hundred meters, but possibly more."

44 Ibid.

There was trouble the day before: two police officers had stated that *Sonderkommando 4a* did not need to be reinforced because of a couple of Jews. But [Obergruppenführer] Jeckeln said that *Sonderkommando 4a* should be reinforced. To avoid any unpleasantness in this respect I should not show myself. Blobel also said to me, 'You were left out of the shootings. I had an unpleasant situation because of you yesterday, so now instead of being punished get to work.' I went forward. The Jews were walking in several rows. They had to hand in their possessions and some even their outer clothing.

In pits three, four, and even five the Jews obediently lay down next to each other.[45] Protection police stood to the right and left. This was an inner cordon.[46] It extended to the Babyn Yar ravine. I had no idea of the concept of Babyn Yar. I first heard about it at the Nuremberg [trials]. About two or three policemen stood about a hundred meters from the ravine to control traffic. Some of the Jews went toward the *Schutzpolizei*, others toward the SS troops. I encountered Grafhorst and one other officer from his company. The executions had already begun. I observed them. With regard to the ravine itself I can say that it was something like a clay quarry about 300–350 meters long; it had a slope whose slant varied. I do not recall either a lateral ravine or a wooden bridge.

The SS troops had a sector about thirty meters in length. Grafhorst told me that the Jews had to lie down on the bottom close to one another. . . . They would lie down this way until the whole bottom was filled. Then everything would start over again. The next ones had to lie down on the dead Jews. Six or seven layers were formed in two days. At first the SS troops used two execution squads to carry out the killings. The entire operation was called an 'action to shoot in the back of the head.' In reality this was not the case. The way the SS troops conducted the killings did not qualify as 'a shot in the back of the head.' I watched all this for a time and stood reeling on the plateau. What else could I do if Grafhorst was still there? Then I went over to the *Schutzpolizei* to see what they were doing. When I came closer, I saw eight to ten execution squads there. Supposedly there were two or three more execution squads, but I could not see them.

At midday Blobel came and said that the SS troops and I would be

45 In the original: "one on top of another."

46 In the original: "agreement."

replaced by *Sonderkommando 4a*. I could go have dinner at the quarters and should return when the SS troops came back. At about half past two we were at the assembly site again. We were replaced again, and when darkness fell the business came to an end. We left for the quarters, and I no longer took an interest in anything.

The next morning was the same. I had to go again. Twelve to fifteen men came from the SS. Only one execution squad shot for them. At midday there was a change again. By midday Grafhorst was no longer there. I heard that he had left that day for Berlin to try to recall his company. Suddenly I was called from behind by my rank. I turned around and saw Brigadeführer Rasch and a crowd of officers. I saw him standing there as white as chalk and looking down into this valley of distress. I said to him, "Herr Brigadeführer, down below it is just as it was ordered above—a flood of blood." He ordered me to get a pistol, jump down, and deliver the final blow. What could I do? I ordered a pistol and jumped down. I probably took several shots to deliver final blows. Rasch moved away, and I returned the weapon. I got out of the pit and went back across the area.[47]

**The Ukrainian Auxiliary Police in late September–early October 1941**

The Ukrainian police appeared in Kyiv in late September 1941. An advanced detachment of eighteen men, headed by Petro Onufryk ("Bohdan Konyk"), arrived from Zhytomyr on 21 September. Two days later a "Cossack squadron" headed by Ivan Kediulych ("Chubchyk") arrived.[48] After his arrival with two assistants on 29 September,[49] Andrii Orlyk became the first commandant of the Ukrainian urban police.[50] Soon after

47 BArch, B 162/17909, Bl. 388-98.

48 Derzhavnyi arkhiv Kyivs'koï oblasti, Fond 2412, Opys 2, Sprava 227, Arkush 2: "Korotkyi narys pro zasnovannia i zorhanizovannia UOP v Kyievi." Petro Onufryk soon left via Poltava for Kharkiv, where he headed the Ukrainian police for a time. He was killed in late 1945 by order of Mykola Arsenych, the chief of the OUN-B Security Service.

49 Andrii Orlyk, or Anatolii Konkel (1899-1989), was Waffen Hauptsturmführer in the SS Division Galicia at the end of the war. He lived in Great Britain after the war under the name Anatolii Orlyk

50 Oleksandr Kucheruk, "Pochatkovyi period diialnosti ukraïnskoï politsiï Kyieva u veresni-hrudni 1941," Ukrainian Website—Orhanizatsiia Ukraïns'kykh Natsionalistiv, 10 October 2016.

Hryhorii Zakhvalynskyi, who had commanded the Zhytomyr oblast police, took charge of the police in the Kyiv oblast.[51] His deputy was Ivan Kediulych.[52] All of these figures belonged to the Melnyk faction of the Organization of Ukrainian Nationalists (OUN).

Sometime in early September, the 454th Protection Police Division in Zhytomyr organized a Ukrainian auxiliary police force for Kyiv, which was subordinated to the 987th Battalion of Ground Riflemen.[53] On 27 September the division ordered its supply officer, Hauptman Dr. Didik, to send the next day from Zhytomyr to Kyiv "one hundred trained Ukrainian auxiliary policemen, part of whom should be familiar with conditions in Kyiv. . . . Until further orders the Ukrainian auxiliary police is subordinated to Feldkommandatur 195. . . . The Ukrainian detachment is to be supplied with provisions for three days."[54]

The Ukrainian police was controlled in September-October 1941 by *Sonderkommando 4a* under SS Obersturmführer Müller. He assigned Oleksii Babii, the Ukrainian interpreter in the force, to report on the mood of its two-hundred-fifty Ukrainians.[55] Babii had been inducted as

51 Testimony given at the Security Police in Zhytomyr on 10 December 1941 by Vasyl Sherei, aide-de-camp to the commandant of the Zhytomyr oblast police in Derzhavnyi arkhiv Zhytomyrs'koï oblasti, Fond r-1151, Opys 1, Sprava 3, Arkush 19zv,

52 Ivan Kediulych was Zakhvalynskyi's deputy until February 1942. When Ukrainian nationalists were arrested in Kyiv, he fled to Proskuriv, where again he was arrested, but escaped to Lviv and sided with Stepan Bandera's forces in the Ukrainian Insurgent Army (UPA), There he headed a training unit and from January1945 headed the Nineteenth Kamianets-Podilskyi Tactical Sector of the UPA. He was killed in a battle with an NKVD unit on 1 August 1945.

53 National Archives and Record Administration, Washington D.C., T 315, Roll 2216.

54 Ibid.

55 Oleksii Babii (1909–1944) joined the Sonderkommando 4a as an interpreter in July 1941and served there until October, when he was transferred in Poltava to Abwehr 202. He was arrested by the Gestapo in Kremenchuh as an OUN functionary on 8 March 1942, and taken away for execution, but managed to escape at the last moment. He was one of the organizers of the UPA in Volhynia. From late November 1943 until July 1944, using the name Petro Levchuk (with the birthdate 1912), he served in the SS Galicia Division with the rank of SS Untersturmführer. He was killed in the Battle of Brody on 20 July 1944. Arkhiv OUN, Kyiv, Fond 1, Opys 1, Sprava 276. Arkush 3: "Spohady pro vtechu vid rozstrilu, Kyiv, 30.3.1942." See also Nestor Myzak, *Za tebe, sviata Ukraïno: buchats'kyi povit u vyzvolnii borotbi OUN, UPA*, Vol. 4 (Chernivtsi: Bukrek, 2004), p. 330.

a rank-and-file member into the force for this purpose.[56]

Oleksa Stasiuk, another member of the Ukrainian Auxiliary Police, described its role during the mass executions at Babyn Yar. According to him, on 29 or 30 September, forty of the policemen, who were then quartered in a school in Kyiv's Podil district, rode in two trucks to the site at Babyn Yar where the Jews' belongings were being confiscated, and then collected and loaded them onto the trucks.[57] Ukrainian policemen also guarded the victims and their belongings at the Lukianivka freight station.[58]

According to Fritz Höfer, a driver with *Sonderkommando 4a*, the Ukrainian policemen not only collected the belongings but helped, if indirectly, to kill the victims.

> When the truck stopped near the heaps of clothing, it was immediately loaded with clothing. The Ukrainians who were there did this. I saw at this spot that the Ukrainians were taking the Jews—men, women, and children—who were arriving. They were sent to various places where they took turns piling up first their baggage, coats, shoes, outer clothing, and also underwear. They were also required to lay down their valuables in a certain place. Each kind of clothing was placed in a separate pile. All this proceeded very quickly, and if any of them lingered the Ukrainians kicked and hit them.[59]

Viktor Trill, a former SS Oberscharführer and driver with Sonderkommando 4a who was directly involved in the killings reported that Ukrai-

---

56 Arkhiv OUN, Kyiv, Fond 1, Opys 1, Sprava 276, Arkush 3:"Spohady pro vtechu vid rozstrilu, Kyiv, 30.3.1942." See also Yuri Radchenko, "The Biography of the OUN(m) Activist Oleksa Babii in the Light of His 'Memoirs on Escaping Execution' (1942)," *Journal of Soviet and Post-Soviet Politics and Society*, VI, 1 (Stuttgart and Hannover, 2020), pp. 239-279.

57 See the interrogation record of Stasiuk at the Ukrainian SSR Ministry of State Security on 1 July 1946, in *Babii Yar: chelovek, vlast, istoriia: dokumenty i materialy*, Vol. 1: *Istoricheskaia topografiia—khronologiia sobytii*, compiled by Tatiana Evstafeva and Vitalii Nakhmanovich (Kyiv, 2004), pp. 280–281.

58 Hinrich Kron's testimony from 1 November 1963 in BArch, B 162/5648, Bl. 1596–97.

59 Hofer's testimony from 27 August 1959 in BArch, B 162/19216, Bl. 9375-9376.

nians guarded the Jews at the place of "resettlement" before the shootings.[60]

There is also information that "Ukrainians" took a direct part in killing Jews. Herman Lass, a former member of the First Platoon, Third Company, 303d Police Battalion, who was inside the cordon around the execution site and witnessed the killings, reported in his postwar testimony that according to "hearsay," "Ukrainian members of the SD" had been involved in killing Jews.[61]

The "Ukrainian members of the SD" were to all appearances Ukrainian interpreters who were serving in Sonderkommando 4a. One of them was Stepan Fedak. He may not have personally participated in shooting Jews at Babyn Yar, but he was involved indirectly in the action. Johannes Materna, an ethnic German from Galicia and former interpreter with the *Sonderkommando* who knew Fedak well, testified while being questioned by postwar German investigation agencies that Fedak himself had told him on 29 September that he had been assigned to the cordon around the road that Jews walked along to Babyn Yar.[62]

**Rescuers**

In a book about Swiss rescuers of Jews, the Swiss historian François Wisard correctly observed that the Holocaust cannot be understood only in terms of an opposition between executioners and victims. There was a third group: those who saved and helped Jews. Although there were few of them by comparison with the indifferent majority of the population, their efforts undoubtedly deserve acknowledgment and respect because what they did is akin to heroism.[63]

Since 1963, Yad Vashem, Israel's Holocaust Martyrs' and Heroes' Remembrance Authority, has been awarding the title of Righteous Among the Nations to those Gentiles who, risking their own lives, rescued Jews

---

60 Trill's testimony from 25 June 1960 in BArch B 162/5641, Bl. 12-15, cited in Aleksandr Kruglov, *Tragediia Babego Yara v nemetskikh dokumentakh* (Dnipro: Tkuma/Lira, 2011), pp. 84–87.

61 Lass's testimony from 10 October 1966 in BArch, B 162/6672, Bl. 377-78.

62 Materna's testimony from 25 April 1966 in BArch, B 162/19206, Bl. 1332.

63 François Wisard, *Les Justes suisses* (Geneva: CICAD, 2007), p. 6.

during World War II. In 2012, the European Parliament set up the Day of the Righteous, which is observed on 6 March. In Ukraine, its parliament passed a resolution on 2 February 2021 to establish 14 May as the day to honor Ukrainians who saved Jews during the war.

As of January 2020, no less than 2,659 citizens of Ukraine had been awarded the title of Righteous Among the Nations.[64] In numerical terms, Ukraine accounts for 9.5 percent of all Righteous and is ranked in fourth place after Poland, the Netherlands, and France. Of the Ukrainian Righteous 155 are from Kyiv.[65]

In 1989 the Jewish Council of Ukraine instituted the title of Righteous of Babyn Yar. The first Righteous were members of the family of the Orthodox priest Aleksei Glagolev. By January 2009, the Righteous of Babyn Yar title had been awarded to 605 residents of Kyiv and surroundings who had rescued in total no less than a thousand Jewish residents of the city.[66] As of January 2010, the Memory of Babyn Yar Fund had registered 607 Righteous, of whom 119 were still alive.[67]

Ukrainians, Russians, Poles, Tatars, Armenians, Moldovans, and Crimean Tatars are among the citizens of Ukraine who rescued Jews. It is also appropriate to mention individual Germans among the occupiers who tried to rescue Jews during the mass executions at Babyn Yar. Paul Wörzberger and Johann Koller were among the Germans who strove to help the victims. Wörzberger was a motorcycle messenger with the Second Company of the Forty-fifth Reserve Police Battalion, while Koller was the personal driver for the company's commander, Kreutzer. On 29 September 1941, Wörzberger drove to Babyn Yar with a dispatch for Kreutzer. As he recalled after the war:

---

64 Yad Vashem, The Righteous Among the Nations Database, (https://www.yadvashem.org/righteous/statistics.html).

65 Yad Vashem, The Righteous Among the Nations Database, https://righteous.yadvashem.org/?search=Kiev&searchType=righteous_only&language=en. For lists of Righteous specifically from Kyiv, see *Pamiati ukraïntsiv, iaki riatuvaly ievreïv pid chas Druhoï svitovoï viiny* (Dnipro: Ukraïns'kyi instytut vyvchennia Holokostu Tkuma, 2021), pp. 84–89.

66 Ilia Levitas, "Kiev," in I. A. Altman, ed., Kholokost na territorii SSSR: entsiklopediia (Moscow: ROSSPEN, 2009), p. 405.

67 Fond "Pamiat BabegoYara," http://babynyar.gov.ua/fond-«pam'yat-babinogo-yaru.

> Near the piles of clothing at the ravine were two women who had been separated from the rest. When I was walking past them, they said that they were Ukrainian and I had to rescue them. They literally attached themselves to me. My friend Koller, who was Kreutzer's driver, was standing near this place. Both women and I went over to Koller, and we started discussing how we could rescue them. I cannot say whether the women were Jewish or really Ukrainian. We agreed that Koller would remove both women from the danger zone in his car. We both realized what would await us if our rescue action were to come to light. But we felt compassion for the women, who were crying badly. Since I knew that Kreutzer [the company commander] was in the ravine, this trip was very risky for Koller [his driver]. I remained at the spot to shield Koller if he were asked.[68]

Koller's account differs somewhat from Wörzberger's.

> During the operation against the Jews, I had to drive Kreutzer to the location. The Jews had already been sent off during this trip. When we arrived at the location, Kreutzer got out of the car and went to a hill. I heard gunfire from where Kreutzer had gone. My task had been completed. While I was standing there, motorcycle messenger Hans [Paul] Wörzberger from Wittenberg (near Dresden) came over to me. A woman was with him. Wörzberger asked me to drive the woman to the city. She was crying. I pondered for a while because it was very risky to drive someone away [from the killing site], and in addition we would have to go back past the entire guarded column. Nevertheless, I agreed. Wörzberger sat beside me, and we put the woman on the back seat. We set off for the city. The woman got out there. Wörzberger had obviously never seen her before. The woman ran off. We were glad that all had gone well.[69]

A certain inconsistency in the details can perhaps be explained by the fact that Wörzberger and Koller related this incident twenty-seven years after it occurred. As for the rescued women, they were apparently seventeen-year-old Genia Batashova and fourteen-year-old Mania Palti (see

68 Wörzberger's testimony from 16 September 1968 in BArch, B 162/6666, Bl. 1000.

69 Koller's testimony from 26 April 1968 in BArch, B 162/6664, Bl. 643–44.

also Chapter 8 below). In Batashova's account the rescue took place after she and other Jews were led to the large level ground near the ravine.

> The Hitlerites were tearing clothes off people . . . and sending them half undressed to the execution site. People were rushing about as if they had lost their heads. Screams from the doomed and bursts from automatics blended with the continuous rumble. I did not completely understand what was happening to me and where I had lost my mother, sister, and brother. In this turmoil I encountered Mania Palti, a fourteen-year-old girl from our courtyard. We took each other by the hand and started searching for rescue. We went up to one of the executioners and began explaining to him that we were not Jewish and had accidentally found ourselves at Babyn Yar simply out of curiosity. He took us to officers who were standing beside a car and started to explain something to them. One of the Hitlerites soon indicated with a gesture that we could get in the car, which we did. The driver covered us up with some sort of clothing and drove off in the direction of the city center. The driver took us to Melnikova Street and let us out.[70]

Despite differences in detail Wörzberger's and Batasheva's testimonies agree on the whole, while Koller's is somewhat different. He may have forgotten many details because he was simply helping Wörzberger. For Wörzberger and Batashova, however, they remembered this event. This is probably better because Wörzberger was the initiator of the rescue, and for Batasheva it was a question of her life.

70 Record of interrogation of Genia Batasheva as a witness by the Ukrainian SSR KGB on 15 July 1980, in *Babii Yar: chelovek, vlast, istoriia*, p. 322.

# Appendix 1: German punitive organs

| Security Police and SD, SS Troops, Protective Police | |
|---|---|
| Unit | Role in Destruction of Jews |
| Higher SS and Police Führer in Russia-South Obergruppenführer Friedrich Jeckeln | Organizer of destruction of Kyiv Jews |
| Staff of *Einsatzgruppe C* | Participation (in the person of Group Chief Rasch) in the preparations for the executions and control over them |
| *Sonderkommando 4a* | Participation (in the person of Commander Blobel) in preparations for mass executions, direct execution of killings, internal cordoning of execution site |
| Operational Command 5 | Direct execution of killings, internal cordoning of execution site |
| Third Company of Special SS Battalion | Directly participating in executions (posting of execution squad), patrolling city, guarding various German departments |
| Staff of Police Regiment Süd | Controlling the course of executions |
| Forty-fifth Reserve Police Battalion (part of Police Regiment Süd) | Combing the city in search of Jews, convoying Jews to execution site, cordoning execution site, posting execution squads |

| | |
|---|---|
| 303d Police Battalion (part of Police Regiment Süd) | Combing the city in search of Jews, convoying Jews to execution site, cordoning execution site |
| Eighty-second Reserve Police Battalion (part of 454th Protective Division | Combing the city in search of Jews, convoying Jews to execution site, cordoning execution site |
| **The Wehrmacht** | |
| Sixth Army Commander General Field Marshall Walter von Reichenau | Approval, if not direct instructions, to conduct an "action of revenge" for the explosions and fires in the city |
| Hans von Obstfelder, commander of the Twenty-ninth Army Corps and chief of the Kyiv garrison until September 2, 1941 | Order to conduct an "action of revenge" for the explosions and fires in the city, involvement in preparing mass executions (discussion of details of the planned action at conferences) |
| Major General Kurt Eberhard, commander of Feldkommandatur 195 and military commandant of Kyiv (after September 24, 1941) | Involvement in preparing mass executions (discussion of details of the planned action at conferences), call to the SD to execute all Jews as revenge for explosions and fires, order for public execution of twenty Jews on September 24,1941, as revenge for explosions and fires |
| Major General Friedrich Zickwolff, commander of the 113th Infantry Division and chief of the Kyiv garrison from September 27 to mid-October 1941 | Involvement in preparing mass executions (discussion of details of the planned action at conferences), assignment of sappers to blow up the brinks of the part of Babyn Yar where executions were carried out |

CHAPTER 6

# Babyn Yar after Babyn Yar

*Vladyslav Hrynevych*

Babyn Yar was part of the family memories of many Kyivites who lived through the German occupation. My grandmother and mother told me about this tragedy when I was a child. My family lived on Zhylianska Street, near the city's central railway station, so they were among the first to see the soldiers of the Wehrmacht arriving on trains. Columns of German infantry entered the city through the Podil district, from where they headed to Khreshchatyk Boulevard. The soldiers were well dressed and equipped, and thus were markedly different from the Red Army units that had just abandoned Kyiv. The preponderant majority of city residents reacted very warily to the Germans' arrival. Some, however, welcomed them as "liberators" with bread and salt. In some areas women danced and sang on the streets, rejoicing at the "flight of the Bolsheviks." When a group of soldiers entered my grandmother's yard, Khaia, her elderly neighbor, addressed them in Yiddish and offered to clean their cauldrons. Seating herself comfortably on the ground, the old woman scrubbed the soldiers' cauldrons thoroughly with sand in the naïve expectation, probably shared by others, that "civilized Europe had arrived," which would put an end to the "barbarism of the communists."

**The tragedy of the Jews: from incomplete to complete suppression**

My mother also recounted how she had accompanied her classmate Mania, who lived in a private house behind the Lybid River, to Babyn Yar. My grandmother often purchased bags of manure for the garden from Mania's father, which he delivered on his cart. It was on this scrupulously cleaned cart loaded with bundles of simple belongings that Mania, her father, and grandmother drove past my family's house on 29 September

1941, on their way to Babyn Yar. My classmate told me that the Germans were sending the Jews to Palestine, so they were heading to the station to board trains. My mother climbed onto the cart next to her classmate and rode with her to Lukianivka, where she was stopped by a police cordon. A policeman said to my mother: "Leave, little girl, you cannot proceed any further." "I am accompanying Mania," she replied. "Get off, you can't go past this point," the policeman replied severely.

Soon afterwards the residents of Kyiv heard the sound of machine guns firing from Babyn Yar. Rumors began circulating throughout the city that the Germans were shooting the unfortunate Jews. This was confirmed later by women whom the occupiers had forced to sort through the clothing, footwear, and other belongings of the executed people. One of them lived in my mother's building.

The residents of Kyiv were stunned and terrified by the news of the mass murder of the Jews. People now realized what could be expected of the Germans' "new order." A survey on the public mood during this period, prepared by the Security Police and the SD in Kyiv, cited a popular saying: "The Germans have come—*gut*. The Jews—*kaput*, the gypsies too. Later for the Ukrainians."[1] Realizing the danger looming over the civilian population, people whispered to each other that "They'll start with the Jews and continue with the Ukrainians."[2]

For my family, the next two years of the German occupation turned into a permanent struggle for survival. Hunger, roundups at bazaars after which you could end up in a gas chamber, prohibitions and intimidation, constant news about shootings, and the seizure of hostages were the features of the daily life of the average resident of Kyiv.

Of course, it was impossible to conceal such a large-scale crime as Babyn Yar. News of the mass murder of the Jews trickled from behind the front line, spread first and foremost by ordinary people who had man-

1 See the report of the head of the security police and SD in Kyiv on the situation in Kyiv general district on 1 December 1942 in Liubov Lehasova et al. eds., *Kyïv ochyma voroha: doslidzhennia, dokumenty, svidchennia* (Kyiv: Aerostat, 2012), p. 334; Inessa Mirchevskaia, *I on podaril mne mamu: vospominaniia* (Kyiv: KMTs "Poeziia," 2005), p. 31.

2 Mykhailo Koval', "Natsysts'kyi henotsyd shchodo ievreïv ta ukraïns'ke naselennia (1941-1944 rr.)," *Ukraïns'kyi istorychnyi zhurnal*, XXXVI, 2 (Kyiv, 1992), p. 27.

aged to leave occupied Kyiv. Reports about Babyn Yar also appeared in the press, initially the foreign press. On 19 November 1941 the central Soviet print media, the newspapers *Pravda* and *Izvestiia*, published information from the New York offices of the Telegraph Agency of the Soviet Union (TASS) about the execution by the Germans of 52,000 Jewish men, women, and children.[3]

The Soviet leadership was already receiving news about the brutal murders of the Jews by the Nazis on the occupied territories from military intelligence and the NKVD in the summer of 1941.[4]

Considering the prewar Soviet practice of destroying millions of innocent people in the Soviet Union, it is unlikely that Stalin was shocked by this news. At the same time, it is highly probable that before the war began the Soviet leadership was fully aware that a possible German occupation represented a clear treat specifically to Jews, if only because special NKVD reports about the Germans' reprisals against the Jews in Germany began appearing regularly, starting in the late 1930s. Based on censored correspondence, letters exchanged between Soviet Jews and their relatives living abroad, these special reports featured crystal-clear descriptions of the Nazis' antisemitic policies and practices, such as, "What Hitler is doing with the Jews defies description," "Jews are being persecuted and restricted in everything," "The Jews in Germany are doomed," and "People are dying because of one accursed person that is sowing all the evil and hatred [...] this is not a human but a devil."[5] Adopting preventive measures to preserve the lives of the condemned Jews—women, elderly people, and children, whose husbands, sons, and fathers had gone to the front at the start of the war—was clearly not one of Stalin's priorities. This is corroborated not only by the Soviet authorities' failure to inform their citizens about the anti-Jewish orientation of Hitler's policy but also by their decision to organize an evacuation that was aimed above all at safeguarding tangible assets.

---

3 "Zverstva nemtsev v Kieve," *Pravda* (Moscow), 19 November 1941, p. 4.

4 Niels Bo Poulsen, "The Soviet Extraordinary State Commission on War Crimes: An Analysis of the Commission`s Investigative Work in War and Post-War Stalinist Society" (Ph.D. dissertation, Copenhagen University, 2004), p. 38.

5 Amir Weiner, *Making Sense of War: The Second World War and the Fate of the Bolshevik Revolution* (Princeton: Princeton University Press, 2001), p. 209.

Nevertheless, one should not downplay the importance of the public declarations and official documents that the Soviet leadership issued at the beginning of the war in connection with the horrific Nazi crimes against the Jews in the occupied territories. On 7 January 1942 *Pravda* published a Note issued by Viacheslav Molotov, People's Commissar of Foreign Affairs of the USSR, condemning the shootings of Jews in Kyiv, Lviv, Odesa, Kamianets-Podilskyi, Dnipropetrovsk, Mariupol, and Kerch:

> A horrific massacre and pogroms were committed by the Nazi invaders in the Ukrainian capital of Kyiv.... A large number of Jews, including women and children of different ages, were assembled; before the shooting everyone was stripped naked and beaten.... They were shot with submachine guns. There were many mass murders...in other Ukrainian cities, and these bloody executions were especially directed against unarmed and defenseless Jews.[6]

On 18 December 1942 the Soviet government signed the Joint Declaration of the governments of Belgium, Great Britain, the Netherlands, Greece, Luxembourg, Norway, Poland, the United States, Czechoslovakia, Yugoslavia, and the French National Committee condemning the barbarous policy of the coldblooded extermination of Europe's Jewish population.[7] The next day *Pravda* published a corresponding declaration prepared by the Information Bureau of the People's Commissariat of Foreign Affairs condemning the "special plan for the total extermination of the Jewish population in the occupied territory of Europe." The declaration emphasized that the "Jewish minority of the Soviet population...has

---

6 "Nota Narodnogo Komissara Inostrannykh Del tov. V.M. Molotova 'O povsemestnykh grabezhakh, razorenii naseleniia i chudovishchnykh zverstvakh germanskikh vlastei na zakhvachennykh imi sovetskikh territoriiakh' on 6 ianvaria 1942," Pravda (Moscow), 7 November 1942, pp. 1-2.

7 "Sovmestnaia deklaratsiia Pravitel'stva Bel'gii, Velikobritanii, Gollandii, Gretsii, Liuksemburga, Norvegii, Pol'shi, Soiedinennykh Shtatov Ameriki, Soiuza Sovetskikh Sotsialisticheskikh Respublik, Chekhoslovakii, Iugoslavii i Frantsuzskogo Natsional'nogo Komiteta o provodimom gitlerovskimi vlastiami istrebleniia evreiskogo naseleniia Evropy," *Pravda* (Moscow), 18 December 1942, p. 1.

suffered particularly grievously."[8] The historian Hennadii Kostyrchenko writes that this document was the last one in which the Soviet leadership assessed the Nazis' crime against the Jews in historically adequate terms.[9] It is revealing that, regardless of widespread Soviet practice, this important declaration was not reprinted in other periodicals, and *Pravda*'s contribution went no further than this declaration; this attests to the newspaper's subordination to exclusively foreign-policy goals.

After Kyiv was liberated in early November 1943, the Extraordinary State Commission for the Investigation of the Crimes of the German-Fascist Invaders and Their Accomplices (NDK) began its work in the city. Established a year earlier, the NDK's goal was to record the crimes committed by the Nazis and to inform the public about them. However, from the very outset the committee did not demonstrate sufficient thoroughness, but its main drawback was that it did not function independently but acted as a political tool of the Soviet government. The concealment of Stalinist crimes and the Soviet government's efforts to distract the public's attention from them played a key role in its activities. For example, as a result of the commission's 1943 "investigation" into the mass burials that were discovered in the Bykivnia woods near Kyiv (where before the war the NKVD secretly buried tens of thousands of executed victims of the Great Terror, as well as Red Army soldiers who were shot after having broken out of encirclement in September 1941), the commission arrived at the "truthful findings" that the mass graves contained the bodies of the "prisoners of the camps [located] in the village of Darnytsia Kyiv oblast" who had been shot by German occupiers.[10] [see Plate **XIV**] In January 1944 the "Special Commission for Establishing and Investigating the Circumstances surrounding the Shooting of Captured Polish Officers by the German-Fascist Invaders in Katyn Forest," which was created within the NDK, also confirmed this "crime of the German-fascist occupiers

8 "Osushchestvlenie gitlerovskimi vlastiami plana istrebleniia evreiskogo naseleniia Evropy," *Pravda* (Moscow), 19 December 1942, p. 1.

9 Gennadii Kostyrchenko, *Stalin protiv "kosmopolitov". Vlast' i evreiskaia intelligentsiia v SSSR* (Moscow: ROSSPEN, 2009), p. 80.

10 Oleh Bazhan, "Represyvna diial'nist' orhaniv VUNK-DPU-NKVS-KDB na Kyïvshchyni u 1919-1980-ti rr.," *Z arkhiviv VUCHK-HPU-NKVD-KDB*, No. 1 (36) (Kyiv, 2011), p. 198.

against the Poles,"[11] which was a blatant act of deliberate falsification.

The NDK undertook practically no large-scale excavations and exhumations of human remains in Babyn Yar. Instead, the public learned that in the summer of 1943, when the front was approaching the Dnipro River, the Nazis formed a special *Sonderkommando* unit headed by SS *Standartenführer* Paul Blobel, which was tasked with destroying all traces of the Nazis' crimes. Under the Germans' supervision, prisoners of war from the Syrets concentration camp were forced to exhume corpses in Babyn Yar, the anti-tank trench, and the area near the Pavlov Psychiatric Hospital and then burn them in large, open ovens, after which they spread the ashes over the ravine. The prisoners, realizing that they were building the last oven for themselves, made a desperate attempt to escape; only 18 out of 327 prisoners succeeded in escaping. These former prisoners recounted the horrors that they had witnessed and in which they had been forced to participate. Their testimonies formed the basis of the commission's findings.[12]

A considerable amount of information about the mass killings of Jews in Babyn Yar also emerged during the trials of the Nazis and their accomplices—former policemen, traitors, and others—which took place immediately after the liberation of Kyiv. The pre-trial investigations revealed the circumstances surrounding the Nazis' non-stop executions in Babyn Yar of prisoners of war, communists, and underground members, as well as the dramatic circumstances relating to some local residents' attempts to save Jews and to the incitement to or involvement in Nazi crimes against others of some city residents. The testimonies of the wit-

---

11 "Soobshchenie Spetsial'noi Komissii po ustanovleniiu i rassledovaniiu obstoiatel'stv rasstrela nemetsko-fashistskimi zakhvatchikami v Katynskom lesu voennoplennykh pol'skikh ofitserov. 24.01.1944," in *Sbornik soobshchenii Chrezvychainoi gosudarstvennoi komissii o zlodeianiiakh nemetsko-fashistskikh zakhvatchikov* (Moscow: OGIZ, 1946), pp. 101-151.

12 *Soobshchenie Spetsial'noi Gosudarstvennoi Komissii po ustanovleniiu i rassledovaniiu zlodeianii nemetsko-fashistskikh zakhvatchikov i ikh soobshchnikov i pricheneniiu imi ushcherba grazhdanam, kolkhozam, obshchestvennym organizatsiiam, gosudarstvennym predpriiatiiam i uchrezhdeniiam SSSR o razrusheniiakh i zverstvakh, sovershennykh nemetsko-fashistskimi zakhvatchikami v gorode Kieve* (Moscow: OGIZ, Gospolitizdat, 1944), p. 12.

nesses P. Savytska, L. Hryhurko, and N. Tkachenko, for example, are revealing in this connection. Until 17 January 1943 these three individuals hid I. Brodsky, a Jewish prisoner of war, until he was denounced by a woman named Shymanska, whose husband served in the Gestapo. For giving assistance to a Jew, all three were arrested but managed to avoid execution. Brodsky, too, survived and subsequently appeared as a witness.[13]

On 12 December 1943 Bondarenko, the head of the NKVD Directorate for Kyiv oblast (UNKVD), sent a memorandum to Serhii Savchenko, People's Commissar of State Security of the Ukrainian SSR, entitled "About the Atrocities of the German-Fascist Occupiers in the City of Kyiv," which clearly indicated that in Babyn Yar the Nazis committed an act of horrific violence against Jews only because they were Jews. The memorandum states:

> Demonstrating special hatred toward the Jewish nationality, the German-fascist bandits in the city of Kyiv destroyed nearly all the Jews.
>
> At the end of September 1941 a German commandant issued a directive ordering the entire Jewish population, including women and children and elderly people, to assemble with all their valuables and property at the Jewish Cemetery, as though they were being sent to the camps. [...]
>
> At the cemetery German soldiers and policemen committed mass robbery; they confiscated all items and valuables from those who had assembled.
>
> After the robbery, all the Jews were led in groups of 100–200 people toward Babyn Yar [located] on the outskirts of the city.
>
> A mass murder of Jews was carried out in Babyn Yar. They were stripped naked and forced to run along the ravine; at this time they were shot with submachine guns and machine guns. Then the killed and wounded, among whom were children who were still alive, were thrown into the ravine and buried. For a long time afterwards groans were heard coming from the ravine; the layer of earth underneath those who had

---

13 Tetiana Ievstaf'ieva, "Trahediia Babynoho Iaru kriz' pryzmu arkhivnykh dokumentiv Sluzhby Bezpeky Ukraïny," *Arkhivy Ukraïny*, No. 5 (Kyiv, 2011), pp. 145-146.

> been shot stirred from the movement of living bodies.
>
> Many people, sensing their death, lost consciousness, tore their hair out, pleaded for mercy, but they received blows in response..
>
> Thus, in Babyn Yar in late September 1941, nearly 70,000 Jews were shot over the space of several days.
>
> During the entire period of the German occupation of Kyiv, Babyn Yar was a permanent site where the shootings of Soviet people were carried out.
>
> According to preliminary estimates, it has been determined that, in addition to 70,000 Jews, nearly 20,000 captured fighters and commanders of the Red Army and nearly 10,000 communists, Komsomol members, [and] non-party Soviet patriots were shot in Babyn Yar during the occupation.[14]

In January the head of the UNKVD for Kyiv oblast also informed Savchenko about the execution of three German accomplices who were directly involved in the Babyn Yar tragedy.[15] In accordance with the sentence handed down by the court-martial of the 8th Guards Tank Corps, Yegor Ustinov (a Russian peasant from Tula oblast, a carpenter by trade), Nikifor Yushkov (a Russian peasant from Orlov oblast, a painter by trade), and Venedykt Baranov (a poor Ukrainian peasant from Vinnytsia oblast, who was employed as a fire protection worker) were hanged on Verkhnii Val Street in the presence of 500 Kyivites. In late September 1941 the three men had hunted down and brutally killed unfortunate Jews who had not obeyed the Nazis' order to go to Babyn Yar. Witnesses testified that the accused buried alive seven people, mostly women. On 30 September one of the criminals, Baranov, dragged a sick, old woman from her bed, dragged her from the fifth floor to the street, then drove

14 Cited in *Kyïv: viina, vlada, suspil'stvo. 1939-1945 rr: za dokumentamy radians'kykh spetssluzhb ta natsysts'koï okupatsiinoï administratsiï* (Kyiv: Tempora, 2014), pp. 630–631.

15 See a special report of the head of the UNKDB in Kyiv oblast Bondarenko submitted to the people's commissar of state security of the Ukrainian RSR Serhii Savchenko on the execution of the active participants of mass atrocities over Kyivites, dated not later than 23 January 1944, in *Kyïv u dni natsysts'koï navaly—za dokumentamy radians'kykh spetssluzhb: naukovo-dokumental'ne vydannia* (Kyiv, Lviv, 2003), pp. 444-445.

her to a garden on Verkhnii Val Street, where the criminals were killing and burying people who were still alive. The next day Baranov discovered a Jewish woman. He "broke into her apartment, looted it, tried to cut her throat with a dull pen knife, after which he threw her out of the window onto the street."[16] Then he buried her in that same garden.

On 19 January 1944 Amaiak Kobulov, Deputy People's Commissar of the NKVD of the USSR, sent a memorandum to the NDK based on the above-mentioned report prepared by the UNKVD for Kyiv oblast dated 12 December 1943. The memorandum reiterated, albeit in an abbreviated form, information about the mass extermination of Jews in Babyn Yar. "The occupiers demonstrated particular brutality in relation to the Jews, having destroyed the entire Jewish population of the city during the occupation."[17]

By the time the memorandum was received, the Extraordinary State Commission had already prepared and disseminated its own draft among its members, in which the tragic fate of the Kyivan Jews was not concealed. In part it read: "The Hitlerite bandits committed a mass, brutal destruction of the Jewish population. They hung announcements ordering all Jews to go to the corner of Melnikova and Dokterivska [actually Dekhtiarivska] streets on 29 September 1941, taking with them documents, money, and valuable items. The executioners herded the Jews who had assembled to Babyn Yar, they confiscated all their valuables and then shot them."[18]

The commission sent the prepared document to Moscow, where problems began to crop up with in connection with its recopying and harmonization in keeping with "political expediency." The text was read personally by Viacheslav Molotov and Nikita Khrushchev. After coordination with the top-ranking figures in the country, Georgii Aleksandrov, the head of the Propaganda and Agitation Department of the CC AUCP(b), edited the document, from which even passing references to Jews were deleted. The final document was endorsed by the commission

16 Ibid., p. 444.

17 Ievstaf'ieva, "Trahediia Babynoho Iaru," p. 147.

18 Cited in Lev Bezymenskii, "Informatsiia po-sovetski," *Znamia*, 5 (Moscow, 1998), p. 192.

in Kyiv, as well as by the distinguished Ukrainian poets Maksym Rylskyi and Pavlo Tychyna.[19]

In late February 1944 the Soviet press published the Extraordinary State Commission's announcement "About the Destruction and Atrocities Perpetrated by the German-Fascist Invaders in the City of Kyiv." The text noted in part: "On 29 September 1941 the Hitlerite bandits herded thousands of innocent Soviet citizens to the corner of Melnikova and Dokterivska streets. The executioners led those who had assembled to Babyn Yar. . . . People recounted seeing the Germans throwing infants into the ravine and burying them alive together with their parents, who were killed and wounded. 'You could see a layer of earth stirring from the movement of people who were still alive.'"[20]

In taking this unambiguous step toward erasing the memory and the destruction of Jewish identity, the Stalinist government thus depersonalized the Jewish victims of the Babyn Yar tragedy. Subsequently, Stalinist propaganda and the Soviet nationality policy in general were increasingly characterized by the practice of dispensing limited amounts of information or blatantly concealing official data on the anti-Jewish nature of Nazi crimes. The situation reached the point that during the war it was forbidden to publish posters about Jewish war heroes and make any references in newspapers to Jews who had been awarded medals for courage and bravery in battle.

Nonetheless, a certain duality existed. On the one hand, in order to mislead the Western democracies, from time-to-time Stalinist propaganda mentioned the extermination of the Jews, especially if they were Jewish victims outside the USSR. On the other, the Stalinist government took into consideration "the possibility of the intensification of antisemitic moods" among its population, and therefore tacitly banned all discussion of the murder of Soviet Jews by the Nazis. In their efforts to

---

19 Ibid., pp. 191-199.

20 "Soobshchenie Chrezvychainoi gosudarstvennoi komissii po ustanovleniiu i rassledovanniu zlodeianii nemetsko-fashistskikh zakhvatchikov i ikh soobshchnikov o razrusheniiakh i zverstvakh sovershennykh nemetsko-fashistskimi zakhvatchikami v gorode Kieve," *Izvestiia* (Moscow), 29 February 1944, p. 2.

conceal the "Jewish topic" for reasons connected with the resolution of "political tasks," the Soviet government and the Soviet press operated in a fashion somewhat similar to the Western media at the time, in which the Nazis' unprecedented destruction of Jews was not overly emphasized (so as "not to provoke antisemitism"). The essential difference between the West and the USSR lay in the fact that toward the end of the war all mentions of Jews in the context of Nazi crimes practically disappeared from Soviet newspapers, and were supplanted by the faceless euphemism "peaceful Soviet citizens."

After returning to the territories that had been under German occupation and the influence of German propaganda for two years, the Soviet government searched for effective ways to re-legitimize itself. This pertained especially to Ukraine, where in the prewar decades the Soviet government was uncomfortably aware of the Ukrainians' low level of loyalty to the Soviet Union. The Soviet security organs, which scrupulously recorded the public mood in the Ukrainian SSR, noted a dichotomy of feelings among Ukrainians, especially in rural areas. On the one hand, they felt relief and joy at having been liberated from the German occupiers; on the other, they felt alarm and fear because of the return of the "Soviets." Ordinary citizens characterized their attitude to the Nazi and Soviet governments with the unambiguous saying, "Let this pass, and may that not return."[21]

Given these sentiments existing against the background of the concealment of the anti-Jewish component of Nazi crimes, the Stalinist government sought to appeal powerfully to Ukrainians' national sentiments, presenting itself as their liberator and defender. Typical in this connection was the preamble to the report prepared by the NDK on the crimes perpetrated by the Nazis in Kyiv. Clearly emphasizing the "crimes of the fascist bandits" against the Ukrainians, it noted that they were treated like "aliens," and discussed the policy of the "Germanization of the Ukrainian people," the suppression and destruction of Ukrainian culture, etc. However, the very structure of the "Announcement" indicated that neither the Ukrainians, nor the Jews, or the loss of human life in general were

21 Arkadii Liubchenko, *Vertep (povist'): opovidannia—shchodennyk* (Kharkiv: Osnova, 2005), p. 112.

recognized and presented as the main war losses. Anyone reading this announcement in the press could not help noticing that the first part of the document was not devoted to war deaths but to the destruction of industry, transport, the municipal economy, and the looting of cultural and historical treasures.[22]

On the other hand, in concealing the Jewish component of the Nazis' crimes, the Stalinist government tried "not to add grist to the mill" of Goebbelsian propaganda and avoided providing "superfluous pretexts" that would "confirm" the myth that the Soviet government represented the rule of the "Judeo-commune." In this case, obviously, the Soviet authorities reckoned on the antisemitic moods that were widespread among part of the Ukrainian population. However, it turned out that owing to its fear of nourishing such sentiments, the Soviet government resorted to actions that were essentially antisemitic. In fact, current research shows that a substantial number of Soviet political figures, including Stalin himself, were not lacking in antisemitic prejudices. The next few years, which were marked by the policy of state antisemitism, confirmed this unmistakably.

**Return of the Jews to Kyiv: antisemitism after the Holocaust**

On the eve of the German invasion, there were 224,236 Jews living in Kyiv, which represented one quarter of the city's population.[23] When the war broke out, some were mobilized or evacuated to the rear areas of the USSR. Most of the Jews who remained in the city and were killed were those who had the least connection to some kind of Soviet government institution, as well as elderly and sick people and children. After Babyn Yar, the once bustling and colorful Jewish life in Kyiv practically disappeared. After the Nazis were expelled from the city, Kyivan Jews began to flock back to their native city. It goes without saying that the mass grave

22 "Soobshchenie Chrezvychainoi gosudarstvennoi komissii. . . ," *Izvestiia* (Moscow), 29 February 1944, p. 2

23 Aleksandr Kruglov and Andrei Umanskii, *Babii Iar: zhertvy, spasiteli, palachi* (Dnipro: Ukrainskii institut izucheniia Kholokosta "Tkuma"; ChP "Lira LTD," 2019), p. 4. Mordechai Altshuler, ed. *Distribution of the Jewish Population of the USSR 1939* (Jerusalem: Hebrew University of Jerusalem, Centre for Research and Documentation of East European Jewry, 1993), 20.

known as Babyn Yar was immediately treated as a place of memory of the Jews who had perished there. Like the Holocaust in general, Babyn Yar became a factor unifying various strata of the Jewish community.

From the very outset, the formation of Jewish memory pertaining to Babyn Yar was influenced by various factors: historical, political, and emotional-psychological. Above all, the families of the victims felt shock, pain, and indignation at the concealment of the Jewish tragedy and the ban preventing Jews from expressing their grief publicly. At the same time, the Babyn Yar tragedy as a symbol prompted people to begin living again, for despite everything, life had to go on.

The Ukrainian-born Yiddish writer Itsik Kipnis wrote the following in an essay entitled "Sered ievreïv" (Among the Jews): "My enemies will not be able to say: 'Babyn Yar is the last refuge of the Jewish people. The final point of Jewish existence.' The last word[s] with which the history of the Jewish people ends [are] 'Am Yisrael chai!' 'The people of Israel live'!"[24]

The popularity of this idea within the Jewish milieu was demonstrated unambiguously by the performances in Kyiv of the Ukrainian State Jewish Theater in 1945 (after the evacuation, the theater was ordered to move to Chernivtsi). When the curtain parted for the performance of Moshe Pinchevsky's play *Ia zhyvu* (I Live) and an inscription appeared with the words "Am Yisrael chai!" the audience gave a standing ovation.[25]

According to research carried out by the Holocaust historian Mordechai Altschuler, during the postwar years Jewish religious communities were often the initiators of commemorative activities aimed at honoring the memory of Holocaust victims.[26] In various locales where the Nazis had committed mass murders of Jews these communities collected and published lists of victims, held commemorative ceremonies in synagogues, and tried to organize memorial gatherings. One such rally was convened in Kharkiv in May 1945, on the third anniversary of the mur-

---

24 Cited Arkadii Zel'tser, "Tema 'Evrei v Babiem Iaru' v Sovetskom Soiuze v 1941-1945 godakh," in *Materialy mizhnarodnoï naukovoï konferentsiï "Babyn Iar: masove ubyvstvo i pam'iat' pro nioho* (Kyiv, October 24-25, 2011), p. 90.

25 Ibid.

26 Mordekhai M. Al'tshuler, "Deiatel'nost' evreev po uvekovechivaniiu pamiati o Kholokoste v Sovetskom Soiuze v epokhu Stalina," *Yadvashem.org.*, https://www.yadvashem.org/yv/ru/pdf/yad_vashem_studies/altshuler.pdf

ders of Jews in that city. However, this was an exception to the rule, and the Soviet authorities soon began treating any outdoor mass assemblies of Jews as manifestations of "political unreliability" and "Jewish nationalism," and promptly banned them.

This happened in Kyiv on the third anniversary of the Babyn Yar tragedy. One of the initiators of a mourning rally was the famous Yiddish poet Dovid Hofshteyn, who spent several months gearing himself up mentally for this event. He recalled later: "I prepared myself for months. I prepared myself for shock, for sufferings. For months I suppressed the first cry that was supposed to break out of me at the very moment that I would see everything that I already knew: our calamity, our catastrophe in its fullest extent."

On 29 September 1944 the Soviet government banned a mass gathering of Jews in Babyn Yar, treating the mourning rally as a manifestation of "Jewish chauvinism" and as an event "fanning antisemitism." Despite the ban, people flocked throughout the day to the site of the tragedy to mourn and remember their relatives in the hopes of alleviating somewhat their pain and despair. Grasping this need, the directors of some institutions permitted their Jewish employees to leave work early that day. Nesia Elgert, who by some miracle survived Babyn Yar together with her son and after the liberation of Kyiv worked in a local institution, was also allowed to leave work in order "to give her a chance to go to the 'vale of tears' to sob out her grief."[27]

A spontaneous mourning procession of Kyiv's Jews to the symbolic grave of their loved ones in Babyn Yar, which took place in the early postwar years, was described by the writer Itsik Kipnis:

> 29 September. People are coming to Babyn Yar from all corners of the city.
>
> In the depths of my soul I am praying for only one thing: my friends, do not travel by streetcar, only on foot. We shall go along that road, along those streets that were filled to the edges with our still-living brothers. [...].
>
> We are approaching the city suburb. Small groups of people from various parts of the city join us. We recognize one another. Those who do not know the route do not ask—everyone is going there.
>
> People are proceeding in a crowd, hardly anyone is talking. [...].

27 Zel'tser, "Tema 'Evrei v Bab'iem Iaru," p. 91.

> We draw close. Quiet weeping is already heard from there. Everyone's faces are darkening, becoming tenser. Weaker people do not endure, and strangled groans and sobs are heard.
>
> The sandy cliffs are crumbling beneath our feet and dragging us down, down. Deep, overgrown cliffs, pits, bushes.
>
> 'Where are we?'
>
> Is this the place?
>
> Our legs are collapsing beneath us...
>
> There are already people here. They came earlier than we did. No one greets each other. And if someone happens to do this, no answer is given. Everyone's hearts and gazes are aimed at one large, overgrown ravine that resembles a square goblet, the only difference being that on the bottom of it there is no wine left undrunk, only blood that has lost its color from the rains and snow. [...]
>
> A few 'living' eyewitnesses remain: charred logs incompletely burned by fire. They recount that which human thought is incapable of grasping and what words cannot describe. People are standing around them since morning. Everyone's eyes are red from tears, hearts are incandescent from crying. And they wait. They do not want to go. Maybe someone will come and respond with at least one word.[28]

However, the majority of the Ukrainian population, which had experienced great tribulations and suffered many losses, was not prepared either to understand or feel the Jews' pain. Neither did the Soviet practice of concealing the Jewish tragedy elicit any astonishment. In the minds of average Ukrainians, this governmental policy fully conformed to the Soviet authorities' policy of concealing and denying the famine in Ukraine that claimed millions of lives in the early 1930s. Moreover, details pertaining to the merciless destruction not only of Jews in Babyn Yar but also prisoners of war, mentally ill people, and ordinary Ukrainians, Russians, Poles, and others, which were made public after Kyiv was liberated, formed the perception that Babyn Yar was a place of many tragedies, and in this context the desperate appeals of Jews to understand the unprecedented nature of the Nazi crime against them were often perceived as the

---

28 Itsik Kipnis, "Babii Iar," *Holokost i suchasnist'. Naukovo-pedahohichnyi biuleten'*, No. 10 (Kyiv, 2003), pp. 1-2..

Jews' own inability and reluctance to feel the pain of "others."

For the most part, the Jews' return to Kyiv did not elicit the support of the city residents, one reason being antisemitic feelings within a segment of the population, which were intensified by the German occupation and the impact of German propaganda, became palpable. There were also certain contradictions stemming from problems connected with the difficult, everyday life in the postwar years. After the war a significant part of Kyiv lay in ruins, and there was a dire lack of suitable housing. A considerable number of homes that were owned by Jews before the war had been looted by their neighbors and now had new owners, who based their right of occupation of these premises on the fact that they remained and had survived the occupation. The attempts by Jews to regain their houses, after all they had gone through during the war, often led to conflicts. The same may be said of their efforts to regain jobs they had before the war. For the most part, their various appeals to fairness, mercy, or professional qualifications had no effect. Instead, new accusations against the Jews emerged along the lines of: "they had hidden in the hinterland" and yet now they were demanding "some kind of rights."

At the same time, Jews' attitudes to their fellow Kyivites were also none too friendly. In addition to the extremely painful problems of daily life, the "shadow of Babyn Yar" also lay behind this unfriendliness, as Jews frequently regarded their former neighbors as having been involved, either indirectly or directly, in the killings of their families and friends. Also shocking were blatant manifestations of antisemitism that went unpunished; for example, the public use of the word *zhid*, offensive to the Jews, which was unimaginable before the war.

On 8 September 1944 Komarov, the head of the militia directorate for the city of Kyiv, prepared a report recording, as of the summer of 1944, manifestations of "antisemitic counterrevolutionary incidents aimed at exacerbating [tensions] between the Ukrainians and the Jewish nationality and the opposite, the Jewish nationality and the Ukrainians."[29] On 13

29 "Spravka nachal'nika upravleniia militsii g. Kieva Komarova 'Ob antisemitskikh kontrrevoliutsionnnykh sluchaiakh, 8 veresnia 1944 r." Cited in Mikhail Mitsel', *Evrei Ukrainy v 1943–1953 gg.: ocherki dokumentirovannoi istorii* (Kyiv: Dukh i litera, 2004), pp. 36-41.

October 1944 the NKVD of the Ukrainian SSR sent Nikita Khrushchev, first secretary of the CC CP(b)U, a special report on manifestations of antisemitism in Ukraine. The document emphasized the rise of "antisemitic manifestations" in the republic, which "in individual cases have a tendency toward flagrant actions of a pogromist nature."[30] The reasons for this were attributed first and foremost to German propaganda, both "German-fascist" and that of the "Ukrainian nationalists." The Soviet secret police also informed the Ukrainian leader about discrimination against Jews (above all, in the refusal to offer them employment), citing concrete examples of everyday antisemitism.

The document also reported on the spread of "provocative rumors" by individual Jews about the antisemitic policy of the Soviet Ukrainian government and its leader Khrushchev, who, it was claimed, was supposed to be removed from his post for condoning antisemitism. Another section of the document reported "nationalistic manifestations on the part of individual members of the Jewish population," for example, conversations to the effect that "Jews in America live far better than [Jews] in the USSR,"[31] sympathy for the Zionist movement, and even the secret compilation of lists of Jews who want to emigrate from the USSR to America, to Palestine, or elsewhere.

On Khrushchev's directive, the secretary of the CC CP(b)U Demian Korotchenko instructed the deputies of heads of Central Committee departments (Organizational Instruction; Cadres; Propaganda and Agitation) to open an investigation. The findings were ready by November. The special report that had been sent by the NKVD was called erroneous and treated as a document that distorted the real mood among the population of Ukraine; in essence, it reflected the moods of Zionist elements that were disseminating "provocative rumors." The NKVD was advised to expose more effectively and isolate "German agents and organizations of Ukrainian nationalists, who are trying to sow national strife," and to improve its work of exposing and putting a stop to the activities of "Zi-

30 Special Report of the NKDB URSR to the secretary of the TsK KP(b)U Nikita Khrushchev "on the antisemitic incidents in Ukraine," 13 October 1944, cited in Kyïv: viina, vlada, suspil'stvo, pp. 769-778.

31 Ibid., 775.

onist elements." The findings included frank criticism of the head of the Cadre Service for countenancing shortcomings in his work with cadres; he was ordered to dismiss the author of the memorandum, Gersonskii, who, as deputy head of the 2nd Directorate of the NKVD of the Ukrainian SSR, was responsible for "work with the operational servicing of the intelligentsia."[32]

Some Jews, encountering manifestations of antisemitism and government apathy day after day, continued to complain to the local and republican authorities; they even wrote to Moscow. Others bottled up their feelings and secretly dreamed of going to Palestine. However, some Jews, mainly veterans who had passed through the crucible of war, were ready to take up arms against their abusers.

In the summer of 1944, an incident took place in the raion division of the NKVD for Kyiv's Zaliznychnyi district, which involved the assistant of the commander of the 191st Guards Air Regiment, Senior Lieutenant Petro Kovtun, who was of Jewish background. Kovtun began his army service in 1941, and he came to Kyiv on business. He appeared at the raion division in a state of semi-inebriation, in the company of a woman named Chemikhova, with whom he began arguing; he even tried to shoot her with his pistol. After he was disarmed, the officer began yelling: "I came from the front to defend the Jewish people, and I will deal with the union of Rus′ people who destroyed the Jews."[33] Kovtun was detained, and the military prosecutor's office of the Kyiv garrison launched an investigation.

Another incident involving a Jewish soldier who used his service weapon against his abusers led to tragic consequences. On 4 September 1945 two Ukrainian Red Army soldiers on a short furlough, Ivan Hrabar, and Junior Lieutenant Mykola Melnykov, who were both tipsy, assaulted Senior Lieutenant of the NKVD Yosyf Rozenshtein, who was dressed in

---

32 Proposals of the TsK KP(b)U following the inspection of activities of the NKDB URSR concerning "the uncovering of the Zionist elements," 28 October 1944, cited in ibid., pp. 778-779.

33 Special Report of the NKDB URSR to the secretary of the TsK KP(b)U Nikita Khrushchev "On the antisemitic incidents in Ukraine," 13 October 1944, cited in ibid., p. 776.

plainclothes and heading home from the bread shop. The soldiers made some antisemitic remarks and then began beating the officer. Passersby came to his aid and stopped the fight. Rozenshtein went home in a fury, put on his military uniform, and went to the courtyard of the building where Hrabar's mother lived, and shot both of his abusers at close range. The mother's cries drew a crowd of people, antisemitic remarks were heard, and Rozenshtein's wife and a Jewish passerby were beaten severely. It was determined that earlier the apartment's previous owner had demanded that Hrabar's mother be ordered to vacate her home. Several days before the tragedy unfolded, her son, the soldier, had gone to the prosecutor's office, where he failed in his attempt to help her mother keep her apartment. He told the prosecutor: "We are fighting, and the Jews are occupying our apartments."[34]

Given the alarming atmosphere in the city, on 5 September party workers made the rounds of various institutions and enterprises, where they engaged in "explanatory work." The two murdered soldiers were buried on 7 September. Nearly 300 people took part in the funeral procession that began at Zhovtnevyi Hospital and ended at Lukianivka Cemetery. Despite the presence of an NKVD escort, it proved impossible to prevent violence. At first the participants of the procession beat two Jewish passersby: Viktor Tomskyi, who worked in the Committee for Art Affairs, and Yakiv Shvartsman, an employee of the oblast department for deaf-mutes. Later, Yosyf Markov, an official employed by the marketplace office, was beaten near Halytskyi Market. Finally, on Dmytrivska Street, some people from the procession who had spotted a Jew standing at the window of a building on Dmytrivska Street began throwing rocks at the windows. The Soviet secret police tried to detain a woman, but a group of soldiers and civilians stopped them and then beat another Jewish passerby.[35]

---

34 Cited in Feliks Kandel′, *Kniga vremen i sobytii: istoriia rossiiskikh evreev*, Vol. 6: *Istoriia evreev Sovetskogo Soiuza (1945–1970)* (Jerusalem: Gesharim/Mosty kul′tury, 2007), p. 20.

35 "Soobshchenie Narodnogo komissara vnutrennikh del USSR V. Riasnogo sekretariu TsK KP(b)U D. Korotchenko o sobytiiakh v Kieve 7 sentiabria 1945 g. 8 sentiabria 1945 g.," in Mitsel′, *Evrei Ukrainy v 1943–1953 gg.*, pp. 65-66.

This event literally shook the city, and the Jews of Kyiv were frightened. In order to prevent further clashes, the authorities intensified police patrols in various parts of the city. As a result of the publicity, on 5 and 8 September the People's Commissar of Internal Affairs of the Ukrainian SSR and his deputy sent special reports with the details of the tragedy to the higher republican leadership. Meanwhile, this incident prompted several Jewish veterans to write an emotional letter to Stalin. Emphasizing the "unbridled antisemitism" in Kyiv, they informed the Soviet leader about the pogrom that had taken place on the day of the two soldiers' funeral. More than a hundred Jews were beaten, thirty-six of whom had to be hospitalized with severe injuries. Five died that day (according to the researcher Mykhailo Mitsel, this information is not supported by archival documents).[36] The authors of the letter explained the killing of the "two antisemites" by the murderer's affective state, caused by rampant antisemitism and the inaction of the Soviet Ukrainian government. Nevertheless, on 1 October 1945, Yosyf Rozenshtein was sentenced to death by a military tribunal.

Although the motive behind this tragic story lay in the sphere of everyday life, its causes ran deeper and attested clearly to the tensions existing in Ukrainian-Jewish relations. To a certain extent the tragedy was also the direct result of the implementation of the government's unpublicized policy of "squeezing" Jews out of Kyiv and Ukraine in general. The "philosophy" behind this policy was explicitly elucidated by Khrushchev himself during his conversation with the old communist Ruzha-Godes, who had survived the German occupation by disguising herself under the name of Khelmynska, but could not find employment after the return of Soviet power because she was Jewish. "In the past Jews committed quite a few sins against the Ukrainian people," Khrushchev told her. "The people hate them for this. In our Ukraine we do not need Jews. . . .It would be better [for them] not to return here. It would be better if they went to Birobidzhan. . . .This is Ukraine here. And we are not interested in seeing the Ukrainian people interpreting the return of Soviet power as the return of the Jews."[37]

36 Ibid., p. 34.

37 Ibid., p. 27.

The following questions should be asked. Did Khrushchev's position reflect only his personal views? Could he have implemented such a policy at his own, without the approval of the Moscow center, assuming he, as the leader of the Ukrainian SSR, was able to act freely at his own discretion? Archival documents indicate clearly that before any decisions were approved in Soviet Ukraine, even those pertaining to the creation in 1944 of the medal "For the Liberation of Ukraine," the top Communist leadership of Soviet Ukraine always had to consult first with The Leader (Stalin, incidentally, refused to approve the creation of that medal). It is hardly possible, therefore, that Khrushchev was in any position to adopt decisions about restricting access to Kyiv for Jews after they returned from evacuation, or about banning Jews from positions in the Communist party Central Committee, in People's Commissariats or other offices. There is no doubt whatsoever that the antisemitic policy was not a "Ukrainian initiative." While it is likely that the Ukrainian authorities were indeed zealous executors of this policy, but in no way were they its ideological masterminds. It is obvious that by the end of the war and in the first postwar years the model of the policy of antisemitism which soon led to a real bacchanal throughout the Soviet Union began functioning precisely in Ukraine.

On 17–28 January 1946 a public trial took place in Kyiv in connection with the crimes committed by the Germans on the territory of the Ukrainian SSR. [See Plate **XVII**] The defendants in the case were General Major Paul Scheer, the head of the police in Kyiv, and fifteen other people. The trial proceedings were widely publicized in the central and republican press. Reports were prepared by the Ukrainian writer Yurii Smolych and the Ukrainian poet Volodymyr Sosiura, and numerous photographers and cameramen were enlisted to take pictures.

One of the witnesses was Dina Pronicheva (Dina Myronivna Wasserman), who survived miraculously. She gave a detailed account of the terrifying day of 29 September 1941, clearly noting that the Nazis' crime targeted Jews specifically.[38] In the opening statement for the prosecution,

38 "Iz protokola doprosa na Kievskom protsesse v kachestve svidetelia spassheisia ot rasstrelov D. Pronichevoi. 12 ianvaria 1946 g.," cited in Tatiana Evstaf'eva and Vitalii Nakhmanovich, comps., *Babii Iar—chelovek, vlast', istoriia: dokumenty i materialy, Vol. 1: Istoricheskaia topografiia: khronologiia sobytiia* (Kyiv: Vneshtorgizdat Ukrainy, 2004), pp. 277-280.

the deputy prosecutor-general of the Red Army, General-Major Aleksandr Cheptsov, declared that "more than four million Soviet citizens, including elderly people, women, and children" were killed and tortured in Ukraine by the Nazis during the German occupation. He called Babyn Yar a grave in which "195,000 victims of bloody fascist terror" were laid to rest.[39] At 5:00 p.m. on 29 January twelve war criminals were executed on the main square of the city in the presence of a large crowd of people.

Two weeks later, during the Nuremberg trials, evidence about the grievous crimes against the civilian population of the USSR was presented by Lev Smirnov, deputy prosecutor for the Soviet Union. He announced that the Extraordinary State Commission had drawn up 54,784 indictments, and he spoke about the atrocities perpetrated by the Nazi criminals. He also presented a document numbered SSSR-9, an announcement published earlier by the NKVD about the events that took place on 29 September 1941 in Babyn Yar, where "thousands of innocent Soviet civilians" were killed.[40]

The German historian Tanja Penter writes that the postwar trials of German war criminals and their accomplices became one of the ways of legitimizing the Stalinist regime both in Soviet society and abroad.[41] Where the Nuremburg trials were concerned, attempts were also made to ensure the "legal consolidation" of the Germans' responsibility for crimes that had been committed by Stalin, particularly the Katyn massacre. As in the case of the mass murders in Katyn, even though the Soviets did not provide sufficient evidence concerning Babyn Yar, no doubts about the Nazis' responsibility for this tragedy surfaced during the Nuremburg trials. In Nuremberg Stalin thus failed in his attempt to shift responsibility for his own crimes in Katyn on the Nazis.

---

39 "Promova prokurora," in *Kyïvs'kyi protses: dokumenty ta materialy*, compiled by Leonid Abramenko (Kyiv: Lybid', 1995), p. 145.

40 "Vystuplenie pomoshchnika Glavnogo obvinitelia ot SSSR L.N. Smirnova," in *Niurnbergskii protsess: sbornik materialov*, Vol. 5 (Moscow: Iuridicheskaia literature, 1991), pp. 80-187.

41 Tana Penter, "Collaboration on Trial: New Source Materials on Soviet Postwar Trials Against Collaborators," *Slavic Review*, LXIV, 4 (Cambridge, Mass., 2005), p. 784.

### State antisemitism: erasing the memory of the Jewish tragedy

During the first postwar years, Jewish communities began adopting active measures to commemorate the victims of the Holocaust but encountered unexpected and harsh resistance from the Soviet authorities. From that point onwards and for many subsequent decades Jewish efforts to preserve this memory and attempts to erase it marked the relations between the Jewish population and the Soviet government.

In 1946 Jews in Ternopil collected funds to tidy up the graves of people who were shot by the Nazis. A monument bearing the following inscription was erected: "Eternal memory and glory to the Jews who were killed by the German fascists." This instantly became the subject of a review that took place during a meeting at the office of the Ternopil oblast committee of the CP(b)U.[42] Most likely the inscription on the monument was altered. That same year the municipal council of Kamianets-Podilskyi forbade the Jews to hold a mourning day to mark the shootings of their coreligionists by the Nazis. For more than three years the municipal government refused to replace the city's stone sidewalks that were paved with gravestones taken from the Jewish cemetery. In July 1948 the Jewish community sent a complaint to the heads of the Supreme Soviet of the USSR, the CC AUCP(b), and the CC CP(b)U.[43]

Proposals had been put forward even during the war years to erect a monument to Jews who perished during World War II and in Babyn Yar (this issue was brought up by Ilya Ehrenburg in particular). Meanwhile, given Kyiv's status as the capital city of Soviet Ukraine, responsibility for efforts to honor the victims' memory passed to the republican government. It goes without saying that the government of the Ukrainian SSR adhered to the official treatment of Babyn Yar as a place where the Nazis murdered "innocent Soviet citizens," without singling out the distinctive fate of the Jews.

On 13 March 1945 the Council of People's Commissars and the CC CP(b)U issued a resolution "About the Erection of a Monument on the

42 Mikhail Mitsel', "Zapret na uvekovechivanie pamiati kak sposob zamalchivaniia Kholokosta: praktika KPU v otnoshenii Bab'iego Iara," *Holokost i suchasnist'*, 1 (Kyiv, 2007), p. 10.

43 Ibid.

Territory of Babyn Yar," which proposed to use the preliminary design and model developed by Oleksandr Vlasov, the chief architect of Kyiv, appoint a sculptor and commission technical drawings, and allocate funds from the republican budget for the monument.[44] Shortly afterwards the Directorate of Architecture contacted Mykola Bazhan, the deputy head of the Council of Ministers of the Ukrainian SSR, in connection with the construction in 1945 of twenty-four installations in Kyiv, including the monument in Babyn Yar. The monument was supposed to be built over a two-year period, 1945–1947, at a cost of three million rubles, half of which amount was allocated for 1946.[45]

The sculptor chosen for the project was I. Kruglov, and the artistic sketches were probably done by Vasyl Ovchynnykov, the director of the Museum of Western and Oriental Art. The municipal party committee also ordered Vlasov to plan the spatial layout of the monument and to tidy up the entire area of Babyn Yar by designing paths, planting trees, and the like. Although, judging by everything, the project design did not feature any distinctively Jewish ethnic symbols, they may have featured in Ovchynnykov's sketches; in any event, the people depicted in the series of paintings on the Babyn Yar theme, which he had completed during this period, had Jewish features. However, the monument project was initially delayed and then collapsed altogether. With the upsurge of antisemitic policies in the Soviet Union during the struggle against "cosmopolitanism" and "Jewish dominance," the commemoration of Jewish victims of the Nazis became virtually impossible. As noted by the historian Mykhailo Mitsel, 1947 marked the beginning of the Soviet government's refusal to allow its citizens to erect Jewish monuments to victims of the Nazis in various oblasts of Ukraine, including Poltava, Kyiv, and Chernihiv.[46]

External political events had an unexpectedly powerful impact on the

44 "Postanova Rady narodnykh komisariv URSR i Tsentral'noho komitetu KP(b)U No. 378 vid 13 bereznia 1945 r.," in Il'ia Levitas, comp., *Babii Iar: kniga pamiati.* (Kyiv: Stal', 2005), p. 489.

45 Tat'iana Evstaf'ieva, "Babii Iar: poslevoennaia istoriia mestnosti," in *Materialy mizhnarodnoï naukovoï konferentsiï "Babyn Iar,"* p. 22.

46 Mitsel', "Zapret na uvekovechivanie pamiati," p. 10.

fate of Soviet Jewry. Seeking to expel Great Britain from Palestine, weaken its position in the Near and Middle East, and create opportunities for penetrating this strategically important region, Stalin initially gave his full support to the idea of founding the State of Israel. On 17 May 1948 the Soviet Union was the first country in the world to recognize the new state, and later condemned the incursion of Arab forces into its territory, and even provided military assistance to Israel (via Czechoslovakia).

Soviet Jews welcomed the news of the founding of Israel with great enthusiasm. This was noted even by the members of Stalin's circle. The wife of National Commissar Kliment Voroshilov, Ekaterina Gorbman, having learnt the news, ecstatically exclaimed that now we, too, have our own fatherland! Friendliness was also shown to Golda Meir, the chargé d'affaires ad interim for the State of Israel, who was a native of Kyiv. Polina Zhemchuzhina, the wife of Viacheslav Molotov, conversed with the diplomat in the language of their parents, Yiddish. In May 1948 the Soviet government even permitted the celebration of the Jewish New Year, Rosh Hashanah, on a grand scale. Tens of thousands of Jews gathered for the celebration in and around the Choral Synagogue in Moscow, which was attended by Meir. Euphoria reigned when the *shofar* (ram's horn) blew, and people began exchanging wishes to celebrate the holiday "next year in Jerusalem."[47]

However, as soon as it became clear that the Jewish state was preparing to ally itself with the United States, Stalin's attitude to Israel changed radically. This had an immediate effect on the fate of Soviet Jews, whose sympathies toward Israel began to be perceived as potentially dangerous and as manifestations of disloyalty and Zionism.

Communist ideologists' view of the emergence of a "second fatherland of the Jews" as a powerful source of the growth of national awareness among Soviet Jews was not unjustified. Their misgivings were confirmed in 1948, in connection with the Israelis' victory in the war of independence. Many Jews did not disguise their willingness to fight for Israel, and there was obvious pride in this victory. These events also encouraged members of the Jewish community to embark on bolder efforts to

47 Timothy Snyder, *Bloodlands: Europe between Hitler and Stalin* (New York: Basic Books, 2010), pp. 350-351.

champion their right to revive Jewish national culture in the USSR. The Stalinist government's response was to launch large-scale repressions against Jews, which were introduced in the propagandistic packaging of a campaign against "rootless cosmopolitans" and "Jewish bourgeois nationalists."

On 16 September 1948 Dovid Hofshteyn, the Yiddish poet, translator, and member of the presidium of the Jewish Anti-Fascist Committee (JAC), was arrested in Kyiv on charges of espionage. His "Zionist moods" had long been under the watchful eye of the Soviet secret police (after the proclamation of the State of Israel, Hofshteyn, among other things, proposed to open a Department of Hebrew at the Academy of Sciences of the Ukrainian SSR).[48] The entire committee, whose activities had long been a thorn in the side of the Soviet authorities, was also targeted.

Since its founding in 1942, the JAC had pursued the goal of establishing international contacts with Jewish communities that were part of the anti-Nazi coalition. Much was done in this direction during the war years. In 1943 the committee's head, the actor and director Solomon Mikhoels, and the writer Itsik Fefer toured the United States, Great Britain, Canada, and Mexico, where they established contact with reputable organizations and gave speeches at well-attended rallies, appealing for help for the USSR. These activities led to some definite results (for example, the Soviets signed an agreement with the American Jewish Joint Distribution Committee about the provision of relief, via the Red Cross, to the Soviet population without distinction on the grounds of nationality, however). Supporting the founding of the State of Israel, the members of the JAC also appealed to the highest Soviet and party leadership to create Jewish autonomy in the Crimea. The Soviet leadership itself actively exploited the committee as a source of information about Israel and the moods among Jews living abroad.[49]

---

48 Volodymyr Prystaiko, Oleksandr Pshennikov, and Iurii Shapoval, "Sprava Ievreis'koho antyfashysts'koho komitetu," in *Z arkhiviv VUCHK-HPU-NKVD-KDB*, No. 3/4 (Kyiv, 1998), p. 13.

49 Il'ia Al'tman, comp., *Evreiskii antifashistskii komitet v SSSR, 1941-1948: dokumentirovannaia istoriia* (Moscow: Mezhdunarodnye otnosheniia, 1996), pp. 74–345.

During the war the Jewish Anti-Fascist Committee had worked tirelessly on a "Black Book," a collection of documents and eyewitness testimonies about the Nazi genocide of the Jews. The representatives of Jewish civic organizations in the United States, Great Britain, and Palestine were invited to take part in this large-scale project, whose goal was to document fully the extermination of the Jews by the Nazis, expressions of human solidarity, that is, the rescue of Jews by Poles, Ukrainians, Belarusans, and Russians, and the Jewish anti-Nazi resistance movement and its struggle against the enemy. Naturally, the Babyn Yar tragedy was regarded as one of the most important topics. At the same time, the compilers of the book, among them the writer Vasily Grossman, wanted to pay tribute not so much to those who had managed to survive as to "the 99 percent of those who were brought to Babyn Yar." In other words, the compilers sought "to present a picture of what happened to those who are silent and can no longer say anything now."[50] Work on the manuscript was completed in the fall of 1945, and one copy was sent to the Soviet prosecution at the Nuremburg trials. The book was published immediately in the United States. In the Soviet Union, however, the manuscript was sent to the printers. The work of typesetting it began but was soon halted. On 3 February 1947 the chief Soviet ideologist Georgii Aleksandrov sent a letter to Andrei Zhdanov, secretary of the CC AUCP(B), about the inadvisability of publishing the "Black Book," reproaching the compilers for presenting a "false picture," especially where Ukraine was concerned, that the Nazis "looted and destroyed only Jews."[51] On 7 October 1947 the Directorate of Propaganda and Agitation of the CC AUCP(B) issued its final decision on the publication: "The book contains serious political errors...owing to which this 'Black Book' cannot be published."[52]

In January 1948 Solomon Mikhoels was killed in Minsk by Soviet secret police agents, who staged the murder as a car accident (he was hit by

50 Idem, "Belye piatna 'Chernoi knigi,'" *Lekhaim*, August 2002.

51 "Dokladnaia zapiska agitpropa TsK A.A. Zhdanovu po voprosu izdaniia 'Chernoi knigi' ot 3 fevralia 1947 g.," in Aleksandr Iakovlev, ed., *Stalin i kosmopolitizm. 1945-1953: Dokumenty Agitpropa TsK* (Moscow: MFD: Materik, 2005), pp. 103-105.

52 "Zakliuchenie upravleniia propagandy i agitatsii TsK VKP(b) o nevozmozhnosti izdaniia 'Chernoi knigi' ot 7.10.1947 g.," *Fond Aleksandra N. Iakovleva*. https://www.alexanderyakovlev.org/fond/issues-doc/68431

a heavy truck). This event was the prelude to the liquidation of the JAC and the launch of repressions targeting its members. On 20 November 1948 the Politburo of the CC AUCP(b) approved a resolution entitled "About the Jewish Anti-Fascist Committee," which was confirmed by a decision passed by the Council of Ministers of the USSR. The Ministry of State Security was instructed at once to disband the organization, now deemed as a "center of anti-Soviet propaganda" that "regularly supplies anti-Soviet information to foreign intelligence agencies" (the order was signed personally by Stalin).[53]

On 3 January 1949 the CC AUCP(b) circulated a secret letter to all oblast and territorial party committees as well as to the central committees of all the Union republics, informing them about the disbanding of the Jewish Anti-Fascist Committee, which was found to be an "espionage organization of Jewish nationalists."[54] This signaled the start of the all-out liquidation of Jewish cultural and scholarly institutions and mass arrests.

On 8 February 1949, responding to the proposal of the writer Aleksamdr Fadeev, head of the Union of Writers of the USSR, the Politburo of the CC AUCP(b) issued a special resolution disbanding the Association of Jewish Writers in Moscow (45 members), in Kyiv (26 members), and in Minsk (6 members). The Yiddish literary almanacs *Heimland* (The Homeland) published in Moscow and *Der Shtern* (The Star) published in Kyiv were also closed down,[55] and Radio Moscow's Yiddish broadcasts ceased in mid-February. In agreement with the CC AUCP(B), the Soviet censorship office Glavlit began removing books by Jewish writers from libraries and the book trade network (the "list of banned literature" compiled by the censors contained 540 titles). In addition, the NKVD fabricated a case involving a "Zionist conspiracy" in the Soviet Union, and dozens of famous Jewish writers, publishers, theatrical figures, and

---

53 "Postanovlenie Politbiuro TsK VKP(b) 'O rospuske Evreiskogo antifashistskogo komiteta' ot 20 noiabria 1948 g.," in Iakovlev, *Stalin i kosmopolitizm*, pp. 193-195.

54 Shimon Redlikh, ed., *Evreiskii antifashistskii komitet v SSSR. 1941-1948: dokumental'naia istoriia* (Moscow: Mezhdunarodnye otnosheniia, 1996), pp. 346-348.

55 "Postanovlenie Politbiuro TsK VKP(b) 'O rospuske obiedineniia evreiskikh pisatelei i o zakrytii al'manakhov na evreiskom iazyke' ot 8 fevralia 1949 g.," in Iakovlev, *Stalin i kosmopolitizm*, pp. 263-265.

scientists were put behind bars.

In Soviet Ukraine the Sixteenth Congress of the CP(b)U held in January 1949 gave impetus to the launch of a struggle against "rootless cosmopolitans."[56] The search for "enemies" and the struggle against "Jewish dominance" encompassed practically every educational, scholarly, and cultural institution and organization in the republic. As a result, the publication of all Yiddish-language newspapers, magazines, and books ceased, and Jewish literature and textbooks were removed from library collections. One after the other, Jewish theaters based in Kyiv, Kharkiv, Odesa, and Chernivtsi were closed down. In Kyiv the Ukrainian Theatrical Society and the Kyiv Conservatory were denigrated as "centers where cosmopolitans were concentrated. In the Academy of Sciences of the Ukrainian SSR the struggle against "Jewish dominance" resulted in the complete destruction of the Office for the Study of Jewish Literature, Language, and Folklore.

Established in 1936 as a result of the reorganization of the Institute of Jewish Culture, the Office for the Study of Jewish Literature, Language, and Folklore was a unique scholarly institution, whose mandate was to preserve the Yiddish cultural heritage. Dozens of eminent scholars, linguists, and writers worked there, grouped in three sections: Linguistics, Literature, and Folklore (there were plans to open a fourth section, History). It was headed by Illia (Elye) Spivak, a distinguished linguist and member of the Jewish Anti-Fascist Committee.[57]

During the war years the Office was evacuated to the city of Ufa, where it continued its scholarly activities. After it moved back to Kyiv in 1944, a commission was formed within the Office for the collection of documentary materials and memoirs slated for the "Black Book," especially those pertaining to the Babyn Yar tragedy. On the basis of these materials, a number of articles were written for the Yiddish-language newspaper *Eynikayt* (Unity). The Office's scholarly associates also did much to expand the collections of folkloric materials. According to some testimonies, they

---

56 Vasyl' Iurchuk et al, eds., *Komunistychna partiia Ukraïny v rezoliutsiiakh i rishenniakh z'ïzdiv, konferentsii i plenumiv TsK*, Vol. 2: 1941–1976 (Kyiv: Vyd. Politychnoï literatury Ukraïny, 1977), pp. 135–136.

57 Oleh Berenshtein, "Elie Spivak: zhyttia, tvorchist', dolia," in *Z arkhiviv VUCHK-HPU-NKVD-KHB*, No. 3/4 (1998), pp. 21-30.

also recorded Yiddish songs about Babyn Yar. In November 1944 a group of scholars headed by the eminent musicologist Moisei Beregovskii went on a folkloric expedition to Chernivtsi, where they recorded 120 new songs, 50 of which they heard from survivors of Jewish ghettos. Based in the Ukrainian capital after the war, the Office for the Study of Jewish Literature, Language, and Folklore revived the tradition of holding creative evenings and encounters with Jewish writers, poets, composers, and singers. These events were extraordinarily popular and attracted large audiences. Kyivites had the opportunity to see performances by such illustrious members of the creative Jewish intelligentsia as the poet Perets Markish, the composer Zinovii Kompaniiets, and many others.[58]

In early January 1949 the Presidium of the Academy of Sciences of the Ukrainian SSR sent an official letter to Leonid Melnykov, first secretary of the CC CP(b)U, proposing that this institution be liquidated at once. The letter stated in part: "The Office's practice of conducting special work on questions of Jewish culture with the Jewish population by creating active members does not foster the inculcation of Soviet patriotism in the Jewish population, but leads to the disunity of the Soviet people, and therefore it is harmful."[59] That month the Office was disbanded, and most of its associates were repressed, including Illia Spivak, who died in prison shortly afterwards.

A secret trial of the Jewish Anti-Fascist Committee began in May 1952. By the summer of that year the Military Collegium of the Supreme Court of the USSR handed down death sentences to thirteen defendants, five of whom were from Ukraine (the writers and poets Dovid Bergelson, Dovid Hofshteyn, Leyb Kvitko, Perets Markish, and Itsik Fefer). They were all executed in August 1952.[60]

Within and outside the "JAC context" thousands of educational, scholarly, and cultural figures, particularly those who sought to preserve

58 I. Pogrebinskaia, "Kabinet evreiskoi kul'tury pri VUAN," in *Ievreï v Ukraïni—istoriia, kul'tura, tradytsii: zbirnyk naukovo-publitsystychnykh statei* (Kyiv, 1997), p. 39.

59 Cited in ibid., p. 42.

60 Redlikh, *Evreiskii antifashistskii komitet*, p. 383; Vasilii Malinovskii, "Poslednii Stalinskii rasstrel," *Vestnik* (Cockeysville, MD), No. 2 (209), 19 January 1999.

the memory of the Jewish tragedy that took place in Babyn Yar, were targeted by accusations of "rootless cosmopolitanism."[61] Thus, in addition to the repressions against Jewish artists, writers, and composers, the very memory of Babyn Yar was suppressed. To this day no one knows what happened to the documented testimonies about Babyn Yar or the numerous folkloric materials that were moved from Kyiv to Moscow by the Office for Jewish History and Culture. Performances of Dmytro Klebanov's symphony, *In Memory of the Martyrs of Babyn Yar*, were banned for many decades, and Vasyl Ovchynnykov's series of paintings entitled *Babyn Yar* was almost completely destroyed. Since Ovchynnykov was an ethnic Ukrainian, he could not be accused of "rootless cosmopolitanism"; instead, his works were criticized mercilessly for "distortions of the images of Soviet people."[62]

The wave of violence unleashed by the Stalinist regime continued to gain momentum. In early 1953 *Pravda* reported the discovery of a "monstrous conspiracy" in which many well-known Kremlin doctors allegedly took part. This was the pretext for unleashing the next antisemitic campaign known as the "Doctors' Plot." The Soviet authorities claimed that by issuing incorrect diagnoses and applying improper medical treatments, the "killers in white coats" tried to murder leading political and military figures. According to the *Pravda* report, "Most of the members of the group were connected with the international Jewish bourgeois-nationalist organization 'Joint.'"[63]

Stalin's death in March 1953 saved Soviet Jewry from a new wave of mass terror. The end of the tyrant's rule signaled the return from imprisonment of individuals who had managed to survive and opened up prospects for finding new ways to honor the Jewish victims of the Holocaust, including those who perished in Babyn Yar.

---

61 Volodymyr Prystaiko, Oleksandr Pshennikov, and Iurii Shapoval, "Sprava Ievreis'koho antyfashysts'koho komitetu," p. 13.

62 Mykhailo Hutor, *Zberezhennia pam'iati pro trahediiu v Babynomu Iaru v chasy radians'koï vlady* (Kyiv: Natsional'nyi istoryko-memorial'nyi zapovidnyk "Babyn Iar," 2019), pp. 12-22.

63 "Podlye shpiony i ubiitsy pod maskoi professorov-vrachei," *Pravda* (Moscow), 13 January 1953.

## After Stalin: memory and the struggle for freedom and dignity

In 1956 the Moscow-based publishing house Sovetskii Pisatel′ released Ilya Ehrenburg's novel, *Ottepel* (The Thaw). Hopes for changes for the better after Stalin's death resound both in the book's title and the character's speeches: "It seems everything has changed," "New people are needed," "We need our own, Soviet humanism," "The time has come to start this," "People have stood up straight. They grumble, but this is a sign of health".[64] These expectations were reinforced by the denunciation of Stalin's cult of personality at the Twentieth Congress of the CPSU (February 1956), the rehabilitation of those who had been repressed, a certain liberalization of sociopolitical life, and improvement of the political climate in the country. Thus, it was understandable that many Jews hoped that, along with the cessation of the absurd "killer doctors" case, the looming changes would also put an end to the state policy of antisemitism.

The first decade after Stalin's death went down in history as the "Thaw." However, the anticipated, radical changes for the better never materialized because the system of power in the USSR remained unaltered. This applied fully to the "Jewish question," as openly aggressive Stalinist antisemitism was supplanted by the policy of concealed state antisemitism. One clear manifestation of this policy was the fifth line (*piataia grafa*) that defined the bearer's nationality in Soviet passports, which served as an unspoken pretext for barring Jews' access to certain schools of higher education, employment opportunities, and movement up the career ladder. Year after year in the Soviet Union the linguistic assimilation—Russification—of Jews intensified, and the disregard of national-cultural features and needs as well as the restriction and infringements of religious freedom remained the stuff of daily reality. Like the permanent defamation of imaginary "internal" and "external" enemies, the accusation of "international Zionism" was typical of the latter category.

The period of the "Thaw" did not bring any changes to the state's interpretations of the Babyn Yar tragedy. As was the case during the Stalinist period, the mass killings of Jews in September 1941 merely because they were Jews were suppressed and obfuscated by the fuzzy formula

64 Il'ia Erenburg, *Ottepel'* (Moscow: Sovetskii pisatel', 1954).

"the killing of peaceful Soviet citizens." There was occasional talk of another "reason" why a monument specifically dedicated to the exterminated Jews was not necessary. Kyiv's own writer and war veteran Viktor Nekrasov himself recalled the following comments: "What monument? To whom? Monuments are erected to heroes. But these people went voluntarily, like rabbits into the jaws of a boa constrictor."[65]

At the same time, public expressions by Jews of their personal attitude to the Babyn Yar tragedy were constantly treated as "fomenting Jewish nationalism" and were thus persecuted. Typical in this regard was an incident that took place in 1959, during the Kyiv performances of the popular singer Nechama Lifshitz, who sang the Yiddish lullaby "Babi Yar" (music: Rivke Boiarska; lyrics: Shike [Ovsii] Driz): "I would hang the cradle from a beam, / And I would rock, I would rock my little boy Yankel./But the house vanished in the flames of a fire,/How can I rock my little boy, my dearest one? . . . I would cut off my braids, my longest ones, / And hang the cradle from them. / But I don't know where the little bones of my children are now, / Help me, mothers, help me, / To cry out my song. / Help me, mothers, help me. / To lull Babi Yar to sleep."[66]

As reported in Lifshitz's memoirs, when she began singing the lullaby, silence descended on the hall and the Kyiv audience rose to its feet. The next day the singer was summoned before the Central Committee of the Communist Party of Ukraine (CPU), after which the rest of her concerts in the Ukrainian capital were cancelled and she was forbidden to perform for a period of one year.[67]

Throughout the 1950s, under the guise of planning new transport routes and constructing residential areas in Kyiv, actives measures were adopted with the goal of physically liquidating Babyn Yar, which was

---

65 Viktor Nekrasov, "Babii Iar, 45 let," *Novoe russkoe slovo* (New York), 28 September 1986.

66 The original poem was written from a male's perspective, but the composer and the singer adapted it for a female voice. The Yiddish original, "Liulenky-liuliu," appeared in Shike Driz's third collections of poetry, *Di ferte strune* (Moscow, 1969); an English version was cited in Dov Noy, "The Model of the Yiddish Lullaby," *Studies in Yiddish Literature and Folklore*, No. 7 (1986), p. 223.

67 "Rasskaz artistki Nekhamy Livshits o pesne Shiki Driza 'Kolybel'naia Bab'iemu Iaru,'" in Efrem Baukh, ed., *Babii Iar* (Tel-Aviv: "Moriia," 1993), pp. 95-98.

viewed as an "inconvenient place." For this purpose, pulp consisting of sandy clay was pumped intensively into the ravine. In late 1958 the Kyiv municipal council passed another decision to dump fill into Babyn Yar.

Members of the public constantly protested against this. For example, Viktor Nekrasov, the Kyiv writer and war veteran who had fought at Stalingrad, published an article in October 1959 entitled "Why was this not done?" in the popular Moscow periodical *Literaturnaia gazeta* (Literary Gazette). In it Nekrasov demanded an end to the abuse of the memory of those who had perished in Babyn Yar and called for their commemoration. "Who could have come up with the idea to fill the ravine, and frolic and play soccer on the site of the greatest tragedy?" Nekrasov asks. "No, this cannot be allowed. When a person dies, s/he is buried, and a marker is erected on the grave. Did the 195,000 Kyivites who were shot brutally in Babyn Yar, in Syrets, in Darnytsia, St. Cyril's Hospital, at the Cave Monastery, at Lukianivka Cemetery not merit this tribute of respect?[68]

But such appeals failed to bring results. Furthermore, on 4 January 1960, in approving the resolution "About the Ordering of Affairs Pertaining to the Construction of Monuments on the Territory of the Ukrainian SSR," the CC CPU and the Council of Ministers of the Ukrainian SSR officially rescinded its earlier resolution, passed in 1945, about constructing a monument to the victims of the Nazis in Babyn Yar because, as it was claimed, this required significant expenditures on anti-erosion works.[69]

As in previous years, the work of dumping fill into Babyn Yar continued, without adhering to crucial technical requirements. This labor continued until 13 March 1961, when disaster struck. Liquid pulp broke through a dam, and a thick wall of pulp four meters high and twenty meters wide went hurtling down with a deafening sound, destroying everything in its path. It flooded part of the Kurenivka district, killing people and destroying residential buildings. It was morning, so many people were getting ready to go to work or on their way. Rescuers had to dig out the bodies of people from places where they were caught: in private homes, in streetcars, and in telephone booths. [see Plates **XVIII** and **XIX**]

---

68 Viktor Nekrasov, "Pochemu eto ne sdelano?," *Literaturnaia gazeta* (Moscow), 10 October 1959.

69 Evstaf'ieva, "Babii Iar: poslevoennaia istoriia mestnosti," p. 23.

According to official data, 145 people were killed in the Kurenivka mudslide. Unofficial data indicated 1,500.[70] The avalanche of mud destroyed 68 residential buildings, 13 administrative-industrial buildings, and a streetcar depot. The KGB then began monitoring the public mood, later reporting "unhealthy opinions," particularly those expressed by Kyivan Jews, to the CC CPU: "A monument should have been erected there instead of launching this kind of development"; "They made up their minds to build a rotten tract instead of constructing a monument to the Jews who were killed there"; "It was the bodies of Jews who were shot by the Germans during the occupation in the city of Kyiv which had risen up"; "They should not have desecrated the memory of those who were killed in Babyn Yar; that's why this disaster happened."[71]

After the Kurenivka tragedy, the Soviet authorities still refused to abandon the idea of redeveloping the Babyn Yar area. The development of the residential area in Syrets continued, and construction began on a new circle (ring) road. In 1962 it was decided to liquidate the cemeteries located on Melnikova Street and build a sports complex. Then the Jewish Cemetery was destroyed, and a sports complex was built there. The construction of a television tower began in the old section of the Military (i.e. Orthodox Bratske) Cemetery. When the cemetery was being dismantled, local residents were invited to move the remains of their family members to another cemetery. Some people did so, but many Jewish people who might have overseen the move of their relatives' remains were not alive either because the Nazis had exterminated entire families in Babyn Yar. The atheistic Soviet government finally ordered the cemetery to be razed, and these "nobodies' graves" were bulldozed into the ground. Exceptions were made when the construction work exposed the remains of Nazi victims; by a decision of the Kyiv executive committee, they were all subject to burial in Lukianivka Cemetery.

---

70 Aleksandr Anisimov, *Kurenevskii potop: Kurenevskaia tragediia, 13 marta 1961 goda* (Kyiv: Kurch, 2003), p. 13.

71 Cited in Tatiana Evstaf'ieva, "Kurenevskaia tragediia v svete novykh dokumentov," in *Materialy shchorichnoï naukovo-praktychnoï konferentsiï "Kyïv i kyiany"* (Kyiv, 22 December 2011); Tatiana Evstafieva, "K 50-letiiu Kurenevskoi tragedii." https://photohistory.kiev.ua/articles.php?a=1

Meanwhile, the 20th anniversary of the Babyn Yar tragedy was approaching. In the summer of 1961, the poet Yevgeny Yevtushenko was in Kyiv, where he visited the site of the massacre together with the young writer Anatoly Kuznetsov. Yevtushenko recalled later that he was deeply moved by what he saw:

> I knew that there was no monument there, but I had expected to see some kind of commemorative marker or some kind of tended spot. And suddenly I saw a very ordinary landfill that had been turned into a sandwich of garbage with a bad smell.... Before our eyes, trucks were arriving and dumping more and more piles of garbage into the place where these victims were lying.[72]

Shortly afterwards a creative evening was held in Zhovtnevyi (October) Palace in Kyiv, where Yevtushenko read his poem about Babyn Yar. In December 1962 the Moscow-based composer Dmitrii Shostakovich presented his Thirteenth Symphony, the first section of which featured vocals based on Yevtushenko's poem. In 1966 the Moscow magazine *Yunost* (Youth) published a shortened version of Anatoly Kuznetsov's novel *Babi Yar*. Thereafter, contrary to the enduring attempts to erase the memory of the tragedy that befell the Jews of Kyiv in September 1941, the Babyn Yar theme entered the Soviet public space and, simultaneously, gained international resonance.

The Soviet authorities could not countenance this. It was decided therefore to revisit the idea of erecting a monument in Babyn Yar, but once again, not a monument dedicated to Jews but to all innocent Soviet citizens. On 30 May 1965 the CC CPU approved a resolution "About Constructing Monuments in Memory of Soviet Citizens and Captured Soldiers and Officers of the Soviet Army Who Died at the Hands of the German-Fascist Occupiers during the Occupation of the City of Kyiv." On 26 July Ivan Kazanets, head of the Council of Ministers of the Ukrainian SSR, requested permission from Moscow to erect two monuments: one on the site of the former Syrets concentration camp and the

72 Cited in Mikhail Buzukashvili, "Evgenii Evtushenko o 'Bab'iem Iare.' Intervew," *Chaika*, (No. 2 (2011). https://www.chayka.org/node/3104

other in Babyn Yar.[73] After obtaining permission, the republican authorities announced a design competition for the monument in Babyn Yar, which was pegged to the 25th anniversary of the tragedy.

Although the competition was a closed one, the public soon became aware of it. Kyivites visited the Architects' Building to discuss the designs, while some people brought flowers that they laid near the design sketchboards. In addition to the proposals that were conceptually inscribed in the official treatment of the Babyn Yar tragedy, the jury also reviewed several designs by Yosyf Karakis, Avraam Miletskii, Volodymyr Melnychenko, Ada Rybachuk, and others, which featured distinctly Jewish motifs. However, none of these designs found favor with the government. A second round of the competition, held under the slogan "The Road: Death and Restoration to Life," did not produce any results. The competition was finally suspended, and all the submitted designs were rejected.[74]

Despite this setback, the twenty-fifth anniversary of the Babyn Yar tragedy did not go unmarked. On 29 September 1966 an unsanctioned, symbolic mourning rally took place there. For several decades afterwards Babyn Yar began to be perceived not only as a "vale of tears" and memory of those who were murdered there, but also as a place for holding demonstratively public rallies organized by Soviet Jews protesting against government persecution and in defense of their identity and the ideals of freedom and dignity.

On the evening of 24 September several dozen concerned citizens—Viktor Nekrasov, the writer; Rafael Nakhmanovych, director of the Kyiv Documentary Film Studio; and Emmanuel (Amik) Diamant, a staff member of the Main Astronomical Observatory, among others—hung a banner on the surviving fragments of the brick wall enclosing the Jewish Cemetery. The banner bore an inscription in Russian and Hebrew: "Babi Yar, 1941; September 1966. Remember the 6 million." The group also placed an invitation to the public to take part in a mourning rally.[75]

---

73 "Istorychna dovidka. Natsional'nyi istoryko-memorial'nyi zapovidnyk 'Babyn Iar,'" *Babynyar.gov.ua*. 17 March 2011. http://babynyar.gov.ua/%D1%96storichna-dov%D1%96dka

74 Evstaf'eva and Nakmanovich, *Babii Iar*, p. 386.

75 Cited in Emmanuil (Amik) Diamant, "Babii Iar, ili pamiat' o tom, kak v narod

On the morning of 29 September people began flocking to Babyn Yar solo or in groups. Nearly a thousand people assembled, mostly Jews. But there were also Ukrainians, Russians, and others who felt compelled by the moral need to demonstrate their sympathy and solidarity with the Jews in the struggle against antisemitism. Among them were the writers Viktor Nekrasov, Ivan Dziuba, and Borys-Antonenko-Davydovych, and the philosopher Yevhen Sverstiuk. The writer Vladimir Voinovich, the editor of the publishing house Sovetskii pisatel Viktor Fogelson, and the literary critic Feliks Svetov came all the way from Moscow to the rally, which was filmed by the documentary filmmakers Rafael Nakhmanovych and Eduard Timlin.[76]

Ivan Dziuba's speech made a powerful impression on the participants. By this time Dziuba had already been classed as "disloyal" for having written his book *Internationalism or Russification?* (1965), a harsh critique of the Communist party's nationality policy. The speech that he delivered at the public meeting soon appeared in the samizdat press and also included in the body of "criminal" evidence that was being scrupulously collected by the KGB (the book was subsequently listed in the indictment as one of several pieces of evidence proving Dziuba's anti-Soviet activities).

Dziuba's speech at Babyn Yar was truly momentous. The young literary critic appealed to Jews, Ukrainians, and the members of the world community to show understanding, urging them to struggle against hatred and respect the most important human value – life:

> Babyn Yar is a tragedy for all mankind, but it happened on Ukrainian soil, and therefore the Ukrainian, like the Jew, has no right to forget about it. Babyn Yar is our shared tragedy; this is a tragedy first and foremost of the Ukrainian and Jewish peoples. This tragedy was brought to our peoples by fascism. But one must not forget that fascism begins not at Babyn Yar and does not end with it. Fascism begins with disrespect toward a person and culminates in the destruction of the person, the destruction of peoples. […]

prevrashchalos' stroptivoe plemia," *My zdes'* (New York and Jerusalem), 15-21 September 2011.

76 Ibid.

The path toward genuine, not false, brotherhood does not lie in selflessness but in self-knowledge, in not repudiating oneself and adapting to others, but in being oneself and respecting others. Jews have the right to be Jews, Ukrainians have the right to be Ukrainians in the full and profound, not merely formal, senses of these words. Let Jews know Jewish history, Jewish culture, language, and may they be proud of them. Let Ukrainians know Ukrainian history, culture, [and] language, and may they be proud of them. Let them know each other's history and culture, the history and culture of other peoples, and know how to value themselves and others as their own brothers. This is difficult to achieve. But it is better to aspire to this than to give up out of indifference and swim with the wave of assimilationism and opportunism; no good will come of them; there will be only boorishness, profanity, and concealed misanthropy. [...]

With our entire lives we should oppose misanthropy and social boorishness. To us there is nothing more important than this now, for otherwise all social ideals are stripped of their meaning.[77]

One of the other speakers at the rally was an actress from the Kyiv Academic Puppet Theater and mother of two children Dina Pronicheva, a survivor of Babyn Yar. The writer Vladimir Voinovich recalled the speech that was delivered by an unidentified man, who took the floor and said the following: "Respected Jews, I ended up here by accident, and I want to express my solidarity. I know that many Ukrainians took part in destroying Jews. I am ashamed of this."[78]

The "unsanctioned rally" attended by crowds of people did not fail to attract the attention of the authorities. [see Plate **XXIII**] The militia rushed in ordered everyone to disperse, and confiscated the film footage from the cameramen. Meanwhile, a group of Ukrainian intellectuals, including Lina Kostenko, Ivan Dziuba, Yevhen Sverstiuk, Mykola Plakhotniuk, and several others went straight from Babyn Yar to Baikove

77 Ivan Dziuba, "U 25-ti rokovyny rozstriliv u Babynomu Iaru," in his *Ukraïna u poshukakh identychnosti: statti, vystupy, interview, pamflety* (Kyiv: "Ukraïna," 2006), pp. 789-795.

78 Vladimir Voinovich, *Avtoportret: roman moei zhizni* (Moscow: Eksmo, 2010), p. 579.

Cemetery, where they held another unsanctioned rally at the grave of the "Ukrainian bourgeois nationalist," the historian Mykhailo Hrushevskyi.

All the participants of the rally that took place at Babyn Yar in 1966 realized that it was a landmark political event; the authorities understood this as well. On 1 October 1966 Oleksandr Botvin, secretary of the Kyiv municipal party committee, submitted a report to Petro Shelest, first secretary of the CC CPU, entitled "About the Case of the Unorganized Rally Held at the Site of the Shootings of Soviet People by the German-Fascist Occupiers in Babyn Yar." At a meeting of the Kyiv municipal party committee held on 12 October 1966, the rally was characterized as an "unauthorized gathering."[79] Nevertheless, these events prodded the authorities into adopting more active measures aimed at "mastering" the process of memorializing the Babyn Yar tragedy. By 19 October 1966 the Kyiv municipal party committee and the municipal executive committee approved a joint decision entitled "About Erecting Commemorative Markers on the Territory of Babyn Yar and in the Square on Pryvokzalna Street in Darnytsia." The Kyivproekt Institute was ordered to prepare, within three days, a design for two commemorative markers, including one that would be installed at Babyn Yar. The order was duly carried out, and shortly afterwards a commemorative marker was installed between Dorohozhytska and Melnikova streets. It was inscribed with the following text: "In this place a monument will be erected to Soviet people, victims of the crimes of fascism during the temporary occupation of the city of Kyiv in 1941–1943."[80]

In order to hinder "unsanctioned gatherings" of Jews near the commemorative marker, the Soviet authorities decided to hold official meetings there. Thus, in subsequent years large gatherings attended by employees of enterprises and municipal institutions, who were obliged to attend them, were held at Babyn Yar in the last days of September. Secretaries of the municipal party and raion committees, war veterans, and front-rank workers, among whom there were always a few token Jews, spoke at these meetings at specially built podiums. The orators proclaimed the achievements of the Soviet government, denounced "inter-

79 Diamant, "Babii Iar, ili pamiat' o tom."

80 Ibid.

national Zionism," and recalled the victims of fascism—innocent Soviet citizens; naturally, the Jewish component of the Babyn Yar tragedy was completely ignored. A brass band performed the "Internationale," after which the rally participants dispersed.

However, the police, KGB "people dressed in plainclothes," and specially dispatched government agitators remained at the site. As a rule, after these official meetings the latter would push their way into the throngs of people and try to convince Jews that Babyn Yar should not be viewed as a symbol of the sufferings only of the Jewish people and that the government was doing much to honor the memory of those who had perished and to ensure a happy future for the Soviet people. Meanwhile, the security officials carried out careful monitoring of "unorganized groups of Jews," making sure that no wreaths bearing "nationalistic" inscriptions and symbols were laid. Another manifestation of psychological pressure was the blatant photographing of Jewish activists (this meant that the government had "taken note" of an activist, who might experience serious unpleasantness at his or her place of work, school, etc.). Those who had the courage to make an overt demonstration of dissatisfaction were taken away to militia branches, where they were subjected, at best, to "preventive treatment" or arrested.[81]

That is precisely what happened to Borys Kochubiievskyi, a thirty-year-old radio engineer who graduated from the Kyiv Polytechnic. During the first official meeting held at Babyn Yar in 1968 he voiced his dissatisfaction with the speeches about "Israeli aggression" and the deaths of "Soviet citizens" at the hands of the Nazis, and the authorities' concealment of the fact that Jews were killed in Babyn Yar. The engineer's apartment was searched, and in early December he was arrested on charges of "disseminating in oral form patently false fabrications that tarnished the Soviet state and social order" (Article 187–1 of the Criminal Code of the Ukrainian SSR). Kochubiievskyi was tried in May 1969 and sentenced to three years in prison. He was released only in December 1971, and then immigrated to Israel.[82]

81 Izraïl' Kleiner, *Anekdotychna trahediia* (Munich: Suchasnist', 1974), pp. 53-60.

82 "Delo Borisa Kochubievskogo," *Khronika tekushchikh sobytii*, Nos. 6,7,9 (Moscow, 1969). Kandel', *Kniga vremeni i sobytii*, p. 516.

Despite government pressure and persecution, the number of people taking part in the "spontaneous rallies" at Babyn Yar increased steadily over the next few years. Whereas between 50 and 70 Jewish activists gathered at the marker in 1968, in 1969 this number rose to 300–400, and in 1970—to 700–800. The KGB monitored these gatherings closely, invariably calling them "antisocial actions" and recording all these "provocative acts" tirelessly. For example, in September 1969 these acts included the laying of a "Zionist star, the lighting of candles, and distribution of leaflets" (according to the reminiscences of Alik Diamant, three young people brought pieces of cloth woven in white and blue colors, which they hung in such a way as to create a six-pointed Star of David; "people in plainclothes" tried to drive them back and destroy it, but were stopped by onlookers).[83] In late September of the following year the KGB recorded the next "Zionist provocation," during which several wreaths with Yiddish and Hebrew inscriptions were laid at the stone.[84]

The subsequent history of Jewish commemoration of Babyn Yar was connected to a significant degree with the specific features of the Jewish national movement that began to acquire certain organized forms in the early 1970s. According to the definition formulated by the Russian human rights activist Liudmila Alekseeva, the most influential trends in this movement were the "kulturniks" and the "immigrationists." Whereas the former focused their efforts on developing the Jewish language and culture, organizing Jewish higher education, creating a network of cultural institutions, and expanding Jewish religious communities in the Soviet Union, the latter staunchly championed the right of Jews to immigrate.[85]

In the summer of 1968, the Soviet government formally reinstated permission for Jews to immigrate to Israel (in the second half of the 1960s, applications to leave the Soviet Union were filed by 5,762 Jewish residents of the Ukrainian SSR, nearly half of the total number of applications submitted in the entire USSR). At the same time, quotas and im-

83 Diamant, "Babii Iar, ili pamiat' o tom."

84 Kandel', *Kniga vremeni i sobytii*, p. 109.

85 Liudmila Alekseeva, *Istoriia inakomysliia v SSSR: noveishii period* (Moscow: Moskovskaia Khel'singskaia Gruppa, 2012), p. 134.

portant restrictions were introduced. For example, people with a higher and specialist education and employees of defense facilities were not allowed to immigrate. Individuals with no relatives in Israel were also not permitted to leave because, in the view of Soviet ideologists, this "compromised living conditions in the USSR." These restrictions led to the rise of the phenomenon of the "refuseniks," whose numbers increased proportionally to the number of rejected immigration applications. For example, in 1968 the Soviet government rejected the applications of 28 Jews; in 1969—1,079, and in 1970—1,439. By the late 1970s between 30 and 60 percent of all applications submitted by Jews in various oblasts of Soviet Ukraine were denied. At the same time in the late 1960s there were 5,762 applications submitted by Jews residing in Ukraine which amounted to almost a half of all such applications across the entire Soviet Union.[86]

This immigration policy spurred the refuseniks into uniting within individual cities, oblasts, and regions, and developing a joint tactic to counteract the Soviet government's efforts. Rallies, demonstrations, and other public events began turning into mass actions, and some of them were held at Babyn Yar.

On 1 August 1971 eleven Kyivan Jews, whose applications to immigrate to Israel were denied without explanation, tried to organize a protest demonstration and hunger strike at Babyn Yar. The KGB got wind of their plans, and several participants were summoned for "preventive conversations" to the Office of Visas and Registration (OVIR) of the Ministry of Internal Affairs of the Kyiv municipal council, but this did not stop the activists. Finally, the participants of the action were arrested "for causing a public disturbance." During the trial that took place the following day militiamen testified that the "arrestees broke flowers and trampled the grass at the monument to the victims of fascism." The ten defendants were sentenced to fifteen days in jail, and one of them was fined ten rubles. However, the matter did not end there. Shortly afterwards an issue of the Soviet opposition's information bulletin, *Chronicle of Current Events*, published a report stating that nine of the illegally

86 Diamant, "Babii Iar, ili pamiat' o tom."

imprisoned Jews had submitted a complaint to court institutions of the Ukrainian SSR in connection with "abuses in prison" (strip searches, name-calling, much harder work assigned to Jews than other prisoners, etc.).[87] The fact that these and similar actions organized by Jews at Babyn Yar were carefully monitored by the government "on the highest level" is attested by a report that the head of the KGB Yurii Andropov sent to the CC CPSU on 10 August 1971. In it Andropov informed the higher party leadership in detail about the events of 1 August and noted the following: "The Zionists' plan was foiled by measures that were adopted."[88]

In 1971 several more notable public actions took place at Babyn Yar. On the Day of Remembrance of the Holocaust and Heroism, which was celebrated that year in Israel on 22 April, Zionists in Kyiv planned to lay wreaths and flowers at the commemorative marker. The KGB instantly learned of this plan and summoned four activists to the oblast administration of the KGB for a "preventive conversation"; in fact, the goal of the meeting was to intimidate them.

The full-scale interrogation that ensued revealed not only the deep ideological divide between the Soviet government and the young Jewish activists but also the utter lack of fear of the regime on the part of the activists and their principled readiness to defend their rights. Aleksandr (Alik) Feldman, one of the Jewish activists, recalled in his memoirs that he was questioned by a "man in plainclothes," who introduced himself as Major Ovcharenko, and then by the deputy head or head of the oblast directorate of the KGB:

> I was asked: 'What action have you planned for tomorrow?'
>
> 'We have not planned any action. If you are interested in what I personally am planning to do tomorrow, I can say that I want to go to Babyn Yar and lay a wreath in memory of the Jews who perished there in 1941.'
>
> 'Why are you honoring the memory only of Jews? After all, Soviet people and other nationalities are buried there.'

87 "Dvizhenie evreev za vyezd v Izrail'," *Khronika tekushchikh sobytii*, No. 21 (Moscow, 1971).

88 "Spetsial'noe soobshchenie KGB USSR o namerenii evreev provesti golodovku v znak protesta protiv otkaza im v vyezde v Izrail' ot 02.08.1971 goda," Haluzevyi Derzhavnyi Arkhiv Sluzhby bezpeky Ukrainy, Kyiv (hereafter: HDA SBU), Fond 16, Sprava 994.

'But only Jews died because they belonged to a certain people. This was genocide. To conceal this means to whitewash the fascist killers. In addition, when we come to a cemetery, we go up to the graves of our loved ones. Does this signify disrespect toward other graves? We grieve for all Nazi victims, but we do not conceal the fact that our hearts ache for the Jews who perished. Is this not natural?'

'For the mourning ceremony, why did you choose tomorrow, when all Soviet people are marking the birthday of V. I. Lenin? This might look like a provocation.'

That's a coincidence. The Jewish calendar is a monthly one, and this year the Day of Remembrance of the Holocaust and Heroism falls on 22 April.

'And in future it will fall on 1 May?'

'No, on 11 April.'

'Why did you mark this day last year?'

'If you are right, I agree with you. This is truly an oversight on our part. I can promise you that this will not happen again.'

'We do not advise you to go to Babyn Yar tomorrow. Laying wreaths with inscriptions in a foreign language and, generally, your defiant behavior could spark a corresponding reaction on the part of the non-Jewish population. Aren't you afraid of this?'

'No, we're not afraid. I know that without your direct instruction, this will not happen. And right now excesses are not beneficial for you.'

'A militiaman, or a vigilante, or any Soviet person does not know what is written on the wreath. And what if it is an anti-Soviet slogan?'

There are 150,000 Jews in Kyiv. You could have a staff member who knows the Jewish language.'

'Nevertheless, we are not advising you to go. Besides laws, there is Soviet rule of law. We will not allow anyone to violate it and hold religious orgies in a public place.'

'We do not need your advice. If you can, ban us from going to Babyn Yar.'

'We cannot forbid [you], but we are warning you: show prudence.'

'Thank you for the warning, and allow me to warn you. Since you are aware that we want to lay wreaths, then you will be responsible for all possible incidents.'

The conversation ended at this point.[89]

89 Cited in Mykhailo Hutor, "Bortsi za zberezhennia pam'iati pro Babyn Iar," *Evreiskii obozrevatel'*, No. 3 (339) (Kyïv, 2021).

Despite brutal government pressure, the planned event took place. Standing at a distance, KGB men monitored the actions of the Jewish activists. However, clearly fearing the mechanisms of international publicity to which the Zionists resorted from time to time, the government did not dare to remove the wreaths that the activists laid at the commemorative marker, and they lay there until the following evening.

The atmosphere was also tense on 29 September 1971, during the ceremony marking the 30th anniversary of the Babyn Yar tragedy, an event for which both the Soviet authorities and Jewish activists prepared. As attested by declassified archival documents, government leaders drew up "a plan to prepare and hold the meeting and to ensure public order." At the appointed time "public representatives and delegations from the collectives of enterprises and institutions in Shevchenkivskyi district," numbering between 3,000 and 3,500 people who had been "mobilized" to attend the official meeting gathered at the commemorative marker. According to established tradition, orators proclaimed ideological slogans from the podium and recalled the "victims of the fascist regime," without mentioning a single word about the Jewish victims of Babyn Yar.[90]

The "unsanctioned" meeting held at the commemorative marker that day drew, according to KGB data nearly 200 people of Jewish nationality and another 200 or so passersby. But the *Chronicle of Current Events* reported nearly a thousand participants, including many young people. From the Jewish inscriptions on the wreaths it was evident that Jewish activists from Moscow, Leningrad, Sverdlovsk, and Tbilisi were also in attendance at the mourning rally in Kyiv. This time the Soviet authorities did not stand on ceremony with the "gathering of citizens of Jewish nationality." Projectors and cameras were aimed at people, and militia units and "people in plainclothes" stationed at the approaches to the commemorative marker tore off anything that could be viewed as "Zionist symbols." "The KGB men, of whom there were very many that day, got down to work," recalled Yosif Begun, a resident of Moscow, former activist of the Jewish movement, and prisoner of the Gulag. "They tore the mourning ribbons from the wreaths. Kippahs were torn off our heads,

90 Alekseeva, *Istoriia inakomysliia v SSSR*, p. 128.

mourning armbands from our arms.... When we were approaching our end goal, there were no longer any 'identifying' Jewish signs either on our persons or our wreaths. Everything had been torn off, thrown out, 'confiscated.'"[91]

### The period of neo-Stalinism to the collapse of the Soviet Union

On 7 September 1972 a group of Kyivan Jews attempted to lay a wreath and bouquets of flowers at Babyn Yar in honor of the eleven Israeli athletes who were brutally murdered by terrorists two days earlier at the Munich Olympics. [see Plate **XXIV**] Militiamen and KGB agents stopped the mourning ceremony, and the twenty-seven activists were arrested. The militia used force in an effort to disperse their relatives and friends, who assembled at the building where the activists were being detained. Two of the arrestees, Yurii Soroko and Zinovii Melamed, recalled afterwards that a KGB officer named Davydenko spoke to them in a threatening tone at the KGB Directorate of Kyiv oblast, declaring frankly that the "circumstances had changed." The KGB's hands were now "untied," and if opposition activities continued, the activists would receive lengthy sentences.[92]

Even though this episode seemed to be true to form, in fact it was quite symptomatic in the context of the fundamental changes in the political climate in the Soviet Union in the late 1960s and early 1970s, with the rise to power of Leonid Brezhnev and his appointee in the Ukrainian SSR, Volodymyr Shcherbytsky. The "Thaw" years were followed by decades of "stagnation," or neo-Stalinism, marked by the restoration of the position of General Secretary of the CC CPSU, the curtailing of criticism of Stalinism, the intensification of repressions targeting oppositionists, who were now being imprisoned not only in the Gulag, but also subjected to forcible treatment in psychiatric hospitals. The government also intensified its ideological struggle against "manifestations of nationalism," especially in Ukraine, where it was waged with particular ferocity against "Ukrainian bourgeois nationalism" and "international Zionism." [see Plate **XXVIII**] The Soviet authorities feared national movements

91 Cited in Diamant, "Babii Iar, ili pamiat' o tom."

92 Ibid.

that opposed the Soviet government both because of the rapid growth of their influence in the country and the international community's powerful support for these movements, especially in the sphere of information. It was clear that the national movements were undermining the legitimacy of communist rule and, in the long perspective, its very existence.

The government's offensive against the Jewish national movement was multi-pronged. In connection with and subsequent to the aircraft hijacking affair of 1970–1971 the Soviet authorities carried out repressions, arresting and imprisoning activists or resorting to expelling the most "odious" of them from the USSR. Numerous artificial obstacles were created for Jews attempting to immigrate to Israel, and prospective émigrés were intimidated by arrests, pogroms, expulsion from institutes, dismissal from work, etc. Finally, both inside the USSR and in the international arena the Soviet authorities conducted a widespread, mass-scale propaganda war against "international Zionism."[93]

On 17 February 1971 the CC CPSU approved a secret resolution entitled "About Measures for Intensifying the Struggle against the Anti-Soviet and Anti-Communist Activities of International Zionism." This document was supplemented by an almost identically titled resolution passed by the CC CPSU on 1 February 1972, "About Further Measures for the Struggle against the Anti-Soviet and Anti-Communist Activities of International Zionism." With the goal of implementing it, on 7 September 1972 the Secretariat of the CC CPSU, including Mikhail Suslov, Fedor Kulakov, Petr Demichev, Vasilii Kuznetsov, and other members, approved the "Plan of Basic Propaganda and Counterpropaganda Measures in Connection with the Latest Anti-Soviet Campaign of International Zionism."[94] A key role in carrying out this plan was assigned to the KGB, which was accountable to the Council of Ministers of the USSR, and its agents were instructed to adopt decisive measures in "exposing

93 In 1970–1971 alone, fifty-nine books with a print run of two million copies in Russian, Ukrainian, Lithuanian, French, Spanish, and Arabic were published in the USSR on the topic of the "reactionary essence" of Zionism. Kandel', *Kniga vremeni i sobytii*, p. 512.

94 Олег Bazhan, "Represyvni zakhody radians'koï vlady shchodo hromadian ievreis'koï natsional'nosti v URSR (1960-ti-1980-ti rr.)," *Z arkhiviv VUCHK-HPU-NKVD-KDB*, No. 1/2 (22/23) (Kyiv, 2004), p. 115.

and halting the hostile actions of the enemy's security services, foreign Zionist organizations, and Jewish nationalists within the country."[95] Approval of these documents signaled a new round of confrontations between the Soviet government and the Jewish national movement in the USSR, in which circumstances Babyn Yar was objectively transformed into an arena of conflict.

On the eve of the commemoration of the next anniversary of the Babyn Yar tragedy, the Kyiv municipal party committee developed a pro-government action plan. On 29 September 1972 the official rally near the commemorative marker began much later than usual, at approximately 6:00 p.m., and it lasted only a short time. In keeping with established tradition, flowers and wreaths bearing "ideologically sustained" inscriptions were laid at the marker. Then an orator delivered a speech in which he emphasized the advantages of life in the "multinational Soviet state," denounced "Israeli aggression against the Arabs," and mentioned the tragedy of Babyn Yar, where during the war "many Soviet people of various nationalities" were killed.[96]

When the official part ended, several hundred Jews tried to pay tribute to their families and friends, but this unofficial part of the ceremony was suddenly taken in hand by the security forces. Numerous militia detachments, stationed earlier on the sidewalks flanking the road leading to the commemorative marker, let through only people bearing wreaths decorated with black and red ribbons, barring access to individuals carrying anything decorated with white and blue ribbons and inscriptions written in Hebrew, on the grounds that "it is not clear what is written on them." At 7:00 p.m. the militia began shoving people brutally away from Babyn Yar, and the electric light near the commemorative marker was switched off. By 8:00 p.m. the area was deserted. Arrests naturally took place. Eleven activists who had defied the Soviet government were detained by the militia and jailed for fifteen days on charges of "violating public order."[97]

On 27 December of that year the Soviet authorities issued a resolution entitled "On the Reimbursement of State Education Expenditures by Cit-

---

95 Ibid.

96 Diamant, "Babii Iar, ili pamiat' o tom."

97 "Repressii na Ukraine," *Khronika tekushchikh sobytii*, No. 27 (Moscow, 1972).

izens of the USSR Leaving for Permanent Residence Abroad," which the Presidium of the Supreme Soviet of the USSR had approved on 3 August. Before leaving the USSR, all émigrés with a higher education were now obliged to repay the Soviet state 6,000 rubles (the average monthly salary at the time was 150 rubles); Candidates of Sciences—15,400 rubles; and Doctors of Science—17,200 rubles. (In 1972 Jews wishing to immigrate reimbursed the Soviet treasury nearly 4.5 million rubles, and more than 1.5 million rubles in the first two months of 1973).[98] In response to this essentially discriminatory decision, the American government signed into law the Jackson-Vanik amendment to the Trade Act of 1974, and in the USSR members of the refusenik movement held mass demonstrations and hunger strikes, and sent petitions and open letters to Soviet government agencies and the international community.[99] Some petitions singled out Babyn Yar as an example of how the Soviet authorities were ignoring the Jews' right to their own memory. In a letter addressed to the American people a Kyivan refusenik wrote:

> We who have been denied this right are behind a curtain of numbers and words about free emigration. We are living in the Soviet Union against our will, the laws of this country no longer protect us. We are threatened with imprisonment for going to a synagogue, for commemorating those who were tortured and killed in Babyn Yar and the Warsaw Ghetto. Most of us have been dismissed from work; we do not know who is deciding our fate and what the future holds for us. The constant threats of arrest by state officials and intimidating articles in newspapers and radio broadcasts are creating an atmosphere of psychological terror around us. We have been stripped of the right to live, and we are not being given a chance to leave. We are turning to you, people of a great country, at this difficult time. Help us.[100]

---

98 Evgenii Zhirnov, "A kogo my ne khotim vypuskat', my ne dolzhny vypuskat'," *Kommersant* (Moscow), 9 March 2018.

99 Alekseeva, *Istoriia inakomysliia v SSSR*, p. 135.

100 Cited in Fred A. Lazin, "Jewish Influence in American Foreign Policy: American Jewry, Israel and the Issue of Soviet Jewry, 1968–1989." *The Lawyer Quarterly*, No. 3 (1) (Prague, 2011), 159-160.

Expecting that the American government would rescind its sanctions, the Soviet government canceled the education tax in March 1973. However, repressions against activists and intimidation of prospective immigrants continued as before. In keeping with the directives of the all-Union party leadership, on 15 August 1973 the CC CPU ordered Soviet Ukraine's Prosecutor's Office, its Ministry of Internal Affairs, and the KGB at the Council of Ministers "to intensify the work of exposing and prosecuting active propagandists of the 'movement' in support of Jewish emigration from the USSR [and] emissaries of foreign Zionist centers."[101] With the intention of implementing these directives, on 29 September 1973 the KGB and the militia were stationed at Babyn Yar, from where they dispersed approximately a thousand Jews who had come to Kyiv from various corners of the Soviet Union.[102]

As in previous years, the Jewish activists put up stubborn resistance to the ban on public manifestations of national identity during commemorations of the victims of the Babyn Yar massacre. [see Plates **XXV** and **XXVI**] Given their experience acquired over the years, the activists had pre-ordered wreaths to be laid at the commemorative marker and had prepared and hidden white ribbons with blue-colored inscriptions in Hebrew and Russian. Wreaths intended for the commemorative marker were carried by men and behind them came women bearing flowers. En route, people joined the procession making its way to the site of the ceremony. After they arrived at the commemorative marker, the activists quickly decorated the wreaths with the white-and-blue ribbons, and also managed to light twenty out of thirty-two candles that they had brought, before the KGB and militiamen pounced and began tearing off the ribbons and trampling the flowers.[103]

In 1974 the persecution of Jewish activists commenced several days before the commemorative days. On 29 September nearly 800 Jews who had gathered at Babyn were surrounded by KGB and militia detachments. The participants of the commemorative ceremony were forbidden to recite the Mourner's *Kaddish* and other prayers. After the mourn-

---

101 Bazhan, "Represyvni zakhody radians'koï vlady," p. 116.

102 "Repressii na Ukraine," *Khronika tekushchikh sobytii*, No. 27 (Moscow, 1972).

103 Ibid.

ing rally ended, several participants traveling home on public transport were subjected to acts of provocation intended to intimidate them.[104] On 28 September 1975 Jewish activists were prevented from holding a commemorative ceremony at Babyn Yar, and two days later several Jewish cemeteries in Kyiv were vandalized.[105]

Back in 1974, eighty-six Jews from Kyiv, Moscow, Tbilisi, and Minsk had sent letters to the CC CPSU protesting against harassment and the Soviet government's obvious procrastination in erecting the long-promised monument at Babyn Yar. They wrote:

> The absence of a monument at Babyn Yar cannot be explained as forgetfulness on the part of the government of Ukraine.... Perhaps it .... does not have enough money. But a monument costs much less than one of the thousands of tanks that are supplied regularly .... to Arab countries. If there is still no possibility to economize the deliveries with at least one tank, then ... the Jews of the USSR are ready to raise the necessary funds to erect a monument.[106]

Jewish activists then announced their readiness to found a public committee for raising funds for the construction of a monument at Babyn Yar.

Such actions on the part of "individuals of the Jewish nationality" were viewed as "provocative." The Soviet authorities banned the creation of this civic committee and, like in previous years, they decided to seize the initiative to construct a monument. On 2 July 1976, thirty-five years after the tragedy, a monument was finally erected at Babyn Yar. This was a multi-figured composition with a metal plaque inscribed with the following words: "Here in 1941–1945 more than a hundred thousand citizens of Kyiv and prisoners of war were shot by the German-fascist invaders."[107]

---

104 "Spetsial'noe soobshchenie V. Shcherbitskomu v dele provedeniia aktsii v Babiem Iaru ot 30.09.1974 g.," HDA SBU, Fond 16, Sprava 1037.

105 Alekseeva, *Istoriia inakomysliia v SSSR*, pp. 68-69.

106 Cited in Oleh Bazhan and Iurii Danyliuk, *Opozytsiia v Ukraïni (druha polovyna 50-kh–80-ti rr. XX st.)* (Kyiv: Ridnyi krai, 2000), pp. 121-122.

107 Cited in Evstafieva, "Babii Iar: poslevoennaia istoriia mestnosti," p. 28.

It was no accident that the date of the monument's unveiling was switched to summertime, the new date being far removed in time from the September days of commemoration. The secret police also took steps to adopt measures aimed at thwarting "provocations" by Jewish activists. The Soviet authorities used a variety of pretexts to prevent a significant number of activists from attending the unveiling ceremony (some people were removed from trains, others were warned about the possibility of arrest, etc.). One participant of this event, Yosif Begun, recalled that in Kyiv several dozen Jews from various cities who were getting ready to bring wreaths to Babyn Yar and take part in the official unveiling of the monument were surrounded, thrown into a bus, and brought to a militia station, where they were detained until late in the evening. These young people were released only at 9:00 p.m., when it was already dark on the streets and the area around the monument was deserted. (The activists brought the wreath that they had intended to lay at Babyn Yar to Moscow, where they showed it to foreign correspondents).[108]

Starting in 1977, official rallies were no longer held at Babyn Yar. The Soviet authorities clearly believed that the political potential of such events had been exhausted. Instead, the monument was often used for propaganda purposes, especially among foreign tourists, whose travel services were provided by the KGB-supervised state agencies Intourist and Sputnik. As noted in a 1978 report written by the head of Intourist, "many tourists express satisfaction as well as surprise at the possibility granted to them to visit Babyn Yar and lay flowers at the monument…, inasmuch as prior to their trip to the Soviet Union they had been warned that 'in Kyiv everything will be done so that tourists do not get to Babyn Yar.'"[109]

Such feelings of "satisfaction and surprise" were an exception to the rule as regards visits to the monument by tourists or official delegations that included members of the Jewish community. In early August 1979 a delegation from the United States visited Babyn Yar; one of its members was Elie Wiesel, chairman of the President's Commission on the

---

108 Bazhan and Danyliuk, *Opozytsiia v Ukraïni*, pp. 121–122.

109 Cited in Mitsel', "Zapret na uvekovechivanie pamiati kak sposob zamalchivaniia Kholokosta," pp. 19-20.

Holocaust. In a speech delivered during the official part of the ceremony, Wiesel emphasized that the memory of the Jews killed in Babyn Yar was honored in the US. He also reminded his listeners that this place became sacred to the Jews long before a monument was installed there. Before his flight to Moscow, Wiesel expressed sharp indignation at the fact that the commemorative plaque next to the monument did not mention a single word about Jewish victims, and he promised to raise this question with the American government.[110]

In late 1979 the Soviet Union launched its military intervention in Afghanistan. Hopes for a reduction of tension between the Soviet and Western blocs, which were sparked by the signing of the Helsinki Accords, proved unfounded. A new round of the arms race and various conflicts erupted between the communist camp and the countries of the free world, the most powerful representatives of which were the USSR and the US. The newly elected US president Ronald Reagan announced a doctrine aimed at curbing communist expansionism the world over, and an arms race that proved to be beyond the capacity of the Soviet economy began.

At this new stage of the Cold War, the Soviet Union intensified its anti-American and anti-Israeli rhetoric in the international arena. In the USSR the Soviet authorities launched reprisals against dissidents who supported the Helsinki process, as well as other opposition forces. Once again, for a lengthy period of time Jews, with few exceptions, were denied the possibility to emigrate from the USSR. Any attempts to hold organized events were punished mercilessly. In order to preempt such events, in the early 1980s the KGB launched repressions against potential organizers of anti-government actions, and in addition to the arrests of Jewish refuseniks, "kulturniks" were persecuted as "agents of international Zionism." In March 1983 the secretariat of the CC CPSU approved the creation of the Anti-Zionist Committee of the Soviet Public (headed by General David Dragunskii), whose mission was to wage a struggle against "international Zionism"; in practice, the committee's efforts were aimed at discrediting the State of Israel.[111]

---

110 Ibid., pp. 23-24.

111 Matvei Geizer, "Istoriia zhizni generala Dragunskogo," *Lekhaim*, No. 6 (98) (Moscow, 2000). https://lechaim.ru/ARHIV/98/geyzer.htm

In the conditions of terror that existed behind the Iron Curtain, the activities of the Jewish national movement decreased significantly but did not disappear altogether. On the eve of the fortieth anniversary of the Babyn Yar tragedy, the KGB implemented a series of "preventive measures" in various cities in order to stop Jewish activists from traveling to Kyiv. On 24 September 1981 Oleg Popov was summoned to the militia in Moscow, where "people in plainclothes" had an unambiguous "talk" with him, warning him in no uncertain terms that if he traveled to Kyiv, both he and his family would end up in "cold lands" instead of gaining permission to immigrate to Israel. The "explanations" of the motivations underpinning the government's position were telling:

> Popov: [...] You do not want the anniversary of the shootings of Jews by the Nazis in Babyn Yar to be marked. By the way, why can't people lay a wreath at the monument in Babyn Yar? Is that against the law?
>
> Unidentified individual: Honest Soviet citizens can. But we will not allow nationalists [to do this].
>
> Popov: Aren't Jews Soviet citizens? How is it that some people can and other people can't?
>
> Unidentified individual: But why do you talk only about Jews? The entire Soviet people suffered during the war, but you are commemorating only Jews. And the wreaths that will be brought are not ordinary ones but beribboned. And the ribbon is inscribed thus: 'We shall remember you in our historical fatherland.' Who gave nationalists the right to consider Israel the historical fatherland of Jews?... We will not allow nationalism to be promoted!... Times have changed.... Do you understand me?
>
> Popov: No, I don't understand. What does different times mean?
>
> Unidentified individual: It's too bad that you don't know.... You preach nationalism. And we will not allow this!... The propaganda of nationalism undermines internationalism. Clear? Is it not? Undermining internationalism is undermining our ideology. Still not clear? Undermining our ideology is undermining our order....[112]

112 Cited in "40 let Babiemu Iaru," *Khronika tekushchikh sobytii*, No. 63 (Moscow, 1981).

That same day, 24 September, Svitlana Yefanova, Volodymyr Tereshchenko, and Borys Kanevskyi were arrested in Kyiv, and were jailed for fifteen days on charges of "petty hooliganism." Several days later Mikhail Elman and Pavel Astrakhan of Leningrad were arrested and jailed for ten days; they had tried to lay a commemorative wreath with a ribbon inscribed with the following text: "Eternal memory to you. Leningrad, 1981." Two Moscow residents, the 70-year-old war veteran Moisei Ravich and Evgenii Nartov, were arrested right at the train station and turned back. But another Moscow resident, Aleksei Lorenstson, was jailed for fifteen days for allegedly "uttering obscenities." The Odesites Oleksandr Kushnir, Yana Mesha, Valerii Pevzher, and Yurii Shvarts were also detained near Babyn Yar and delivered to the airport. But the young people returned and managed to lay flowers at the monument and recite the *Kaddish*. Later the militia drove them to the train station and waited until the train pulled away. On 27 September at least a hundred militiamen and "people in plainclothes" were stationed near the monument to the victims of Babyn Yar. In addition, four buses were sent there to pick the arrested "hooligans," and the militia and KGB men controlled all the streets leading to Babyn Yar.[113]

Outraged by the government's actions, eighty Jewish activists wrote a letter to Leonid Brezhnev demanding that he stand up for the unjustly convicted activists and put an end to the "outrageous abuse of the sacred memory of the war victims." The letter stated in part:

> For many years Babyn Yar has remained a wilderness. A monument was erected only five years ago; its inscription conceals the fact that this is a place of Jewish suffering. However, Jews from throughout the Soviet Union and from other countries always came here on 29 September to honor the memoir of the nameless victims. Any attempt to impede the desire to honor those who were killed would be profane. Nonetheless, such profanity did indeed take place. . . . What happened in Kyiv is terrible. This is an insult to the memory of war victims, an insult to Soviet Jews, an insult to everyone who fought and is fighting against fascism.[114]

113 Bazhan and Danyliuk, *Opozytsiia v Ukraïni*, pp. 125–126.

114 Cited in ibid., pp. 125–126.

A group of Soviet dissidents also reacted to the government's actions in Babyn Yar. Three members of the Moscow Helsinki Group—Elena Bonner, Sofia Kalistratova, and Naum Meiman—drafted a special declaration that read in part: "The events in Kyiv attest to the authorities' desire to erase the memory of Babyn Yar. At the same time the authorities used the fortieth anniversary of the mass killings of Jews near Kyiv as a pretext to launch the latest repressions against those Jews who want to emigrate from the Soviet Union."[115]

On 29 September Ukrainian television aired a propaganda film entitled *Babyn Yar: Lessons of History*. The author of the script, the Kyiv-based playwright Aleksandr Shlaen, was dismissed from his job for refusing to obey party ideologists' orders that he introduce material aimed at "unmasking Zionists." As the film director Volodymyr Heorhiienko recalled later, all the "recommendations" were ultimately included in the final product. In addition to "exposing" Zionists, the film also included material on the "atrocities committed by the American military clique in Korea and China." An English version of the film, completed shortly afterwards, contained material on the "role of Ukrainian policemen."[116]

The latter was clearly connected with the Soviet government's desire to preclude the formation in the international area of any united "bloc" of Zionists and "Ukrainian bourgeois nationalists." The existence of such a strategy is attested by documents drafted by Soviet political and secret police agencies. A 1980 report prepared by the KGB of the Ukrainian SSR, in the section entitled "About Attempts to Create an OUNite and Zionist Bloc," describes joint Jewish-Ukrainian actions connected with the creation of Babi Yar Park in Denver, Colorado. According to KGB data, these actions were viewed as the "first practical step toward the realization of the Jewish-Ukrainian agreement on cooperation, which was supposedly adopted in Israel in 1979 by the members of the World Jewish Congress and the Ukrainian Congress Committee of America." The document noted that "the republican Committee of State Security is

115 Cited in ibid., p. 127.

116 "Aleksandru Shlaenu – 70 let!," in *Khar'kovskii muzei Kholokosta: Daidzhest E*, No. 6 (23) (Kharkiv, June 2001).

carrying out measures to counteract the formation of a bloc uniting the Ukrainian nationalists and the Zionists."

The history of the creation of Babi Yar Park in the United States merits separate attention. In general, little is known about how this park came to be. The idea to create a park emerged in the late 1960s–early 1970s. The initiative came from the local Jewish community, which included natives of Kyiv whose families were killed in Babyn Yar. The Jewish community raised $140,000 for the project, and the federal and municipal governments donated an additional $750,000. The city granted twenty-seven acres of land for the park.[117] At a certain stage, friction arose between the local Jewish and Ukrainian communities, sparked by different visions of the project, the traumatic experience of World War II, and—quite likely—targeted KGB provocations. For a certain period of time two parallel organizations existed: the Babi Yar Park Foundation and the Ukrainian Babyn Yar Committee. However, in August 1980 the two communities reached an understanding and formulated a joint plan to carry out the project. The Ukrainian community launched a fundraising campaign in order to make its own contribution to creating "the only memorial park in the world together with the Jews" and to pay homage to the "shadows of those whose lives were cut down prematurely by the brutal hurricane of war of German Nazism." One publication issued by the Ukrainian Babyn Yar Committee noted:

> No matter from which point of view we approach in assessing the Ukrainian role in building the memorial park in Denver, we reach the conclusion that it has and will have a positive meaning for us and therefore it deserves our efforts and funds.... First, it is proof that we, like all cultured nations, honor the memory of the numerous victims among the Ukrainian people, and second, it is exemplary evidence that Ukrainians and Jews, with good will, can pave the way to better coexistence.[118]

While Jewish activists in Kyiv who tried consistently to honor the

117 Nataliia Shchur, "K 72-i godovshchine rasstrela evreev v Babiem Iaru: vechnaia pamiat," *Zemliaki* (Chicago), September 2013.

118 Cited in ibid.

memory of the Jews killed in Babyn Yar continued to be terrorized and persecuted on the eve of and during the 40th anniversary of the tragedy, in the free world the Ukrainian Babyn Yar Committee published long lists of donors and reported on the funds that were raised in the United States, Canada, and Europe for the creation of the memorial park. The park was officially opened on 2 October 1983. A few days earlier, on 27 September, the Babi Yar Committee, along with Secretary Gallagher, organized a meeting between the Denver community and General Petro Hryhorenko (Petr Grigorenko), who had been expelled from the USSR.

The park was designed by Lawrence Halprin and Satoru Nishita, who devised the entrance to the path as a kind of purgatory taking the form of a narrow passage between two black granite monoliths flanked by trees, which by its configuration is reminiscent of the gates leading to the Garden of the Gods. The left stone is inscribed with the following words in Ukrainian: "In Memoriam to the Two Hundred Thousand Victims Who Died, Babi Yar, Kiev, Ukraine, USSR September 29,1941–November 6, 1943 / The Majority Jews with Ukranians [*sic*] and Others [Ukrainian] in Babi Yar / ETERNAL MEMORY to all the victims of terror." The right stone is inscribed with a poem written in English: "Decades Ago… / Still the Aching Sadness / Innocents . . . / People Who Loved / Forever Silenced by Nazi Terror / Sharing Eternally . . . / The Mystic Number . . . Six Million / A holocaust for the Jews of Europe / A tragedy for all humanity / Remember . . ."[119]

Mikhail Gorbachev's rise to power in the mid-1980s ushered in another wave of liberalization in the Soviet Union. The activities of oppositionist national movements were finally legalized, and formal obstacles to Jewish emigration from the USSR were abolished. A plaque inscribed in Yiddish appeared next to the monument at Babyn Yar. There was obvious progress in international relations, especially after Soviet troops were withdrawn from Afghanistan in February 1989 and the Berlin Wall was dismantled in November 1989.

Nevertheless, practically until the collapse of the USSR, there was a distrustful Soviet attitude to the State of Israel in the international arena

119 Cited in ibid.

and specific approaches to the "Jewish question," which were marked by considerations of "political expediency." Despite the détente, in 1989 the Soviet Union refused to acknowledge the erroneousness of the UN General Assembly's 1975 resolution defining Zionism as "a form of racism and racial discrimination." Furthermore, in actively exploiting for political purposes the theme that organizations of "Ukrainian nationalists" were involved in killing Jews during the Holocaust, the Soviet leadership refused to take responsibility for the decades of state antisemitism or publicly acknowledge the fact that the Nazis killed Jews in Babyn Yar only because they were Jews.

According to Gorbachev's personal assistant, the possibility of his visit to Kyiv was discussed on the eve of the 50th anniversary of the Babyn Yar tragedy. The main points of his speech were drafted quietly, and it referred "directly to Stalinist antisemitism and to the emigration of talented fellow citizens, and to the great nation, and to the lessons that we took from our own, not just Nazi, antisemitism."[120] In the end, Gorbachev decided not to attend the commemoration ceremonies in Kyiv. Instead, on 2 October 1991 he met with Shoshana Cardin, chairperson of the National Conference on Soviet Jewry. When he was asked the straightforward question of why the leadership of the Soviet Union, despite the conditions of democratization, still had not condemned antisemitism, the last leader of the Soviet Union not only dodged the question but commented, entirely in the spirit of all his predecessors, that "placing special attention on antisemitism" was not feasible. "We have 120 nationalities in the Union. Singling out one means to give preference to someone. And nationalistic manifestations exist not only in connection with the Jews."[121]

A month later the USSR ceased to exist. The question of whether to take on the burden of responsibilities for the policies and practices of Soviet state antisemitism and for the participation of a segment of "ordinary Soviet people" in the destruction of their Jewish neighbors during the Holocaust now emerged as a moral choice for the independent states that were created from the ruins of the USSR and for each of its citizens.

---

120 Cited in Anatolii Cherniaev, *1991 god: Dnevnik pomoshchnika prezidenta SSSR* (Moscow: TERRA; Respublika, 1997), p. 71.

121 Cited in ibid., p. 115.

**Babyn Yar in Ukraine's official politics of memory**

On 24 August 1991 an extraordinary session of the Supreme Soviet of the Ukrainian SSR approved the Act of Declaration of Ukraine's Independence. The presidential elections were set for 1 December, as well as a referendum with which the Ukrainian people were supposed to confirm their decision to leave the Soviet Union and begin building a sovereign, democratic state. In these circumstances, the commemoration of the 50th anniversary of the Babyn Yar tragedy acquired special importance. Recognition of the Jewish component of the tragedy that took place in September 1941 was supposed to demonstrate that its disgraceful concealment was now a thing of the past and to attest to the new Ukrainian state's commitment to democratic and humanistic values that had been ignored for so long in the USSR.

On 10 September 1991 the cabinet of ministers of Ukraine handed down a resolution that spelled out a number of measures for the state commemoration of the upcoming anniversary of the massacre of Jews in Babyn Yar. The week-long commemorative events were slated to take place between 29 September and 6 October 1991.[122] [see Plates **XXIX-XXX**]

On the eve of the commemoration, posters were hung on Khreshchatyk, the main boulevard of the Ukrainian capital, bearing the following inscription in four languages: Ukrainian, Russian, Yiddish, and Hebrew: "Eternal memory. The Babyn Yar tragedy must never be repeated." That week the Menorah Monument (sculptor: Yurii Paskevych) was unveiled at the site of the shootings; various individuals were granted the title of Righteous Among the Nations, an international conference "Babyn Yar: History and Its Lessons" was held; and film screenings and documentary exhibitions took place. At the site of the tragedy the American actors Cliff Robertson and Tony Randall, the Israeli actor Chaim Topol, and the Ukrainian actor Bohdan Stupka gave a public reading of excerpts from the *Black Book*, published in Kyiv, and together with Yevgeny Yevtushenko, they recited his poem "Babi Yar." The performance of the Ukrainian composer Yevhen Stankovych's work *Babyn Yar Requi-*

---

122 "Postanova Kabinetu Ministriv Ukraïny № 192 'Pro zakhody u zv'iazku z 50-richchiam trahediï Babynoho iaru'," Verkhovna Rada Ukraïny, 10 September 1991. https://zakon.rada.gov.ua/laws/show/192-91-%D0%BF#Text

*em-Kaddish*, set to the words of the poet Dmytro Pavlychko, was one of the highlights of the commemorative week.[123]

On 5 October 1991 several thousand people gathered at Babyn Yar for a mourning rally, having traversed the same "death road" along which the Jews of Kyiv had walked to their place of execution in the fall of 1941. Hundreds of foreign guests took part in the official ceremony, among them the Ambassador of Israel and representatives of the German and US governments. Aleksandr Yakovlev was sent to Kyiv as a delegate by the all-Union Soviet leadership. Among the participants of the mourning rally were numerous public figures, particularly activists of the Jewish and Ukrainian national movements, as well as many ordinary citizens.[124] The researcher Anatoly Podolsky noted that many of the Jews who came that day to Babyn Yar for the very first time were convinced that KGB agents would be in attendance, taking down their names; it was difficult for them to believe that it was now possible to honor the memory of the Jewish victims without fear of repressions.[125]

At the commemorative rally Leonid Kravchuk, head of the Verkhovna Rada of Ukraine, delivered a speech that raised a whole array of political and worldview perspectives. After decades marked by the suppression and denial of the Jewish tragedy, the following points were acknowledged on the official state level for the first time. Babyn Yar was the first act of the "final resolution of the Jewish question," and Jews were killed in Babyn Yar only because they were Jews. Kravchuk also mentioned the tens of thousands of Poles, Russians, Ukrainians, Lithuanians, Soviet partisans, underground members, and hostages who were murdered later by the Nazis. He emphasized: "Babyn Yar became an international mass grave. Babyn Yar was a testing site, where mass methods of destroying people were carried out.... It will forever be an eternal reproach to humankind, a testament to one of the most shameful of its evildoings."[126]

---

123 Alexander Burakovskiy, "Holocaust Remembrance in Ukraine: Memorialization of the Jewish Tragedy at Babi Yar," *Nationalities Papers*, XXXIX, 3 (Basingstoke, England, 2011), pp. 371-389.

124 Ibid., p. 379.

125 From the author's personal archive.

126 "Vystup holovy Verkhovnoï Rady Ukraïny L. Kravchuka na memorial'nii tseremoniï u Babynomu Iari," *Holos Ukraïny* (Kyiv), 8 October 1991, pp. 1-2.

In recognizing that the Babyn Yar tragedy was the logical culmination of the monstrous theory and practice of antisemitism and emphasizing that Hitler frequently speculated on the slogans of waging a war against international Jewry, and that from the standpoint of a civilized person such slogans are the work of savagery, Kravchuk acknowledged the inadequate assessments of Zionism contained in the United Nations resolution of 1975 as a vestige of the past era of old quarrels, and announced his support for United States president George Bush's initiative to review it those decisions.

Leonid Kravchuk devoted part of his speech to the difficult and dramatic history of Ukrainian-Jewish relations. "In it there have been both bright and dark pages. None of us has the right to forget anything. But let us remember them not in order to reopen old wounds, but to prevent them in the future. Let that which unites rather than separates our peoples enter our recollections."[127]

The Ukrainian leader spoke at length about the fundamental principles of state building and policies of today's Ukraine, the main ones being the imperative to guarantee equal rights and respect regardless of national or social origin, race or skin color, political convictions or religious beliefs; equal opportunities for all national minorities to take part in building the Ukrainian state, and respect for their languages, traditions, culture, and spiritual characteristics.

Kravchuk went on to condemn the Soviet policies of ignoring human rights and concealing and suppressing the truth about the Babyn Yar tragedy. He then issued an apology to the Jewish community:

> Before the entire world, today we declare the inadmissibility of the ideological considerations of the former regime in Ukraine, which trampled over the rights of the individual and the rights of nations, concealed from the people the historical truth about the Babyn Yar tragedy, about the fact that the majority of the victims of the mass shootings were Jews. This was genocide, and responsibility for it lies not only with the fascists but also with those who did not stop the murderers in a timely manner. We accept part of it on ourselves. Today's sad observances are also a fit-

127 Ibid.

ting occasion to apologize to the Jewish people, against whom so many injustices were committed in our history. This is difficult. But it is necessary for people to acknowledge mistakes and to apologize. Without this, progress is impossible. It is better to do good than to sow hatred [...].

Even today, the recollections of the mass killings of people, which the fascist executioners perpetrated in Babyn Yar, give us no peace. The ashes of the victims of genocide beat at our breasts. Can such a thing be forgotten? Never. The death of memory is the death of the soul.[128]

Kravchuk ended his speech with the following greeting in the Ukrainian and Yiddish languages: "Peace and happiness to you, the long-suffering Jewish people. Sholom eykh/could not verify this word/ tayere idn![129]

On 1 December 1991, nearly 32 million citizens of Ukraine (84.2 percent of the electorate) took part in a nationwide referendum, in which an overwhelming majority of 90.3 percent of voters approved the declaration of Ukrainian independence.[130] That same day Leonid Kravchuk was elected president of Ukraine. A new era began in the life of the Ukrainian people. It was symbolic that by 26 December 1991 Ukraine and Israel established diplomatic relations.[131]

### Historical memory in Europe and Ukraine

Sociopolitical events that took place in the last decade of the twentieth century—the velvet revolutions, decommunization, and the unification of Europe—had an essential impact on European countries' approaches to forming official politics of memory, which are marked by fundamental differences in western and central/eastern Europe.

Western Europe, which rests on the ideological heritage of enlightenment and humanism and the experience of World War II, set out to

128 Ibid., pp. 1-2.

129 Ibid., p. 2.

130 Petro Kahui, "Arkhivni foto. Referendum za nezalezhnist' Ukraïny 1 hrudnia 1991 roku," *Radio Svoboda*. 29 May 2021. https://www.radiosvoboda.org/a/referendum-pershoho-hrudnia-1991-roku-pro-nezalezhnist-ukrayiny-arkhivni-foto/30287132.html

131 "Politychni vidnosyny mizh Ukraïnoiu ta Izraïlem," statement issued by the embassy of Ukraine in the State of Israel, 1 May 2020. https://israel.mfa.gov.ua/spivrobitnictvo/429-politichni-vidnosini-mizh-ukrajinoju-ta-izrajilem

create a new culture of memory. The Nazi destruction of the Jews, who lived in practically every country of Europe and comprised a significant proportion of these countries' societies, was recognized as a tragedy of all the European people. At the same time, this perception also included a sense of blame, as part of the population of both aggressor-countries and victim-countries was implicated in this crime, having contributed one of the most shameful pages in European history. These ideas determined the centrality of the Holocaust as a symbol in the historical memory of western Europe, an important element of whose culture became repentance.

Meanwhile, central and eastern European countries, following decades of communist rule, defined their priorities for restoring/forming their historical memory by emphasizing national and cultural renaissance. Post-communist countries, having suffered huge losses at the hands of both the Nazis and the Soviets, displayed a tendency toward victimization of their national histories, from which the Holocaust was excluded here and there.

Following the unification of Europe, the process of integrating the concept of the Holocaust into national memory models was launched in the new member countries of the European Union. As the British historian Tony Judt commented, awareness of the Holocaust became a kind of "train ticket" to European integration.[132] In the post-Soviet space, however, the re/formation of historical memory acquired its own clear-cut features. In Russia and Belarus, where authoritarian regimes emerged, emphasis was placed on the Great Victory in the war against Germany, heroism was accented, and a cult of leaders was glorified. Moreover, the Holocaust and Stalinist antisemitism did not occupy an important place in the official politics of memory. Where Ukraine is concerned, the formation of a contemporary historical memory model was unmistakably marked by the struggle between the post-Soviet, pro/Russian, and various versions of the Ukrainian national memory model, as well as by the

132 Tony Judt, "The Past Is Another Country: Myth and Memory in Postwar Europe," in István Deák, Jan Gross, and Tony Judt, eds., *The Politics of Retribution in Europe: World War II and Its Aftermath* (Princeton, N.J.: Princeton University Press, 2000), pp. 293–325.

features of various presidents' strategies for governing the state.

The first president of Ukraine, Leonid Kravchuk, sought to distance himself from the "extremes of communism and nationalism," and tried not to raise complex and painful historical issues that might "irritate" Russia, which stance was also adopted by the Ukrainian parliament, comprised mostly of former communists, and by the divided Ukrainian society. Admittedly, in the early years of independence the old, official Soviet memory model was removed from school textbooks, and the Ministry of Education became one of the key institutions for implementing desovietization and Ukrainization. The term "Great Patriotic War" was expunged from textbooks, the crimes of Stalinism and Nazism were condemned equally, and topics related to the Holodomor and the activities of the Organization of Ukrainian Nationalists and the Ukrainian Insurgent Army were introduced into curricula. Meanwhile, the Holocaust topic was not implanted in the education process, and it was inadequately covered in the media. After his memorable 1991 speech at Babyn Yar, Kravchuk practically never raised this topic during his presidency, believing that the question of rendering an apology to the Jews was now closed. Nevertheless, in the external political arena he expressed regret several times for crimes that were committed by Ukrainians against Jews, for example, in 1993, during his speech in the Knesset.[133]

The next president, Leonid Kuchma, a former "red director" from eastern Ukraine, won the elections, running on a campaign to grant Russian official-language status. During his presidency he too underscored the importance of restoring historical memory, a return to the origins of national identity, and the restoration of Ukrainian national traditions. The formation of a historical memory model throughout Kuchma's two terms in office took place mostly via the Ukrainization of old Soviet myths, particularly the myth of the "Great Patriotic War." Emphasis was placed on Ukrainians' heroism and self-sacrifice as soldiers of the Red Army during the war.

133 "Address of Ukrainian President Mr. Leonid Kravchuk to the Knesset Plenum Jerusalem," 12 January 1993 (unofficial translation of the speech delivered in Ukrainian). https://www.knesset.gov.il/description/eng/doc/speech_kravchuk_1993_eng.pdf

In 2000 the Verkhovna Rada of Ukraine, acting on a proposal submitted by the Veterans' Organization of Ukraine, approved a law entitled "About the Commemoration of Victory in the Great Patriotic War of 1941–1945," recognizing Victory Day as an official Ukrainian state holiday that was aimed at preserving the old, ritual symbolism.[134]

Against the background of this Sovietized historical memory, Babyn Yar was transformed de facto into a place visited once a year by government officials laying wreaths and uttering the customary phrases at a commemorative rally. This formality was violated in 2001, when, two weeks before the 60th anniversary of the Babyn Yar tragedy, terrorists attacked the World Trade Center in New York City. In his Address to the Ukrainian People, President Kuchma linked the mass killings in the US with the Nazi crimes of 1941, describing them as "genocide and [as] an extreme form of terrorism raised to the level of state policy."[135]

During his presidency public attention was abruptly focused on the tragedy that befell Ukraine's Romani people, who were among the Germans' first victims in Babyn Yar. Back in 1966, members of various civic organizations in Kyiv tried to organize the installation of a metal monument designed in the shape of a "gypsy caravan" to honor the memory of the Roma who perished in Babyn Yar. Encountering stiff opposition from the Kyiv authorities (who controlled the territory of Babyn Yar at the time), this idea never came to fruition. The caravan ended up in the city of Kamianets-Podilskyi, where it became the first monument dedicated to the genocide of the Romani people.[136] By the end of the Kuchma presidency, the Ukrainian state finally recognized this genocide. On 8 October 2004 the Ukrainian parliament passed a resolution entitled "On the Commemoration of International Roma Holocaust Remembrance

---

134 "Zakon Ukraïny 'Pro uvichnennia Peremohy u Velykii Vitchyznianii viini 1941-1945 rokiv'," Verkhovna Rada Ukraïny, 20 April 2020. https://zakon.rada.gov.ua/laws/show/1684-14#Text

135 Leonid Kuchma, "Tol'ko sovmestnoe protivodeistvie terrorizmu pozvolit izbezhat' povtoreniia novykh Bab'ikh Iarov – takikh zhe zhestokh i stokrat bolee strashnykh po svoim masshtabam," *Fakty* (Kyiv), 2 October 2001.

136 Andrei Kotliarchuk, "Natsistskii genotsid tsygan na territorii okkupirovannoi Ukrainy: rol' sovetskogo proshlogo v sovremennoi politike pamiati," *Holokost i suchasnist'*, No. 1 (12) (Kyiv, 2014), p. 45.

Day," to be celebrated on 2 August (the date of the "Night of the Gypsies" in Auschwitz-Birkenau).[137]

> Three weeks later, on 27 October 2004, during the celebrations of the sixtieth anniversary of Ukraine's liberation from the Nazis, President Kuchma offered his personal take on the history of World War II. Recalling the shootings in Babyn Yar of Jews, Ukrainians, and Russians, he also—unexpectedly—mentioned Ukrainian nationalists who also perished there. He went on to propose a qualitatively new historical memory model for the consolidation of society, the foundation of which would be the condemnation of all those who were involved in Nazi crimes and the rejection of the mechanistic exploitation of the thesis, imposed by Soviet propaganda, that all the members of the OUN and the UPA were criminals. According to Kuchma:
>
> 'The 'new order' was revealed in Kyiv's Babyn Yar, where—in addition to tens of thousands of Jews—Ukrainian, Russians, and members of the Organization of Ukrainian Nationalists were shot. The history of World War II still contains many conflicting pages that are perceived ambivalently by our contemporaries. In particular, these are questions relating to prisoners of war and the activities of the OUN and the UPA. Without a doubt, all those with innocent blood on their hands deserve condemnation. However, it would be unjust to put forward such accusations against all the members of the insurgent movement. The search for compromises and possibilities for mutual reconciliation among various political forces, including the veterans' milieu, is the only path to the consolidation of Ukrainian society.'[138]

The "memory wars" in Ukraine escalated significantly during the presidency of Viktor Yushchenko. He came to power in the country in the wake of the Orange Revolution and sought to make a radical change in

---

137 "Postanova Verkhovnoï Rady Ukraïny 'Pro vidznachennia Mizhnarodnoho dnia holokostu romiv,'" Verkhovna Rada Ukraïny, 8 October 2004. https://zakon.rada.gov.ua/laws/show/2085-IV#Text

138 Leonid Kuchma, "Vyzvolennia Ukraïny – odna z naivydatnishykh storinok svitovoï voiennoï istoriï: vystup Prezydenta Ukraïny na urochystomu zibranni z nahody vidznachennia 60-ï richnytsi vyzvolennia Ukraïny vid fashysts'kykh zaharbnykiv," *Uriadovyi kur'ier* (Kyiv), 29 October 2004.

Ukrainian politics of history by focusing on the crimes of the communist totalitarian system. Henceforward, the Stalinist USSR in the Yushchenko memory model was identified as an empire, and Ukraine—as a post-totalitarian, post-colonial, and post-genocidal state.

Babyn Yar and the Holocaust occupied a prominent place in Yushchenko's history policies. By his own admission, the Jews' tragedy was also part of his own family history. His father was a prisoner of Auschwitz, "and he was there with the Jews at a time when 25,000 people were exterminated in a single day, and during this period no one divided people into Ukrainians, Russians, or Jews; no one gave a thought to whom he was giving a piece of bread."[139] During the war President Yushchenko's grandmother and mother, who lived in his native village of Khoruzhivka, in the Sumy region, hid three little Jewish girls in the family home.

In 2005, the first year of his presidency, Yushchenko directed the Cabinet of Ministers to study "the question of creating in the established order the Babyn Yar Historical and Cultural Preserve."[140] Since Yushchenko viewed Ukraine's tragedy during the World War II period through the prism of the crimes committed by the two totalitarian regimes, Stalinist and Nazi, he drew a direct equivalence between Auschwitz and the Gulag and the Holocaust and the Holodomor. He also made consistent efforts to integrate into the Ukrainian memory model the idea of reconciliation between two groups of World War II combatants: veterans of the Soviet army and the Ukrainian Insurgent Army. At the same time, he began focusing attention on Ukrainian nationalists who were executed in Babyn Yar.

On 22 May 2006 President Yushchenko issued a decree entitled "On Commemorating the Centenary of Olena Teliha's Birth." Teliha was a Ukrainian poet and member of the Melnykite faction of the OUN, who

---

139 "Syn v'iaznia №11367 ïde v Osventsim," *Ukraïns'ka pravda* (Kyiv), 19 January 2005.

140 The Cultural Preserve was founded in 2007 under the Ministry of Culture and Tourism and transferred in 2008 to the jurisdiction of the Ukrainian Institute of National Remembrance; on 24 February 2010 President Yushchenko issued a decree granting Babyn Yar the status of a national historical and memorial preserve. "Istoriko-memorial'nyi zapovednik 'Babii Iar' poluchil status natsional'nogo," *Khreshchatyk* (Kyiv), 25 February 2010.

was shot by the Germans in Babyn Yar on 22 February 1942. The decree mandated that official and cultural events take place from July to September 2006. Over the course of two-year period (2006–2008) a "monument to Olena Teliha and her companion in arms" was erected on the territory of the Babyn Yar Memorial Complex (the monument was supposed to replace the wooden cross that activists had erected in 1992).[141] At this point the monument installation project ground to a halt. Yet on 1 December 2009 a monument was erected at Babyn Yar in honor of Tania Markus, a member of the Soviet underground, on whom President Yushchenko conferred the title "Hero of Ukraine" on 21 September 2006.[142]

In the fall of 2006, the sixty-fifth anniversary of the Babyn Yar tragedy was marked on the state level. President Moshe Katsav of Israel flew to Kyiv to take part in the commemorative events, which included an official mourning ceremony, a litany served by the hierarchs of most of the traditional churches, and a themed exhibit held in Ukrainian House in downtown Kyiv. A highlight of the commemorative events was an international forum, "Let My People Live," organized by the government of Ukraine, the World Holocaust Forum, and Yad Vashem. The forum was attended by nearly a thousand foreign guests from over fifty countries. In his speech to the forum, President Yushchenko emphasized that "today Ukraine is speaking to mankind for the first time in the voice of the world catastrophe." He recalled the words of the Musaf Prayer for the Day of Judgment, "These things I remember, and pour out my soul within me," assuring his listeners that there would be no place in Ukraine for national or religious intolerance.[143]

The commemoration of the victims of Babyn Yar on the sixty-sixth anniversary of this tragedy was marked by special features. After a wreath was laid at the 1976 monument, President Yushchenko, together with the head of the Kyiv oblast administration Vira Ulianchenko, deputy

141 "U Babynomu Iari vstanovliat' pam'iatnyk Oleni Telizi," *Istorychna pravda* (Kyiv), 10 November 2013.

142 "Pidpil'nytsi Tetiani Markus postavyly pam'iatnyk," *Khreshchatyk* (Kyïv), 4 November 2009.

143 Cited in Iuliia Kundeleva, "Prezidenty Ukrainy i Izrailia prizyvaiut pomnit' o zhertvakh tragedii v Babiem Iaru," *MediaPort* (Kharkiv), 27 September 2006.

premier Dmytro Tabachnyk, and the secretary of the National Security and Defense Council of Ukraine Ivan Pliushch, laid flowers at the memorial cross, the approximate spot where the Nazis shot a group of OUN members and the poet Olena Teliha (in subsequent years this ritual was repeated by prime minister Julia Tymoshenko and the head of the Ukrainian parliament, Arsenii Yatseniuk). In 2007 Yushchenko issued a decree granting the title of "Hero of Ukraine" to Roman Shukhevych, commander in chief of the UPA, and in January 2010—to Stepan Bandera, the leader of the OUN(B).[144] Yet, in his official speeches he never once raised the difficult topic of the "idealistic" and "ordinary people" among those Ukrainians who helped the Nazis in their killing spree during World War II. This was a clear indication of his narrow view of the official memory model of a European Ukraine. At the same time this circumstance, taken against the background of President Yushchenko's decisions mentioned above, made him sensitive to the harsh criticism of his opponents both inside and outside Ukraine.

The expression "Forward to the past!" best characterizes the official politics of memory pursued by Viktor Yanukovych, the fourth president of Ukraine. Compared to all the previous presidents, who had proclaimed, clearly or not very plainly, their desire for the restoration and formation of Ukrainian identity, Yanukovych was the only one who showed absolute indifference and even hostility to this question.

During Yanukovych's presidency, President Yushchenko's flawed but consistent policy of dissociating the country from communism and condemning the crimes of the Stalinist empire began to be supplanted by the policy of reviving the old, heroized Soviet heritage; these efforts taking place against the background of unmistakable attempts to dilute Ukrainian identity with Russian. Holding a majority in the Ukrainian parliament, the president's Party of Regions and its communist allies approved laws and resolutions that recreated the old Soviet-Russian models of the historical memory of the war. At the same time it was obvious that this process was not simply a matter of copying Russian politics, but

144 "Ukaz Prezydenta Ukraïny 'Pro prysvoiennia S. Bandery zvannia Heroi Ukraïny." Verkhovna Rada Ukraïny, 20 January 2010. https://zakon.rada.gov.ua/laws/show/46/2010#Text

that it was being determined in no uncertain terms in Moscow. Such official acts as Yanukovych's public refusal to recognize the Holodomor as an act of genocide, the revival by the Ukrainian parliament of the practice of holding a grandiose Victory Parade (2010), and the passing of contradictory resolutions on the eve of the sixty-fifth anniversary of the Nuremberg trials and the "Law about the Red Flag" (2011) not only did not bring any peace to Ukrainian society but caused even more turmoil.[145]

The conflict between the new and old politics of memory was also reflected in the official practices of honoring the memory of the victims of Babyn Yar. For several years in a row, in late September, the area surrounding the 1976 Soviet monument was covered with red flags and banners, where communists and their ideological allies, like the members of the Anti-Fascist Committee of Ukraine founded in 2006, ruthlessly denounced "Ukrainian national fascists" and the "criminal organizations OUN-UPA,"[146] exactly as they had once condemned "international Zionism" and the "Israeli military clique." Some speakers voiced programmatic slogans against Ukraine joining NATO and in favor of restoring the "everlasting fraternal relations with Russia, Belarus, and other countries of the Commonwealth of Independent States."

On 5 July 2011 the Verkhovna Rada of Ukraine approved a resolution entitled "About the 70$^{th}$ Anniversary of the Babyn Yar Tragedy," establishing 27 January as Holocaust Remembrance Day. Despite the fact that the Parliamentary Committee on Questions of Culture and Spirituality had proposed that Jews and Romani be singled out expressly, the promulgated resolution, similar to the Soviet-era practice, concealed these specific victims behind the euphemism "people of various nationalities."[147] How-

---

145 "Ianukovych: Holodomor nespravedlyvo vyznavaty henotsydom ukraïntsiv," *Radio Svoboda*, 27 April 2010. https://www.radiosvoboda.org/a/2025786.html; "Zaiava Verkhovnoï Rady Ukraïny 'Do 65-oï richnytsi Niurnberz'koho protsesu nad fashysts'kymy zlochyntsiamy', 19 April 2011," *Holos Ukraïny* (Kyiv), 7 May 2011; "Ianukovych pidpysav Zakon pro Chervonyi Prapor," *Tyzhden.ua*, 21 May 2011. https://tyzhden.ua/News/23070

146 "Antyfashysts'kyi komitet Ukrainy zavtra v Kyievi provede aktsiiu 'Den' borot'by z natsional-fashyzmom'," *UNIAN* (Kyiv), 13 October 2010.

147 "Postanova Verkhovnoï Rady Ukraïny 'Pro 70-richchia trahediï Babynoho Iaru'," Verkhovna Rada Ukraïny, 5 July 2011. https://zakon.rada.gov.ua/laws/show/3560-VI#Text

ever, in addition to civilians, prisoners of war, communists, and Soviet underground members and partisans, the list of people whom the Nazis murdered in Babyn Yar included Ukrainian nationalists, who could not be expunged from the list once the story about the Nazis murdering hundreds of OUN members became public knowledge.[148]

The tendency of repeating the Soviet-era practice of ignoring the Jewish victims of Babyn Yar was also revealed in no uncertain terms in Viktor Yanukovych's Address to the Ukrainian People on the occasion of the seventieth anniversary of the Babyn Yar tragedy, which mentioned, once again, only "the civilian population."[149] On 3 October 2011 the official ceremony organized to mark the anniversary of the tragedy attested to the deep divide between the Ukrainian government and society. The main feature of those commemorative events was the government's overt dissociation from the Ukrainian public and the "ceremonial indifference" to the tragic date that was supposed to become one of the main instruments for uniting Ukrainian society.[150] President Yanukovych's rejection and very real denial of democratic values, all the while declaring them, particularly in the sphere of the official politics of memory, was one of the causes behind the Revolution of Dignity (Maidan) in 2014, which put an end to attempts to preserve the traditions of the Soviet past and to halt Ukraine's move into Europe.

The current stage of forming the Ukrainian model of historical memory is proceeding in the extraordinarily complex conditions of Russia's annexation of the Crimean Peninsula and the hybrid war raging in Ukraine's Donbas region. The process of Ukraine's withdrawal from the influence of the Russian/Soviet empire is drawing to a close, and a new Ukrainian

---

148 The memorial cross erected in honor of Ukrainian nationalists at Babyn Yar was vandalized from time to time, as was the Menorah Monument.

149 "Ianukovich: v Ukraine net mesta rasizmu i nasiliiu," *Obozrevatel'* (Kyiv), 29 September 2011.

150 "Tseremoniia pokladannia kvitiv do 'Pam'iatnyka radians'kym hromadianam ta viis'kovopolonenym soldatam i ofitseram Radians'koï armiï, rozstrilianym nimets'kymy fashystamy u Babynomu Iaru." Natsional'nyi istoryko-memorial'nyi zapovidnyk 'Babyn Iar'," 4 October 2011. http://babynyar.gov.ua/tseremon%D1%96ya-pokladanya-kv%D1%96t%D1%96v-do-pamyatnika-radyanskim-gromadyanam-ta-v%D1%96iskovopolonenim-soldatam-%D1%96-o

civic identity is forming. On 9 April 2015 a majority of Ukrainian parliamentarians adopted four laws, the so-called "decommunization packet": (1) "On the Condemnation of the Communist and Nazi Regimes," which bans the propaganda and symbols of these regimes; (2) "Regarding Access to the Archives of the Repressive Organs," which declassifies the archives of the All-Union Cheka, NKVD, and KGB; (3) "Regarding the Commemoration of the Victory over Nazism," which supplements the 9 May date with 8 May, the Day of Memory and Reconciliation, and replaces the official use of the phrase "the Great Patriotic War" with "the Second World War; and (4) "About the Legal Status of Fighters for Ukraine's Independence," which recognizes as such not only those who fought in battles between 1941 and 1945 but also all members of anti-Soviet movements from the 1920s to 1991.[151] The decommunization legislation is based on the experience of central and eastern Europe, the Baltic countries, and Georgia. Despite some shortcomings, this packet of laws is of strategic importance for Ukraine's future.

Today the Holocaust, which was suppressed for so long in the USSR, occupies an important place in Ukraine's politics of history. In fact, the prospects for consolidating democracy in Ukraine, as well as the literal prospects for the country's integration into the family of European nations, depend on the degree to which this issue becomes a component of Ukrainian identity. President Petro Poroshenko's decree of 12 August 2015 entitled "Concerning Measures in Connection with the 75th Anniversary of the Babyn Yar tragedy" is the first time that this place of memory was linked directly with the Holocaust on the highest state level. The decree also refers to many other victims who are buried in this mass

---

151 "Zakon Ukraïny 'Pro zasudzhennia komunistychnoho ta natsional-sotsialistychnoho (natsysts'koho) totalitarnoho rezhymiv v Ukraïni ta zaboronu propahandy ïkhnioï symvoliky,'" Verkhovna Rada Ukraïny, 9 April 2015; "Zakon Ukraïny 'Pro dostup do arkhiviv represyvnykh orhaniv komunistychnoho totalitarnoho rezhymu 1917-1991 rokiv,'" Verkhovna Rada Ukrainy, 9 April 2015; "Zakon Ukraïny 'Pro uvichnennia peremohy nad natsyzmom u Druhii svitovii viini 1939-1945 rokiv,'" Verkhovna Rada Ukraïny, 9 April 2015; "Zakon Ukraïny 'Pro pravovyi status ta vshanuvannia pam'iati bortsiv za nezalezhnist' Ukraïny u XX stolitti,'" Verkhovna Rada Ukraïny, 9 April 2015. https://zakon.rada.gov.ua/laws/show/314-19#Text

grave, including members of the Ukrainian liberation movement.[152]

President Poroshenko's speech in the Knesset on 23 December 2015 was a momentous event in terms of Ukraine's integration into the European culture of memory, the culture of grief and repentance. Emphasizing that Babyn Yar is a shared, open wound of Ukrainians and Jews and the place where tens of thousands of Jews were murdered only because they were Jews, and noting that 1.5 million Ukrainian Jews perished during the Holocaust, Poroshenko paid tribute to the Righteous Among the Nations who, risking their own lives, rescued Jews. He also spoke about negative episodes in history and about collaborationists, who "unfortunately, existed practically in all European countries that were occupied by the Nazis, and helped those monsters to implement the "final resolution of the Jewish question."[153] The president of Ukraine apologized for this to the children and grandchildren of Holocaust victims, and emphasized that future generations would be raised in the spirit of rejecting crimes, such as the Holocaust and Babyn Yar.

These words, reflecting the Ukrainian state's official politics of memory, hold great symbolic significance. They attest to Ukraine's decisive readiness to disengage itself from the Soviet past, adopt European values, and become an equal member of a united Europe.

---

152 "Ukaz Prezydenta Ukraïny 'Pro zakhody u zv'iazku z 75-my rokovynamy trahediï Babynoho Iaru'," Verkhovna Rada Ukraïny, 12 August 2015. https://zakon.rada.gov.ua/laws/show/471/2015#Text

153 "Vystyp Prezydenta Ukraïny u Knesseti Derzhavy Izraïl'," *Galinfo* (Lviv), 23 December 2015.

CHAPTER 7

# Babyn Yar in Personal Accounts

*Asia Kovrigina*

...and as smoke
you shall climb to the sky
then you'll have a grave in the clouds
it is ample to lie there ...
– Paul Celan

I have come to you, Babi Yar. [...]
Pleading, I stand on this soil,
If I don't go mad, I will hear you, soil –
Talk to me.
– Lev Ozerov

I have chosen these two verses for the epigraph of this chapter for several reasons. First, to show that the smoke of Auschwitz and the earth of Babyn Yar gave rise to two different images in art, hence in our memory. Second, to demonstrate that in the former Soviet Union it was impossible to write the same way as in the West.

Writing in the former Soviet Union was closely tied to politics. This was especially the case when it concerned the genocide, which was passed over in silence, and Babyn Yar, which was erased from the face of the earth. As a Jewish-Ukrainian poet living in the Soviet Union, Lev Ozerov could not write like his contemporary, the Bukovinian Jewish poet from Romania, Paul Celan. And, finally, the last reason for my choice of verses in the above epigraph is to show that there is a very fine line between literature and memoiristic writing. Both employ one and the same images. Literature is fed by memoirs, and vice versa. Moreover, poets write memoirs. These three aspects are the axes on which my reflections will revolve.

Paul Celan wrote very little prose and he left behind only poetic memoirs. He conveyed his past exclusively through poetic language that is manifestly somber, compact, and dense as black basalt. A native of Chernivtsi, he was forced into a ghetto and then sent to Romania's wartime Tabareşti labor camp. While he survived, his parents perished in camps in Transnistria. After the war Celan decided to leave communist Romania and in 1947 fled to the West, where he was eventually recognized as a major German-language poet of the twentieth century. He wrote generally about the Holocaust, but his poetry was interpreted as being focused on Auschwitz. Well versed in Russian literature, in 1962 Celan translated into German Yevgeny Yevtushenko's famous poem, "Babi Yar."

**Smoke and earth: Auschwitz and Babyn Yar**

Auschwitz hangs like a black sun over European culture and thought. It became a universal criterion of political thought, and stimulated the creation of art, novels, and literary criticism. The world has been branded by Auschwitz, which today is considered an "unprecedented" event that left history fractured and forced the individual to reassess the limits of reality.

Auschwitz swallowed up more than a million victims, turning them into smoke. The gas chambers produced death on a daily basis, mechanically, without leaving any waste materials. The "production of corpses" – the all-out destruction that was organized at this factory of death – became a paradigm of contemporary barbarism and an embodiment of evil in the twentieth century. Together, the inconceivable number of victims and industrial progress turned inside out, destroying instead of producing, confirmed Auschwitz in our awareness as the center of the destruction of European Jewry. For a long time Western reflections were focused precisely on the technocratic aspect of the Holocaust, to wit, the extermination of the Jews by Zyklon B, an organic compound first used as an anti-flea pesticide. From now on there would be history before and after Auschwitz; poetry before and after Auschwitz; prose writing before and after Auschwitz. Is there writing before and after Babyn Yar?

For many years Babyn Yar was overshadowed by Auschwitz. The massacre in Babyn Yar was not industrial genocide, nor a distorted mirror of technical progress. And, despite the fact that the Nazis carried out Operation 1005, the code name for the secret campaign to erase the evidence of the mass murders they had perpetrated in eastern and central Europe, and notwithstanding the Kurenivka mudslide tragedy and the continuing urban transformation in this part of Kyiv, to this day Babyn Yar has preserved the remains of the victims who perished there. The ravine is a grave. One can still visit it and bow down, as did Lev Ozerov and many others who will be discussed in this essay.

The ritual of mourning and grief on the steep slopes of Babyn Yar was described by Elie Wiesel:

> A second woman was pointed out to me in the synagogue. She, too, lives in another world, but she was not among those taken out to be shot. She had managed to hide and escape. Her husband . . . . was caught and killed with the others. After the liberation, his widow somehow received a long letter he had left for her. She shut herself in her room and for three days and three nights read the letter, over and over, hundreds of times. . . . Then she went to Babi Yar and called to her husband in a loud voice. The next day she did the same. Now that is all she does, every day of the year, except for Sabbaths and holidays.[1]

It is impossible to mourn Auschwitz, for it is a monster, a machine-monster. But it is possible to grieve in Babyn Yar, even if it drives one insane.

The non-technocratic nature and non-novelty of the Babyn Yar tragedy ("old-style mass murder" in the style of the execution of the Polish officers in Katyn), the subsequent imposition of Soviet censorship, the Iron Curtain, and the Cold War between the Soviet Union and the West are all factors which explain why so few people in the West were aware of the mass killings in Babyn Yar. Much less writing was devoted to Babyn Yar than to Auschwitz, and it barely registered in the world's understanding of the Catastrophe.

### Behind the Iron Curtain

We owe one of the most penetrating and poetic descriptions of Babyn

1 Elie Wiesel, *The Jews of Silence: A Personal Report on Soviet Jewry* (New York: Holt, Rinehart and Winston, 1966), p. 36.

Yar published in the West to Elie Wiesel. In 1965 this renowned former prisoner of Auschwitz traveled to the Soviet Union on a fact-finding mission for an Israeli newspaper. "You must go and see," he was told by the Israelis who sent him to the USSR. "You have already been a witness; now you should go and find out the way things really stand with Soviet Jews and testify on their behalf."[2] So, Wiesel went as a witness in order to find out what happened in the past and what was still happening to Jews in the Soviet Union, where they were living in the conditions of state-sanctioned antisemitism and were cut off from the rest of the world. An observant and no-nonsense traveler, Wiesel visited Moscow, Leningrad, Kyiv, and Tbilisi, and came home "transformed." From that time onwards, he regarded himself as an emissary of Soviet Jews. In the opening lines of his book, *The Jews of Silence: A Personal Report on Soviet Jewry*, Wiesel wrote: "The pages that follow are the report of a witness. Nothing more and nothing else. Their purpose is to draw attention to a problem about which no one should remain unaware."[3]

Wiesel's report on Soviet Jewry echoes his first book, *And the World Remained Silent* (1956), whose nine hundred pages are filled with detailed eyewitness testimonies of people who had survived the Nazi concentration camps. In the *The Jews of Silence*, Wiesel tries to explain what is happening in the Soviet Union and why not only its Jews but also their coreligionists and the entire world community remained silent about their plight. From the other side of the Iron Curtain he raised his voice in an impassioned appeal for action, publicizing the grave situation of Soviet Jewry and reminding his readers that the world was silent when the Jews were being exterminated during World War II. The journey to the Soviet Union merely confirmed Wiesel's conviction that "To remain silent and indifferent is the greatest sin of all."

A separate chapter in his book is devoted to Babyn Yar. Its first two lines read: "Kiev brings to mind Babi Yar. Kiev *is* Babi Yar."[4] But Wiesel does not find Babyn Yar on any map of the city, and it is not on the itinerary of any sightseeing tours. He asks a taxi driver to take him to

2 Ibid

3 Ibid., p. vii.

4 Ibid., p. 33.

Babyn Yar and is brought to an empty field in a suburb of Kyiv. There is nothing there, not a single marker, and it is impossible to determine if this field really is Babyn Yar. Wiesel realizes that even though Babyn Yar has disappeared and is therefore not indicated on maps or marked by a single commemorative plaque or gravestone, it is both nowhere and everywhere: "Finally the realization comes that there really is no need for you to be shown that spot. . . . The government guides are right; there is no reason to go there, there is nothing to see at Babi Yar. You can see it downtown, in every square and on every street; nothing and everything."[5]

After *The Jews of Silence* was published in 1966, the West could no longer remain unaware of Babyn Yar, the place where a completely different plan of extermination was employed and where tragedy was erased from maps and the face of the earth through the efforts of the Soviet government. Within a year after Wiesel's book was published, a trial began in October 1967 in the German city of Darmstadt. In the docket were former members of *Einsatzgruppe 4a*, which on 29 and 30 September 1941 carried out the extermination of nearly 34,000 Jews. Thanks to the publicity surrounding the Darmstadt trial, Babyn Yar entered the Western media space. Then, in 1966, Anatoly Kuznetsov burst onto the literary scene with his novel, *Babi Yar*.

Three years later, on 20 July 1969, during a trip to England to collect materials for another novel, Kuznetsov managed to shake off his KGB chaperone (popularly called *mamka*) and requested political asylum. The desperate and risky escape of one of the most brilliant, progressive, and privileged Soviet writers was a knife in the back of the Soviet authorities. Kuznetsov was roundly condemned at a meeting of the Union of Writers, and all Soviet newspapers, even those based in the most far-flung corners of the Soviet Union, joined in the campaign of persecution. Amidst the hounding, accusations, and revela- tions about a writer who had been read widely before this wave of persecution, Kuznetsov's critics mentioned only his conformist, socialist-realist style, and best-selling novel *Prodolzhenie legendy* (Sequel to a Legend, 1957), all the while ut-

5 Ibid., p. 33-34.

terly ignoring *Babi Yar*. Nevertheless, in 1966 two million copies of the magazine *Yunost*, which originally published the novel, were sold.[6]

Despite having been thoroughly censored, Kuznetsov's *Babi Yar* which had nothing novelistic about it, had the effect of a bombshell. In the Soviet Union, where there was no free press and no freedom of expression, literary texts played a preeminent social and political role, and it may be argued that in no other society was literature the object of such keen public attention. Totalitarian systems established special relationships with art, whose creative results were used for propaganda purposes. Soviet literary texts are marked both by traces of state violence and, most often, the traces of efforts to evade it. History thus invades the very heart of art. Like the Soviet press, literature was constantly subjected to the manipulations of censorship, which sculpted a text into an instrument of propaganda. At the same time, literature generated immense interest among readers who were on a perpetual quest for "truth." Literature was the place to be. It was the ringside seat where a face-to-face encounter took place between the government and Soviet citizens who had learned how to dodge the direct blows of censorship and read between the lines.

Kuznetsov's *Babi Yar*, cut down by approximately one-third of its original length by Soviet censors, was read precisely this way: between the lines. Therefore, the taboo that was placed on the novel after the author's defection in 1969, its confiscation from libraries, and its expungement from history cost Soviet collective memory of Babyn Yar dearly. This work, so fundamental to Soviet literature and journalism, was kept out of the public eye until the collapse of the Soviet Union, that is, for more than twenty years. Of course, it was not the censored version of Kuznetsov's novel that was circulated in samizdat. It is problematic, however, even to compare the print run of this secretly circulated work with the print runs of publishing houses that had published this leading Soviet writer prior to his defection.

Kuznetsov left the Soviet Union precisely for the sake of *Babi Yar*, sewing photographic film containing the unabridged version of his novel

6 After its appearance in installments in the Moscow journal *Iunost'*, the novel was published separately: Anatolii Kuznetsov, *Babii Iar: roman dokument* (Moscow: Izd-vo Moloddaia Gvardiia, 1967).

into the lining of his light coat. He was convinced that he should publish the novel, the major work of his life, in its complete form, without any distortions.

Censored versions of *Babi Yar* very soon appeared in the West. The English translation was published in New York by The Dial Press, known for its many publications on eastern Europe. The translator Jacob Guralsky, through no fault of his own, misconstrued the innovative nature of the genre proposed by Kuznetsov. For example, the foreword, in which the author explained the meaning of the phrase "document in the form of a novel," was removed by censors from the Soviet edition. Using the Soviet censored version for his translation, Guralsky gave *Babi Yar* the subtitle, "a documentary novel."[7] What is more, the American edition was illustrated in the socialist-realist style, which was absolutely at odds with the tone of the book.

A French translation of the censored version of Kuznetsov's work was published in Paris by Français Réunis, a publishing house controlled by France's Communist party.[8] The book did not enjoy great success because even the pro-Soviet reading public was struck by the oddity of the novel, mangled by censorship, while anti-Soviet readers were loath even to look at the book. This was, after all, a time when the Iron Curtain divided space into socialist and capitalist spheres which were not just geographic; mentally it separated the free West from the enchained East.

### Testimonies about the catastrophe and belles lettres

The Western public heard about Kuznetsov because of his "non-return." On 8 August 1969, *Time* magazine published a three-page article about him, comparing his sensational defection to the West with the defection of Stalin's daughter just two years earlier. The article mentions *Babi Yar* only in passing as a book that "recounts the Nazi massacre of thousands of Russian Jews outside the author's native [city of] Kyiv and implies that

7 Anatoly Kuznetsov, *Babi Yar: A Documentary Novel*, translated by Jacob Guralsky (New York: Dial Press, 1967).

8 Anatoly Kouznetzof, *Babi Yar*, translated by André Robel (Paris: Editeurs Français Réunis, 1967).

many Russians were not displeased to see the Jews gone."[9] Kuznetsov attracted the West's attention more as an un- expected dissident who was exposing repressions on the other side of the Iron Curtain than as a direct eyewitness who had survived the occupation of Kyiv.

In August 1969 the British newspaper *The Sunday Telegraph* published an interview that Kuznetsov gave to David Floyd, a well-known London journalist, Slavist, and future translator of a new version of *Babi Yar.*[10] In the interview Kuznetsov made an open and naive admission about his links with the KGB and how he had been recruited by the Soviet secret police and agreed to cooperate with the Soviet secret police in order to be allowed to travel abroad. After this admission, a considerable number of people who had welcomed Kuznetsov with open arms turned away from him in disgust.

Today, with all the available historical research and testimonies about the Soviet period, we understand that reality was never so clear-cut. But in the late 1960s it was difficult for the public to distinguish between victim and de nouncer. Notions of black and white would finally merge, on the border, into an indistinct gray zone, where moral principles are forcibly erased or completely absent. Thus, in 1970, when Kuznetsov published his polyphonic work, now titled *Babi Yar: A Document in the Form of a Novel*, under his new, "free" name of A. Anatoli,[11] far less attention was paid to it than to the infamous 1969 interview in London's *Sunday Telegraph*.

Why do I use the word "polyphonic"? Because three voices coexist in this novel: the voice of a Soviet writer who, regardless of state antisemitism, decided to write about Babyn Yar (this text appears in an ordinary font); the voice of censorship, which gutted the novel and custom-fit it to the official version of history (this text appears in italics); and the voice of an author living in liberty in the West (this text appears within square

9 A. Anatoli, "I Could No Longer Breathe", interview in *Time* (New York), 8 August 1969, p. 30.

10 David Floyd, "Anatoly Kouznetsov: Interview," *The Sunday Telegraph* (London), 16 August 1969.

11 A. Anatoli (Kuznetsov), *Babi Yar: A Document in the Form of a Novel* (New York: Farrar, Straus and Giroux, 1970).

brackets). This is a trio of voices that often sound harmonious. Kuznetsov was the first writer to employ the italics-stratagem in order to permit a multilevel reading of the novel, reveal the traces of state violence within a literary text, and create a political palimpsest. The glasnost period of the late 1980s and early 1990s witnessed the phenomenon of the "return" of literature formerly banned in the Soviet Union, which was then on the point of collapse. The multiple-font scheme is also present in *The Complete Black Book of Russian Jewry*, to be discussed below.

In England Kuznetsov obtained access to works that had never been published in the Soviet Union. Comprehending how the twentieth century had changed literature, and coming to grips with the naive soap bubble in which Soviet literature was forced to exist, Kuznetsov came to the realization that he was not, after all, a writer. Therefore he did not write anything while in emigration. In 1979, two months before his fiftieth birthday and before his premature death, he declared: "Now that I have read real [books], I have realized that I have no reason to sully paper."[1212] For him, "real" works were written by the likes of Proust and Kafka, Borges and Faulkner. Therefore, he, Kuznetsov, was no writer; he was a witness, or, to be more precise, a witness who became a writer in order to bear testimony.

The twentieth century gave rise to a new type of literature, or anti-literature. This was literary testimony; testimony that has a literary character, a literary idea. And although the social practice of testifying through writing was born in the trenches of World War I and during the Armenian genocide, the real impetus for the development of this type of writing was given by the deportations of European Jews to Nazi concentration camps and the Holocaust. After the barbed wire surrounding Auschwitz was dismantled, three different but active figures appeared on the Western historical landscape: the Survivor, the Witness, and the Witness Who Became a Writer.

The Survivor tries to return and to adapt to a normal life, and sometimes – to forget everything and to be forgotten. By contrast, the Witness takes the word and heads for the podium in order to recount how he/

12 A. Anatoli, "Anatoly Kuznetsov, Wrote *Babi Yar*," *The Washington Post* (Washington, D.C.), 15 June 1979, p. 14.

she survived and to talk about those who did not. Finally, the Witness/Writer seeks to convey through literature what he/she has seen behind the barbed wire. Literary testimony seeks to express a situation that by its degree of brutality cannot be expressed, to give voice to it, to recreate it, and to enroot it in reality. When the language with which it became possible to describe the genocide emerged, the horror emerged as well.

Immediately after the liberation of the Nazi death camps, newspapers were flooded with texts written by witnesses. For example, over 140 memoirs of former prisoners were published in France between 1945 and 1948. For the most part, these were fact-based texts offering a straightforward, non-metaphorical description of the mechanism governing the concentration camp in action. They served as sources for historians and prepared society for the reception of texts written by writers acting as witnesses and of literature about the Holocaust, whose emergence required time and a text's artistic maturation.

The precursors of literary testimony are memoirs and diaries. However, a new dimension appeared in twentieth-century literary testimonies, which was not present in nineteenth-century memoirs. Owing to its narrative model, literary testimony is closer to a judicial act, somewhat like a speech before a court, than it is to the novelistic model of belles lettres. The goal of the "judicial act" that these witnesses employ lies in writing and publishing a detailed account of the extreme brutality of history to which they were witness and presenting it to the court of public opinion. They are driven by the thirst and imperative to tell their stories. And even if these texts cannot be attached to a set of written criminal charges, they are designed to ensure that the court of history will take place one day.

Therefore, literary testimony is characterized by a special type of narrative as well as by an author's own and inalienable experience and degree of inclusion in the described event. The genre affiliation of literary testimony is often declared by an author on a boundary level, and the text is created on the border of one genre overlapping into another. This attests to the author's experimental quest that underscores the ambivalent affiliation of the text with literature. Peter Weiss, author of the play *The Investigation: Oratorio in 11 Cantos* (1965), defines his work as "documentary theater." Kuznetsov accomplishes a similar quest for genre affiliation, the result of which is his "document in the form of a novel."

In the Soviet Union, Kuznetsov worked in conditions where thought was fettered and in complete isolation from the process that was taking place in Western literature "after Auschwitz." Nevertheless, he was able to create one of the first literary testimonies in the fullest sense of this term. He intuited the many specific features of this genre, including the role of literature in the transmission of a document. He proposed a document that was created with the aid of literature.

Kuznetsov was not in the ravine in Kyiv and, therefore, only an indirect wit ness of the genocide against the Jews. His work, however, blends a first-person account with the accounts of those who survived Babyn Yar. The Holocaust is conveyed from various positions, and its various stages are recreated. The Babyn Yar massacre is viewed through the perception of the author-witness Kuznetsov, but the actual shootings are recounted by Dina Pronicheva and the functioning of the Syrets concentration camp and efforts to destroy the traces of the Babyn Yar massacre are described by Volodymyr Davydov. Kuznetsov fills in the gaps in his knowledge by inserting testimonies and documents into the novel.

Kuznetsov's novel is fully sustained within the discourse of eyewitness testimonies. Written in the first-person, it is "I" who recounts the story and also offers readers an opportunity to hear a polyphony of voices. Furthermore, the author himself emphasizes the importance of testimony, constructing his novel to resemble a speech in court: "I am writing it as though I were giving evidence under oath in the very highest court . . ."[13] In the paragraphs in which he addresses the reader, we seem to sense the author's gestures on a physical level. This is very intuitive and non-literary writing, a type of narrative born out of an absolute impasse. Hence the intrusive and constant emphasis on credibility, a quality that did not exist in Soviet literature.

### The *Black Book*: a document that became literature

In 1943 Ilya Ehrenburg, one of the most influential Soviet writers during World War II, began working in collaboration with Vasilii Grossman on

13 Anatolii Kuznetsov, *Babii Iar: roman-dokument* (Moscow, 2014), p. 39.

*The Complete Black Book of Russian Jewry.*[14] The idea to write this book that recounts the catastrophe that befell Soviet Jews through the voices of witnesses – both those who survived and those who perished – was Ehrenburg's. It probably came to him when Albert Einstein suggested that the Jewish Anti-Fascist Committee compile a commemorative book about the Nazi destruction of the Jews and publish it in many languages. Like the Jewish Anti-Fascist Committee, created with Stalin's permission at the beginning of 1942 in order to convince its "Jewish brothers in the entire world" to come to the Soviet Union's assistance, Ehrenberg's book project initially received the Communist party leadership's approval. The literary commission overseeing the Soviet *Black Book* included a considerable number of well-known writers. Their task was to edit testimonies written by people who had either survived or were direct eyewitnesses of the Holocaust, as well as testimonies sent from the various places that were affected by the hurricane of genocide.

It is still a mystery who came up with the title of the book. In any case, the project is not the only "black book" in existence. A Romanian publication, *Cartea Neagra – Holocaust in Romania*, and its Polish counterpart, *The Black Book of Polish Jewry*, were compiled at the same time as the Soviet book project.[15] The Holocaust gave rise not only to a new kind of writing but also a new type of compilation. The phenomenon of "black books" continued to spread throughout the world during the second half of the twentieth century.[16]

The destruction of the Jews on Soviet territory also sparked a flood of testimonies, although their numbers did not compare to the volume

---

14 Ilya Ehrenburg and Vasily Grossman, eds., *The Complete Black Book of Russian Jewry*, translated by David Patterson (New Brunswick, NJ and London: Transaction Publishers, 2003).

15 Matatias Carp, ed. *Cartea Negra—Holocaust in Romania: Facts and Documents on the Annihilation of Romania's Jews, 1940-1944*, translated by Sean Murphy (Safety Harbor, FL: Simon Publications, 2001); Jacob Apenszlak, ed., *The Black Book of Polish Jewry: An Account of the Martyrdom of Polish Jewry Under the Nazi Occupation* (New York: Roy Publishers, 1943).

16 Stéphane Courtois, Nicolas Werth et al., *The Black Book of Communism: Crimes, Terror, Repression* (Cambridge, MA and London, England: Harvard University Press, 1999), translated from the original French edition: *Le livre noir du Communisme* (Paris: Robert Laffont, 1997).

produced in the West. Nevertheless, a large number of texts were written in the Soviet Union both during the Holocaust and immediately after the war ended. Their authors were people who had never before been tempted to take up their pens. Most of these texts belong to the factographic genre (diaries, letters, ghetto chronicles). Among them are poems, songs, and descriptive accounts, that is, works that display a pronounced tendency toward literature.

The testimonies that appeared during and immediately after the Holocaust is explained, in addition to the need to express oneself and give voice to pain, by Jewish religious culture, which requires that the memory of the Jewish people be preserved. In Judaism's sacred texts the Hebrew word *zakar* (remember) is an absolute commandment to preserve the memory of the Jewish people, who are in danger of extermination. The secularization of this tradition became noticeable already during the pogroms that swept through the Russian Empire in the late nineteenth and early twentieth centuries. That was a time when the poets S. Ansky and Perets Markish appealed to writers to preserve the Jewish world with the aid of written testimonies. Therefore, when the Holocaust began and when it was impossible to preserve life, the imperative "to record" and preserve memory became paramount. Before he was shot in a ravine near Riga in December 1941, the Jewish historian Simon Dubnow implored his friends to not forget and to write down their own stories.

But unlike Western witnesses who, upon returning from the camps, talked about Auschwitz openly and widely, Soviet witnesses were denied the right to testify publicly. The silence surrounding the genocide, as well as the repressions that targeted Soviet Jews during the period of postwar antisemitism, stripped them of the opportunity to publish their testimonies. Then, in keeping with an old Russian tradition, witnesses began writing to authors, whom they regarded as patrons and defenders of a downtrodden people. The largest number of letters containing testimonies were sent to Ilya Ehrenburg, whose table was literally covered with envelopes.

In the Soviet Union, a witness was forced to have a witness; in other words, there had to be a person who was narrating (the witness) and the one who was recording and then publishing (a writer). In the conditions of Soviet totalitarianism this kind of collaboration was mandatory. Since Holocaust survivors were denied the right to bear testimony openly and in full voice, writers felt a responsibility to convey the witness's painful experience in their own words by capitalizing on their popularity. *The Complete Black Book of Russian Jewry* is an illustrative example of this kind of collaboration between the witness and the writer.

Toward the end of the war, when Ehrenburg was compiling material, he had few testimonies specifically about Babyn Yar. Most of what he eventually published were obtained later in 1945, thanks in no small part to the Research Center of Jewish Culture in Kyiv, which was collecting testimonies about the Babyn Yar massacre.

In October 1944, during a meeting of the literary commission, Ehrenburg expressed concern that there was no text about the infamous "ravine of death." "Of the great tragic cities, Kyiv is missing in the first volume. . . . It is a crying shame that the city which acquired symbolic importance will not be in the first volume, but Kyiv might be done only if someone can travel there."[17] Shortly after the commission's meeting, Ehrenburg came across Lev Ozerov and convinced him to go to his native city Kyiv and write a text about Babyn Yar.

After arriving in Kyiv, Ozerov first had to suppress his pain and control his emotions because he had lost family members in Babyn Yar. Many years later Ozerov recalled his wartime visit to Babyn Yar:

> I saw a ditch. Not all the bodies had been burned, not all the bones had been ground into dust. We could not speak. A scene out of Dante. A sense of ca- tastrophe, destruction hung in the air. Eventually I found out all the details. . . . I questioned people who had been in hiding; very few of them are left. . . . But I especially looked for people who had managed to crawl out of the ravine from underneath a pile of bodies and not be killed by the Germans, who were checking to see if any people were still alive in the ravine. It was very difficult to write. Among those who perished were many people from my family. . . . It was difficult for those people who saved themselves to tell me everything; in recounting, they re-

17 Transcript of a meeting of the literary commission, 13 October 1944, Gosudarstvennyi Arkhiv Rosiiskoi Federatsii, Fond 8114, Opis 1, Delo 912, List 8.

> lived something that was unendurable. Literary talent was not adequate for this account; one had to be capable of sensing the move- ments of the human soul in these extreme conditions. I decided to stick to the facts.[18]

Thus, Ozerov decided intentionally to create a journalistic document about Babyn Yar, and to express his "I" in poetry. The text, placed at the outset of *The Complete Black Book of Russian Jewry*, has no author, because he has been erased or killed: "Old men and women walked along supporting each other. Mothers carried their infants in their arms or pushed them in baby carriages. People were carrying sacks, bundles, suitcases, and boxes. Children plodded along with their parents. Young people brought nothing with them. . . . The city fell silent."[19] The silence is maintained not just by the city. Its residents are silent, we do not hear their sighs or their sobs; we do not even hear the shooting going on in the ravine. Before us is a silent film; a reel of film turns on the projector, there is a constant change of frames, in which the same heroes are repeated but in various settings. The settings are truth, the reel is a documentary.

The first phrase/subtitle is short and self-contained: "German troops entered Kyiv on 19 September."[20] It appears against a gray background; it needs no illustration. The creaking of the movie projector; the first frame is a general long shot, without a close-up, of the looting and beatings taking place at the Bessarabka marketplace. In the second frame Nesia Elgert opens the doors of her apartment in a building located at 40 Saksahanskyi Street, and the beseeching glances of her entire large family are aimed at her. Elgert is one of the characters who is seen throughout the reel: remember her. Two days are skipped over. The third frame is 21 September. Nesia's father is taken away and she goes off to find him. The reel speeds up; from now on the frames are monotonous in their horror: a German commandant; insults; Jews being forced to dance; Jews who are falling down; Jews being beaten. On 22 September the explosions on Khreshchatyk Boulevard are in the background; in the foreground a

18 Lev Ozerov, "Pourquoi vous jetez du sable sur mes yeux?", interview in *Liberation* (Paris), 16 November 1995

19 Lev Ozerov, "Babi Yar," in Ehrenburg and Grossman, *Complete Black Book*, p. 7.

20 Ibid., p. 3.

German is running; he makes a slicing motion across his neck: "Partisans and Jews – *Kaput*."[21]

One could continue breaking down into frames Ozerov's entire text, which is fully sustained in this severe, cinematic-photographic style. It consists of gestures and clearly thought-out scenes. On the fifth day after the Germans' arrival in Kyiv, a Jew named Liberman appears in the frame. Hoping to save himself, he is pretending to be a Karaite named Libermanov. We are witness to his arrest and release, and then plunged into the epicenter of the explosions going off on Khreshchatyk Boulevard. We see smoke and fire, this time much closer. In the last frame of this fragment, we look, through Liberman's eyes, at a "scrap of blue sky" from inside a shelter fashioned by his wife: "In the evenings the sky was tinged with the crimson reflection of a gigantic fire. Put to the torch the Khreshchatyk was ablaze for six days."[22]

The second phrase/subtitle, which begins the next sequence, is an announcement to "the Jews of the city of Kyiv and [surrounding] vicinities." From now on it is difficult to keep track of the characters, as one is replaced by another. One of the many who perish in Babyn Yar is the composer Chaim Yampolsky; a violin and a conductor's baton appear briefly in the foreground. The maestro is led right out of a rehearseal. There is no music. Short, stabbing phrases break off the existence of people even before we have a chance to get a good look at them.

The third sequence is the murky dawn of 29 September. Amidst the flow of people, for a second we spot Nesia Elgert; it is a blurred, distant frame. Then Nesia reappears in a close-up. She is not wearing any clothes now; she is pressing her son Iliushka to her and moving toward the edge of the ravine, and then . . .

Writers and artists will spend a long time reflecting on how to recreate what came next. This dispute over creative devices for depicting mass death and fashioning pathos-filled descriptions of pre-death erotica continues to trouble critics. Annette Wieviorka, the French historian of the Holocaust, was the first to write about the flow of testimonies following the genocide: "What comes next – there is nothing to say and practically

21 Ibid., p. 3.

22 Ibid., p. 5.

nothing to write about. Not because of some difficulty or lack of literary talent or lack of words. Hereinafter is only a mass of people who are dying from suffocation by gas, who are then either buried or burned. Any account, whether literary or historical, involves development within time. Here time does not exist. . . . Here it lies in the repetition of quasi-'industrial' gestures that convey what cannot be conveyed. . . ."[23]

Ozerov had no time to reflect on how to depict what came next; he needed to write. The fundamental difference between literature and journalism lies precisely in the time dimension. Literature is aimed at the future; before it lies eternity. Journalism is aimed at the present time.

There is an obvious difference between urgent pressing testimony and testimony that is left for the future, for the next generations. Special, unconditional urgency is characteristic precisely of documentary, factographic testimony that must be brought to the immediate attention of the reader or listener. Literary testimony can also possess this urgency, but besides this, the interlocutor of literary testimony is found in the absolute future. A literary text has immortality in order to make an impression. Eternity is literature's time. Accordingly, a fundamental difference exists between the need to bear testimony (to transmit to others one's extreme experience of surviving in a historical cataclysm) and the desire to create a literary text.

*The Complete Black Book of Russian Jewry*, which began as a journalistic project, became a collection of "people's documents" and was slated for immediate publication. Its compilers, Ehrenburg and Grossman, realized that the Soviet authorities were deliberately suppressing information about the Holocaust of European Jewry. Once the book was released, they hoped to use it as a counterpoise to the outbreak of antisemitism that was rising to appalling heights in the Soviet Union. Yet, their hope of seeing the book in print began to evaporate almost immediately. Already in 1945 Ehrenburg abandoned the project, while his collaborators who continued working on the manuscript were aware that the book would not be published any time soon. At the same time they were cognizant of the fact that the book did not belong to the present time but to eternity. In 1948 the galleys of *The Complete Book of Russian Jewry*

---

23 Annette Wieviorka, *Déportation et génocide: entre la mémoire et l'oubli* (Paris: Hachette "Pluriel", 2003), p. 123.

were destroyed, the archives were sequestered, and soon a considerable number of writers were arrested.

In my view, *The Complete Black Book of Russian Jewry* belongs not just to history but also to literature, and in this way it differs from its Polish and Romanian counterparts. The collaboration of writers on the Soviet publication, the repressions to which they were subjected, the several layers of censorship that were applied to the testimonies, and the metaphorical survival of the book make it a literary work rather than a collection of fact-based testimonies.

Annette Wieviorka's remark about time frozen in the epicenter of destruction, the absence of developing action, and, as a result, the impossibility of conveying the Holocaust through an artistic story line pertains specifically to Auschwitz. In a gas chamber there is no time, and the people who survived are absent. In Babyn Yar there is time, and what happens next is conveyed by some heroes in Ozerov's unsigned text that opens the Soviet *Black Book*.

In that text Ozerov introduces the account of Olena Borodianska-Knysh, who escaped from the ravine with her four-year-old daughter. The account is brief but memorable for its happy ending. After crawling out of Babyn Yar, Olena moistens the lips of her dead daughter with dew, and she comes back to life. Many years later, in 1991, Liudmyla Borodianska wrote a testimony about Babyn Yar and the war. From this text we learn some details about her mother, Olena Borodianska, about whom we learn nothing from Ozerov's text except for her name and the complex trajectory of her survival after escaping from Babyn Yar.

The shootings in Babyn Yar were only the first in an endless string of trials and tribulations that included denunciations, flight, and survival. In testimonies, particularly those written after the collapse of the Soviet Union, the Babyn Yar shootings themselves most often occupy a vivid, morbid, but comparatively insignificant place. These texts resound with echoes of the pogroms, the Great Famine (Holodomor) of the early 1930s, and the Stalinist repressions. Layered over Babyn Yar are the horrors of the war and betrayal at the hands of trusted people and neighbors. The fear experienced during the period of postwar antisemitism rings out like a concluding chord.

In Borodianska's testimony all the lines of twentieth-century Soviet history intersect fantastically (and within the parameters of a single individual's life) and ominously. Before us is an intricate story unfolding over time, which is primed for a creative account. Liudmyla's mother was an elementary school teacher, and her father was a soldier. Her father was shot in 1937, during the Great Terror. Liudmyla has only a vague recollection of the first year of the war, since she was barely five years old. Her testimony is a calm, even-handed account of what she was told later about the war. But in the most dramatic moments, the child's confused awareness breaks into this serene account. The text quickens. One can feel breathing or even shortness of breath:

> Then I heard a woman's hysterical screaming. They were taking her fifteen-year-old daughter from her, but she was not giving her up; then they hit her with a buttstock, they probably killed her, and the Germans stripped her daughter and dragged her off somewhere. I became very frightened then and began pressing closer to mother. . . . Then I saw a German with a folding knife approaching an old man, he said something to him, then he grabbed him by the beard, and with all his strength began pulling him by the beard. The old man started yelling loudly, blood poured down his face, and the beard was left in the fascist's hands. Seeing this, I began to scream and cry, asking my mother to leave this bad place, where aunty and grandpa are being killed and we might be killed. Then they began rounding us up, and like a herd, we were driven ever closer to the precipice. It was already dark outside, and projectors were blazing all around.[24]

After little Liudmyla's sudden burst of awareness, once again we plunge into her equable account of spending several days in a cellar before being rescued by her mother's friend, Valia Litoshenko, who lived near Babyn Yar next to Saint Cyril's Church. Here the narrative is intersected by a new line that brings us to the future, the year 1961, when Litoshenko dies in the Kurenivka mudslide, her house swallowed up by the debris flowing down the steep hill from Syrets. Next comes a succinct descrip-

---

24 Liudmyla Borodianska, " Mesto smerti – Babyn Yar," in Boris Zabarko, ed., *Zhizn' i smert' v epokhu Kholokosta: svidetel' stva i dokumenty*, Vol. I (Kyiv, 2008), p. 184.

tion of a number of rescues, encounters with good people and evil ones, Ukrainian songs, and roundups of people who are sent to Germany to work as slave laborers. Suddenly, there is another projection into the future. During the Chornobyl nuclear accident Olena Borodianska, who was born in the village of Varovychi, finds herself in the Chornobyl Exclusion Zone until the entire family is resettled.

The text concludes with another vivid burst of childhood memories, in which the Germans bring Liudmyla's mother into a church, which they nail shut with boards and then douse with gas:

> I ran after them, shoeless, wearing only a shirt. I wanted to be with mama. But I didn't see her anywhere. And people were being led into the church that was secured on all sides by the Germans. They did not let me come closer. In my way stood a German, I remember him even today; he was so young. He looked both ways (to see if anyone was looking), tossed a candy to me (which consisted of slices). I took it. I'm standing in front of him and crying. I beg him to let me go to my mother, but he chases me away from the church.[25]

By some miracle, the mother Olena Borodianska survives, because, at the last minute, hostages were released from the church. In describing these events fifty years later, her daughter says that it is difficult for her to recall them and write about them, and her narrative breaks off here.

### "Me" in the face of history

Testimonies and memoirs often conclude, not with an admission of the narrator's fear of the past and helplessness when confronted by a blank piece of paper, but with words about how important it is for a survivor finally to enter the category of witness and leave his or her first-person account. Becoming a witness means finding one's voice and understanding one's "me" in history.

The detailed memoirs of Zakhar Trubakov begin and end with an emphasis on the paramount importance of finally writing and publishing that which could not be published earlier. Whereas Liudmyla Borodi-

25 Ibid., p. 191.

anska wrote her testimony at the request of the Ukrainian historian Borys Zabarko, it was Trubakov's decision to write about his experiences, although after an interval of fifty years.

A former prisoner of the Syrets concentration camp and member of Operation 1005, whose task was to exhume and burn the corpses of Babyn Yar, Trubakov recorded the main facts while his memory was still fresh, immediately after the liberation of Kyiv. Later he became friends with Anatoly Kuznetsov, who convinced Trubakov of the crucial need to describe everything that he had witnessed. By the time Kuznetsov's *Babi Yar* was published, the former concentration camp prisoner Trubakov knew that at the very first opportunity he would supplement the information and publish his notes. The opportunity arose only in 1990s, after he immigrated to Israel and began working on his autobiography. And even though he called his work a novel, *Taina Babego Yara* (The Secret of Babyn Yar), it is unquestionably the autobiography of a witness.[26] This is because Trubakov not only places events in their historical context, but also describes his experiences as a person that encountered the brutality of history.

At the heart of his story is not Babyn Yar but the authorial "me", torn and broken by Babyn Yar. Trubakov does not begin his account in September 1941, when the Germans entered Kyiv, but with a description of his childhood, youth, and married life. This is a personal and rather self-referential work. The word "Secret" is part of the title not only because Operation 1005 was supposed to turn the Babyn Yar massacre into a secret, but also because for the rest of the author's life the secret of what took place in the ravine in Kyiv continued to maim his life. His book is a depressing, painful, and belated confession of all the events that took place in the Syrets concentration camp. The executions, gallows, stench of corpses, and escape are refracted through the prism of the author's awareness and memory.

The narrator emerges with all his human frailities and unheroic fears. Nevertheless, despite the author's all too obvious desire to create a purely personal narrative, the reader senses some kind of unconscious "coding

26 Zakhar Trubakov, *Taina Bab'ego Iara* (Tel Aviv: Izd-vo Krugozor, 1997).

of suffering," and the softened descriptions, characterized by the Soviet style and Newspeak, are unmistakable. Suffering and the authorial "me" have been forced out of the book by Soviet clichés. It is clear that Zakhar Trubakov did not possess an adequate verbal palette or tools to convey a new self-awareness born of the Holocaust and World War II. A different language, other than that of the Soviets created to describe the happy socialist future, is necessary for recounting horrific death and stomach-turning survival. What is required is language that is maimed.

Autobiographical writing was not intrinsic to Russian and Eastern European culture, but rather was a product of the West's culture of individualism. In the 1930s, after the introduction of Socialist Realism, autobiography became the most disgraced genre in the Soviet Union. It was considered a bourgeois relic that overemphasized the moral worth of the individual and psychoanalytical self-discovery. Totalitarianism banned psychoanalysis and placed a ban on talking about one's "me" as a separate persona. Autobiographies would be supplanted by accusatory collective meetings focused on expulsions from the Communist party, while personal history would be supplanted by general history. A careful reading of *The Complete Book of Russian Jewry* reveals that it does not contain profound personal histories but moves continuously from personal catastrophe to historical catastrophe. The only thing left of the witness, as in the case of Olena Borodianska in Ozerov's essay, is a name and a brief account of survival. From the very outset, Soviet authors rejected desperate, personal testimonies that sounded like shouts, in which one can hear the rudiments of a "verbal spasm," to recall the words of the Bukovinian Jewish poet Paul Celan.

The testimony of Ida Belozovska was stored in the archives of the Jewish Anti-Fascist Committee. She did not go to Babyn Yar but was hidden by her Russian husband. Her entire family perished in Babyn Yar: mother, father, nieces, and nephews. She knew that they would be killed, but she was powerless to save them. Her five-page text is one sustained, confusing account of inner struggle, self-accusations, nightmares, and the constant desire to stop living – to disappear. The followings are fragments of her text not included in Ehrenburg and Grossman's *Black Book*: "I felt a strong desire to sprinkle my head, my whole self with ashes, to hear nothing, to be changed into dust. . . . What should I do? Why should I live? Have I got the right to live while those around me, who mean the most to me, have to die such a horrible, violent death? . . . I was buried, I no longer existed, I had disappeared from among the living."[27]

Soviet witnesses were not permitted to suffer, to describe experiences connected with physicality (pain, hunger, cold), or to expound on these questions that are so characteristic of people who have survived historical cataclysms. From the standpoint of Soviet ideology, experiences that presented an individual's unheroic conduct during the war were untypical and disgraceful, and thus under a strict taboo. Death was depicted as sacrifice, illness as a trial, and physicality was either absent or the body streamed with myrrh, like Christian relics. The official Soviet discourse sought to propel positive characters to the foreground; it demanded the transmission of an exclusively constructive message and abstention from the tragic. The principles and aspirations to create such a description of the Holocaust are in absolute contradiction to the essence and substance of the act of bearing testimony, which is always spontaneous and impulsive, reflects the destruction and death of the "Me", and portrays the loss of all that is human, as well as horrific death.

Western testimonies written by survivors of Auschwitz are distinguished by their specific narrative mode. The survivor, switching throughout his or her account from "Me" to "We", seeks to recount everything on behalf of everyone. In the text, s/he talks not only in his/her own name but also in the name of those who did not return, who did not survive. Prisoners of concentration camps and ghettos knew that someone had to return in order to bear witness and to say "We" on behalf of those who can no longer speak. For example, the three-act tragedy written by the former prisoner of Auschwitz Charlotte Delbo is entitled *Qui rapportera ces paroles?* (Who Will Carry Forth These Words?). But those who survived Babyn Yar encountered a different "We", one that was grand and patriotic, and imposed by Soviet literature and the official discourse. This heroic "We", the victors, imposed by the Soviet state,

27 Ida Belozovska, "My Life in the Occupied Kiev," in Joshua Rubenstein and Ilya Altman, eds., *The Unknown Black Book: The Holocaust in the German-Occupied Soviet Territories* (Bloomington, IN, 2008), pp. 53-59.

supplanted the individual voices of victims who remained tormented by questions and feelings of guilt.

In the Soviet Union, the "We" that survived or disappeared in the ravine could not break through the official vision of history; it was proclaimed as uninteresting for the future. The prohibition against people bearing witness and the loss of the right to express one's tragic voice precluded the transformation of the survivor into a witness, and the witness into a writer. "We", which had a sincere desire to bear testimony and might have emerged (something clearly evident in the texts sent to the compilers of *The Complete Book of Russian Jewry*) was crushed by propaganda and Soviet epic literature. These texts were not read or used. For decades, the weak voices recounting, through their "Me", the horrible death that befell "We" remained buried in the archives. The amputation of the role of witness took place in Soviet society. Thanks to its very non-Soviet narrative, "confessionality," and physicality, Kuznetsov's novel won the admiration of Soviet readers. Ultimately, the Soviet censor, who whitewashed passages about collaborationism, the Holodomor, and the Great Terror, was unable to eliminate the "Me" crushed by history from the novel.

In the late 1980s and early 1990s, alongside the political movements of *perestroika* and *glasnost*, the Soviet Union experienced an awakening of historical awareness and thus finally entered the era of the witness. Soviet society began coming out actively against ideology and demanding the demystification of history. It turns out that nothing had been forgotten, and testimony as a personal document finally found its true worth. The collapse of the Soviet Union was essential to the emergence of testimony that recounts the collapse of "Me" in the twentieth century.

## CHAPTER 8

# Babyn Yar as Oral History

*Gelinada Grinchenko*

> I am not a historian, but I was born and grew up in Kyiv,
> and even met people who lived through the occupation.
> One granny told me that it was not just
> Jews who were shot in Babyn Yar;
> there are also Russians and Ukrainians there, anyone you like,
> but only the Jews were shot because they were Jews.
> That is the essence of the Holocaust.
> Incidentally, this granny was not a historian either
> and did not have documents corroborating her words;
> she simply saw this with her own eyes, and I believe her. That's all.
>
> *A post on Facebook*

Oral histories, that is, audio or video recordings of survivor and witness accounts of the shootings that took place in the ravine in Kyiv known as Babyn Yar during World War II, occupy a singular place among documents containing accounts of this mass murder. The process of collecting such oral histories intensified immediately after the collapse of the Soviet Union, as it was impossible to undertake such work during the existence of the Soviet state.

Oral history as a historical research method is predicated on sincere, frank, and honest communication between a researcher and a witness of an event. The main goal of such research is to obtain personal experience, private recollections, and the witness's subjective attitude to what he/she has lived through. Given the imposed, "ideologically correct," hence one-sided understanding of events pertaining to the war that was proposed in Soviet times, personal recollections were inevitably tailored to fit the generally acceptable version. Any divergence between the "official" and individual points of view put paid to the publication of the latter type of accounts.

The very subjectivity of a personal recollection, a private memory of a person, and his/her personal assessment of experienced events, distinguishes oral histories from "classic" paper documents. Furthermore, oral histories are usually recorded within a certain period of time after the event that has been experienced—and sometimes long after it. This interval of time may dim some recollections but not others. The interval also allows for the saturation of memories with experience that has been gained over a lifetime, and blends a person's personal knowledge with that proposed by the mass media, literature, cinematography, and the like. Thus, according to contemporary oral historians, even though witness accounts may add little to the study of the factological aspect of an event being studied, they offer something different: the subjective importance of a given event to the narrator, as well as the unique emotions and experiences of a person who has lived life in history.

The narrators of accounts that were recorded after the collapse of the Soviet Union experienced the tragedy of Babyn Yar in various ways. Stored in the collections of various research institutions are interviews with Jews who managed to escape being shot, often at the very last minute, and with people who were heading to the ravine but, for some reason, did not arrive, lost track of their family members en route, and then came back home. There are interviews recorded with Jews who were not in Kyiv at the time of the shootings, but who lost their relatives and close friends in Babyn Yar. These collections also contain numerous oral histories of non-Jewish residents of Kyiv who knew about the mass executions because they had lost friends and neighbors. There are interviews with people who, risking their own lives, helped to hide Jews throughout the Nazi occupation and therefore saved their lives. Such individuals would eventually be recognized as the Righteous Among the Nations and the Righteous of Babyn Yar. Finally, there are recollections of Kyiv residents who recount the events of 29–30 September 1941 not from their personal experience but mostly from rumors that they recreate on the level of retold testimonies that have now become part of a collective, rather than personal, memory.

Oral histories typically feature testimonies about the Babyn Yar tragedy, which differ in terms of content. As this article will demonstrate, witnesses have different ways of recalling the period before the war and reporting how well or little informed they were about the persecution of the Jews in Europe. They recreate in various ways the text of the order that preceded the dreadful events of 29–30 September 1941, and offer differing descriptions of the procession of people who made their way to Babyn Yar. Even though the general, factological picture created by the accounts of those who escaped Babyn Yar is undisturbed, their stories differ from each other. This very dissimilarity constitutes the main value of the recorded accounts, precisely because they contain uniquely personal interpretations and private observations as well as subjective assessments. All this in its totality contributes to an understanding of the course of a concrete event and general historical phenomenon from the perspective of the memories and feelings of their direct participants and witnesses.

Two separate subjects are highlighted in this chapter: recollections of life before the war and the beginning of the war; and accounts about two specific days, 29 and 30 September, on the part of people who managed to return from Babyn Yar. I have included numerous quotations because oral history embodies, first and foremost, the meanings and content that belong to those who speak, whether the eyewitness, participant, observer, or contemporary of a certain event.[1]

**Do you remember how the war started?**

Practically every interview begins with the start of the war and the first encounters with the Germans. After the symbolic words, "On 22 June at exactly four o'clock," the narrators recall what they were doing and what they were feeling. Almost all of them learned that war had broken out that morning or sometime during the day; those who heard explosions

1 All quotations in the chapter are taken from materials held in the United States Holocaust Memorial Museum (hereafter: USHMM), Washington, D.C., and the USC Shoah Foundation Institute.

say they thought they were part of some maneuvers or training exercises. One person came home late at night from the theater or a walk and was still sleeping soundly in the morning; someone else was getting ready for the opening of the central stadium and only found out that the war had begun because the opening was cancelled; another person heard the terrible news on a streetcar while running errands in the city; someone else saw the first first to be wounded; another did not understand what was happening for some time.

For many narrators, the immediate awareness of the war was triggered by the announcement of general mobilization and the subsequent evacuation. They recall the great impact that the much-repeated government propagandistic slogan had on the city's residents: "Kyiv was and will be Soviet." Thanks to this, most the residents did not panic and remained in the city. Thus, their astonishment and fear was all the more devastating once they realized that the Soviet military was abandoning Kyiv.

For many narrators, the German arrival in Kyiv on 17 September became fixed in their memories because that day was marked by chaos and the "shameless" (to quote the eyewitness Serhii Ivanov) looting of stores:

> As soon as the question arose that the Germans are approaching Kyiv and that Kyiv might be surrendered, people began looting stores. This looting was shameless. We, young boys, were not ready for this. But adults looted; men and women. Past the bridge in our area there was a huge department store. And we simply went to see how everything that could be dragged out was being hauled off. Not just goods but furniture, too. People were carrying everything out of all grocers' shops, stores, counters. This was right before the Germans arrived. This picture is deeply engraved [in my memory]. [2]

Another eyewitness, Viktor Berezin, provides more details: "The Central Department Store was so looted that it was terrible to see; windows and storefronts were smashed and everything was dragged out of there; people fought among themselves, they grabbed things from each other,

2 Serhii Ivanov, USC Shoah Foundation Institute, interview code no. 47287–55, 18 August 1998, Kyiv, Ukraine.

rags."[3] Kostiantyn Miroshnyk devotes a considerable part of his eyewitness testimonies to these events:

> The Red Army left. I don't know where the German troops are. . . . In Kyiv were no authorities. . . . Wide-scale public destruction began, destruction of shops in the city center, including various department stores. Well, when I ran over there, I saw people dragging and grabbing everything. It was awful. Simply a horror. I, too, slipped into the city's Central Department Store. Everyone was taking something; they were carting [stuff] on wheelbarrows and carts, [or] simply with their hands. I got hold of two shoe brushes that I grabbed somewhere, I ran outside, opposite a grocery shop. I'm thinking: 'Grab something here too!' After all, food is very important. I ran into the grocery store, where everything had already been raked out and looted; I found a can of food and threw it into my knapsack. Then I went home. Night fell on the city. I woke up in the morning and, like always, I ate something and rushed outside to find out what was happening now. A neighbor met me on the street and said: 'Why are you walking around here? The Germans are on Khreshchatyk Boulevard!' 'What do you mean, the Germans? There was no battle, there was no attack, there was nothing!' 'Just go and look.' I approached the city center and there, where the street slopes steeply downward from the Golden Gates and to the Khreshchatyk, I could see from a distance that some kind of columns are coming, marching. . . . People were standing on the sidewalks on both sides of the street. Right down the center [the Germans are marching] with such an easy gait, beautifully dressed, pompously. Well, I don't mean pompously; but, in any case, this was an army that was marching. There were officers, some on horseback and in cars. This was a parade of troops in very good form. Well-fed, clean, shaved, they entered Kyiv. There was a variety of moods among the people. Me, I was just watching. There were some who were very happy about this. And some German officers were on horseback, not just in cars, which is why girls, women, and men threw flowers that they had brought at them. The Germans were welcomed ecstatically. But I also saw gloomy people. Locals. They were gazing so gloomily at all of this . . .[4]

3 Victor Berezin, USC Shoah Foundation Institute, interview code no. 45743–55, 12 June 1998 Kyiv, Ukraine.

4 Kostiantyn Miroshnyk, USC Shoah Foundation Institute, interview code no. 21998–13, 31 October 1996, Jerusalem, Israel.

After describing the Germans' entry into Kyiv, the eyewitness accounts become denser, as though compressed in time. They often mention, in passing and without any details, the first attempts to recreate normal life under the occupation, the destruction of Khreshchatyk Boulevard which was mined with explosives, and the rumors that the Jews and communists had done this. One interviewee suggests that the Jews were eventually accused not of blowing up the Khreshchatyk, but of damaging the hoses bringing up water from the Dnieper River to put out the fires. In fact, this episode—the destruction of Khreshchatyk Boulevard and the accusations leveled against the Jews—serves as a prologue to recollections of the Babyn Yar tragedy, which its narrators most often begin with the notorious order commanding the Jews of Kyiv to assemble on Monday, 29 September 1941, at 8:00 a.m.

**"There is an order, it must be obeyed. We have to get ready"**

Narrators recreate the text of this order in a variety of ways: some verbatim, others introduce mistakes, still others are completely wrong about the date, place, and goal of the roundup. Reactions to the order also vary. Kateryna Kovalenko, for example, talks straightaway about a bad omen: "All Jews are to appear with their belongings and appear by order there and there. And the street is terrifying, a feeling of some sort of pogrom."[5] Some narrators, like Vira Lukanina, who were young when the order was issued, nevertheless remember it and recall the experiences of their family members.

> And so, one day mama was walking and saw an announcement stating that all the Jews of the city of Kyiv must take their valuables and appear at 9:00 at the corner of Melnikova Street. Mama wanted to tear down this announcement, but someone grabbed her and said: 'What are you doing? Do you want to end up at the Gestapo?' So mama continued on. After coming home, she told us everything. We wanted to do something to help.[6]

5 Kateryna Kovalenko, USC Shoah Foundation Institute, interview code no. 38314, 25 November 1997, Kyiv, Ukraine.

6 Vira Lukanina, USC Shoah Foundation Institute, interview code no. 36456–48, 1 September 1997, Kyiv, Ukraine.

A stark note of anxiety runs through the recollections of Valentyna Berezliova, who was an adult when the German occupation began. Throughout all the years spent "under the Germans," she hid her future husband in her apartment. (They finally married, but not until 1974 because, according to Berezliova, superstitions about what she had lived through prevented her from agreeing to an official marriage before then).

> In the evening I went to Volodymyrska Street to get water and read a blue-colored poster, the kind they used to wrap a lump of sugar. It said: 'All Jews residing in Kyiv and its vicinities are to appear with their valuables and warm clothing at 7:00 at the Jewish cemetery.' I no longer remember how I made my way home, and instantly told my husband everything. . . . I will tell you right now that this was around the 28th; the 29th was Judgment Day, and everyone was supposed to go on the 29th. They wrote this dazzling, beastly announcement in less than a day.[7]

From the early morning of 29 September people began gathering on the street indicated in the announcement. They were Jews, who came with their entire families; with them were some Ukrainians and Russians who were helping those who needed assistance by carrying their belongings or transporting them. Witnesses who saw the procession of Jews on 29 September mostly emphasize that the assembled people did not know or understand where they were going and what would happen later. From the sidelines, it resembled a mass resettlement operation. In the words of Zoia Popova:

> here comes a women hitched to a small cart, a two-wheeled cart. [She was] a young woman; walking next to her is a small child holding her by the hand; on the other side is an elderly woman. And sitting on the cart is an old man, there are some things wrapped in a bundle, but what caught my eyes was a broom! They were bringing a broom with them. This means that people really believed that they would be transported somewhere. And that's the kind of domestic 'treasure' they were bringing with them; and so, we reached Hohol Street, and from every alleyway

7 Valentyna Berezliova, USC Shoah Foundation Institute, interview code no. 38234–48, 5 September 1997, Kyiv, Ukraine.

and from every street people were gradually merging into this crowd.[8]

Some narrators cite conversations that took place either within their own families or a neighboring Jewish family on the eve of 29 September. The conversations make it clear that the Jews of Kyiv also figured that the ominous order about "all the Jews of the city" had to do with further resettlement. "There is an order, it has to be obeyed. We have to get ready," says Kostiantyn Miroshnyk, recalling the words of his grandfather, after which the old man told Kostiantyn's grandmother and aunt to gather up their belongings.[9] People tried to take all their valuables, like jewels, dinner sets, and fancy dresses that a mother had recently sewn for her daughter. For the impending journey the mother dressed her in both of them, with an old dress on top, because she thought that in the new place of settlement it would be necessary to barter them for something.

Vira Lukanina mentions all the above in her interview and then recounts a moving story about the Chudnovska family. This newlywed couple—Olena, who was Ukrainian, and Marko, who was Jewish—were expecting a child. They went to Babyn Yar together and perished there.

> My mother went to see her niece Lialia [dim. of Olena—Marta], a Ukrainian language teacher. She went to her house, she had a husband named Mara, they had completed their studies at the pedagogical institute at the same time. He looked like Pushkin. Lialia was expecting. [Olena's] mother, Hanna Oleksandrivna, and Tania lived with them. Tania was saying: 'Don't go, Lialia, don't go! And Mara, don't go either! I will bring you to the countryside in Makariv raion. People will hide you. Let's go!' Mara said: 'Well, Lialia, we won't go anywhere! No one will take us! Are the Germans really such barbarians? I am a scholar, I'm a philologist. See how many books I have! Will I really abandon all this?' This was before Babyn Yar. But he already realized that there was nothing more to say, and they simply began to get ready. Hanna Oleksandrivna tells Lialia to stay because she is not a Jew, but Lialia could not abandon her

---

8 Zoia Popova. USHMM, interview code no. RG-50.575*0046, 1 August 2008, Kyiv, Ukraine.

9 Kostiantyn Miroshnyk. USC Shoah Foundation Institute, interview code no. 21998–13, 31 October 1996, Jerusalem, Israel.

> husband, and that's why she was going. And Tania, and Mara, and Lialia went to Babyn Yar. . . . Lialia went with them, they ran into their friends. There was a lawyer; in general, all the young people. They were walking and joking. It was difficult for people to believe that other people were capable of such savagery. . . . A German shoved Lialia and said: 'Go away, you Russian woman!' She said something to him in Hebrew, and he let her through. We never saw them again.[10]

Recollections of young people who, in keeping with all the laws of nature and the world, should have lived and prolonged their family lines, are shared by Nelli Baianova. In her memory the dreadful existential discordance between blossoming youth and inevitable, very sudden death was forever etched: "I must tell you that everyone went: old people, children. But for some reason the memory of one couple has remained with me my whole life. She was a very young girl of astonishing beauty, he a young fellow. Either they had gotten married recently or they were brother and sister; they were pushing a baby carriage. I remember their faces even now; they affected me extraordinarily."[11]

But despite feelings of foreboding and pleas to disregard the German order, the people who came to see off their Jewish friends or who were simply watching the procession were generally convinced that a resettlement operation was underway. Hence, they discussed the possible destinations of their resettlement. In the oral histories that I analyzed, the two places that were mentioned most often were Palestine (some narrators say "Israel") and Russia (the phrase used is "to Stalin"). It is interesting to note that, in reply to the interviewer's question to Zoia Popova, "Is this what you think right now? Did you hear this from someone?" she said: "No, we were talking about this among ourselves, we rejected it outright

---

10 Vira Lukanina, USC Shoah Foundation Institute, interview code no. 36456–48, 1 September 1997, Kyiv, Ukraine. This story, written by Nina Kryvoruchko, was published in the newspaper *Ievreis'ki visti* (Jewish News), nos. 17–18 (253–254) in September 2002. Olena Chudnovska was the sister of Kryvoruchko's maternal great-grandmother. See http://2queens.ru/Articles/Besedka-dlya-Romantikov-Zapiski-romantika/Mark-i-Elena-ili-Pravda-o-vernosti.aspx?ID=62

11 Nelli Baianova. USC Shoah Foundation Institute, interview code no. 44901–0, 31 May 1998, Kyiv, Ukraine.

because of the warm clothing; why do you need warm clothing in Palestine?; this means that they will be sent to Russia."[12] People hypothesized about a ghetto and some notional places, where the Jews would be forced to work. Here the witnesses allude to the German penchant for practicality.

People who witnessed the procession of deportees recall seeing many people accompanying the Jews (Ukrainians and Russians), who, unaware of the end goal of this march, had come to help their Jewish friends and neighbors carry their belongings or simply to say goodbye to them. According to the narrators, the crowd of people consisted mostly of women and their children, and elderly individuals. Among the latter were many old people who, for various reasons, had not been evacuated together with their families to the Soviet East, but had stayed behind in Kyiv. Kostiantyn Miroshnyk recalls the following incident: "Everyone who was leaving asked and begged their grandfather, grandmother, Aunty Rokhl: 'Come with us!' And the old man would refuse. First of all, he said: 'All of you are going, we are staying, and we will look after your apartments, your property.' Then, he said: 'Where will you take me if I agree? Where will I go? And will there be a synagogue where you bring me? You don't know. No, you go and I will stay.'"[13]

Terrible things happened to the elderly even before they reached Babyn Yar. Valentyna Berezliova recounts a dreadful story about her neighbor, an elderly Jewish woman named Busel, who asked the narrator to help her with her things on the morning of 29 September:

> At that very moment Busel knocks at my door and says: 'Valia, you promised to accompany me.' I say: 'Yes.' I left with her, she took a small bundle of things, she left all her belongings in her apartment. Where would she go, this old granny, who was 78 or 79 years old? I reached the grocery store with her; you know it, it's the 'Morozov Building'; every Kyivite knows it, on the corner of Volodymyrska Street and another street, I forget. And she fainted. A stocky German was walking by, some lady with

12 Zoia Popova. USHMM, interview code no. RG-50.575*0046, 1 August 2008, Kyiv, Ukraine.

13 Kostiantyn Miroshnyk. USC Shoah Foundation Institute, interview code no. 21998–13, 31 October 1996, Jerusalem, Israel.

> him saw everything, how these unfortunate, exhausted, maimed people are moving. He takes out a pistol and kills her right in front of me. Can you imagine what I saw? I saw this with my very own eyes![14]

Then the narrator pronounces awful words that reveal the horrific essence of the tragedy that took place several hours later:

> She was gone in a second, and it was very good that this happened because if she had gone to Babyn Yar, they were not shooting and killing there; they were covering wounded people with earth, this earth there was moving from blood and from everything. Not all of them were killed; they could not kill them all; a machine gun was standing there, they could have killed everyone. So, it is very good that she was killed that way. Later I thought that with this one shot maybe God saved her from all her sufferings.[15]

**"I was thinking at the time . . . . that I was going to my death"**

Of all the recorded oral histories about Babyn Yar, the interview with Genia Batashova is one of the longest. It consists of eight parts, each lasting one hour. The recording was made on 30 April 1992 as part of an Israeli documentation project, and three years later was sent to the archives of the United States Holocaust Memorial Museum in Washington, D.C. Batashova's account begins with a recollection of her childhood and life with her parents, twin sister Liza, and younger brother Grisha. She recalls the Ukrainian famine of 1933, her schooling, and several stories about her twin sister, for whom she was often mistaken. The narrator shifts very soon to the early days of the war and devotes the main part of her account to recreating the events of 29 September. What follows is the story of how she was rescued from Babyn Yar together with a neighbor girl, Mania Palti; how she was hidden by neighbors; and then how she fled eastward from Kyiv. At the end of the interview Batashova talks about her return to Kyiv, postwar life, her two husbands, and immigrating to Israel.

---

14 Valentyna Berezliova. USC Shoah Foundation Institute, interview code no. 38234–48, 5 September 1997, Kyiv, Ukraine.

15 Ibid.

Batashova begins her account of Babyn Yar with a recollection of her neighbor, Mykola Soroka,[16] or "Uncle Kolia," as he was called. A few days after the Germans entered Kyiv, he revealed to Genia's mother that he was a member of an underground organization. On the eve of the massacre in Babyn Yar he warned her family not to obey the Germans' order on 29 September but to wait until he verified if there was impending danger. Jumping ahead, I must mention that it was Soroka who, in saving the girls, sent Genia and Mania out of Kyiv after they returned home on 29 September, and explained the details of their escape route from Kyiv.

Batashova's account of the evening before 29 September is quite lengthy. She recalls that her mother was crying nonstop, repeating to her children that "I did not safeguard you." The neighbors brought some food for the road, and took Genia and her sister to spend the night at their house. "I have been tormented my whole life, and I cannot forgive myself for going," the narrator states. "Well, maybe because I did not believe that such a horror could happen, that this would be the last night of our life together. Perhaps I did not understand this? Still, I have reproached myself my entire life for having done something very wrong. To this day I don't know what my mother's last night was like. This has tormented me my whole life."[17]

On the morning of 29 September Batashova's mother and her three children, together with Mania Palti's mother and her three children, were at home waiting for "Uncle Kolia." Genia's mother began to fret because it was long past 8:00 a.m., so they decided to go by themselves: the four members of the Batashov family and the four members of the Palti family. They set off along Turgenev Street, then reached Artem Street, where there were a lot of people already, according to Batashova. The two-family procession stopped near the Lukianivka marketplace and sat down to rest. Mykola Soroka caught up with them there, and once again he begged them not to go but wait for further news from him. But the two mothers were getting nervous, and they decided to go on with their

16 Mykola Arseniiovych Soroka, b. 1899, city of Kyiv, a carpenter employed by Bread-Baking Plant No. 3. He was a member of an underground group helping to free prisoners from jails. He was murdered by the Gestapo on 6 January 1943.

17 Genia Batashova. USHMM, interview code no. RG-50.120*0008, 30 April 1992.

children. There is a striking detail in this scene, when the families are resting. Batashova points out that while they were sitting there, some people rushed up and said that the first convoy of people had already gone. When she heard this, her sister Liza began checking her belongings and became terribly sad that she had forgotten to bring salt from home: How could you set out on a journey without salt?

Continuing her account, Batashova says that after they passed Pugacheva Street, she did not see any more wagons; people were going on foot. At the end of this street she saw a fence. "Why did we not hear the shots there, beyond Pugacheva Street?" the narrator asks herself.

> I can't understand. . . . In my opinion we should have heard the shots. But we did not hear them yet. Well, it's obvious that they had planned everything because if people had heard. . . . So, we walked a short distance from Pugacheva Street, and there on both sides stood anti-tank hedgehogs. . . . with a passageway down the middle. We could walk to this passageway. We could still move toward this, toward these antitank hedgehogs. We could turn around. And a lot of things were already scattered next to these antitank hedgehogs. Farther on there was nothing, but right in front of this, people were already throwing down such heavy, portable things. And I remember this one episode. Some Russian came there and was choosing clothing for himself. He picked up one article, looked at it, put it down, looked [some more]. He was putting something aside. It was disgusting. And from out of the crowd, a Jew, a man came up to him. They got into an argument. He struck him. But we went on. Something began back there, but I don't know how it ended.[18]

Batashova recalls that standing next to the passageway were guards who were not letting people go back. A little farther away, at the entrance to the passageway, the narrator saw sacks into which you had to throw documents, money, and valuables. They threw in their documents and some money; they did not have any family valuables with them. Then they stepped onto the road alongside of which trees were growing in even rows. It was here on this road that they heard shots and realized what was happening.

---

18 Ibid.

For Batashova this road represented the gates of hell, a place of no-return where a horrific fate awaited the people heading to Babyn Yar. On this road she saw policemen and Germans, but she speaks mostly about the Germans:

> There were Germans here: And they were standing with dogs, with submachine guns, and clubs. At this point they were not standing on ceremony. They drove us like cattle. I always use this word because no other word will do. They drove us, those who were walking, properly—with clubs. And if people stopped, they set the dogs [on them]. . . . Mama was crying so much that I became rigid. I remember mama and Liza crying, but Grisha and I were not. I was simply rigid. If I tell you what I was thinking at the time [*sic*]. I realized that I was going to my death. And I thought: my teeth will never hurt again. I suffered a lot, my teeth often hurt me. This was the only way I could help myself. Crying, mama somehow tried the whole time. I remember her hands, the whole time she tried . . . to protect us with herself. The whole time. . . . She cried so much along the way, she cried so much. And then, this road was not a long one. On this road people were already tearing out their hair. And there was such shouting![19]

The road led to a small square measuring approximately 250 by 150 meters. This little square was already Babyn Yar, she emphasizes. At the end of the square were chutes with artificial gangways, behind which was "death, they were already shooting there, machine guns were clattering away uninterruptedly."[20] There was an incessant clamor, people were rushing about, wailing, they tried to dodge the blows and get away from the dogs. In this particular portion of her testimony, the narrator emphasizes that resistance was no longer possible. This is the only part in the interview where Batashova digresses from her straightforward account and makes an emotional declaration in defense of those terrorized and confused people, who could not fathom what was going on or put up resistance because they had no way to do so:

---

19 Ibid.

20 Ibid.

> People often ask me: 'How is it possible that people did not put up resistance?' You know, I have lived a long time, I turned fifty after Babyn Yar, and I have been encountering this question literally my whole life. First of all, this is a provocation; it was said that the echelons are already departing, and people were going around, special people. Second, it was known that there is really a railway line there. But once people entered these passageways, they were in a vice, they were already surrounded on all sides. And it was already dangerous . . . especially once they came onto this road with trees; it was even risky to turn your head. A wrong move here and you might get a bullet or a dog and a club.
>
> You know, I feel responsible before those who perished so that they are not accused of not having resisted. They absolutely could not put up resistance. And you know, I feel like shouting that to the whole world. They could not, they were deceived, and once they realized [it], they had no possibility even to turn their head. This is my answer. Especially here, in Israel; I was in Jerusalem for the commemoration of the fiftieth anniversary [of Babyn Yar], and I spoke about this, too. Because I want to defend them. I bow to the memory of not only my family, I bow to the memory of all those who perished there. And I want people to understand, so that it does not occur to anyone to say [that], so that not even a shadow will fall on the memory of these people. Because they are not guilty; they did not have a chance to resist. And, after all, who was there? Who could have put up resistance there? Do you think there were young men there? There were children, old people, people past middle age. The bulk was at the front, there were sickly people there.[21]

After these remarks, the narrator resumes her description of the small square located in front of the execution site. Again and again she mentions the shouting and the sound of people being beaten. She says that the Germans were tearing people's clothes off and constantly driving them in the direction of the entryways. Genia and her family came into the square together, but suddenly she saw a swathed baby lying on the ground and screaming. "Her mother probably dropped her, could not go with her little ones to the entryway. The baby was screaming so loudly, so loudly; I turned toward it, and right then and there a German or a po-

---

21 Ibid.

liceman came up and smashed this baby's head in with a cudgel. When I saw this, I was gripped by such horror that I fainted."[22]

Batashova cannot remember how long she was unconscious, but when she came to, her family was no longer beside her. "I was in such despair that I was going to die alone, without them." She began running around, looking for her family. She was beaten and driven forward, but she was nimble and managed to wriggle out. Suddenly she spotted her mother and Grisha. She watched Grisha running up to a policeman, grabbing him by the arm, and pleading with him: "Uncle, save me, I didn't do anything wrong!"[23] The policeman was pulling away, and Genia was now hanging onto his arms, also begging to be saved. But the policeman shoved them and struck Grisha and Genia. Genia fainted again. When she came to, her family had disappeared again. She began running around the square and suddenly spotted a neighbor girl with whose family her own family had set out on the road to Babyn Yar. It was Mania Palti, who was already undressed, also alone, without her family.

Mania was a beautiful blonde, while Genia had light brown hair and did not consider herself to look Jewish. This circumstance led the girls to embark on an action that saved their lives. They decided to approach a couple of policemen and tell them that they were Russians and that, while accompanying some Jews, had entered the passageways by accident, out of mere curiosity. The first policeman chased them away with the words, "I saw that you are not Jewesses, but now that you've come, stay." But the second policeman, "Very well, I will try to help you."[24]

Batashova recalls that they could not believe their luck. In recounting her miraculous rescue, she says that it was as though everything that was taking place around her was not happening; it's as if she were recounting someone else's story, not her own. That's how incredible the scene was. The policeman led the girls to some Germans standing next to a passenger car, and began explaining in broken German that the two girls were sisters. One of the Germans asked them their names. Genia replied that her name was Batashova, but for some reason Mania used the name of

22 Ibid.

23 Ibid.

24 Ibid.

another woman, Uliana Chernetska, who lived in the same building as Mania's family. The German began snarling and yelling that they were not sisters, that they were lying. But Genia suddenly realized what was happening and said that they were cousins. Then the Germans asked them where they lived and ordered them to get in the car.

> From the ground he lifted up a small sack and draped a brown beaver-lamb coat on Mania. He picked up a small bag of kopecks from the ground. Before the war children would collect kopecks, and you could get little [trinkets] with these kopecks. He gave me the kopecks, and my hands were burned because I realized that the child [who dropped them] may have been shot already. In the back of the car was a small window; I turned my head and suddenly in the passageway I saw all of my relatives. Grisha was with mama. To this day I remember how mama was standing. They were not looking where death was; they were looking and searching for me. And when I saw her, I moved forward; I dropped the kopecks, they scattered in the car and on the ground. The German was pointing at my head, [showing] how I had dropped the kopecks. If the car had not started moving, I would have definitely jumped out of the car. And the car started moving. I was only looking, and [Mania and I] held hands; the whole time [the German] was pointing at my head.[25]

The above incident did not mark the end of that dreadful day, 29 September. The girls were let out of the car on the corner of Melnikova and Pugacheva streets, and at first they did not even comprehend that they were being released. They got out of the car timidly and stood there in a state of semi-awareness. Neither girl—one was seventeen, the other thirteen—remembers how they got home. They did not dare go through the front entrance because next to it they saw a lot of people who were discussing the events of that day. They managed to knock on the semi-basement windows of the Lushcheiev family, whose daughter, Olia, was a close friend of Genia's sister Liza. The window opened, and Genia and Mania did not jump but literally fell[26] into the arms of Olha

25 Ibid.

26 Genia Batashova emphasizes this phrase, as uttered by Olia. In an interview recorded in 1995 Olia Rozhchenko (née Lushcheieva) also underscores the fact that

(Olia) and her mother, Hanna Lushcheieva.[27] "Uncle Kolia" came in the evening, and he questioned the girls and soothed them. They spent the night at the Lushcheievs, and in the morning they heard Germans outside looking for the Chernetsky girls. Batashova offers an interesting explanation for this search: "They did not doubt that we are Russians. But very often the Russians whom they had saved, who had been caught in some extreme situation, they saved them in order to exploit them in certain situations. They needed such people. And here they had come to the courtyard to look for the Chernetsky girls."[28]

No one betrayed the girls, and during the search they hid in a small closet. After a while Mykola Soroka brought them a certificate stating that they were students, Halyna and Mariia Kovalchuk, who were studying at a trade school. He said that the girls had to leave Kyiv, head in the direction of Kharkiv, and cross the front. For their journey they were given some clothing and a bit of money, fifteen rubles, and a map of Ukraine torn out of a school atlas, on which Soroka had indicated their route. "Incidentally, Olia still has this atlas. She showed it to me; one time I even said to her: 'Olechka, give it to me as a present.' But she told me: 'No, this will be for little Zoia', for her daughter. 'Once we are gone', she says, 'this will be for Zoiechka.'"[29]

This concludes Genia Batashova's account of the events of 29 September and her departure from Kyiv. What follows is a lengthy, detailed story of the two girls' journey to Kharkiv then farther east to Saratov, Tashkent, and Barnaul, where she lived until the end of the war. Genia returned to Kyiv in 1946 and immigrated to Israel in the 1990s, where died in 2002.

**"I was not crying out of fear, I was wailing in this hell; it was a real hell!"[30]**
The oral history of Mariia/Mania Zusivna Grinberg, née Palti, was re-

---

the girls literally fell into their arms.

27 For hiding and saving Genia Batashova and Mania Palti, Hanna and Olha Lushcheieva were recognized as Righteous Among the Nations and Righteous of Babyn Yar.

28 Genia Batashova. USHMM, interview code no. RG-50.120*0008, 30 April 1992.

29 Ibid.

30 Mariia Grinberg (Palti). USHMM, interview code no. RG-50.226*0012, 2 August 1994.

corded on 2 August 1994 in Kyiv and sent to the archives of the United States Holocaust Memorial Museum in March 1995. This interview is much shorter and, in contrast to the one given by Genia Batashova, it was recorded in several places: in Grinberg's home; on the street near the place where their two families had lived; near and outside the building where Olha Lushcheieva had lived; and on the way to the Babyn Yar site. Below are fragments from the first uninterrupted recording, which lasts approximately one hour. It was very difficult for Grinberg to speak. She often interrupted her account to wipe away tears or seek help from Olha Lushcheieva, who was also present when the interview was recorded (although she does not speak on tape). At first, Grinberg talks briefly about her family, including her father, who was a very devout man. Very soon the interviewer asks questions about the beginning of the war and whether the Palti family tried to join the evacuation operation. From that point the narrator begins talking about the war and about Babyn Yar.

In the first days of the war Mania's father was sent to the front, and before his departure he told his wife to take the family and leave Kyiv. The mood among the Jews, as the narrator emphasizes, was that the Germans were not feared. Their arguments were the traditional ones: the Germans had been in Ukraine during World War I, and at that time they had not done anything bad to the Jews. Before the Germans entered Kyiv in September 1941, some Jewish families were still living in the building, among them Genia Batashova's family. The mothers of Mania and Genia, despite the difference in their ages (Mania's mother Gita Palti was ten years younger than Genia's mother), were great friends. Mania says that her mother was always saying, "We'll go away," but Genia's mother would say, "We have to wait."

On 29 September the two families headed in the direction designated in the Germans announcement. Mania Grinberg's account lacks the details present in Batashova's. Instead, she offers a more general, panoramic picture of what happened on the way to Babyn Yar and at the place where she was saved. In response to the interviewer's question about what people were thinking when they were getting ready to leave their homes, she says that everyone thought they were being evacuated, that they would be transported from Kyiv, that the Germans themselves were circulating these rumors. These stories were believed by the Jews themselves and by those who saw them off. Grinberg soon mentions Melnikova Street, the beginning of the cemetery, and her realization of what was going on because shots could be heard:

> There were people all around . . . some who were seeing [people] off were standing and looking, and they too did believed that the Jews would be transported somewhere. But once they began approaching Melnikova Street, closer to the cemetery, people there now realized what this was connected with, because shots were heard; you understand, people now realized that they were doomed.[31]

What Grinberg describes next is a reverberation of people's shouts and fear concentrated into a few sentences, compressed into a dreadful, infernal clump, and filled with pain and tears stemming from the tragedy that in an instant, as the narrator states, took everything from her—her mother, her family, and her home. Her profound loneliness and helplessness was expressed in the following:

> I was undressed, and maybe I was standing close to the field of vision, I think this was an interpreter; I will close my eyes, and if I were shown what he looked like then, I would recognize him instantly because this was a boy, a Russian or a Ukrainian, I don't know, in civilian clothing, and ... maybe I was standing within the field of vision, not far from him, so he obviously turned his attention to me; I was undressed, with a blond braid, and perhaps he did not recognize me as a Jewish girl; I was not crying out of fear—I was wailing in this hell; it was a real hell. And suddenly in this hell I heard a human word; he asked me: 'Little girl, how did you end up here?' Right there I grabbed his hand, and to this day I think that no force on earth could have prised my arm from his, I was trembling so much; he asked me how I had ended up here; he began patting me on the head, saying: 'Calm down, we will drive you home'.[32]

According to Grinberg, at this very moment she saw Genia Batash-

31 Ibid.

32 Ibid.

ova, who came up to her and asked her to say that she was her sister. They were led to a group of women who had accidentally stumbled into the area past the fence, and told to wait there. The girls waited with this group until evening and arrived home very late, after curfew. Grinberg often says that she was so frightened and confused that she does not remember many details, such as telling her name and address to the German, or waiting until evening, or how they managed to make their way home. She also talks about the coat that the German put over her before she was driven from Babyn Yar, and it is mentioned again in connection with the Germans who came looking for her and Genia the next day. Unlike Batashova, Grinberg had no idea why they came, but the coat could have given her away, which, fortunately, did not happen: "Oliunia's mother [Hanna Lushcheieva] and aunt took me and Genia and hid [us] in a closet; everyone was very frightened, you understand, and this coat had been left on the bed; Oliunia remembered the coat; she ran home and grabbed this coat and threw it under the bed. He [the German officer] was running there and he saw a girl and says that she was this kind of girl, he says, but not this one, a different one, fair-haired, but no one in the courtyard knew that we had survived, so he ran and ran, and left."[33]

According to Grinberg's recollections, she and Genia Batashova left the Lushcheiev family not the next day but several days later, and she devotes the second part of her interview to the journey to Kharkiv. It was a very complicated route, and Grinberg a says that it was the mothers' souls—her mother's and Rakhil Batashova's—that protected them on their journey. After Kyiv was liberated, Mariia Grinberg came back home. At first, she lived with her father and later with her aunt, until she got married and had her own family. She recalls bitterly that the long journey on foot from Kyiv to Kharkiv, which took place in the cold and rainy autumn, damaged her health, and that neither she nor Genia Batashova ever had children.

### "There were even some Germans who rescued Jews..."[34]

The interview with Ruvim Shtein was recorded on 14 November 1999

33 Ibid.

34 Ruvim Shtein. USHMM, interview code no. RG-50.657*0001, 14 November 1999.

for a documentary film entitled *Who Destroyed Kiev?* (1999). Two years later it was transferred to the archives of the United States Holocaust Memorial Museum in Washington, D.C. Shtein recounts his story at the very spot where he managed to escape from Babyn Yar. Here and there he replies to questions, but for the most part he constructs his own narrative. After complying with the interviewer's request to provide some information about himself and his family, he begins talking about the beginning of the war, the destruction of Khreshchatyk Boulevard with mines, the accusations that the Jews were responsible for this, and about his personal attitude to the German announcement ordering the Jews of Kyiv to assemble on the morning of 29 September.

> I watched many films before the war, and newsreels were already showing that the Germans were doing away with the Jews. And I told my mother that we did not have to go anywhere in compliance with this announcement because we would be shot. But rumors were circulating continuously in the city, and many people said that we would be sent to Palestine, that perhaps we would be sent to a ghetto somewhere, that we would simply be transported out of the city and settled somewhere else. And no one believed that we would be shot and that we would be tortured to death. And we were hoping that somehow we would survive, that they could not [kill] thousands of people, women, children, elderly people—because the men were all at the front—that such a thing could happen to us![35]

But Shtein's mother did not believe him, and he was unable to convince her. So, "where the mother goes, there go the children." On 29 September, obeying the Germans' order, the Shtein family set out with a few suitcases, leaving behind some valuables, furniture and dishes.[36] He says that they walked in the direction of the Syrets rail spur, because

> there was a rumor that we are being brought to the [Lukianivka freight] station; it is obvious that they are going to load us into train cars and

35 Ibid.

36 On the morning of 29 September Ruvim, along with his mother and sister, set out for Babyn Yar. His father died in 1938.

> transport us. That's what. And no one was talking, but some said: 'Where are you going? They are shooting there.' Some local people, Ukrainians by nationality or Russians, who were living [in the vicinity] also spoke, maybe they knew. But none of the Jews believed they could all be killed. And here was this crowd of many thousands, which had been walking since morning, and we went at around 11–12.[37]

Continuing his account, Shtein says that when the street along which they were walking ended and the cemetery appeared, there was already a barrier in this spot, the road was blocked off, and people were being counted off in columns of 150–200 and assembled for the next part of the journey. Then the road curved in another direction, and those who were walking at the back did not see where the ones walking up front had disappeared. There was another curve,

> and a terrible picture opened up there, and we realized instantly that it would be bad for us as soon as we were brought there. They began to take all this away, well, these German occupation troops, who were obviously the field gendarmerie, obviously the SS, Nazis, special troops, you understand, which dealt with this. In one place they were taking documents, and what is interesting is that they were instantly throwing the documents that they were confiscating onto a bonfire. And passports, and photographs, and documents that people had. They were already depersonalizing the people, you understand. We were brought to another spot; there they were confiscating belongings. Suitcases: there was such a mountain of these suitcases already; a huge one, you understand! As though half the world had brought those things there; like a mountain, you understand. In a third area, valuables that people had on them [were being confiscated]: wedding rings, earrings, bracelets, chains. Well, everything that people valued most; they were confiscated there, and all this was placed in chests. In a fourth area, outer clothing was removed: coats, jackets, woolen things, well, whatever people were wearing. They were left only in their underclothing: underwear, such light clothing, you understand.
>
> And they began sorting the people: women and children, including

37 Ruvim Shtein. USHMM, interview code no. RG-50.657*0001, 14 November 1999.

infants, were placed into a vehicle with closed bodywork, and the doors were shut tightly. What was this, were these mobile gas chambers or were these simply closed doors, so that nothing could be seen? That is why great horror, crying began; people were screaming for help, mothers were tearing out their hair. Everyone realized now that if everything is being seized and you are left with nothing, then you are only being led away somewhere to be exterminated. And columns of teenagers, men and teenagers, were formed, and they were sent under escort on the road to Babyn Yar. Because in the place where everything was being confiscated, there was nothing there; no one was even being beaten. That is, they did not create a panic, so that there would be no panic. So there.[38]

Shtein says that this was where he was separated from his mother and led to a column guarded by armed soldiers. Then he realized that he had not even managed to say goodbye to her. Despite the fact that they were walking under escort, he decided to escape. He edged over to one side of the column and saw water drainage ditches on both sides of the road, under which lay metal pipes half a meter in diameter. In one spot he could not get his bearings and could not escape. But in another spot, he managed to jump into the ditch and hide inside a pipe.

I crawled into the pipe, it was wet there, there was water there, there was water. And I lay there until evening. My legs grew numb, turned blue, it was already getting dark. When I saw that no one was walking on the road, I crawled through the fence of this old Lukianivka cemetery, through this fence, and through the old graves, through the old cemetery I came out onto Parkhomenko Street, that is, to the freight station. And from there, already late in the evening, through this old cemetery and freight station, I came home to my house.

I had the key to the building, I opened [the door], entered my apartment, and shut myself in. I lived at home for seven days, for seven days I lived in the building without going out. Pardon the word, but there wasn't even any place to relieve myself because we did not have a lavatory in the room; there was a general room. It was separated from the corridor, and I would go on a piece of paper and hide it in the oven. And when, after

38 Ibid.

> these seven days, I heard—we had crackers at home, some food was left over—whatever there was I ate it. And when I heard someone opening the door and trying to come in, I went out of the second-story window down the drainpipe and fled.[39]

Shtein recalls how he spent the night in various parts of the city: in an attic, an abandoned shed, and cellars in old buildings, where no one lived except rats. But there was nothing to eat, so he decided to go to his friends' house, with whom he had gone to school and was on very good terms. When he arrived at their place, their mother fed him quickly and hid him. This was the Bobrovsky family—"These are my righteous ones," says Shtein: the mother, Mariia Panasivna, her children Mykhailo, Mykola, and Olha, as well as Yurii Tansky, who later helped Shtein acquire documents.

This concludes Shtein's account of his escape from Babyn Yar. Next, he talks about his departure from Kyiv and the journey to Briansk oblast (Russia), being drafted in 1943, the end of the war in the Baltic republics, his temporary residence in Baku [in the Caucasus], his return to Kyiv, and his postwar life in the Ukrainian capital.

"That is my short biography," says Shtein, after which the interviewer asked him some questions for the purpose of clarification. In replying to them, the narrator cited several new details and explanations of what happened to him on 29 September. For example, in response to a question about whether there were Ukrainian policemen and translators, besides Germans, in the place where people's belongings were being confiscated, he said:

> There were. And the Ukrainian police was there. But they did not play a main role. They were like auxiliaries, you understand. There were even some Germans who rescued Jews. There were some Germans, officers who took a child away, you know, children. The mothers would leave, but they would give their children away in order to save them. This was on the street where we were walking, when, you understand, it was no longer possible to go, so you only had to hand [a child] over to someone.

---

39 Ibid.

***This was still on Melnikova Street?***
This was still on Melnikova Street, yes. Well, at the end of Melnikova already there people were stopping, everyone was stopping, people had already begun to be agitated; they saw that they would die, and gave their children away.
***And later you went to the left? Where the things were, the clothing?***
Yes.
***And [people] from the Einsatzgruppe were there and ordinary German soldiers, and the Ukrainian police? Or just German soldiers and the Ukrainian police?***
Yes, there were only German soldiers there, those special detachments, the special unit, that one. Well, there were policemen because they had armbands; they were dressed worse than the Germans, you understand. But this was evident because they spoke Russian; this was evidently the police.
***In Russian or Ukrainian or both?***
Either Ukrainian or Russian, well, some spoke one or the other. Well, the speech was understandable. So, what did they do? They did as they were ordered, they...
***And later, when the people went farther, then there was this special group?***
And farther away, where people were already being shot, those cut-throats, yes, those real fascists, the Nazis, who were armed with machine guns. Even in the evening, the evening, when I was still sitting in the pipe, I peered out [and saw] vehicles, vehicles were arriving and delivering lime. They poured lime so that when the killed Jews fell into the pit, after some time, an interval, the vehicles poured out the lime. Well, so that there would be no...so that the corpses did not decompose or something, you understand.
***And you were sitting inside the pipe and heard everything?***
Yes, I was sitting inside this pipe. I heard people screaming and I heard the shots. This was very close, well, it may have been 300 meters; 300–400 meters at the most.[40]

Ruvim Shtein is one of a handful of narrators who talks about having had to conceal this dreadful experience for the rest of his life. He never

40 Ibid.

spoke about his escape from Babyn Yar until 1991, and when he was accepted into the Communist party he was forced, in his own words, to "gloss over" certain information about his life.

**"... they put on loud music so that the voices would not be heard"**

The story that Mykhailo Sidko recounted for the documentary film *The Last Witness of Babyn Yar* is about 30 September and the amazing rescue of the six-year-old Mykhailo.[41] He and other children were set free either by a policeman or a German, but to this day Sidko does not know who it was. "Mama was taken away, and I was standing with this crowd until we were given the order, 'Disperse!' Well, you know what a bunch of children is like; they ran like hares in all directions. This [man]—I still can't remember, don't understand—was a policeman or a German, but when we began to scatter, he fired his submachine gun into the air and killed a couple of children. Well, clearly this was so that he would be able to justify himself: You can't kill all of them, they're scattering."[42]

He begins his story with an account of how his family was supposed to evacuate Kyiv and was already on the train. But his brother suddenly remembered that he had not let the pigeons out of their cage, and he jumped out of the train car. At this very moment the train began moving. "Like every Jewish mother," Sidko says, "how can she go anywhere without her son? She threw all three out of the train car, and the train departed. And we went home."[43] Their father left on the train with their belongings, and Sidko's mother and siblings returned to Kyiv, where they lived quietly until the Germans arrived.

His family reacted in the following way to the order for the Jews to assemble at a designated spot on 29 collections. Sidko's uncle harnessed the small horse with which he earned a living as a private carter; his neighbor, Uncle Vasyl, also decided to go with him because he wanted to take the horse and cart later for himself. Both of them died in Babyn Yar, says Sidko. But his mother up and returned from Babyn Yar that day. Her neighbors told her: "Berta, where are you going, you have Russian chil-

41 The film is available at: http://www.agenda-tv.com/2014/04/blog-post.html

42 Quoted from ibid.

43 Quoted from ibid.

dren and a Russian surname."[44] But the next day, 30 September, "Lushka, the caretaker's wife," yelling, "Hey, you Jews, get ready, let's be off!," led two policemen into the building, who forced Sidko's mother to go back to Babyn Yar.[45]

Sidko's account is the only one that describes the events of 30 September, instead of 29 September. Therefore, I am citing it below with some minor excisions:

> So, we walked along Zhylianska Street, we came out onto the Yevbaz, now called the Ploshcha Peremohy [Victory Square]; and as soon as the road began below, on Yevbaz, this is Poltavska Street, where guards appeared right away—policemen mixed with Germans. And that way there was already a corridor to the very place of the shootings, all the way to Syrets. There was no return for anyone who ended up in this current, in this flow of people; at this point, everyone was supposed to walk only to Syrets. After the Zhytnii marketplace, on Artem Street, there was dense encirclement. In front of this place, where the assembly was designated in the order, a barrier had been erected because many people are on the move; a crowd is walking, as though during a demonstration. True, the weather was [bad], some rain, sleet with snow; it was raw and cold. But the people were walking nonetheless; one had a bag tucked under an arm, another had children. In a word, they were going straight there, without reaching the barrier; the column was stopped, 300–400 people were let through to the second barrier. Those standing here were waiting next to the first [group of people], and those are already being led to the place of execution. This means that in this second zone people were being stripped of belongings, money, documents. Everything that they had—all of it was taken away. And if someone had beautiful clothing, they were made to undress, and the person went practically naked there, to the pit, to the place of execution. And so that they would not come back, not scream, and not be agitated...the Germans did this: There, in the place where they were shooting, I know, at the execution site, they put on loud music so that the voices would not be heard, they muffled the shots.[46]

---

44 Mykhailo Sidko's mother, Berta Yudivna Kohan, was Jewish. His father, Petro Andriiovych Sidko, was Ukrainian.

45 Quoted from the film *The Last Witness of Babyn Yar*

46 Quoted from ibid.

Mykhailo Sidko says that on 30 September the Germans began sorting people for several purposes, something that had not happened on 29 September, and he ended up with a group of children who were probably selected for medical experiments. His brother, Grisha, also ended up in this group. Sidko recalls his mother's farewell cry: "Mishka, take care of Grisha, you are of one blood!" Then she went to the ravine with her three-year-old daughter Klara and four-month-old Volodia.... His mother and the children were led away, while Mykhailo continued standing with the group of children until he heard the order, "Disperse!"[47]

He came back home, where once again he was betrayed by the same caretaker's wife, Lushka, after which he was arrested by the Gestapo, and then sent to a children's barrack called the Prytulok (Refuge) at the Syrets concentration camp, where medical experiments were conducted on him. Further misery in occupied Kyiv awaited him. In 1944 his father returned to Kyiv, and Mykhailo went to live with him.

According to the leading researcher in the field of memory studies, Aleida Assmann, contemporary society is living in a time of transition from the political to the moral paradigm of examining the past. This transition lies in the displacement of the commemoration of heroes, who were active fighters and gave up their lives for certain ideals, by the commemoration of passive and defenseless victims of violence, who experienced collective persecution and extermination.

In this ethical and moral shift from heroization to victimization in the discourse of memory, oral histories of the Holocaust occupy a leading place. They heighten society's moral sensitivity, define new legal and ethical standards, make history emotional, and place emphasis on suffering and trauma as the main object of the work of memory. It is my view that in this work of memory, which does not permit us to forget about suffering and trauma and teaches us to have sympathy and empathy and be attentive to another's pain, the study of the oral histories of survivors and witnesses of tragic events offer the best opportunities for constructing a commemoration policy based on the conscious decision to prevent the reoccurrence of similar events in the future.

47 Quoted from ibid.

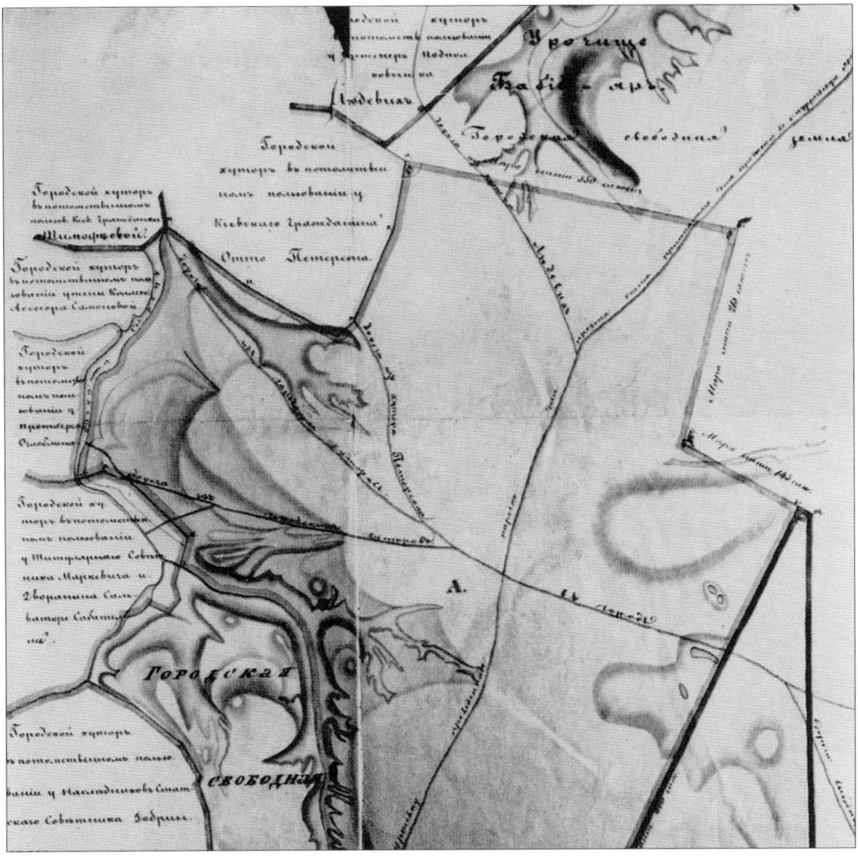


Fragment of a Kyiv site plan marked "Babyn Yar Tract" (1869).

Main entrance to St. Cyril's Hospital (Kyiv, 1914–1916)

Main entrance to the Jewish Cemetery in Lukianivka (Kyiv, 1910)

Army camp divisional church (Kyiv, early 20th century)

Panorama of the "Kyivan Switzerland" with streetcar route. Postcard, early 20th century.

"During his lifetime this sick person will cost the people 60,000 Reichsmark. Citizens, this is also your money! (Nazi poster, ca. 1938)

Der Stürmer

Deutsches Wochenblatt zum Kampfe um die Wahrheit

HERAUSGEBER: JULIUS STREICHER

41 | Nürnberg, im Oktober 1936 | 1936

Das Lügenmanöver

Hinter den Kulissen des Moskauer Prozesses

Unersättlich

The demonization and dehumanization of Jews in the newspaper *Der Stürmer* (Germany, 1936)

Nazi book burnings (Germany, 1933)

Signing of the German–Soviet Non-aggression Pact (Molotov-Ribbentrop Pact) (Moscow, 23 August 1939)

Prisoners executed by the NKVD before the Red Army's retreat (Lviv, July 1941)

Nazi Germany attacks the Soviet Union. A German sentry on the Great Bell-Tower, panorama of the Caves Monastery against the background of the burning Navodnytskyi Bridge spanning the Dnieper River (Kyiv, 23 September 1941).

A little boy and his mother observe a German motorcyclist on a city street (Kyiv, 3 November 1941).

A fire in the city center (Kyiv, September 1941).

The reverse side of this photograph is inscribed in German: "The Soviets have been expelled from the blooming and beautiful Ukrainian capital. All the important residential quarters have been blown up by the Soviets or the Jews" (Kyiv, 24 September 1941).

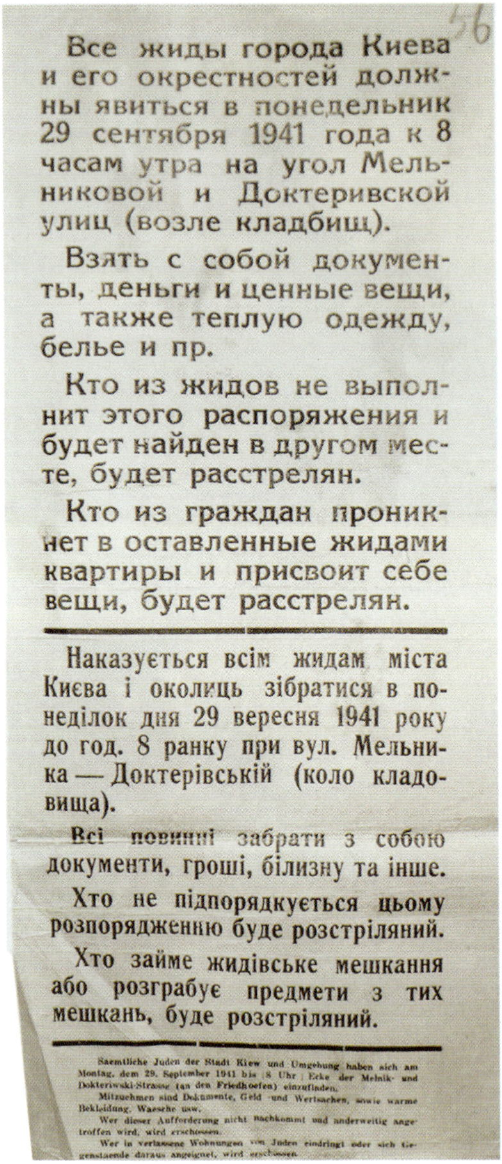

Все жиды города Киева и его окрестностей должны явиться в понедельник 29 сентября 1941 года к 8 часам утра на угол Мельниковой и Доктеривской улиц (возле кладбищ).

Взять с собой документы, деньги и ценные вещи, а также теплую одежду, белье и пр.

Кто из жидов не выполнит этого распоряжения и будет найден в другом месте, будет расстрелян.

Кто из граждан проникнет в оставленные жидами квартиры и присвоит себе вещи, будет расстрелян.

---

Наказується всім жидам міста Києва і околиць зібратися в понеділок дня 29 вересня 1941 року до год. 8 ранку при вул. Мельника — Доктерівській (коло кладовища).

Всі повинні забрати з собою документи, гроші, білизну та інше.

Хто не підпорядкується цьому розпорядженню буде розстріляний.

Хто займе жидівське мешкання або розграбує предмети з тих мешкань, буде розстріляний.

---

Saemtliche Juden der Stadt Kiew und Umgebung haben sich am Montag, dem 29. September 1941 bis 8 Uhr Ecke der Melnik- und Dokteriwski-Strasse (an den Friedhoefen) einzufinden.

Mitzunehmen sind Dokumente, Geld und Wertsachen, sowie warme Bekleidung, Waesche usw.

Wer dieser Aufforderung nicht nachkommt und anderweitig angetroffen wird, wird erschossen.

Wer in verlassene Wohnungen von Juden eindringt oder sich Gegenstaende daraus angeeignet, wird erschossen.

German order directing all the Jews of Kyiv to assemble at 8:00 a.m., on 29 September, and to bring their documents, money, valuables, and warm clothing (Kyiv, 28 September 1941).

Jews, alone or with their families, heading to Babyn Yar. Drawings by the artist and ethnographer Yurii Pavlovych (Kyiv, September 1941).

**Babyn Yar.**

Photographs taken by the German army photographer Johannes Hähle, Kyiv, early October 1941.

Soviet POWs next to the sorted belongings of executed Jews

SS men rummaging through the belongings of murdered Jews

Some belongings of the murdered victims:
photographs, clothing, women's and children's footwear, a prosthesis.

Як репресивні заходи, з приводу акту саботажу, сьогодні 100 мешканців міста Києва були розстріляні.

ЦЕ Є ПОПЕРЕДЖЕННЯ.

Кожний мешканець Києва є відповідальним за кожний акт саботажу.

Київ, 22.10. 1941 р. КОМЕНДАНТ МІСТА.

Wegen eines Sabotageaktes wurden heute 100 Einwohner von Kiew als Repressalie erschossen.

DIES DIENE ZUR WARNUNG!

Jeder Bewohner von Kiew ist für einen Sabotageakt mitverantwortlich.

Kiew, den 22.10. 1941. DER STADTKOMMANDANT.

№ 43—2.000.

Announcement by the occupation authorities about the execution of 100 city residents "for committing sabotage" (Kyiv, 22 October 1941).

Victims executed under a sign that reads: "A fine for removing a helmet from the grave of a German soldier" (Kyiv, no later than 6 November 1943).

People being deported to Germany for forced labor (Kyiv, late 1941-early 1942).

Nazi propaganda posters (in Ukrainian and Russian) in Nazi-occupied Ukraine.

Mud huts of the Syrets concentration camp (Kyiv, 1943).

POWs at the Darnytsia concentration camp (1941).

Soviet POWs, guarded by German soldiers, burying the bodies of Jews who were shot in Babyn Yar (early October 1941).

2 КРАСНАЯ ЗВЕЗДА 29 февраля 1944 г., вторник. № 50 (5730).

# СООБЩЕНИЕ

Чрезвычайной Государственной Комиссии по установлению и расследованию злодеяний немецко-фашистских захватчиков и их сообщников и причиненного ими ущерба гражданам, колхозам, общественным организациям, государственным предприятиям и учреждениям СССР

## О разрушениях и зверствах, совершенных немецко-фашистскими захватчиками в городе Киеве

### Разрушение промышленности, транспорта и коммунального хозяйства города и ограбление населения

A page from the newspaper Krasnaia zvezda, 29 February 1944.

A woman standing in front of bodies exhumed at the Syrets concentration camp (Kyiv, 1943).

**Trial of Nazi criminals. Photographs by H. Uhrynovych, Kyiv, 17-28 January 1946.**

Session of the military tribunal.

Public execution on Kalinin Square, Kyiv, 29 January 1946.

**The Kurenivka tragedy**
**Destruction caused by a river of mud (Kyiv, March 1961)**

Residential buildings on Frunze Street flooded to the ceilings and windows.

Overturned streetcar and trolleybus.

Destruction at the Babyn Yar site.

Destroyed neighborhood.

The poet Yevgeny Yevtushenko (center) and the young writer Anatoly Kuznetsov (left) after their first visit to Babyn Yar (Kyiv, 1961).

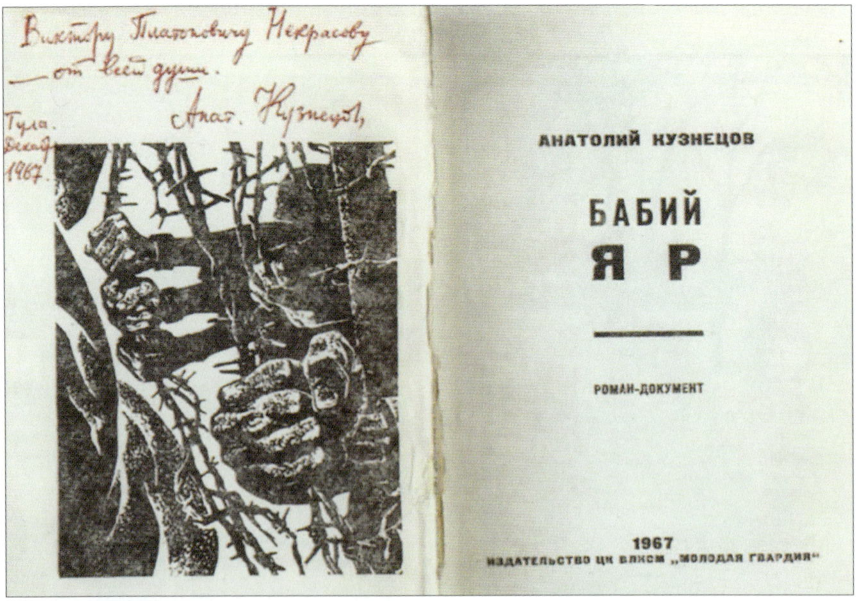


Copy of Anatoly Kuznetsov's book Babi Yar, with the author's dedication: "To Viktor Platonovich Nekrasov, Sincerely, Anat. Kuznetsov" (Tula, December 1967).

Composer Dmitrii Shostakovich of *Symphony No. 13*, opus 113 (subtitled "Babi Yar"), set to the poems of Yevgeny Yevtushenko.

Composer Dmytro Klebanov of Babyn Yar, the first-ever symphony dedicated to the tragedy (1945).

The score of *Symphony No. 13*.

The Jewish Cemetery in Lukianivka.
Photographs by Eduard Timlin, Kyiv, 28 September 1966

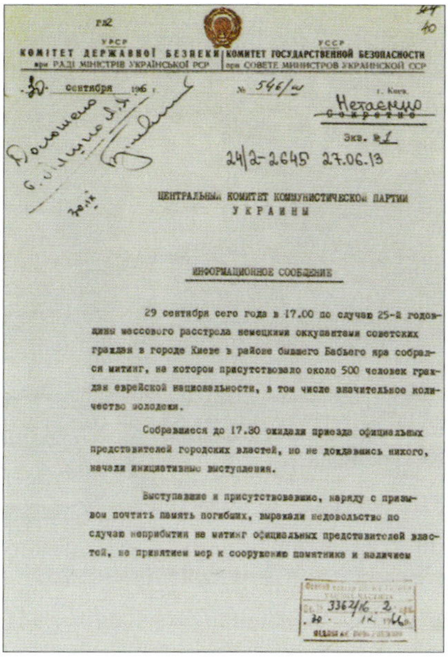

УРСР
КОМІТЕТ ДЕРЖАВНОЇ БЕЗПЕКИ
при РАДІ МІНІСТРІВ УКРАЇНСЬКОЇ РСР

УССР
КОМИТЕТ ГОСУДАРСТВЕННОЙ БЕЗОПАСНОСТИ
при СОВЕТЕ МИНИСТРОВ УКРАИНСКОЙ ССР

30 сентября 1966 г. № 546/ш г. Киев

Несекретно
~~Совершенно секретно~~

Экз. № 1

24/2-2645 27.06.13

ЦЕНТРАЛЬНЫЙ КОМИТЕТ КОММУНИСТИЧЕСКОЙ ПАРТИИ УКРАИНЫ

ИНФОРМАЦИОННОЕ СООБЩЕНИЕ

29 сентября сего года в 17.00 по случаю 25-й годовщины массового расстрела немецкими оккупантами советских граждан в городе Киеве в районе бывшего Бабьего яра собрался митинг, на котором присутствовало около 500 человек граждан еврейской национальности, в том числе значительное количество молодежи.

Собравшиеся до 17.30 ожидали приезда официальных представителей городских властей, но не дождавшись никого, начали инициативные выступления.

Выступавшие и присутствовавшие, наряду с призывом почтить память погибших, выражали недовольство по случаю неприбытия на митинг официальных представителей властей, не принятием мер к сооружению памятника и наличием

3362/16 2
30 12 1966

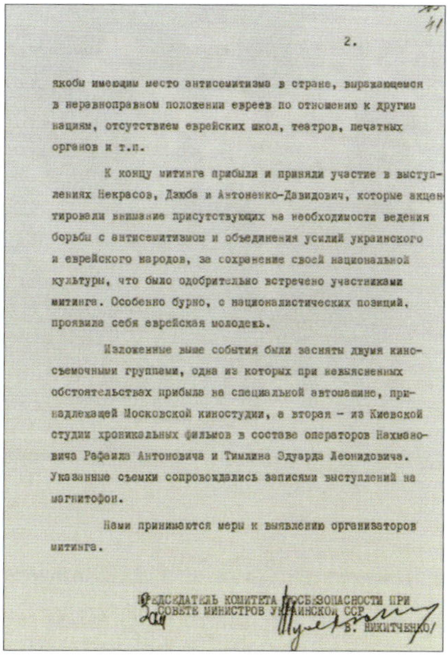

2.

якобы имеющим место антисемитизма в стране, выражающемся в неравноправном положении евреев по отношению к другим нациям, отсутствием еврейских школ, театров, печатных органов и т.п.

К концу митинга прибыли и приняли участие в выступлениях Некрасов, Дзюба и Антоненко-Давидович, которые акцентировали внимание присутствующих на необходимости ведения борьбы с антисемитизмом и объединения усилий украинского и еврейского народов, за сохранение своей национальной культуры, что было одобрительно встречено участниками митинга. Особенно бурно, с националистических позиций, проявила себя еврейская молодежь.

Изложенные выше события были засняты двумя киносъемочными группами, одна из которых при невыясненных обстоятельствах прибыла на специальной автомашине, принадлежащей Московской киностудии, а вторая – из Киевской студии хроникальных фильмов в составе операторов Нахмановича Рафаила Антоновича и Тимлина Эдуарда Леонидовича. Указанные съемки сопровождались записями выступлений на магнитофон.

Нами принимаются меры к выявлению организаторов митинга.

ПРЕДСЕДАТЕЛЬ КОМИТЕТА ГОСБЕЗОПАСНОСТИ ПРИ СОВЕТЕ МИНИСТРОВ УКРАИНСКОЙ ССР
/В. НИКИТЧЕНКО/

Report issued by the KGB of the Ukrainian SSR, dated 30 September 1966, on the unsanctioned rally marking the 25th anniversary of the shootings in Babyn Yar.

Unofficial rally at Babyn Yar (Kyiv, 29 September 1966).

Jewish activists next to the commemorative marker at Babyn Yar (Kyiv, 1972).

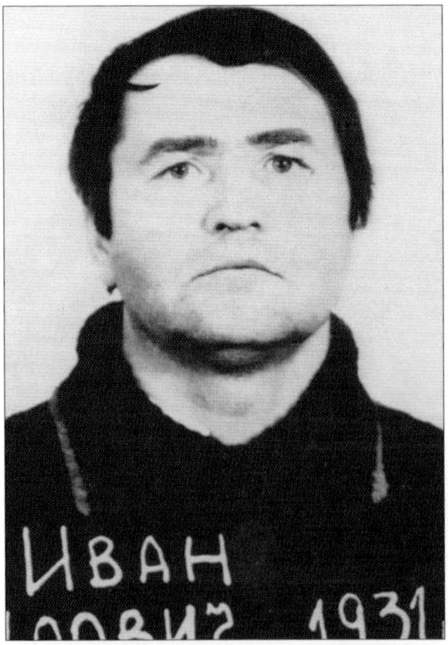


Police file photograph
of Ivan Dziuba after his arrest
(Kyiv, 1972).

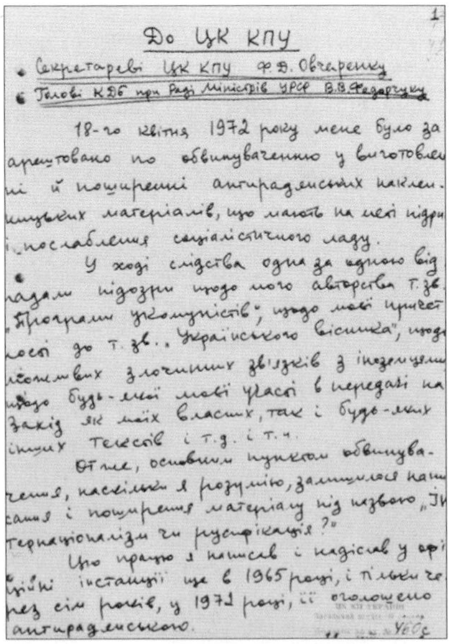

1

До ЦК КПУ

Секретареві ЦК КПУ Ф. Д. Овчаренку
Голові КДБ при Раді Міністрів УРСР В. В. Федорчуку

18-го квітня 1972 року мене було за
арештовано по обвинуваченню у виготовлен
ні й поширенні антирадянських наклеп
ницьких матеріалів, що мають на меті підри
і послаблення соціалістичного ладу.
У ході слідства одна за одною від
падали підозри щодо мого авторства т. зв.
„Програми укомуністів", щодо моєї причет
ності до т. зв. „Українського вісника", щод
можливих злочинних зв'язків з іноземцями
щодо будь-якої моєї участі в передачі на
Захід як моїх власних, так і будь-яких
інших текстів і т. д. і т. п.
Отже, основним пунктом обвинува-
чення, наскільки я розумію, залишилося нап
сання і поширення матеріалу під назвою „Ін
тернаціоналізм чи русифікація?"
Цю працю я написав і надіслав у офі
ційні інстанції ще в 1965 році, і тільки че
рез сім років, у 1972 році, її оголошено
антирадянською.

Fragment of Ivan Dziuba's letter to the
Central Committee of the Communist
Party of Ukraine (Kyiv, 18 August 1972).

The young Jewish activists Aleksandr Feldman and Aleksandr Tsatskis (foreground), and others with wreaths to be laid at Babyn Yar (Kyiv, 1973).

Unsanctioned meeting in Babyn Yar;
second from right: Leonid Finberg (Kyiv, 1970s).

Government organized rally of workers from Kyiv's Shevchenkivskyi district at Babyn Yar (late 1960s/1970s).

Jews who were saved from Babyn Yar standing next to the monument "To the Soviet citizens and captured soldiers and officers of the Soviet Army": Ya. Steiuk, Z. Trubakov, Ya. Kaper, D. Budnyk, F. Zavertannyi (Kyiv, 29 September 1978).

**Anti-Zionist propaganda in the Soviet Union/Soviet Ukraine**

"In one harness" [Zionists and Ukrainian bourgeois nationalists].
Editorial cartoon from the magazine *Perets'* (1981).

Book cover of T. K. Kichko, *Iudaïzm i sionizm* (Judaism and Zionism, 1968).

Book cover of Iulian Shulmeister, *Sluzhiteli ada* (Ministers of Hell, 1985).

**The indestructible ones: Ukrainian and Jewish dissidents**

Josef Zissels

Yevhen Sverstiuk

General Petro Hryhorenko

Semyon Gluzman

**Commemoration of the 50th anniversary of the Babyn Yar tragedy**

Posters displayed on Kyiv's main thoroughfare, Khreshchatyk Boulevard, with the inscription: "29.09—6.10 Babyn Yar Memorial Days, 1941-1991."

Gathering at the monument dedicated to the victims of Babyn Yar.

Photographs of family members and friends who perished in Babyn Yar.

The composer Yevhen Stankovych and the poet Dmytro Pavlychko.

Official ceremony to lay flowers at the monument.

U.S. President Bill Clinton
at the Menorah Monument in Babyn Yar (Kyiv, 1995).

Pope John Paul II
and Ukraine's chief Rabbi,
Yaakov Dov Bleich
(Kyiv, 2001).

**Official events marking the anniversary of the Baby Yar tragedy (Kyiv, September 2014)**

President of Ukraine, Petro Poroshenko

# CHAPTER 9

# Babyn Yar in Belles Lettres

*Iryna Zakharchuk*

Coming to grips with the tragedy of Babyn Yar in literature involves various dimensions both in its chronological and cultural-generational aspects. Above all, this is connected with the change in reception models of World War II and the dynamics of the moral, psychological, and intellectual climate within society. In the sphere of artistic creativity, the war brought to the fore numerous challenges that demanded different approaches. A key problem was the need to overcome the pressure exerted by established ideological schemes and to find new resources for reproducing the collective trauma.

The essence of the challenges facing artists was described by Alexander Dovzhenko at a meeting of filmmakers that took place in 1942: "Today and tomorrow we will have to push the limits of what is permissible in art. Today unprecedented baseness and crimes are crying out to be depicted on screen, as are sadism and abuse, hatred of the individual, and hatred of humanism. Today the mass, fascist child-killer, hangman…killer of wounded people, old people, and children…the killer of entire nations should come to the screen."[1] In bringing to light the tragic dimensions of the war, the Babyn Yar theme shifted the emphases to the category of victims, resistance to violence, and responsibility for perpetrated crimes.

### Earliest writings

Already during the war, information about Babyn Yar appeared in the Soviet press, in official statements issued by the Ministry of Foreign Af-

1 Cited in Valerii Fomin, comp., *Kino na voine* (Moscow, 2005), p. 5.

fairs, and in eyewitness testimonies. The first news about the mass killings appeared in the pages of *Pravda* in November 1941, when the perception of the tragedy was still especially acute. Particularly important in this regard was the Yiddish-language newspaper *Eynikayt* (Unity), the official mouthpiece of the Jewish Anti-Fascist Committee, which began to appear in June 1942. Among the contributors to this newspaper were Itsik Fefer, Dovid Bergelson, Ilya Ehrenburg, Vasilii Grossman, and other writers.

Several strategic directions predominated in *Eynikayt's* coverage of the war. Its editors collected and systematized materials on the mass killings of the Jewish people, which were perpetrated by the Nazi occupiers. The newspaper also devoted much attention to the selfless struggle of Jewish fighters in the ranks of the Red Army, emphasizing their readiness to fight, active resistance, and desire to revenge their people's collective suffering. These strategies were bound together by moral and ethical reflections on the scale of the national catastrophe and by considerations of the spiritual breakdown in national awareness.

A veritable symbolic chronicle of Babyn Yar was recorded systematically and comprehensively in the pages of *Eynikayt*. First and foremost, the newspaper published testimonies of people who had managed not only to survive but also escape from occupied Kyiv. The atmosphere of moral devaluation and cynicism was reflected in the diary of a Nazi corporal named Herbert Becher, who carried out the shootings in Babyn Yar. In October 1942 the Soviet writer Ilya Ehrenburg published fragments from the killer's diary for the purpose of eliciting the reader's condemnation. In this way, the voices of both executioners and victims created a mirror image of the crime, which gave an impetus to understanding the scope of moral degradation.

The truth about the Nazis' efforts to conceal the traces of their crimes in Babyn Yar was recounted in the pages of *Eynikayt* by participants in an uprising that took place in the early morning hours of 29 September 1943. Relying on their testimonies as well as on materials gathered by the Office of Jewish Culture in Kyiv, Ikhil Falikman and Moishe Myzhyritsky published articles recounting the preparations for and the evolution of the uprising. In a speech delivered at the third anti-fascist meeting of "representatives of the Jewish people" held in Moscow in April 1944, Itsik Fefer (whose relatives were killed in Babyn Yar), noted that the "ashes of Babyn Yar are scorching our hearts."[2] Over the next several decades this image would become a major theme in belles lettres.

In October 1943 Vasilii Grossman's essay "Ukraine," which discussed the Babyn Yar tragedy, was published in the Yiddish-language Soviet newspaper *Eynikayt*. The following month, the newspaper published another of his articles, "Ukraine Without Jews." The writer perceived this tragedy of the Jewish people as a personal drama whose reverberations he projected onto Ukraine's history, culture, and family memory. He used the "tree of life" metaphor, noting that the mass killing of the Jews is the "death of roots, not just branches and leaves." For this literary artist, this is tantamount to the "murder of a people, of homes, entire families, books, faith… This is the murder of a people's morals… memories, folk poetry, of cheerful and simultaneous bitter life."[3] Grossman thus clearly codified the category of victims as a key topos in the construction of the narrative about the experience of war. His system of moral priorities obviously clashed with the official Soviet interpretation of the war, which was dominated by emotional and entreating intonations that emphasized the feats of the Soviet armed forces at the same time that it concealed the tragic and multifaceted experience of life under the German occupation. It is not surprising, therefore, that the Soviet authorities sought to limit Grossman's readership and curb access to his frank and courageous statements. This explains why Grossman's Russian-language article, "Ukraine Without Jews," was never published in the original language.

The de-occupation of Soviet Ukraine led to an increase in the number of articles about the crimes committed in Babyn Yar. They were published in *Izvestiia*, *Krasnaia zvezda* (Red Star), *Radians'ka Ukraïna* (Soviet Ukraine), among other newspapers by such writers as Aleksandr Avdeenko (Oleksandr Avdiienko), Kostiantyn Bukovskyi, Vadym Sko-

2 Cited in Arkadii Zel'tser, "Tema 'Evrei v Bab'em Iaru v Sovetskom Soiuze v 1941–1945 godakh." In *Babyn Iar: masove ubyvstvo i pam'iat' pro n'oho: materialy mizhnarodnoï naukovoï konferentsiï 24-25 zhovtnia* (Kyïv, 2017), pp. 83-101.

3 Vasilii Grossman, "Ukraina bez evreev", *Eynikayt* (Moscow), 25 November 1943.

morovskyi, and others. In other words, there was ample information in the press about Babyn Yar to provide a deeper understanding of the tragedy in the sphere of belles lettres.

The ways of narrating the Babyn Yar massacre, however, depended to a significant degree on the government's position in the sphere of nationality policy and the integration of culture into the official models of remembering World War II. In fact, it was the war itself that introduced a palpable imbalance into Soviet nationality policy. During the first phase of the war, when the Soviet-Nazi conflict was at its most complex stage, there was a marked tendency to revive certain national components in the rhetoric of propaganda and to restore national symbols and key figures of national history to the system of military awards, theater repertoires, agitational brigades, and literary texts. Eventually, an imperialistic and chauvinistic attitude came to dominate the Soviet government's cultural strategy, as part of its general concern with the exceptional achievements and selfless struggle of the Russian people. In this context, the treatment of the Babyn Yar theme in official publications was characterized by a lack of consistency and double standards, which ranged from the use and exploitation of symbols of national awareness as an active instrument and powerful mobilizational resource to the gradual neutralization and repression of individual national cultures.

It is generally assumed that literature is particularly sensitive to problems of national identity, suffering, and death, as well as to new meanings of life that war brings to the experience of the individual and society. Writers believed it was their moral obligation to express the tragedy of Babyn Yar in belles lettres. This attitude was also determined by the creative atmosphere in the literary milieu during the war, which was marked by the easing of censorship and control on the part of Soviet institutions. This breath of freedom gave grounds to hope for an expansion of creative horizons and the possibility that writers might be able to speak with their own voices and not be at the mercy of instructions dictated from above. But the introduction of Babyn Yar into the literary space also demanded civic courage because, one way or another, this theme was embedded in the national memory, philosophical dimensions of life and death, religious tradition, and prayer practices; that is, the breadth of experiences that had been proscribed in Soviet literature before the war. No one could predict the government's reaction to such "free-thinking," so that the threat to life and death hung like the sword of Damocles over every creative person.

Another problem concerned the artistic factor itself. The Babyn Yar narrative required a fundamental renewal of stylistic manner and content-based emphases: the existing technique of writing, which was activated by the recreation of battle scenes and descriptions of armed resistance at the front or selfless labor in the rear, turned out to be ineffective where the mass killing of civilians was concerned. The scale of the Babyn Yar massacre and its transcendental dimension, along with the intonations of pain, sympathy, shared suffering, and calls for revenge, which are understandable in such situations, also required psychological distance from the language of agitation leaflets, propagandistic slogans, and aggressive patriotism—and, above all, civic courage to embark on an open dialogue with the reader.

**Babyn Yar in Soviet literature during World War II**

The first literary texts to record an emotional and psychological reaction to the tragedy of Babyn Yar were works of poetry. The reason for this is that poetry is always fluid in reproducing lived experience, and dynamic in its reaction to painful shocks. The first writers to respond to the massacre in Babyn Yar were two female poets, Olga Anstei and Liudmyla Titova, who lived in Kyiv during the Nazi occupation, and for whom the mass murder became part of their personal experience of the war. Their texts were written between 1941 and 1943.

Olga Anstei (née Steinberg) was born in 1912 in Kyiv. Jewish and German branches interwove in her family tree: her mother was Jewish; her father, a russified German. Kyiv played a special role in her writings as a source of inspiration that awakened her artistic self-awareness. It is no coincidence that Anstei referred to the initial stage of her writing career as the Kyiv period. Her first poems date back to the 1930s, but she neither published them in the press nor produced a separate volume of collected poems in the interwar period. Her creative growth was supported by Maksym Rylskyi, who spoke favorably of her poetry, while being fully aware that her works did not fit into the ideological imperatives of totalitarian literature and could not appear in print.

Anstei managed to survive during the Nazi occupation thanks to her good command of German and self-identification as an ethnic German (*Volksdeutsche*). In 1943, she left Ukraine together with her husband, the poet Ivan Elagin, and they soon found themselves in DP camps. This was the beginning of her emigré period. There she published "Kirillovskie iary" (The Kirillov Ravines), a series of poems about the tragedy of Babyn Yar. They first appeared in a literary magazine (1948) and the following year were included in a book of poems *Dver' v stene* (The Door in the Wall).[4]

In the series, Anstei employs the name for Babyn Yar which was used by the locals, Kirillov Ravines, thus emphasizing the continuity of historical memory and pointing to the irreversible losses in Kyiv's national and cultural landscape. The poem involves the images of the valley of tears, a giant cemetery, and places of funeral prayer. There is also a highly distinct appeal to the religious tradition, which, according to the author, is a powerful spiritual resource for re-living the tragedy.

> The last cup. That place
> Where nature sleepily whirled,
> To this strange, endangered people
> Became the Calvary, the place of the cross.
> Listen! They were lined up,
> Their belongings stacked in piles on slabs.
> Half-dead, half-gone,
> They were half-slain by foreign soldiers…
> Can you see the old ladies in handkerchiefs,
> Elders, stately like Abraham,
> And, as in Bethlehem, curly babies
> Held by their mothers?[5]

---

4 Ol'ga Anstei, *Dver' v stene* (Munich, 1949), https://www.liveinternet.ru/users/4652778/post208473970

5 Ol'ga Anstei, "Stikhotvoreniia," in *Dver' v stene* (Munich, 1949), http://laidinen.ru/women.php?part=528&letter=%C0&code=3352

Anstei clearly points to the ethnicity of the victims through the use of phrases like "a holey tallis", "scraps of the Talmud", and "tattered, rain-soaked passports." It is crucial for the author that the national and universal dimensions of the tragedy coexisted organically in the experience of collective memory. The pathos expressed in her verses is aimed at being heard and making a compelling case with her poetic testimony.

The poem was originally written in Russian but was later translated into Ukrainian by the author. This suggests that Anstei felt the need to redefine the image of her homeland by injecting the Ukrainian factor as an integral component of her cultural consciousness. It can also be argued that the translation reflected the poet's desire to expand her readership by integrating the tragedy of Babyn Yar into the Ukrainian literary experience.

Another author, Liudmila Titova, grew up in an environment similar to that of Anstei. A survivor of the Nazi occupation in Kyiv, Titova was one of the first to depict the tragedy of Babyn Yar in writing. She compared the crimes committed in Babyn Yar with the devolution of humankind to animal instincts and arbitrary aggression: "no longer do I believe that there was once the *Appassionata* [the colloquial name for Beethoven's *Piano Sonata No. 23 in F minor*, Op. 57—translator]."[6] Titova conveys the anomaly of the terrible events through the image of bloody snow: as it falls over Kyiv, everything around turns crimson. Thus, the tragedy of Babyn Yar was first interpreted by women, and their poetic voices are close to weeping and lamentations over the dead. Both Titova and Anstei try to relate the traumatic, spiritual, and commemorative dimensions of the crime. In their artistic versions, they pay special attention to the moral humiliation of the victims and the physical torture they endured.

The postwar experience of the two authors was different. While Titova was not active in the literary scene and was basically unknown, Anstei published her works in Russian literary magazines in exile. It is no wonder that their works took a long time to reach readers in Ukraine, which effectively happened only after the country became independent.

6 Cited in https://en.wikipedia.org/wiki/Liudmila_Titova

The poems of both Titova and Anstei were included in the anthology *Vidlunnia Babynoho Iaru* (*The Echoes of Babyn Yar*), first published in 1991 and reprinted multiple times.[7] The anthology was dedicated to the fiftieth anniversary of the tragedy in Babyn Yar. It can be argued that Ukraine's independence enabled its literary memorialization at the public level and had a significant impact on restructuring Babyn Yar's genealogy by highlighting in collective memory Kyiv's status as the primary locus of attempts at comprehending the tragedy through literature. In this way, the poems by Titova and Anstei prove that artists whose life was linked to Ukraine were best able to understand the tragedy. Anstei penned her texts on the Nazi atrocities in Babyn Yar in December 1942, while research suggests Titova's poems date from 1941–1942. Their works are still in the process of being integrated into Ukrainian literature and literary consciousness.

After Kyiv was liberated from the Nazi occupation, Ukrainian writers were among the first to address the tragedy of Babyn Yar. Among them was the poet and front-line soldier Vasyl Shvets, who fought throughout the entire war and was wounded. War poetry and the actualization of Shvets's wartime experience characterize his work. In the poet's archive the poem "Babyn Yar" is dated 3 March 1944, that is, the artistic embodiment of the Kyivan tragedy took place relatively long after the massacre. It is highly likely that this fact defined to a significant degree the text's palette of intonations, in which moods of grief and sadness are predominant, and represented by the image of a mother crying over unborn children. The poem expresses agonizing reflections on the sundering of generational continuity and the loss of the tree of life and the spiritual code.

From beneath the earth rise our children,
Tortured to death, suffocated, killed,
Loved incompletely by us and the world
Unschooled in how to walk firmly.[8]

---

7 Iurii Kaplan, comp. *Vidlunnia Babynoho Iaru* (Kyiv, 2001).

8 Vasyl' Shvets', "Babyn Iar," manuscript copy in the Tsentral'nyi derzhavnyi arkhiv, Muzei literatury i mystetstv Ukraïny, Fond 949, Opys 2, Zbirka 2, Arkush 25-25 zvorot.

The poem "Babyn Yar" was not included in any collection published during the author's lifetime. The policy of distinct antisemitism at the state level, which prevailed in the first postwar years, evidently prompted him to leave the text in the "archives of memory."

The experience of Jewish Yiddish-speaking writers is crucial for understanding the evolution of receptive models of the Babyn Yar tragedy. In 1946, the eminent Jewish poet Peretz Markish completed his epic poem "Milkhome" (War), which includes a section on Babyn Yar. Because it was written in Yiddish, it remained inaccessible to Ukrainian and Russian readers for a long time. Some excerpts, including the part about Babyn Yar, were translated into Ukrainian by Valeriia Bohuslavska and included in another collection of Markish's poems. [9] Another outstanding Jewish poet, Shike (Ovsei) Driz, wrote a poem, "A Lullaby to Babi Yar," with the haunting verses:

> I do not know where to look for the little bones now,
> The dear little bones of both my children.
> Help me, mothers, help me,
> To wail to the end my melody.
> Help me, mothers, help me.
> To lull Babi Yar to sleep.[10]

For many writers, the experience of living in German-occupied Kyiv became part of their family history and personal drama, onto which were overlaid intensified feelings of national identity and a paradigm shift in understanding cultural and religious traditions. In discussions of the most famous texts that became landmarks of Soviet Russian literature, critics traditionally focus their attention on two poems written in 1944-1945 by Ilya Ehrenburg and Lev Ozerov, each of which is entitled "Babi Yar."

The eminent Soviet writer and wartime journalist Ilya Ehrenburg devoted to the Holocaust several poems: "Screbet sebia na peple Iov" (Job

---

9 Peretz Markish, *Narechenyi zaviriukhy: virshi i poemy* (Kyiv, 2000), pp. 125-128.

10 Shike Driz, Di ferte strune (Moscow, 1969). An English version, cited here, comes from Dov Noy, "The Model of the Yiddish Lullaby," *Studies in Yiddish Literature and Folklore*, No.7 (Jerusalem, 1986), p. 223.

Scrapes Himself on the Ashes, 1943), "V eto getto lyudi ne pridut" (People Won't Come to This Ghetto, 1944), and "Za to, chto znoy poludennoy Esfiri…" (For Keeping the Heat of the Southern Esther, 1944). He also expressed his moral solidarity with the victims in his poem "Babii Iar," first published in 1946. Actually, the poem was given no title and there was not a single mention of Jews or any sign of a Jewish narrative. This posed for the authors an unprecedented challenge: How to recreate in writing a tragedy that defied description; and how to recount a trauma, in comparison with which all words seemed trite. The author admitted frankly that this was by no means an easy task, which is why his poetic language is extraordinarily restrained, even frugal, and the pathos that is typical of Soviet war poetry is muffled.

> What use are words and what use is the pen,
> When this stone on the heart,
> When, like a convict with a ball and chain,
> I drag someone else's memory?[11]

Intonations of grief predominate in Ehrenburg's text, which includes an appeal to observe a personal moment of prayerful silence that is essential for symbolically uniting the living and the dead ("Blow out the light. Lower the flag."). The author explained that his duty was to become a voice of collective memory, its cultural emissary to a wide readership. It is worth noting that Ehrenburg penned his poetic text about Babyn Yar at a time when he was also publishing journalistic pieces exhibiting a clear anti-German stance as well as ideological messages of the Soviet authorities. The topic of Babyn Yar restructured Ehrenburg's political and artistic identity, and it enabled him to focus, if only indirectly, on the ethnic experience. The best example of this new focus appeared in the novel *The Storm*, for which Ehrenburg was awarded the Stalin Prize in 1948.[12]

*The Storm* is organized in a largely cinematic manner: the lives of many heroes are interwoven in the text; the events of World War II are re-interpreted; and the issues caused by the crisis of humanism are highlighted.

---

11 Il'ia Erenburg, *Sobranie sochinenii*, Vol. 3 (Moscow, 1964), p. 455.

12 Il'ia Ehrenburg, *Buria* (Moscow, 1960).

The eighth chapter focuses on the occupation of Kyiv and the shooting of Jews in Babyn Yar. The writer recreates the fate of Jewish families left to fend for themselves in a duel with death. In terms of mood, Kyiv is portrayed most palpably, as it turns from a space of life into a territory of death and despair. The infamous road to Babyn Yar is depicted in detail. It is fixed in the mind of an old Jewish woman who is being driven to the place of death together with her granddaughter: "No, this road is not to life! Everyone is crying; women are tearing their hair out; old people are praying as if before death."[13] Ehrenburg then describes various reactions of the victims—from fear and despair to curses and threats against their murderers. At the last moment before the shooting, girls sing lines from "The Internationale" with a smile on their faces: "Arise, ye prisoners of starvation! Arise, ye wretched of the earth!". Grandmother Khana exclaims: "The Red Army shall come! You shall pay for everything, beasts!"[14]

Undoubtedly, Ehrenburg deliberately added ideological coloring to the victims' reactions. Such an approach was one of the components in his version of the war. Hence, in order to voice this version more deeply and philosophically, the author resorted to well-established propagandistic schemes. It is important to note that the publication of the novel chronologically coincided with the launch of the antisemitic campaign and the persecution of Jewish artists in the Soviet Union. Ehrenburg, however, was one of the few who managed to avoid repression and continue writing. In official government presentations, his name actually served as a major counterargument to accusations of antisemitism. In other words, Ehrenburg functioned as a kind of alibi for the authorities: a Jewish writer who is respected, not persecuted, and is allowed to realize his full creative potential.

Naturally, the question arises as to how, amidst of the struggle against the "rootless cosmopolitans", a novel like *The Storm* could be officially published and receive a literary award to boot. There are several possible answers, all of which suggest that behind the novel's external ideological framework there lies hidden complex existential and social issues. Thus,

13 Ibid.
14 Ibid.

there is a need to re-read the novel as a text that laid the foundation for the interpretation of the Holocaust in world literature.

It seems that the contemporary Russian literary scholar Dmitrii Bykov has offered one of the most meaningful and intellectually profound interpretations, pointing out for the first time that the deep semantic structures of the novel needed to be revealed.[15] As Bykov points out that *The Storm* is an attempt to create a full-scale military epos, but that such an artistic canvas is impossible to create for a writer like Ehrenburg, who was integrated into the system of totalitarian literature. Any author who sets out to write a war epic must, according to Bykov, be imbued with a holistic, ontologically complete worldview. Since Soviet literature removed transcendental components and historiosophy as a worldview tool from its artistic foundations, it was impossible to create a true war epic within the Soviet value system. Instead, the Soviet cultural doctrine encouraged mimicry as an integral part of the writer's identity. As a result, Ehrenburg was not completely sincere in *The Storm*. He often resorted to "Aesopian language," not for fear of Soviet censorship but because he did not dare speak out with certainty. Bykov put it, "mimicry is in his blood," something that is noticeable in the entire Jewish discourse of Ehrenburg's writings.[16]

It is, in fact, the Jewish discourse of Ehrenburg's novel to which Bykov draws the reader's attention. He interprets the very title as a philosophical phenomenon, noting that the "storm" is actually the internal state of Ehrenburg's mind, that is, it is reflective of his worldview and his unrest about everything. This is a Jewish rather than artistic trait, the inner hell of an eternal stranger who is alien to all people in Europe. In Bykov's version, it is precisely because Ehrenburg "showed" (or really was) the type of Jew with his eternal inner chaos, skepticism, insecurity, and "internal storm" that he survived amidst repressions. Bykov notes further that in the Stalinist era, only an artist who embodied a certain pre-established character and demonstrated certain completeness stood any chance of survival. It was this integrity that gave him a chance to live because Stalin

15 Dmitrii Bykov, *Il'ia Erenburg: kurs sovetskoi literatury*, in https://www.youtube.com/watch?v=XDnU46rnjc0

16 Ibid.

simply did not like complexity. The Soviet leader formed an opinion of a person, and if that person did not correspond to his understanding, he perceived this as a betrayal. Ehrenburg most consistently "stayed within the image." His "inner hell" seemed most convincing and found an axiological interpretation in *The Storm*.

At the same time, Ehrenburg's novel gave rise to the iconic models of Holocaust interpretation. For example, the worldview of *The Storm* became the philosophical foundation for *Zhizn' i sud'ba* (Life and Fate) by Vasilii Grossman. Bykov also believes that *The Storm* served as a matrix for Jonathan Littell's novel *Les Bienveillantes* (The Kindly Ones, 2006), in which Ehrenburg's anthropologist becomes a German esthete. According to Bykov, in terms of passionate hatred towards the dehumanization of society and exposition of the destructive power of bigotry, Ehrenburg's *The Storm* is more fascinating than Grossman's *Life and Destiny* and much deeper than Littell's novel. Thus, we are still faced with the problem of re-reading *The Storm* in order to put it into the right artistic niche and gauge its role in shaping interpretive models of the topos of Babyn Yar.

Lev Ozerov's interpretation supplements and expands Ehrenburg's poetic vision. In 1943 the poet visited Kyiv after its liberation and then wrote an essay about the victims of Babyn Yar. Shortly afterwards Ozerov wrote the poem "Babi Yar." As the writer later recalled: Kyiv was part of his youth and family history:

> Born in 1914, I experienced all the wars of the century and three famines, especially the famine in Ukraine of 1930–1933, which the Ukrainians refer to by the much more profound word *holodomor* [murder by starvation]. We were hanging on by a thread; how we survived is difficult to comprehend. I had already then...begun to write; I received positive responses, but because of the famine I had to drop everything and hire myself out as an unskilled laborer at the Arsenal Plant in Kyiv. . . . They were happy at home because I would bring a small handful of groats and a fishtail.[17]

17 Lev Ozerov, recollections in http://ju.org.ua/ru/literature/241.html

Ozerov's "Babi Yar" generalizes the accumulation of several traumas caused by both the Soviet and Nazi totalitarian regimes. The poem recreates the lyrical hero's symbolic road to Babyn Yar. Along the way he bids farewell to people who are dear to him, and honors their memory; there is no doubt whatsoever that this path leads from the depths of his conscience. According to the German dramatist, poet, writer, essayist, and theater director Heiner Müller, trauma is an explosion of a memory set off after a long, latent period. For Ozerov, the detonator of memory is the symbolic return to the tragedy that took place in September 1941, and the recreation of the moods and psychological state of the people who went to their death.

> And the autumn day is transparent, slow, eternal.
> The crowds flow, dark in the light.
> The last candles on poplars tremble quietly,
> And in the air:
> — Where are we? Where are they taking us?
> — Where are they taking us? Where are they taking us today?
> — Where? — eyes question in final supplication.
> And the long and endless procession
> Walks to its funeral.
> Everything is understood now. And the pit is open, like a pool.
> And the distance is lit up with the light of final moments.
> Death too has an anteroom.
> The fascists, business-like, remove
> Clothing from the newcomers and lay it in a pile.[18]

The author uses the language of cinema, recording sequences that reveal the fine line between life and death: a little girl being buried alive, who begs her tormentor not to throw sand in her eyes; a small boy with trusting eyes asks a policeman stripping the condemned of their clothing if he should take off his stockings. At the same time, the lyrical hero is wracked with guilt because he could not save his loved ones from death. Interspersed throughout his internal monologue are notes of self-reproach and the

---

18 Lev Ozerov, "Babii Iar," in his *Izbrannye stikhotvoreniia* (Moscow: Khudozhestvennaia literatura, 1974), p. 451.

question of whether it would have been better to perish together with the people he loved most: "We would have embraced each other in the final dream/ And fallen together to the bottom/ For I will be tormented as long as I shall live/ That we did not die all together."[19] The private component humanizes the text of the poem and intensifies the intonations of confession and repentance. The poet's artistic attitude may be summarized with the words of the Jewish-American scholar Yohanan Petrovsky-Shtern: "to help victims of violence find their voice."[20] Self-identification with victims is precisely the position that will define the creative quests of many writers who, during the war and immediately after its conclusion, were the first to explore the tragedy of Babyn Yar in their works.

**Babyn Yar and Ukrainian writers**

Ukrainian writers also posed questions about the moral consequences of the German occupation and the reverberations of the Babyn Yar massacre in the lives of Kyivites and the life of their city. The encounter with the Ukrainian capital and especially its surviving inhabitants after the expulsion of the Nazi occupiers had an oppressive effect on many writers. This is corroborated by entries in Alexander Dovzhenko's journal:

> What affected me most, what plunged me into unforgettable sorrow and despair and anguish, was the people. The people of Kyiv. There were none. The city was empty. I saw a total of approximately a hundred people either individually or in small groups. For the most part these were elderly people and invalids, cripples. But all of them had that harrowing look that no one in the world can ever forget. They were half-mad, thin, in rags, yellow, with unnatural, hysterical gestures and wide-open, unhealthy eyes. . . . This was the state of people after an unprecedented earthquake or some other kind of geological catastrophe. These were people in the aftermath of extraordinary misfortune, abuses, and that lawless, daily and hourly danger that brings a person to the semi-mad state of a tormented human being. It is difficult to describe, difficult to recall.[21]

19 Ibid., p. 453.

20 Yohanan Petrovsky-Shtern, *The Anti-Imperial Choice: The Making of the Ukrainian Jew* (New Haven and London: Yale University Press, 2009), p. 227.

21 O.P. Dovzhenko, *Shchodennykovi zapysy, 1939–1956*, edited by A. A. Artizov et al.

Poetic reflections on Babyn Yar also appear in the work of the Ukrainian writers Mykola Bazhan, Volodymyr Sosiura, and Oleksa Yushchenko. Both chronologically and atmospherically, their works are consonant with the texts of Ehrenburg and Ozerov. Mykola Bazhan's poem "Yar" appeared in 1943, that is, in the first months after Kyiv was liberated of the Nazi forces. Like the works of other Ukrainian writers, this text is an important argument in building the significance of the Ukrainian-centric Holocaust reception. Bazhan's poetry is distinctive for the particularly emotional intransigence that he expresses in the poetic slogan, "We shall not forget, we will not forgive!" Like his fellow poets, Bazhan conveys his impressions of a visit to Babyn Yar, over which a "wind from the grave" blows and the "fumes of fatal fires, the bodies of smoking cinders" are sensed. In the poet's perception, the silence around Babyn Yar is deceptive; it is rent by the voices of the murdered innocents. "No, this is not silence! This is the inextinguishable cry of a hundred thousand hearts, a despairing cry before death." The poet is affected by the visible traces of that horrific crime.

> The curly and delicate gold of hair
> Has not been hidden in the soil, has not decayed.
> Shining in the wet mud of the steep ravines
> Is the shattered glass of an old person's glasses,
> And a bloody children's shoe tossed aside
> Is rotting.[22]

Bazhan uses the truncated version *Yar* rather than the full toponym *Babyn Yar*. The critic Yurii Barabash rightly notes that Bazhan's poem does not contain a clear reference to the Jews. In other words, there is no distinct ethnic connotation. Instead, the poet points to the Jewish background of the victims indirectly through semantic allusions and as-

---

(Kharkiv: Folio, 2013), p. 301.

22 Mykola Bazhan, *Polit kriz' buriu: vybrani tvory* (Kyiv: Krynytsia, 2002), p. 197.

sociations, such as "no rot, no hiding for the golden curls." [23] Later in the text, *Babyn Yar* does appear as the name of the crime scene and a symbol of revenge.

The indirect manner in which the ethnic identity of the victims is revealed invites a deeper analysis of the author's approach. The poet clearly strives to speak in line with the official formulations of the authorities which unequivocally characterized the tragedy of Babyn Yar as the murder of "peaceful Soviet citizens," the formula used to replace the term "Jews." As the editor of the newspaper *For Soviet Ukraine* and a person close to government circles, Bazhan certainly knew about these political attitudes and was, in consequence, torn between the need for an adequate formula to express his artistic vision and a desire not to deviate from the official rhetoric. As Barabash notes, "this was not a 'surrender' or a capitulation—merely a forced compromise—but it was probably enough for a dramatic emotional conflict."[24]

Bazhan's artistic reception of the Holocaust found expression in some of his other works, including the poem "Deborah." The stimulus for this poem came in 1967, when Bazhan visited a place called Sukha Balka in the Cherkasy region where the Nazis killed Jews during the war. First published in the magazine *Vitchyzna* (Fatherland) in 1968, the poem "Deborah" does not speak directly about the events of the Holocaust. There are, however, clear psychological parallels between the tragic history of the Ukrainian and Jewish peoples in an era of social upheaval and trial. The publication drew the ire of censors. An official letter from the Soviet Writer's Publishing House claimed that "the parallels drawn in the poem between the events in Uman during the Civil War [1919] and the Nazi invasion of 1941 are somewhat biased and obviously not entirely legitimate."[25] Despite numerous changes that Bazhan was forced to make, "Deborah" was not included in his 1972 collection *Umanski spohady* (Uman Memories).

23 Iurii Barabash, *Chuzhe-Inakshe-Svoie* (Kyiv, 2020), p. 143.

24 Ibid., p. 144.

25 Volodymyr Panchenko, "*Po zharyshchu pidem udvokh* . . . Pro poemu Bazhana 'Debora,'" *Slovo Prosvity* (Kyiv), 23 July 2015, in http://ju.org.ua/ru/publicism/695.html

The trial of the individuals involved in the mass shootings during the Nazi occupation took place in Kyiv between 17 and 28 February 1946. Present in the courtroom were the Ukrainian writers Volodymyr Sosiura and Yurii Smolych. Based on his courtroom experiences, Sosiura wrote the following lines.

> The hour of judgment for Babyn Yar has come!
> For our blood, for the arbitrary oppression of darkness,
> These are the evils of monsters, and folly, and filth.
> The hand of vengeance.
> Try them, try them in the name of the people,
> In the name of the dead and the living,
> In the name of life and happiness and freedom
> O, righteous judges, try them, the accursed ones.[26]

The poet give emphasis to the concept of "righteous judgment," which is simultaneously the "hand of vengeance." The motif of the inevitability of retribution becomes a dominant one in many poetic texts during the first stage of the literary interpretation of the Babyn Yar tragedy.

The first stage of the literary response to Babyn Yar may be dated tentatively to 1943–1946. In terms of genre, it was mostly poetic texts that emerged in Soviet literature. A ground-breaking prose work that would become a fact of cultural awareness during the war and the first postwar decade had not been created yet. This lacuna may be explained by artistic and political factors, the most pivotal of which was the intensification of governmental control over the interpretation of the war.

In the Soviet cultural space of the first postwar decade a celebratory, victorious version of the war became the order of the day. It was distinguished by a bombastic code featuring feats of heroism. Victory in the war became a powerful propagandistic device for promoting the superiority of the Soviet regime. The replication of symbolic military myths took place in cultural awareness; for example, the leading role of the Communist party, the friendship of peoples, the liberation mission of

---

26 Volodymyr Sosiura cited in "Voennye prestupniki: vozmezdie," in https://babiy-yar.livejournal.com/3601.html

the Soviet army, and others. Official literature was enlisted to promote actively these myths, with the result that the entire multifaceted experience of the war was standardized and pushed into identical, explanatory schemas marked by several negating oppositions: ours and outsiders, enemies and heroes, heroic deed and treason. The non-celebratory version of World War II, which exposed psychological and spiritual traumas, national problems, the Holocaust tragedy, and the Soviet government's responsibility for the price of victory, was relegated to the archives of memory, where it remained for a long time.

During this first period of the literary interpretation of Babyn Yar, writers faced several fundamental problems, above all, the redefinition of identity. For many writers there began a move away from the Soviet matrix to the realization of a dual codification of sameness: Soviet-Jewish, Russian-Jewish, Ukrainian-Jewish, Soviet-Ukrainian, etc. Positioning within the framework of a dual identity expanded the range of possibilities for creative realization, and laid the foundations of intercultural dialogue and new forms of cultural memory (first and foremost, Ukrainian-Jewish and Russian-Jewish). But the creative development of writers in the force field of dual identity was brutally halted by the government-inspired political campaign of 1945–1948, which went down in history as the "struggle against cosmopolitanism" concurrently with the "struggle against Ukrainian bourgeois nationalism." Writers thus often found themselves in the crossfire of accusations. Overt antisemitic rhetoric as well as the psychological harassment and physical liquidation of well-known Jewish artists led to the prohibition, concealment, and marginalization of the Babyn Yar theme.

**Ukrainian émigré literature**

There was an alternative to the Soviet techniques of obliteration and consignment to oblivion. That occurred, however, outside the borders of the totalitarian Soviet state, on the pages of Ukrainian émigré literature where a frank discussion of the Ukraine's experience of World War II was possible. One of the first efforts to portray the Babyn Yar tragedy in Ukrainian literature is Dokiia Humenna's epic novel, *Khreshchatyi yar: Kyiv 1941–1943* (The Cruciform Ravine: Kyiv 1941–1943), which was written immediately after the end of the war. This novel is called a chronicle, reflecting of Humenna's desire to describe her experiences from the perspective of an eyewitness and artistic analyst. During the Nazi occupation the writer lived in Kyiv, where she witnessed various incidents revealing how humans behave in extreme situations.

During the Nazi occupation, Dokiia Humenna was in Kyiv where she experienced first-hand a variety of forms of human conduct in extreme situations. As Myroslav Shkandrij notes, "Humenna's writings appear to be some of the first by a Ukrainian eyewitness to describe the Holocaust in Kyiv. They predate by more than a decade Anatolii Kuznetsov's *Babii Yar*, which first appeared in heavily censored form in Russian in the Soviet Union and then caused a sensation when it was published in English translation in 1970, shortly after the author escaped to Britain. "She deserves credit for portraying a range of public attitudes toward the Holocaust, for problematizing the issue of violence and the question of who forms part of the nation." [27]

Given that the Ukrainian literary space of the first postwar years was dominated by heroic and victim narratives, it can be argued that Hummena's novel emerged as an artistic alternative to such models. At the same time, the author painted a collective portrait of Ukrainian artists in whose lives the traumas of the Holodomor, Stalin's repressions, and the Holocaust tragedy were interwoven. Humenna builds a dialogue with European literature by describing how violence was an integral part of the colonization of Ukrainian space and culture by the Soviet and Nazi regimes. Fundamental to the novel was the reproduction of multiple experiences of war in the ethnocultural, axiological, and gender dimensions and a desire to integrate them into the private and public narrative. For Humenna, the interwar period was marked by a thorny dilemma: a desire to find her place in the writing milieu and a realization that creative fulfillment was impossible to attain living in a totalitarian state.

Humenna's formative years as a writer coincided with the 1920s, a period marking the dynamic and creative burgeoning of Ukrainian literature. This was followed by the decade of the 1930s, which came to be

27 Myroslav Shkandrij, *Jews in Ukrainian Literature: Representation and Identity* (New Haven, CT: Yale University Press, 2009), p. 204.

known as Ukraine's "executed renaissance." This was a time when the majority of Ukrainian artists were liquidated by the Soviet totalitarian regime. Those able to survive endured severe moral tribulations, which for many provided a genuine experience in their psychological and artistic mastery of trauma.

For Humenna, the perception of collective trauma is connected with the destruction of the Ukrainian countryside. In 1928 she worked as a special correspondent of the journal *Pluh* (The Plow), and spent time in the southern regions of Ukraine (the Dnipropetrovsk region and Zaporozhia) and the Kuban. This experience resulted in a cycle of travel essays entitled *Lysty iz stepovoi Ukrainy* (Letters from Steppe Ukraine) and *Ekh, Kuban, Kuban* ( Eh, Kuban, Kuban), published in the journals *Pluh* and *Chervonyi shliakh* (Red Pathway). Published in 1928–1929, these provide a frank and truthful account of the situation in Ukraine's rural regions: the suffering, the curses directed at the Soviet government, and the evil specter of famine against a background of the destruction of established moral principles that traditionally governed relationships in rural communities. Humenna thus exposed the very problems that the Soviet authorities (and officially sanctioned literature) were ignoring and silencing.

The reaction of the Communist party leadership to Humenna's publications was harsh. At various official meetings the general secretary of the Central Committee of the CP(b)U Stanislav Kosior delivered speeches that were highly critical of her writings. The editors of the All-Union Communist party's official organ *Pravda* also harassed Humenna, publishing a denunciatory exposé entitled "Prokazy teti Khivri" (The Pranks of Aunty Khivria).[28] Subsequently, Humenna was forbidden to publish, banned from Ukrainian literature, and in a real sense trapped between life and death, between despair and mobilization of her spiritual resources to counteract falsehood and humiliation.

All these experiences were transformed into the creative dimensions of the novel, *Khreshchatyi yar* (The Cruciform Ravine), in which the occupation of Kyiv is presented as a story about moral challenges, tests, and

28 Cited in Liudmyla Hrynevych, *Khronika kolektyvizatsiï ta holodomoru v Ukraïni, 1927–1933*, Vol. 1, pt. 2 (Kyiv: Krytyka, 2012), p. 107.

personal choice. Rather than building a dialogue with the reader through the condemnation of some and the glorification of others, Humenna reveals the variability of people's roles and statuses in life-threatening conditions. Her focus is on the life stories of various characters: those who sympathized with the Soviet regime; those who pinned their hopes on the Nazi invaders; those who felt for the Jews; and those who participated in their persecution. The city of Kyiv itself is a symbolic character in the novel rendered in different incarnations—Ukrainian, Soviet, German, and Jewish—which are represented through the life events of the protagonist, Mariana Veresoch, for whom the war becomes a chance to restructure identity. We learn that Mariana's youth coincided with Ukraine's short-lived statehood in 1917-1920. During the subsequent Stalinist period her relatives perished in exile or in forced labor camps, while the heroine herself was branded as a "relative of an enemy of the people" and forced to conceal her thoughts and convictions.

At this time a Jewish family becomes her spiritual refuge. In this family headed by a rabbi, Mariana hears about the outbreak of World War II. In the early months of the war, Kyiv, itself a symbolic character, emerges as a city of diverse and frequently contradictory moods and expectations of the war. The inhabitants grow increasingly distrustful of the government's official announcements about the situation at the front, and the city is filled with conflicting rumors. The double standards and morals nourished by totalitarianism are portrayed against this background. At official, obligatory meetings intellectuals make pompous declarations about the "beloved leader" and "our military and political might." At the same time, we read about the panic-stricken flight of high-ranking officials and their families, who manage, nevertheless, to cart away a considerable number of assets. Then there is the forced evacuation of all suspect citizens; robberies; and looting incidents. Giving way to feelings of alarm and uncertainty, the rabbi's family is also evacuated hurriedly. "I don't know anything," the Rebbe replies perplexedly. "All I know is that wherever Hitler comes, our lives are in danger."[29] During the German occupation Mariana goes back to the home of her good friend. It has

29 Dokiia Humenna, *Khreshchatyi iar (Kyïv 1941–1943): roman-khronika* (Kyiv: Vydavnytstvo im. Oleny Telihy), 2001, p. 5.

been looted and plundered, and the heroine grabs the owner's books and papers and takes them to a safe place. The ruined house of the rebbe and occupied Kyiv symbolize the loss of home as a spiritual homeland.

Humenna recounts the tragic fate of the Jews in occupied Kyiv and the challenges that the Holocaust presented to Ukrainian society. With particular warmth the author recreates the life story of Mariana's friend, a Jewish woman named Roza, who, because of her family circumstances, is detained in Kyiv. She fails in her attempt to leave the city at the last minute, before the Germans arrive. Roza's home is occupied by the Germans, and she seeks shelter with Mariana. After a fire breaks out in downtown Kyiv, both women become homeless and end up in a building packed with other people who have lost their homes. One of them is the wife of a caretaker named Tykhohlasykha, whose main job under Soviet rule was to spy on people and denounce the residents of her building to the authorities. "Tykhohlasykha exchanged knowing looks with her female neighbors. It must be said...that there are Jews among us. They began whispering and dashing out somewhere. Snippets of conversation: 'We're not going to shelter them.'"[30] A German officer arrives eventually. He brutalizes the Jews (among whom are many elderly and sick people), beats them, and evicts them from the premises. Mariana is in despair over not being able to help Roza and protect her from death. Roza hides in bushes and parks, finds refuge in the odd building, and is finally denounced. As for Mariana, the German administration constantly evicts her from her lodgings, and she has to move several times. In her fourth temporary lodgings she discovers a photo album belonging to the previous owners. From the very first page of the album Roza gazes at Mariana. She is young, surrounded by a nimbus of happiness. Mariana recalls that Roza's husband was killed at the front and their young son was left in the countryside. She reflects that Roza accepted all the burdens of this terrible time.

The motif of homelessness, lack of protection, and impending death of all those who are trapped in the occupied city is repeated throughout the novel. Singled out is the dramatic story of Semen Kucheriavyi,

30 Ibid., pp. 155-156.

who is married to a Jewish woman. He makes a conscious decision not to abandon Kyiv and convinces his wife that the rumors about the Nazis' savagery are all lies. He clings to an old illusion that the advancing Germans are those whom he remembers from his youth. In his dreams he imagines that prosperity, order, and "our own Ukrainian state" will arrive along with the Germans. Kucheriavyi's anticipations complement the palette of other moods prevalent among the residents of Kyiv. "Some want the return of Ukraine, others want 'a [Russia] one and indivisible', while others do not care, as long as 'they bring in goods.'"[31] Everyone is seeking a return to the past, but reality turns out to be terrible and cruel. For a while Kucheriavyi hides his Jewish wife, but some neighbors denounce her to the Germans, and she dies at the hands of the Nazis. Left alone with his three children, homeless, and with no means of survival, he has paid dearly for his naivety, and he sinks into disillusionment and depression.

Humenna does not conceal the population's collaboration with the German authorities or the fact that, for various reasons, some local residents revealed the hiding places of Jews. At the same time, But at the same time she convincingly proves that the reaction of most Kyivites to the killings in Babyn Yar was almost universally negative. At first, they are in a state of shock and unable to comprehend the unthinkable. Shock is then replaced by feelings of sympathy for the victims and condemnation of the Germans' actions. The author describes the atmosphere in the city, filled with rumors that made one's "hair stand on end." The inhabitants of Kyiv are stunned by accounts of:

> how a machine gun . . . clattered away above the ravine and swept [people] into the ravine, how the Germans threw one or two grenades, and the earth covered thousands of perhaps fatally wounded people, possibly still alive, how they killed with an electric current. . . . There is no one in Kyiv who was not repulsed and did not shudder inwardly from the Hitlerites' savage reprisals against the Jews. . . . No, the Hitlerite bloodbath is not to the Kyivites' taste, there are no voices of the malicious joy that Hitler was probably expecting. Hitler perpetrated a loathsome act

31 Ibid., pp. 104-105.

> against the Jews! It would have been better if they had all left than for this to have happened in Kyiv.[32]

As Myroslav Shkandrij noted, this novel "is perhaps the most thoughtful attempt to grapple with the Holocaust and with Jewish-Ukrainian relations in Ukrainian fiction of the postwar years, and raises issues that only entered wider public discourse in later decades: political conformism, guilt felt by silent witnesses, responses to limit experiences, and the need to construct a narrative for even the most traumatic events."[33] Humenna broaches the psychological changes that occur in the consciousness of Kyiv residents as a result of the Babyn Yar massacre. Their feelings of marginality and defenselessness in the face of violence and fear of the future are exacerbated, and their daily life is filled with worries about their physical survival and how to avoid being deported as slave laborers to the German Reich. In a certain way, the obsession of Kyiv's residents with their own troubles reduces their openness to others' sufferings; each person becomes a hostage to his or her own tragic history.

Humenna's artistic depiction reveals the dramatic experience that was later systematically summarized by Karel Berkhoff in his study *Harvest of Despair*. Describing the moral and psychological climate in Reichskommissariat Ukraine (which included Kyiv), the researcher compares it to the regime of Nazi concentration camps: "the pervasive terror; the obligation to witness public beatings or executions; the happy music during sad occasions; and the frequency with which captors observed their subjects with disgust or pretended not to see them at all."[34] Accordingly, the symbol of Babyn Yar in Humenna's novel is integrated into the coordinates of values-based priorities. For Mariana Veresoch, the German occupation creates the problem of existential choice. The heroine overcomes her fears and seeks support through spiritual resistance to both the Soviet and Nazi totalitarian regimes. The experience of living

---

32 Ibid., p. 169.

33 Shkandrij, *Jews in Ukrainian Literature*, p. 202.

34 Karel Berkhoff, *Harvest of Despair: Life and Death in Ukraine under Nazi Rule* (Cambridge, Mass. and London: The Belknap Press of Harvard University Press, 2004), p. 309.

under the occupation teaches her not to curry favor with any powers that be, not submit to the temptations of all-out hatred and moral deafness, and not lose the capacity to empathize with another's pain. At the same time Mariana realizes that the Ukrainians failed to gain a political state or spiritual fatherland under both Soviet and Nazi rule. Whereas at the beginning of the novel Kyiv is "on the alert" prior to the arrival of the German army, by the epilogue the city is "bewitched by fear."

Hummena ends the novel with the main heroine setting out on a journey. Contextually, this is not simply flight from the approaching Soviet army but, above all, an attempt to find new spiritual reference points; a longing for genuine—not simulated—liberation from violence. It is not accidental that encoded in the title *Khreshchatyi yar/The Cruciform Ravine* are direct parallels to the toponym "Babyn Yar": A common, unifying point in the novel is the memory of suffering, victims, and the assertion of the value of human life.

Thus, Humenna's novel revealed the need to address painful and complex issues related to the experience of occupation and the Holocaust. Her work became a reliable basis for reinterpreting Ukrainian-Jewish relations during World War II and for exposing the complex problems that people faced in situations where they had to make a moral choice and assume responsibility. Noteworthily, the author integrates into Ukrainian cultural memory the narrative of Jewish suffering and links it to the history of Ukrainian suffering. The combination of these narratives changes the notion of national identity into one that is open to the integration of multiple ethnic experiences and their cultural memorialization. Shkandrij rightly notes that by addressing the sufferings of both Ukrainians and Jews during World War II, Humenna re-creates the idea of the nation as a spiritual family. The spiritual family of Mariana, the protagonist of *Khreshchatyi Yar*, includes "Ukrainians and Jews, and the loss of Jewish friends is mourned as a loss of family members."[35] Remarkably, her version is not a "competition of victims". Rather, she emphasized that, by being open to the sufferings of another person, you can better understand who you really are and discover yourself in another human being.

35 Shkandrij, *Jews in Ukrainian Literature*, p. 202-203.

Thus, *Khreshchatyi Yar* became the first significant attempt at outlining the Holocaust trauma in Ukrainian emigration prose and set Ukrainian literature on the course of decolonization.

### The Sixties Generation

In the late 1950s–early 1960s, under the influence of social changes that sparked a wave of spiritual emancipation in art, a fundamental reconsideration of the war and its overloaded memory took place. A new generation of writers appeared in literature. Known as the *Shistydesiatnyky* ("The Sixtiers"), its members distanced themselves from the political and cultural legacy of Stalinism. One of the representatives of this generation, the Ukrainian writer and journalist Yevhen Sverstiuk, noted that the "sixties were a period of great upheavals throughout the world. Young radicals were entering the arena. They rejected the world that their parents had created for them."[36]

It was the Sixtiers who established a new moral and critical response to the war. At its heart lay attention to the fate of concrete individuals and the glaring incongruity between the optimistic and victorious representation of the war, as cultivated in the Soviet Union, and the private, mostly traumatic and tragic, experience of the war. In Soviet Russian literature, a wave of "lieutenant's prose" appeared, its authors portraying the war as a set of moral tests, extreme psychological states, and the dilemma between choice and personal responsibility. Among the texts revealing this new moral and analytical dimension of the war are Boris Balter's novel *Do svidaniia, malchiki* (Goodbye, Lads), Viktor Astafev's novel *Zvezdopad* (Starfall), Vasilii Rosliakov's novel *Odin iz nas* (One of Us), Konstantin Vorobev's *Ubity pod Moskvoi* (Killed at Moscow) and other works.

Other Ukrainian prose works of the sixties, such as Hryhir Tiutiunnyk's short stories "Smert kavalera" (Death of a Hero), "Obloha" (The Siege), and "Klymko"; Yevhen Hutsalo's short story "Mertva zona" (Dead Zone); and Volodymyr Drozd's novel *Zemlia pid kopytamy* (The Land under the Hooves), stand out in marked contrast to the bombastic pa-

36 Ievhen Sverstiuk, *Bludni syny Ukraïny* (Kyiv, 1993), p. 23.

thos and grandiloquence that frequently defined the war theme in literature. Instead, this new generation of Ukrainian writers focused their attention on the trauma of a war childhood, incomplete families, and survival strategies to cope with life under German occupation.

Against the background of social changes and the revival of literature, the Babyn Yar theme acquired new topicality. The unique poetic detonator that awakened the artistic milieu from its spiritual sleep and garnered a broad response among readers was Yevgeny Yevtushenko's poem "Babi Yar," whose opening line reads: "No monument stands over Babi Yar" (in the English translation by Benjamin Okopnik). Yevtushenko wrote the poem following his trip to Kyiv in August 1961, during which he visited Babyn Yar together with the writer Anatoly Kuznetsov. [see Plate **XX**] Stunned to see that the site of the mass executions was utterly neglected and resembled a huge, appalling garbage dump, Yevtushenko was moved to write his poem, first read publicly in September 1961 at a literary evening held at the Polytechnical Museum in Moscow. The members of the audience listened with baited breath, then burst into a frenzy of applause and demanded an encore; they listened to the second reading of "Babi Yar" standing at attention.

For a long period of time Yevtushenko was not able to publish the poem, although it finally appeared in *Literaturnaia gazeta* (Literary Gazette). No reader could remain indifferent to the poem, which soon became the subject of energetic discussions and impassioned arguments. Some writers accused Yevtushenko of a lack of patriotism, cosmopolitanism, and 'forgetting about his own Russian people." The majority of reputable literary figures, however, including Samuil Marshak and Konstantin Simonov, publicly supported the poet in their writings.[37]

The opening lines of Yevtushenko's poem sounded like a symbolic indictment of the Soviet government and the double standard in its attitude to the memory of the victims of Babyn Yar: "No monument stands over Babi Yar./ A steep cliff only, like the rudest headstone." Then the poet diagnoses the spiritual abyss in the Soviet Union, from which an exit was possible only through liberation from the burden of the ste-

37 "My reshili byt' uvolennymi", in https://babiy-yar.livejournal.com/6149.html

reotypes imposed by the authorities. The burden in question is the imperialistic legacy of antisemitism, the language of suspicion, innuendo, and mutual recrimination. The poet's persona rebels against this state of affairs, so that the feelings of blame and responsibility acquire a particular resonance.

> Wild grasses rustle over Babi Yar,
> The trees look sternly, as if passing judgement.
> Here, silently, all screams, and, hat in hand,
> I feel my hair changing shade to gray.[38]

Like his predecessors Ehrenburg and Ozerov, Yevtushenko identifies himself with the victims of violence. Yet at the same time he is well aware of his obligation to awaken deadened memory.

> And I myself, like one long soundless scream
> Above the thousands of thousands interred,
> I'm every old man executed here,
> As I am every child murdered here.[39]

In discussions about the tragic past, the supreme authority for the poet is truth. The perception of the other as hostile and potentially dangerous is a disgraceful page that must be turned over forever. This statement became the poem's symbolic slogan and artistic platform of the generation of Sixtiers.

> May [the] "Internationale" thunder and ring
> When, for all time, is buried and forgotten
> The last antisemites on this earth.[40]

Literary scholars noted that Yevtushenko's poem became a phenomenon not only in cultural but also in sociopolitical life. In December 1962 the poet read a fragment of his poem at a meeting attended by Niki-

---

38 Evgenii Evtushenko, *Stikhotvoreniia* (Moscow, 1988), p. 72.
39 Ibid., p. 74.
40 Ibid.

ta Khrushchev. The Soviet leader's reaction was categorically negative. Khrushchev called such texts irrelevant and politically harmful, and accused he Yevtushenko of "singing in a foreign voice." The Soviet government thus continued to think in oppositional terms and wielded the language of political accusations.[41]

Yevtushenko's poem was a turning-point on literature's path to finding its own voice and the courage to oppose the authorities. Spiritual continuity with the main principles of Yevtushenko's civic stance was manifested with particular clarity in mass rallies that took place on 29 September 1966 to mark the twenty-fifth anniversary of Babyn Yar. A public meeting held in Kyiv was attended by the Russian writer and journalist Viktor Nekrasov, and his Ukrainian colleagues, the literary critic Ivan Dziuba, the writer and translator Borys Antonenko-Davydovych, the writer and director Helii Sniehiriov, and others.

In his address, Dziuba noted that various norms of social behavior regarding attitudes to Babyn Yar were now current in Kyiv. Drawing a clearly demarcated line between unofficial memory and the government's official position, Dziuba declared:

> Some Kyivites went out on this day with bouquets of flowers and black mourning ribbons, heading for the outlying district of the city whose name has become sadly notorious throughout the world: Babyn Yar. Meanwhile, other Kyivites wracked their brains, trying to prevent a large gathering of the former at this site. Still other residents of Kyiv, on orders from the second group of Kyivites, monitored the members of the first group, and, in case of need, 'adopted measures' against those of us who were most enthusiastic.[42]

### The impact of the first commemorations

The symbolic space of Babyn Yar thus came to embody various values-based priorities. For some it was viewed as a place of grief and remembrance; for others it became a political instrument of control, black-

41 "My reshili byt' uvolennym," in https://babiy-yar.livejournal.com/6149.html

42 Ivan Dziuba, "U 25 rokovyny rozstriliv u Babynomu Iaru: promova, 29 September 1966," Iehupets', No. 1 (Kyiv, 1995), pp. 4-8.

mail, and intimidation. The latter factor undoubtedly played a decisive role in the fact that in the postwar decades no prominent cultural figure ever took part in the annual mourning processions of Kyivites to Babyn Yar, or delivered any eulogies at the victims' graves.

In September 1966 an especially large crowd of people came to the ravine in Kyiv. The presence of well-known artists created a special psychological and emotional atmosphere. As Dziuba recalled:

> People's faces were frozen with suffering, and their eyes were otherworldly: they gazed into the depths of time and saw a dreadful picture of what was not and would never become the past for them. The shadow of the bygone horror and a kind of human bewilderment reigned over Babyn Yar, and thousands of people, mute in petrified trepidation, seemed to be permeated with the mute cry of an entire people. The crowd remained silent. But this was a pressing, questioning kind of silence. People wanted to listen, they rushed toward us, they grabbed us in various directions. . . . Each one of us was surrounded by a dense crowd demanding: 'Tell us something!'[43]

The words of Ivan Dziuba, one of the intellectual leaders of the Ukrainian Sixtiers, rang out powerfully that day. First and foremost, he emphasized the "conspiracy of silence" that had risen around the semantic field of Babyn Yar. In his considered opinion, this long-lasting silence "was becoming an accomplice of untruth and unfreedom."[44] Second, Dziuba integrated the Babyn Yar tragedy into the coordinates of the Ukrainian experience, collective memory, and cultural awareness. A concerted effort to gain an understanding of the tragedy, one that transcended the limits of national identification and opened up new horizons for a different set of philosophical and psychological optics, was the very approach that failed to be reflected in a full-fledged manner in the space of Soviet (and Soviet Ukrainian) literature during the postwar decades. In a certain sense, Dziuba's speech played a compensatory role with regard to the moral dilemmas that had fallen out of the analytical

43 Ibid.

44 Ibid.

field of Ukrainian literature but which had to be expressed in order to overcome the colonial way of thinking.

Dziuba's stirring speech not only issued an appeal to the past, it also outlined prospects for the future, linking them with the development of new communications practices, in which culture would be called upon to carry out a leading role. Accordingly, the lessons of Babyn Yar envisioned a dialogue among cultures and nations.

Viktor Nekrasov, one of the organizers of the 1966 commemorative event, later recalled Dziuba's speech warmly. He commented that the Soviet state security service duly noted the writer's participation in the ceremony to honor the victims of Babyn Yar, adding it to the list of political accusations against Dziuba, who was later imprisoned on charges of "Ukrainian bourgeois nationalism." But the public meeting, as well as its scale and the questions that were posed that day, spurred the party leadership into co-opting the initiative and imbuing future commemorations of the Babyn Yar massacre with ideological and ritual content.

For the purpose of comparison, it is worthwhile recalling the words of Nekrasov, who noted the "governmentalization" of the commemorative tradition. His reflections exposed the Soviet government's efforts to strip Babyn Yar of its intellectual voice and to supplant the commemoration of its victims with exclusively Soviet ideological content.

> And now, every year on 29 September (the day set aside to honor the victims of the temporary German-fascist occupation), not far from the rock a podium is being constructed, from which the secretary of the Shevchenko raion party committee is delivering a speech devoted mostly to the achievements in fulfilling the plan in various branches. Later, speeches are made by a few factory workers recognized for their initiative or exemplary work, among whom there is one token worker of the Jewish nationality (today it is not acceptable to say simply a Jew), and he talks about the Zionists' savagery in Israel. After the speeches the hymn is performed and the meeting is declared closed. At this very moment people with flowers and wreaths appear. But it turns out that it is no simple matter to lay them. Members of the militia and their doubles, dressed in civilian clothing, carefully inspect the inscriptions on the wreaths, and if they find something suspect ('And what language is this

> written in? Translate it.'), the people holding the wreaths end up in 'Black Marias' [security service vehicles] that are idling nearby. Elderly people with small bouquets are let through without hindrance. Well, maybe, someone is photographed.[45]

Nekrasov incorporated his reminiscences and impressions of the 1966 Babyn Yar commemoration into his novel, *Zapiski zevaki* (Notes of a Bystander). This work, written during his forced emigration (1976), may be regarded as the confessions of a Kyivite, which gushed out in the form of a frank conversation about values and about an individual who seeks the profound meaning of life. In addition to other urban centers (Paris, New York, Warsaw), Nekrasov reconstructs the image of his native Kyiv, a city that is immeasurably dear to him and which vanished without a trace or was obliterated from the map of memory by the winds of history and the actions of politicians.

Babyn Yar occupies a singular place in Nekrasov's text, and acquires universal, symbolic meaning. The writer inserts it into the cultural space of Kyiv and his own life story. The supreme importance to him of this part of the Kyiv landscape is attested by the fact that before emigrating, Nekrasov visited the site of Babyn Yar. This farewell pilgrimage turns into an analysis of past experience and a quest for spiritual support in the future. The author's look at Babyn Yar is multifaceted. Above all, his novel *Zapiski zevaki* is a reconstruction of the mass killings that took place there during World War II. He also describes the postwar life of Babyn Yar as a place of special commemorative unanimity. "A small hill of flowers. Wreaths. Large, small; simply bouquets of flowers. On the wreaths are ribbons with inscriptions saying 'To father, to mother, to grandfather—from your sons, daughters, and grandchildren'; 'To the children who were not destined to reach adulthood.'"[46]

Nekrasov does not overlook the Kurenivka mudslide of 1961. He traces the tragedy's roots to acts of vandalism that mock death itself in the form of the planned destruction of a Jewish cemetery located near Babyn Yar. During the 1941 occupation of Kyiv, the main cemetery alleyway

45 Viktor Nekrasov, *Zapiski zevaki* (Moscow: Vagrius, 2003), p. 40.

46 Ibid., p. 38.

was destroyed by the Germans. The destruction of Jewish gravestones was continued later by Kyiv's city authorities. Nekrasov compares his impressions of this destruction from various perspectives of time: the late 1950s, when he first discovered traces of the ruins, and the mid-1970s, on the eve of his departure from Kyiv: "I was there at the time; in fact, before my departure. After fifteen years. . . . Everything was overgrown with bushes and grass. The ruined gravestones had been carted off somewhere. But not all of them. Here and there half-broken pedestals, stairs, bits of marble, and labradorite gleam whitely. And bulldozers. They are rumbling, and through the metal screeching they are laying a road on the site of the main alleyway. . . . There are no people. It is empty. Dead . . . and terrifying."[47]

Nekrasov treats the Babyn Yar massacre during World War II, the destruction of the Jewish Cemetery by both totalitarian regimes, the dam collapse in Kurenivka, and, finally, the spatial disappearance of Babyn Yar as manifestations of the "captive mind" (to quote Czesław Miłosz), submission to evil, and descent into a state of moral nihilism. Nekrasov's unwillingness to reconcile himself to this situation was a decisive factor in his participation in the dissident movement and lengthy spiritual duel with the Soviet government.

For Nekrasov, the culmination of his chosen path was the 29 September 1966 commemoration, which the writer recorded with painstaking precision. Describing his feelings, he accentuated the spiritual freedom that filled his being. He had every reason to feel this way because he had not coordinated his speech in advance with anyone, and it had not been vetted by any oversight institution. In other words, no censorship of any kind had influenced his thought processes. For this former front-line soldier and author of the masterpiece *V okopakh Stalingrada* (Front-Line Stalingrad), the war found its continuation and gained new meaning precisely at the site of Babyn Yar, and it became a struggle for human dignity and memory. In a certain sense, the struggle for memory is one of the most important subjects raised in Nekrasov's *Zapiski zevaki*, in which the author recalls his impressions of the various entries that were submit-

---

47 Ibid., p. 45.

ted to a design competition for a monument intended to commemorate the victims of Babyn Yar. The submission terms and conditions included clear-cut ideological criteria: "The monuments should reflect in artistic form the heroism, invincible will, courage, and fearlessness of our people in the face of death at the hands of the German executioners; they should depict the beastly faces of the Hitlerite invaders, and they should also convey the nationwide grieving for the thousands of nameless heroes."[48]

It is no wonder that Nekrasov rebelled inwardly against the majority of the submitted designs. For this writer, who had direct experience of the war (and not in the way Soviet propaganda portrayed it), it was important to liberate memory from the patriotism of hatred. His top priority in the process of comprehending the tragedy was to apprehend the philosophy of death. In his view, the attitude to death is a marker of a society's spiritual maturity. He realizes with bitterness that a profanation of death is taking place within Soviet totalitarian society, especially through the negation of its sacred, religious dimension and denial of the transcendental sense. What is obvious to the writer in this context is the culpability of ideologically subordinated art that generates simple, standardized answers to complex and debatable questions.

On the whole, there is a very personal dimension to Babyn Yar in *Zapiski zevaki*. In a certain sense, it became part of the author's treasured memories of his childhood, youth, and civic maturation. At the same time, Nekrasov's version of Babyn Yar signifies the problem of choice: between freedom of self-realization and conformism; between truth and the "conspiracy of silence." In those social confrontations that the writer was destined to experience, Babyn Yar became the source of spiritual strength, impregnability, and the capacity to remain his own person.

The Babyn Yar tragedy found its fullest possible artistic expression in Anatoly Kuznetsov's novel *Babi Yar: A Document in the Form of a Novel*, a work that played a special role in the author's life and became a unique literary phenomenon in the era of the Sixtiers. Kuznetsov recalled that the publication of his novel was dictated by the government's attempts to dampen the public's response to Yevtushenko's poem. Literary ide-

---

48 Ibid., p. 42.

ologists sought to prove that Kuznetsov's novel utterly contradicted the main ideas of Yevtushenko's tribute to Babyn Yar. Kuznetsov rejected these claims, emphasizing that his novel was not a polemic against Yevtushenko's poem but a continuation and substantial expansion of a set of problems pertaining to Babyn Yar.

From the pen of the writer whose childhood and youth were linked indissolubly with Kyiv (Kuznetsov and his family lived in Kurenivka, the district adjacent to Babyn Yar) came the artistic and documentary embodiment of multiple dimensions of meaning layered over the symbol of Babyn Yar. The occupation of Kyiv had a decisive, formative influence on the writer. Kuznetsov, who began taking notes in his adolescence, returned constantly to his wartime experiences and eventually created a document in the form of a novel.

Kuznetsov's work encountered numerous obstacles. His novel first appeared in abridged form in three issues (nos. 8–10) of the journal *Yunost* (Youth) in 1966; a year later, the Molodaia gvardiia publishing house released it as a separate book. [see Plate **XX**] From both versions the censors mercilessly excised excerpts containing what they considered "anti-Soviet content." The author later recalled: "Writers in the Soviet Union are always confronted with a dilemma: whether they should be published at all, or whether they should publish only what is permitted by censorship. Many believe that it is better to offer the reader something rather than nothing. I too thought that."[49] When, in 1969, Kuznetsov was sent on an assignment to London, he requested political asylum and announced his refusal to return to the Soviet Union. His decision sparked a wave of indignation and political accusations in Soviet governmental circles. Placed on a list of "traitors and enemies," Kuznetsov's novel was banned for several decades. Its complete text, along with additions that the writer made in 1967–1969, was published abroad in 1970.

The book's complicated trajectory was determined not only by Kuznetsov's political choice (he was branded as a defector) but, above all, by those questions that he brought into the public space of literature. They struck a discordant note within the totalitarian system of political

49 Anatolii Kuznetsov, *Babii Iar: roman-dokument* (Kyiv: MIP "Oberih," 1991), p. 7.

directives, above all through his call to resist the attack on the space of freedom and human dignity. The final lines of his novel proclaim: "No social crime will remain unknown. Something can be burned, dispersed by the wind, covered up with earth, and trampled down, but human memory remains."[50] In fact, memory is one of the main heroes in the novel, and the author's interlocutor.

Kuznetsov begins his symbolic journey into the depths of memory with episodes that had a decisive impact on the writing of his novel. First and foremost, the author revisits his impressions of Kyiv during the German occupation, when for two years he heard machine-gun fire coming from Babyn Yar, and noticed thick, black smoke rising from the ravine for several weeks. When he went to the ravine later, he spotted many white stones at the bottom of a little stream. Picking one up, he realized that it was a charred fragment of a human bone. Reaching the end of the stream, he noticed that the sand was gray, and realized that he was walking on human ashes. The writer reinterprets this symbol and declares that the "ashes of Klaas knock at my heart"[51] (a reference to *Till Eulenspiegel*, an impudent trickster figure originating in German folklore, who carries his father's ashes in a bag around his neck—translator). Kuznetsov's work thus became a symbolic step to ensure that human memory will not be transformed into the ashes of oblivion. At the same time, this is a story about the ways one individual survived in a totalitarian society, as well as about the tragedy of an artist stripped of the freedom to create.

Kuznetsov insisted that his novel was based entirely on documentary materials. His main goal was to convey as much truthful information as possible and thus distance himself from socialist-realist texts. He opted for confessional writing, a style that allowed him to present the historical, social, and psychological characteristics of a particular era. The novel begins in the mid-1920s and ends in the late 1960s. Such a broad chronological sweep allowed the novelist to recreate major historical events and to recount the history of numerous heroes, as well as his own family history.

One of his first conscious memories of childhood was overhearing

50 Ibid., p. 349.
51 Ibid., 17.

adults' conversations about the famine that ravaged Ukraine in 1933 (marked by incidents of cannibalism), the New Year tree, and a song about "this wonder tree that Postyshev has brought us." In one scene little Tolia is shocked to see his mother burning "dangerous" books on the stove; in another, he and his friends are watching their favorite movies: *Chapaev*, *Shchors*, *Bohdan Khmelnytsky*, and *Esli zavtra voina* (If War Comes Tomorrow). This kaleidoscope of childhood experiences is layered over the life stories of the people who are dearest to him: his grandparents, his mother, and the parents of his childhood friends. In Kuznetsov's view, the multitude of problems that were exacerbated by World War II are rooted in the situation that existed before the war, with its repressions, lies, and atmosphere of fear and mutual suspicion.

The arrival of German troops becomes engraved in the memory of the teenaged Kuznetsov as a result of the following incident. A female neighbor, who had rushed over to his parents' house, was "excited, not herself; she was shouting in joyful astonishment and exultation: 'Why are you just sitting here? The Germans have come! Soviet rule has ended.'"[52] The writer supplements his account with other examples demonstrating the priorities in the expectations of Kyiv residents, for whom the end of Soviet rule is a more important event than the arrival of a foreign army. He writes convincingly and truthfully about the rapid onset of disillusionment and despair, and the tragedy of life under the German occupation. At the same time he introduces psychological parallels, showing how hope gave way to the disillusionment and fear that were everyday features of people's lives during Soviet and German rule.

Kuznetsov reproduces the varied topography of the crimes committed in occupied Kyiv: the explosions detonated on Khreshchatyk Boulevard and in the Kyivan Cave Monastery; and the death camp for Soviet prisoners of war in the Darnytsia district of Kyiv. Into this space of violence and death he inscribes Babyn Yar. The author confesses that this place had a lethal effect on him because forever after he was plagued by dreams in which he heard the voices of people being shot, and imagined scenes in which he himself was being led away to be shot. However, Kuznetsov's

52 Ibid., p. 21.

novel cannot be reduced to a psychological release from childhood trauma. There is no question that unexpressed pain and the process of pushing into the subconscious information begging to be recorded on paper were part and parcel of a situation that was typical of all Soviet literature in the first postwar decade. But, in addition to Post-Traumatic Stress Disorder, the writer outlined the war's new dimensions of meaning: state violence against the individual and the loss of preventive ethics with regard to evil.

The writer portrays the beginning of the occupation of Kyiv also through the deformation of the information space, which, in his estimation, became a component of physical violence. Kuznetsov cites announcements, orders, and directives issued by the German administration that communicates with the civilian population in the language of threats, intimidation, and a list of punishments to be meted out in the event of noncompliance. One such announcement that the twelve-year-old Tolia Kuznetsov happened to read proved fatal for many thousands of Jews living in the Ukrainian capital.

Kuznetsov recreates the tragic death route that wound its way through the streets of Kyiv on 29 September 1941 by conveying moods of anxiety, uncertainty, fear, and impending doom among the Jewish population (he was struck by the large numbers of sick, elderly, and weak people), as well as sympathy, indifference, and malicious joy expressed by the local citizenry. Despite the varied reactions of Kyivites, the writer underscores the fact that the residents of the Ukrainian capital were shocked to their core by the shootings in Babyn Yar.

While Kuznetsov was working on his novel, he met many people, who not only recalled the dreadful years of the German occupation, but also their personal stories to him. In his novel the storytellers are not just eyewitnesses but active figures in a grand history that was often excessively brutal toward them. The multiplicity of voices allows the reader to comprehend how Ukraine lived through the largest war of the twentieth century, to become aware of the dramas and tragedies that played out on its territory, with its heroes and antiheroes, and to understand how the writer resisted the temptations of falseness and untruth.

Kuznetsov recapitulates the life stories of several individuals who managed to save themselves from the deadly hell (Dina Pronicheva, Volodymyr Davydov) and talks about the Kyivites who helped some to survive. He significantly expands the martyrology of victims and recalls the Ukrainian poet Olena Teliha, the editor of the newspaper *Ukrainske slovo* Ivan Rohach, the Roma people, and the extermination of patients at the Pavlov Psychiatric Hospital, Soviet prisoners of war, and underground members who were shot in Babyn Yar.

The writer describes in detail how the German occupation authorities manipulated the vanquished by provoking them into engaging in mutual suspicion and spying on each other. "Woe to you if you had an enemy or someone envied you. In the past, someone might write a denunciation stating that you are against Soviet power, therefore an enemy of the people, and you disappeared without a trace. Now that person might write that you are against German power, therefore an enemy of the people, and Babyn Yar awaited you. Even the German terminology was the same: 'enemy of the people'!"[53] For Kuznetsov, Babyn Yar becomes a symbol of the totalitarian ghetto; it is the road traversed by the writer in order to cast off his political and spiritual chains.

Kuznetsov's novel achieved several strategic goals. One of the main ones was breaching the information blockade by literary means. By combining the formats of reminiscences and journal entries, the writer created an emotionally arresting account of violence, terror, and people's capacity to counteract them by marshaling their spiritual reserves. One of the book's main commandments is that truth is the most potent weapon in the struggle against violence. The standard of openness and moral responsibility that was put into practice by Kuznetsov was definitive in the formation of the world perceptions and principles of many writers.

The capacity to be oneself and not betray one's chosen principles is especially prominent in the works of the talented and original Ukrainian writer Leonid Pervomaiskyi. The theme of the Holocaust and Babyn Yar is foremost in his creative explorations.

Leonid Pervomaiskyi was born in 1908 into a Jewish family in the Ukrainian region of Poltava. He began his literary career in the late 1920s

---

53 Ibid., p. 15.

as a poet and prose writer. His choice to link his destiny with Ukrainian literature was unusual in his milieu, as the majority of his peers aspired to realize themselves creatively within the dominant culture of the Soviet state—Russian. But Pervomaiskyi deliberated chose integration into the Ukrainian cultural space. This choice became a values-based priority which was to define the philosophical principles of his creativity. In the perceptive words of Yohanan Petrovsky-Shtern: "Pervomaiskyi identified with the deprived shtetl Jews and the silenced victims of the Ukrainian famine, the anonymous Red Army soldiers perishing on the front during World War II and the voiceless Holocaust martyrs, the persecuted literati of various epochs and nations, and the executed Soviet Yiddish writers. At the end of his career, he came to identify with the martyrdom of creative writing, with persecuted poets such as himself, and with the suppressed voice of Ukrainian poetry."[54]

In 1949, during the "struggle against rootless cosmopolitans," Pervomaiskyi was powerless to escape the accusations and humiliating jibes that were aimed at him. The direct response to his spiritual conflict with the Soviet government was the poem, "Na ukrainskii zolotii zemli" (On the Ukrainian Golden Land). The writer had fought at the front, and when the war ended, he worked as a military correspondent for the newspaper *Pravda*. The Babyn Yar tragedy could not fail to affect him, whether as a writer whose life before the war and creative formation were inextricably tied to Kyiv, or as a Jew who had survived and felt a spiritual kinship with the victims of the Holocaust.

At the same time, what makes Pervomaiskyi stand out is his sense of guilt before the victims, which is why the topic of the Holocaust has a special place in his oeuvre and runs through his postwar poetry ("Melnikova Street", "Wild Honey", "In Babyn Yar"). Pervomaiskyi is also of interest with regard to the limits of the permissible in Ukrainian literature as defined by the imperial cultural policy. To quote again Petrovsky-Shtern: "The area of the 'legally allowed' was much narrower for a Ukrainian writer than for a Russian one. National endeavors within Russian national perceptions were censored, whereas such endeavors

54 Petrovskyi-Shtern, *Anti-Imperial Choice*, p. 166.

within Ukrainian national feelings were expurgated. The regime would frown on certain Jewish motifs in Russian-Jewish literature but would immediately stifle recognizable Jewish hints in the texts of Ukrainian-Jewish writers."[55] For Pervomaiskyi to address Holocaust issues was in itself an act of civic courage, and, at the same time, a testament to new approaches of describing the tragedy. The poet localized the spatial dimensions of the Holocaust, outlining them in the parameters of family history, emphasizing not so much the acts of violence and cruelty as those of kindness, compassion, and rescue. In the words of Yohanan Petrovsky-Shtern, he "found voiceless victims . . . and helped them speak."[56]

Pervomaiskyi's reinterpretation of the Kyivan dimension of the Nazi German occupation was reflected in both his prose and poetry. In his short story "Vulytsia Melnykova" (Melnikova Street), Pervomaiskyi reveals the moral and psychological challenges that the Holocaust introduced into the lives of ordinary Kyiv residents.[57] The Ukrainian–Jewish couple, Klava and Mosia, get married before the war. When the war breaks out, Mosia is sent to the front, and his pregnant wife remains in occupied Kyiv. Klava is about to give birth, and while waiting for labor to begin, she reads some announcements that have been plastered all over the city, ordering all Jews to assemble at the corner of Melnikova and Dehtiarivska streets. The young woman rents an apartment from Aunty Nastia and tells her landlady who the father of her child is. Aunty Nastia becomes preoccupied with her thoughts and with various evil presentiments. She is afraid for her life and does not know what to do. The birth of Klava's child coincides with the first days of the executions in Babyn Yar, and at this very time some policemen come to the flat to check passports. Aunty Nastia convinces them that Klava is her niece, and thus saves the mother and her newborn. This ordinary woman achieves the greatest possible victory, triumphing over her own terror and hopelessness.

55 Ibid., p. 277.

56 Ibid., p. 227.

57 Leonid Pervomais'kyi, "Vulytsia Melnykova" in his *Tvory*, Vol. 3 (Kyiv: Dnipro, 1985), pp. 416-429.

It is precisely through the exploration of such extreme situations that Pervomaiskyi exposed new psychological dimensions of Babyn Yar. In other words, even while being defenseless against the government, a person is nonetheless able to resist. In the author's interpretation, the day of death becomes the birthday of a new life, and this life is stronger than fear and despair. Hence the semantics of death is not dominant in this version. Instead, the author reveals sources of spiritual strength and solidarity. For example, ordinary women experience a powerful transformation and turn into warriors in spiritual confrontation. Such spiritual power cannot be overcome by physical means. As Petrovsky-Shtern reminds us: "whatever the real number of righteous gentiles in Kyiv in 1941, the most important lesson one may draw from [the short story] "Melnikova Street" is that marginalized individuals can and should actively oppose violence."[58]

Not unexpectedly, echoes of Babyn Yar also appear throughout Pervomaiskyi's poetry. One poem, symbolically entitled "Popil" (Ashes), conveys his fear and bitterness at the state of spiritual amnesia that reigns in society.

It lay on guard over conscience,
But we, living and existing passersby,
Shake that dread dust off our boots,
Is it because the crime has not ended,
That we fear future bloodshed
That we have no strength to stop?[59]

Another poem "V Babynim Yaru" (In Babyn Yar) reproduces a heart-wrenching and extraordinarily caring conversation between an elderly Jew and his son a minute before their execution.

Stand next to me, stand, my son,
I will cover your eyes with my palm,
So that you will not see your death,

---

58 Petrovsky-Shtern, *Anti-Imperial Choice*, p. 203.

59 Leonid Pervomais'kyi, *Vybrani tvory u dvokh tomakh*, Vol. 1 (Kyiv: Dnipro, 1978), p. 230.

Just my blood in my fingers in the sun,
That blood which also became your blood
And is about to pour onto the ground . . .[60]

The absence of traditional curses and accusations directed at the murderers is striking. Instead, the main emphasis is shifted to the father's love for his son, which is stronger than death.

Pervomaiskyi was one of the first writers to explicate clearly the main mission of artists when dealing with the Holocaust—memorialization. Writers must become the voices of those "who are being killed" and recreate their life stories for posterity. This explains the reappearance of the image of the elderly Jew, who addresses the poet as the mouthpiece of the nameless victims.

And when I was falling dead into the ravine
Into the terrible clay of bloody bodies,
I stubbornly believed that you would inevitably
Come to resurrect me![61]

Pervomaiskyi turned to the Babyn Yar theme in moments when he himself was experiencing crisis situations linked to questions of creative solitude, a reassessment of values, and states of "inner emigration." Creative insight into the tragedy also became a kind of psychological bulwark and a new understanding of the mission of art. It is no accident that the poem "V Babynim Yaru" was included in a collection entitled *Uroki poezii* (The Lessons of Poetry).[62] At the same time, Babyn Yar became a projection of Pervomaiskyi's philosophical reflections, according to which supreme wisdom and truth are on the side of martyrs and sufferers.

**Recent Ukrainian-language belletrists**

This particular attitude is also common to the artistic construction

60 Ibid., p. 180.

61 Ibid.

62 Leonid Pervomais'kyi "Babynim Iaru," in *Uroky poezii* (Kyiv: Radians'kyi pysmennyk, 1968), p. 29.

and new interpretation in the works of several late twentieth-century Ukrainian poets. It is worth mentioning poems by Moisei Fishbein ("Yar"), Leonid Vysheslavsky ("Olena Teliha's Cross"), Yurii Kaplan ("Babyn Yar," "Self-Portrait"), Dmytro Pavlychko ("Requiem", "Walking near Babyn Yar"), Abram Katsnelson ("Grandson's Monologue"), and Dmytro Palamarchuk ("A Vision of Babyn Yar").

In his interpretation of the Babyn Yar tragedy, Fishbein, a Ukrainian-Jewish poet, adopts a metaphorical model blending biblical associations (Rachel weeping for her murdered children), folkloric symbols (the image of cranes flying over the ravine is more eloquent than words), and the perception of the tragedy as a component of his own spiritual landscape. The poet raises his voice in defense of women and children, the most vulnerable and defenseless victims of Babyn Yar.

> They are walking
> on the cold, hard pavement,
> Thousands of people
> are walking between the hard, implacable walls,
> they carry
> Rachel without a hole in her temple,
> Here it is, the temple,
> a child's temple without a hole,
> they are carrying her there, to the machine guns.
> Shuffling. Tramping. Creaking. Noise.
> From the sky,
> birds gaze at the earth.[63]

In Iurii Kaplan's poem "Babyn Yar," he spoke about "the 100,000 [people] sleeping" in it, with "their names forgotten forever."[64]

Each of these writers relived the tragedy through an imaginary reconstruction of events which restored the victims' personal stories and integrated memory into the moral climate of contemporary life. A prominent feature of this poetic polyphony is the perception of Babyn Yar as a space for the reconciliation of memories.

63 Moisei Fishbein, "Vechir bez kolyskovoï," *Suchasnist'*, No. 5 (Munich, 1983), p. 3.

64 Iurii Kaplan, *Iurkovitsa* (Kyiv, 2010), pp. 238-248.

At the turn of the twentieth century the poetic counterpoint of Babyn Yar remained the most productive in literature, which was poignantly revealed in several anthologies. For example, the anthology *Vidlunnia Babynoho Yaru* (Echoes of Babyn Yar) compiled by Yurii Kaplan was reissued a third time to mark the sixty-fifth anniversary of the tragedy. The book featured the poems of writers who were not published in the Soviet Union: Liudmila Titova, Olga Anstei, and Naum Korzhavin ("Poema sushchestvovaniia" [A Poem of Existence]). The third edition also included Paul Celan's "Fugue of Death," translated by the Ukrainian poet Vasyl Stus, and the poems of Yurii Kaplan, Dmytro Palamarchuk, and others.

Several trends have been observed in the prose writings devoted to the theme of Babyn Yar in the first decades of the twenty-first century. The first and main one is linked to values-based approaches to the experience of World War II on the whole. The new generation of Ukrainian writers focuses attention, first and foremost, on Ukrainian projections of the war in the anti-totalitarian, anti-imperialist, religious, national, and psycho-emotional dimensions. In recent years, evocative works of Ukrainian prose, such as Oksana Zabuzhko's *Muzei pokynutykh sekretiv* (The Museum of Abandoned Secrets), Volodymyr Lys's *Stolittia Yakova* (Jacob's Century), Yurii Vynnychuk's *Tango smerti* (Tango of Death), Andrii Kokotiukha's *Chervonyi* (Red), Tetiana Belimova's *Vilnyi svit* (Free World), Lesia Stepovychka's *Nimtsi v horodi* (Germans in the City), Vasyl Shkliar's *Troshcha* (*The Reed*), and Sofia Andrukhovych's *Amadoka*, depict many traumatic experiences that intersected during the war. The private stories on which these writers focus their attention help to reveal various strategies of behavior and to delineate the changeability of roles. Depending on circumstances and moral priorities, during the war one and the same person was capable of demonstrating immense courage and heroism, and after a short period of time—becoming a coward and betrayer.

Within the dimension of private stories, the image of the enemy has undergone fundamental restructuring. Above all, it has been stripped of demonizing, irrational patterns that were cultivated in the space of Soviet literature, which for the longest time portrayed the enemy only as a base individual deserving of hatred, contempt, and liquidation. Contemporary literature, which is restoring full-fledged, vital space to the enemy, exposes his various faces (often contradictory) and studies the transformations that the war brought into his life.

An alternate view of victims and criminals, whose life stories emerge not within a system of oppositions, but as self-sufficient and equivalent, is presented in Mykola Mashchenko's novel *Dytia ievreiske* (The Jewish Baby, 2008). The author, a well-known Ukrainian film director, constructed his work in the form of a melodrama, blending elements of a detective novel with a love story. The novel centers on the fate of a Jewish woman named Ida Fridman and the Nazi officer Wilhelm Hauptmann. On 29 September 1941, on the way to Babyn Yar, Ida seizes an opportunity to hide her daughter in some bushes. The child is later found and hidden by a Ukrainian family, and Major Hauptmann saves the mother from being shot.

Wilhelm's encounter with Ida on the very day of the Babyn Yar shootings marks the start of a new war—with himself and the system. He refuses to carry out his superiors' order and does not take part in the executions. "Even Hitler himself cannot save all of you, although it is he who handed down the death sentence to your entire nation. I am fatally guilty in that I am not shooting the Jews right now in Babyn Yar. All of Germany is shooting hundreds of thousands of you. But I am saving a single Jewish baby and its mother ...in order to prolong the Jewish line. My entire soldier's crime and great human deed lie only in this," says Wilhelm to Ida.[65] The love-based motivation in the Nazi officer's change of life strategy is very important, but no less significant for the author is an individual's capacity to issue a challenge to the entire machinery of government and collective will, and to resist evil by realizing his/her own responsibility. It is precisely this choice that sets in motion the hero's spiritual healing and regeneration.

Mashchenko, who died in 2013, was the creator of such Soviet cult films as *Komisary* (The Commissars, 1969) and *Yak hartuvalasia stal* (How the Steel Was Tempered, 1973). The artist's path from cinema, in which life is sacrificed for ideology, to the novel *Dytia ievreiske* that con-

65 Mykola Mashchenko, *Dytia ievreiske* (Kyiv: Dukh i litera, 2008), pp. 78-79.

firms life as the highest value, reveals a profound internal evolution in understanding the nature of violence and, ultimately, changing one's life priorities. In the foreword to his novel Mashchenko noted: "Today the world of goodness, love, human civilization are in the same kind of jeopardy as all the most tragic epochs in the history of the planet. . . . *Dytia ievreiske* is a warning about the threat that new Babyn Yars may take place! I pray that nothing like that will ever happen again in the world. This is a painful plea to treasure God's supreme grace: human life."[66]

In recent years, independent Ukraine's changes in literary space have become a powerful impetus to the reception of the Holocaust experience. An important confirmation of these processes is the collective monograph *Holokost: khudozhni vymiry ukraïns'koï prozy* (The Holocaust: Artistic Dimensions of Ukrainian Prose).[67] Its authors draw attention to an impressive array of works, previously published in independent Ukraine, that provide a powerful stimulus to comprehend the Holocaust from a new analytical perspective. Examples of such works include: *V yaru zhasaiuchykh zirok* (In the Ravine of Fading Stars, 2007) by Raisa Plotnikova; *Cherevychky Bozhoi Materi* (The Shoes of Our Lady, 2013) by Maria Matios; *Vohnenni stovpy* (Pillars of Fire, 1999–2012) and *Torhovytsia* (The Merchant, 2012) by Roman Ivanychuk; *Vidlunnia: vid zahybloho dida do pomerloho* (Echoes: From the Fallen Grandfather to the Deceased, 2012) by Larysa Denysenko; *Sonia* (2013) by Kateryna Babkina; *Ya, ty i nash maliovanyi i nemaliovanyi Boh* (I, You, and Our Painted and Unpainted God, 2016) by Tetiana Pakhomova; *Istoriia varta tsiloho yablunevoho sadu* (A Story Worth an Entire Apple Orchard, 2017) by Maksym Dupeshka, and *Vynova hora* (Wine Mountain, 2017) by Nadiia Morykvas, and *Amadoka* (2020) by Sofia Andrukhovych.

All these works incorporate the Holocaust into their narrative and actualize memorialization practices that have arisen through family memory and moral challenges caused by a combination of an internal existential crisis and the crisis of social order. As far as the analysis of the Holocaust is concerned, researchers emphasize its relation to the histo-

66 Ibid., p. 8.

67 Natalia Horbach et al, *Holokost: khudozhni vymiry ukraïns'koï prozy* (Dnipro, 2019), p. 41.

ry of previous genocides in Ukraine. Attention is given to reformatting cultural memory, to narrating the Holocaust in terms of the ontological designations Ours and Theirs, and to establishing the genre and style attributes of texts depicting the tragedy. This recent emergence of a significant number of works on the Holocaust in modern Ukrainian literature has provided a solid foundation for the eventual appearance of new texts of artistic quality with a focus on Babyn Yar.

A landmark in this new cultural development is a collection of poems *Babyn Yar: holosamy* (Babyn Yar: In Voices, 2017) by Marianna Kiyanovska. The book became a momentous event in Ukraine's literary life because it introduced a new artistic metalanguage to speak about trauma. Kiyanovska said that she constructed her book on the principle of a choir, that is, choosing poems so that they would sound in tune. Since her poems tell multiple stories of Babyn Yar victims, Kiyanovska provides an individual voice for each victim. In the words of one critic, readers can "see the world through someone's eyes and listen to the world on their behalf."[68]

Kiyanovska does not limit the space of death to Babyn Yar only. Rather, she traces its origins to Stalin's prewar crimes and extends the coordinates of violence to all of Kyiv, to its basements, attics, and the hideouts of the Jews. Hence, her poems present the psychology of a person that lives in constant apprehension of mortal danger coming from either the bullets of Nazi invaders or civilian denunciations.

Featured are the voices of men and women of all ages and social status: Jews, Roma, and victims of the Holodomor and other Stalinist repressions of the 1930s. All are united by the figure of the Eyewitness who seeks to inscribe individual traumatic experiences in the collective memory—to survive in order to testify. Kiyanovka's poems provide a powerful transcendent foundation that genealogically goes back to the sacred biblical story and that reveals the strategy of confronting evil in the existential dimension. Kiyanovska's texts are also a reflection on the murder of the Human Being, which is the essence of all totalitarian regimes:

68 Olga Tokarczuk, "Te, shcho ne rozkazane, perestaie isnuvaty, vmyraie," in https://culture.pl/ru/article/olga-tokarchuk-te-scho-ne-rozkazane-perestae-isnuvati-vmirae

nothing or nothing save maybe tears saves me anymore
tears that break the background surface and the remainders of the body
to survive I must have it in my vessels at the bottom and at the bottom of the suitcases
the heavy mechanisms of inventing displacement wings wings.[69]

The story of how Kiyanovska's texts emerged is symbolic in many ways. Most were written in 2016, the third year of the Russian-Ukrainian war. According to the author herself, the current war prompted the need for a powerful reset of historical memory in Ukrainian literature. In the case of the Holocaust, it was now possible to develop plots and intellectual reflections that either had been voiced sporadically or not at all, or displaced into the subconscious. In Kiyanovska's poetic version, the narratives of Babyn Yar and the Russian-Ukrainian war create an organic unity and complement each other. Moreover, the poet notes that she originally intended to recreate her impressions specifically of the war in eastern Ukraine, but that this revision of the modern military confrontation in terms of values led her to the topic of the Holocaust: "when I write some of my poems about what happened in Babyn Yar, for me it is an experience of both what was then and what is now happening in the Donbas. It's a special experience of trauma."[70] In the search for a new metalanguage to describe modern warfare, Kiyanovska turned to the experience of World War II, in which the topic of Babyn Yar was decisive. As Iya Kiva points out, "the book *Babyn Yar: In Voices* is an attempt to understand (literally: to hear) the future through the past and to understand today's war through the past war and thereby overcome the language of hate by creating a supranational language of the victim."[71]

Kiyanovska cites distance in time as one of the factors that enabled her collection of poems. She counts herself as a member of the first generation educated and formed spiritually in independent Ukraine, that is, a generation free from the fear that an artistic interpretation of the Ho-

69 Marianna Kiianovs'ka, *Babyn Iar: holosamy* (Kyiv, 2017), p. 7.

70 Marianna Kiianovs'ka, "Holokost stav chastynoiu istoriï Ukraïny," interview in https://hromadske.radio/podcasts/zustrichi/golokost-stav-chastynoyu-istoriyi-ukrayiny-marianna-kiyanovska-pro-babyn-yar-golosamy

71 Iia Kiva, "Plach Rakhyli, *Zbruch*, 25 July 2017, in https://zbruc.eu/node/68821

locaust may have negative consequences for the author or cause repression by the authorities. It was this generational change and distance from the experience of Soviet totalitarianism that prompted contemporary authors to seek an artistic language freed from imperial myths and stereotypes. Thanks to Kiyanovska, Ukrainian literature has been enriched with a new quality of writing and new interpretive practices consistent with the experience of present-day European intellectuals.

Most appropriately, Kiyanovska's book won Ukraine's highest literary award, the Taras Shevchenko Prize, in 2020. This extraordinary event in Ukraine's cultural life proved that the tragedy of Babyn Yar became an integral component of Ukrainian cultural identity and Ukrainian culture of memory.

The literary interpretation of Babyn Yar has motivated artists of different generations and eras. Each of them destroyed the "zone of silence" and constructed the analytical and cognitive space necessary for spiritual growth. At the same time, the topic of Babyn Yar has taken on multiple characteristics that have yet to be made sense of by each new literary generation. With regard to the present Ukrainian cultural consciousness, the emergence of new artistic strategies is associated with the final liberation from the cultural domination of imperial rule and from the language of hatred and aggression.

Thus, the third millennium has brought new challenges that inevitably will spur writers to seek answers to problems of contemporary life in the experiences of the past. In these quests literature may become an advisor, a wise interlocutor, and a valuable reference point as well as—perhaps—a ray of hope.

CHAPTER 10

# Babyn Yar in Cinema

*Karel C. Berkhoff*

Some fiction films make the past come alive and attract large audiences, including the very many people who do not wish to watch documentaries or to read. They allow them to empathize with the people from the past. This is also the case with films about genocide and crimes against humanity, such as the Holocaust. Even critics of the American television series *Holocaust* and the film *Schindler's List* often admit that these opened the eyes of many poorly informed people. It offered what the Dutch writer Jessica Durlacher has called *emotional knowledge*.[1]

Meanwhile, many prominent intellectuals and thinkers have warned against mixing fiction novels or films with the Holocaust. The strongest objections are religious. Elie Wiesel, American citizen and the world's best-known Holocaust survivor, appreciates that some fiction films about the Holocaust move people and are not laden with what he calls "cheap sentimentality." But the "sacred" Holocaust may never be insulted, and here he refers specifically to Kyiv: "To direct the massacre of Babi Yar smells of blasphemy. To make up extras as corpses is obscene."[2]

Whether one agrees with Wiesel or not, Holocaust films do require special caution on the part of their creators. Fiction about genocide is unlike other kinds of fiction. Filmmakers (and writers) use their imagination, but the facts of the genocide, to the extent that historians have discovered them, remain important. Moreover, viewers should be disturbed. In short, extreme inaccuracy, including happy endings, and voyeurism (as if watching a slasher movie) ought to be avoided. The ques-

1 Jessica Durlacher, *Op scherp* [On Edge] (Amsterdam: De Bezige Bij, 2001).

2 Annette Insdorf, *Indelible Shadows: Film and the Holocaust*, 3rd ed. (Cambridge: Cambridge University Press, 2003, or. 1983), p. xii.

tion arises: how has Babyn Yar faired on screens? With some exceptions, such as a Soviet Ukrainian documentary from the 1980s, the following discussion deals with cinematic attempts to reenact Babyn Yar.

**Babyn Yar in passing and as site of reenactment**

Babyn Yar was first filmed, without sound, in November 1943 for a Russian-language film, *Victory in Right-Bank Ukraine and the Expulsion of the German Invaders from the Boundaries of Soviet Ukrainian Lands.* It was directed by Alexander Dovzhenko and Yuliia Solntseva and shown in Soviet cinemas in 1945. The segment used in this film lasted only nineteen seconds and showed the mass grave and some corpses, while a voice-over said:

> In Babyn Yar alone, the murderers shot more than one hundred thousand ill-fated citizens. Babies in arms were buried alive in the earth with their murdered mothers, and the earth could be seen rippling, shuddering from the movements of living people. Here people cried, screamed, cursed, and bid final farewells. Here small children saw sights unknown to the imagination of the great Dante, who wrote the *Inferno*.[3]

Jews were not mentioned at all, matching the official line of the Soviet Information Bureau and the tendency of the rest of the Soviet media.

Early in 1946, the theme of Babyn Yar reappeared briefly twice on screens. A special edition of the Soviet Ukrainian newsreel "Radianska Ukraïna" included Dina Pronicheva, a woman who had survived the shootings of 1941. The image and sound were recorded during her testimony on January 24 of that year at a Soviet military tribunal in Kyiv. (The accused were one Austrian and fourteen Germans, most of whom were hung.) Far less compelling on Babyn Yar, for lacking a survivor's voice, was *Film Documents of the German Fascist Invaders' Atrocities*, a documentary hastily prepared in 1945 for the Nuremberg Tribunal of the Major War Criminals before the International Military Tribunal, and shown there on February 19, 1946. It only included half a minute of footage of Babyn Yar.

3 Jeremy Hicks, *First Films of the Holocaust: Soviet Cinema and the Genocide of the Jews, 1939–1946* (Pittsburgh: University of Pittsburgh Press, 2012), p. 130.

The real surprise of the 1940s was a Russian-language fiction film produced by the Kyiv Film Studios, today the Dovzhenko Studios: *Nepokorennye* (*The Unvanquished*), shown in Soviet cinemas in late 1945. [see Plate **XLVI**] The film was remarkable because it showed a procession of Jews being led to their death and then their murder in a massive Nazi shooting. No fiction film anywhere in the world had ever done either. The film was also unique in Soviet cinema of those days for insisting that the victims were Jews, and for not claiming that suffering could somehow be balanced by vengeance or victory. Director Mark Donskoi was an award-winning filmmaker, who during the war had been filming propaganda shorts (*boevye kinosborniki*) and the fiction film *Raduga* (*The Rainbow*), but none of these had said a thing about the persecution and murder of the Jews.

The film, *The Unvanquished*, derived from a novel, *Semia Tarasa* (Taras's Family), that was serialized in the main Soviet newspaper *Pravda* in 1943. The novel, by one of *Pravda*'s own correspondents, the Russian Boris Gorbatov, was also read out on the radio and appeared as a book with a new title, *The Unvanquished*, in a large print run. It describes life and death in the fictional Donbas town of Kamennyi Brod after the arrival of the Germans and Italians in July 1942 and ends with liberation by the Red Army. Much of the content derived from Gorbatov's impressions of his native city of Luhansk (then called Voroshylovhrad), where he met acquaintances who had survived Nazi rule and read the notes made by a former underground activist.

The story's main character is Taras Yatsenko, a sixty-year-old metal worker with a strong faith in the Soviet system. With him are his wife, daughter, and two daughters-in-law and their children. His three sons have left home, however: one is carrying out a Communist party order to conduct underground work; another is a prisoner of war in German hands who manages to rejoin the Red Army; and the third survives the Battle of Stalingrad. In the film, the town is unnamed. The words *Ukraine* or *Ukrainians* are absent, but so is any glorification of the Russian people. Nevertheless, one sees much that suggests a Ukrainian setting and heritage; for instance, Taras's family is shown reading Nikolai Gogol's story *Taras Bulba*.

In Gorbatov's novel, the Holocaust appears briefly but distinctly. An elderly doctor called Aron Davidovich Fishman used to treat Taras's family. Now he wears a bandage with a Star of David. Upon seeing this, Taras bows deeply to acknowledge "you and your suffering." Later, Dr. Fishman walks with other Jews toward his death, guarded by auxiliary policemen and German submachine gunners. The novel put it as follows: these Jews shall be shot outside the city but "don't know and don't believe" it. Again, Taras is a witness; he says to himself, "Goodbye Doctor Aron Davidovich! Don't condemn me; I cannot save you. We ourselves are awaiting execution."[4]

Donskoi's film *The Unvanquished* showed both scenes. Taras was played by the Ukrainian Amvrosii Buchma (simultaneously artistic director of the Kyiv Film Studios), Fishman by the Yiddish Lithuanian actor Veniamin Zuskin. In the film as in the novel, Taras is the only non-Jewish person seen as reacting to the upcoming massacre. His behavior as he sees the death march surprises the doctor: "Are you bowing for me?" The reply: "I bow for your suffering, doctor."[5]

The novel and the film also depict a young Jewish girl who is hidden by many. In effect, every night she is passed on to another family. It is pure chance that she is captured in Taras's house. Unrealistically, no one is punished. Unlike in the novel, her murder is prevented by an auxiliary policeman who is a secret informant of the Soviet partisans.

Donskoi's film reenacted a mass shooting. It probably mattered that Gorbatov had just visited the liberated Nazi death camp of Majdanek, and that Donskoi was a Jew from Odessa, whose Jewish inhabitants had been murdered. From June 1944, he moved freely about Kyiv as a "special war correspondent," speaking about Babyn Yar with locals, including even survivors, and with a cameraman who had filmed there. As Donskoi later recalled: "At every step we met people who became our assistants, people who reestablished the truth and who understood the nature

4 Boris Gorbatov, *Nepokorennye: (Sem'ia Tarasa)* (Moscow: Izdatel'stvo "Pravda," 1945), pp. 23-24 and 44-45.

5 The scene can be viewed at https://phantomholocaust.org/films/the-unvanquished/ [last accessed June 3, 2021].

of the Germans all too deeply and exactly."[6]

Filming at the real Babyn Yar took place in October 1944. No one expressed any concern with on-site reenactment atop the human remains of the real victims. But Donskoi did not aim to reenact the Babyn Yar massacre. Instead, evidently inspired by the Odessa Steps sequence in Sergei Eisenstein's *Battleship "Potemkin"*, the killers are a line of advancing soldiers who shoot Jews who are standing at the same level, facing them. A wounded girl stumbles toward her executioners. Also, unlike the reality of Babyn Yar of September 1941, Donskoi's film has Jews wearing armbands; guards in uniforms of the Ukrainian Police; and does not show undressing. In the short Babyn Yar scene, the images of murder are interspersed with images of dark clouds, and there is loud music.

Like Gorbatov's novel, Donskoi's 90-minute film, *The Unvanquished*, is remarkable in another way. The Jewish victims are presented as largely passive and are not condemned for this. At the shooting, they just stand and wait and utter no words of defiance or patriotism. Instead, there are images of implied prayer.

The last half hour of the film does not have anything about Jews and is optimistic. Taras begins a journey and meets people from all walks of life. In the novel, he is looking for food and for "unravaged land."[7] The film does really not explain why he leaves, but repeats the term "unravaged land," which, perhaps intentionally, brings to mind the Jewish notion of the Promised Land.[8] The individual quest becomes a group journey whereby Ukrainians from different regions are somehow placed in the role of the murdered Jews.

In June 1945, the Artistic Council of the State Committee for Cinematography—Goskino, which was the body governing the Soviet film industry, convened to pass judgement which could either make or break the film. Almost all members of the council said they did not understand Taras's journey, and some expressed unease with the execution scene. One film director (Ivan Pyrev) opposed what he called singling out Jew-

---

6 Hicks, *First Films of the Holocaust*, p. 142.

7 Gorbatov, *Nepokorennye*, pp. 83-84.

8 Olga Gershenson, *The Phantom Holocaust: Soviet Cinea and Jewish Catastrophe* (New Brunswick, N.J.: Rutgers University Press, 2013), p. 47.

ish victims. But the novelist Gorbatov intervened: he had no complaints about the way his novel was adapted. Support for the film was also expressed by Eisenstein and Mikhail Romm, a director who said it was about time for Soviet films to talk about "the extermination of three and a half million Jews."[9] The Artistic Council's meeting, chaired by Ivan Bolshakov, decided in favor of mass release and even *praised* the execution scene. At the same time, however, the resolution that was adopted foreshadowed the attack on Jewish identity of the late 1940s, since it referred only to "Soviet citizens" and complained that the film's makers had been "carried away with the development of secondary characters"—that is, the Jews.[10]

Mark Donskoi's *The Unvanquished* premiered in eleven Moscow cinema theaters on October 15, 1945. It was shown in several of these until the end of November. Its time in Kyiv was much shorter, however. Within days after the premiere in four theaters on October 23, two theaters withdrew the film and by November 3, it was fully gone. The problem was that when distribution began, the film contrasted with the state's official dogmas and artistic guidelines. Hence, it received an ambivalent review in *Pravda*, which described the victims as too passive – "Aron Davidovich submits to his fate too much."[11] In other words, that part of the film had nothing to uplift the viewer.

In 1947, Stalin abolished the celebrations of Victory Day, and any realistic depictions of war losses became taboo. The next year, he began persecuting prominent Jews under the guise of a campaign against "cosmopolitanism." This led to the murder of Solomon Mikhoels, director of the Moscow State Jewish Theater, who was replaced by Veniamin Zuskin. He, too, faced the same fate as his predecessor. On the night of December 24, 1948, the MGB awoke Zuskin from a hospital bed and arrested him. Eventually, the man who had played the victim of the Nazi shooting in *The Unvanquished* was himself shot on August 12, 1952. As for Donskoi, he was lucky in merely being told to leave Moscow and settle in Kyiv.

9 Gershenson, *The Phantom Holocaust*, p. 50; Hicks, *First Films of the Holocaust*, p. 144.

10 Gershenson, *The Phantom Holocaust*, p. 52.

11 Hicks, *First Films of the Holocaust*, pp. 152-153.

Outside the Soviet Union, *The Unvanquished* was praised at the Venice Film Festival in September 1946. British distributors declined the film, but it was shown in Poland, East Germany, France, and Italy. A shortened version (82 minutes) premiered in New York City as *The Taras Family* on December 7, 1946. The *New York Times* praised it, called the shooting scene both "dramatic and horrible."[12] The show-business daily *Variety* also was impressed by the scene, despite what it called sloppy camera work.

In the 1960s, *The Unvanquished* was shown on Soviet television, but with cuts. The original film is little known outside eastern Europe, as there exist no copies with a translation. But the execution scene has received a life of its own. First it appeared in the Russian-language documentary *Deti iz bezdny* (*Children from the Abyss*, directed by Pavel Chukhraj, 2000), which was shown on Ukrainian television and also worldwide as part of the mini-series *Broken Silence*, produced by Steven Spielberg. A documentary from France, *Einsatzgruppen: The Death Commandos* (released French and English versions in 2009), presented the scene as historical footage, its writer and director Michaël Prazan wrongfully convinced that the footage was actually filmed in 1941 and only recently discovered.

**Reenactment for American television**

For more than three decades, no new cinematographic material depicting Babyn Yar appeared anywhere. Footage of the unsanctioned commemoration of 1966 was confiscated. In 1967, the Leningrad film studios offered to make a film on the basis of Anatoly Kuznetsov's book on Babyn Yar, but nothing came of the plan after the Moscow-based State Committee for Cinematography replied that this was a matter for the Ukrainians. During the following two decades, no one dared propose a fiction film about Babyn Yar. The new initiative came from across the Atlantic: in the 1970s and 1980s, two large American productions included brief reenactments. The first was the 9.5-hour-long television mini-series *Holocaust*, first broadcast by the NBC channel on four evenings in

12 Hicks, *First Films of the Holocaust*, p. 153

April 1978. *Holocaust* was directed by Marvin J. Chomsky, who used a script written by the Jewish American novelist Gerald Green. It told an implausible, continent-wide story from the perspective of two fictional German families: the Weiss family, Jewish, unsuspecting and all but one murdered; and the non-Jewish Dorf family, ambitious and callous.

The Babyn Yar shooting scene, filmed at an undisclosed location, lasted four minutes and appeared in part 2, *The Road to Babi Yar*, which aired on April 17, 1978. The perspective was that of onlookers, alternating between that of two Jews and two SS men. The first two were the fictional Rudi Weiss from Germany and Helena Slomová from Slovakia. One of the two Germans was supposed to be Paul Blobel, the actual commander of *Sonderkommando 4a*, the SS unit that played a leading role at Babyn Yar (along with the Staff of the *Einsatzgruppe C* and German police battalions 45 and 303). Blobel's role was played by the Irish actor Thomas McKenn. The other German, Blobel's fictional SS colleague Erik Dorf, was played by the American Michael Moriarty. Each pair observes from high above the shooting site, which is depicted as an even ground full of trees.

The first to arrive are auxiliary policemen, who, as Dorf notes, "don't march very well, do they?" Blobel responds, dismissively, "Ukrainians." More than thirty-thousand Jews are down there, he says. Dorf finds it "astonishing how they cooperate," which, Blobel add, "proves they don't deserve to live. Ah, there they come."[13]

The viewer then gets a view of Jews who surrender clothing and two brief glances at the rear of naked people, who are shot from behind. We see no beatings, no blood, and hear no screams. The victims seemingly endure the horror in silence. (In that sense, an earlier scene in *Holocaust*, of an SS shooting of Jews in a Ukrainian village, where Dorf is initiated into murder, was much more shocking.) Rudi, who alone of the Weiss family will survive the Holocaust, urges Helena to stop watching and says, "No-one will believe any of this. They'll say, we lie. Because nobody could do this to other people."

The mini-series won awards, was seen by hundreds of millions of

13 DVD set "Holocaust" (Dutch Filmworks B.V., 2008), chapter 13.

watchers globally, and helped turn the word "Holocaust" into the standard term for Nazi German persecution and murder of the Jews. Soviet citizens never got to see it.

The second American re-enactment of Babyn Yar, also not available in the Soviet Union, could be seen in the thirty-hour television series *War and Remembrance*, first aired by the ABC channel in 1988. *War and Remembrance* was presented as an adventure about Americans in World War II, but it included vivid reproductions of mass murder. Among other things, the ambitious television drama shows how a Jewish-American woman is deported from Italy and how Jews are murdered in a gas chamber reconstructed by the film crew in Birkenau just fifty meters away from the ruins of Crematorium IV. The producer and director of the series was Dan Curtis, who co-wrote the script with the highly successful historical novelist Herman Wouk, the son of Jewish immigrants from Belarus. When Wouk adapted his novel of 1978 of the same name, he wanted "to make those great and terrible days live again, graphically and truthfully," in "entertainment on the grand scale." Thus he hoped to influence a large audience: "It may grieve the judicious that the great public learns much of its history from works of entertainment. But such is the case."[14] For the Holocaust scenes, the series' producers were advised by the Simon Wiesenthal Center for Holocaust Studies, including its founder, Rabbi Marvin Hier. The series was also, as the credits stated, recommended by the National Education Association and the American Federation of Teachers.

The Babyn Yar scene was filmed in communist Yugoslavia, in a quarry, using five hundred extras including children, who rehearsed for a week. The scene was broadcast on November 23, 1988, as part of an eleven-minute section entitled "White Russia" in Episode 7. ABC kept its promise not to cut anything. Lasting four minutes, the massacre scene is entirely narrated from the perspective of Blobel, played by the British actor Kenneth Colley. In Belarus in the middle of 1943, this SS man has just proudly shown a German visitor how his organization forces prisoners to unearth and burn the corpses of murdered Jews. In a car on the

14 Booklet included in DVD set *Herman Wouk's War and Remembrance* (Orland Park, Ill.: MPI Home Video, [2008?]).

way back from this brief tour, Blobel then tells him how bad things used to be back in 1941. Horrific images of the Babyn Yar massacre are shown, including the undressing, beating, lines before the entry of the ravine, and shootings. Jews tumble down and SS men walk over bodies to finish off survivors. Many naked people are seen.

The camera watches from various angles, mostly from the ground. Among those who force the Jews to undress are auxiliary policemen in uniforms which they actually could not have worn at the time. Blobel looks on in distress. He is not horrified, but rather worried about the inefficiency. The procedure was a "botch," he says, for Ukrainian and German "sightseers" were allowed to stand next to the killings (which was historically inaccurate).[15] Indeed, we are shown civilian onlookers, including a man taking pictures and—ludicrously—a woman eating ice cream. And, as Blobel recalls in a voice-over, the clothes of the victims were thrown into the mass grave on top of the bodies. They went to waste. (This was not historically accurate either.) The reenactment ends before the shootings are over, and does not show what happened to the clothes.

Despite some errors, *War and Remembrance*'s section on Babyn Yar was vivid and in many ways realistic. It seems that the script writer had closely read Anatoly Kuznetsov's book Babyn Yar, with its narrative of the story of survivor Dina Pronicheva. For years the scene could only be seen by purchasing the full, expensive set of DVDs, but sections now appear on YouTube.

**One man's truth and Soviet lessons**

In the mid-1970s, in Kyiv, the Jewish theatrical director, scenario writer, and author Aleksandr Shlaen began urging the authorities to allow him to make a documentary film about Babyn Yar. This was not a logical step for then, as always, the Soviet leadership refused to acknowledge that the massacre of September 1941 was an unparalleled war crime, namely, an attempt to kill every single Jew in the city at the time. But to Shlaen it was personal, for his grandmother and aunt had died at Babyn Yar.

Several years later, Shlaen's project took off. The Communist par-

15 DVD set *Herman Wouk's War and Remembrance* (Orland Park, Ill.: MPI Home Video, [2008?]), part VII, chapter 4.

ty of Ukraine had been ordered by Moscow to step up its propaganda against "Zionism," and one of its responses was to order a documentary that would "expose the slanderous inventions of the Zionists regarding Babyn Yar." The CPU also ordered documentaries about "the crimes of the Ukrainian bourgeois nationalists (including against Jews), and their servility toward Hitlerite fascism during the Second World War."[16] Evidently, the authorities felt that a film about Babyn Yar could strike hard at both Jewish and Ukrainian opponents of the Soviet system. That Shlaen's goal was different—a film about Jews murdered simply because of their Jewishness—at first did not seem problematic to him.

The film director Vladimir Georgienko searched for materials and filmed survivors, witnesses, as well as the Russian poet Yevgenii Yevtushenko at the ravine. The documentary film, completed in 1980, with commentary in Ukrainian and following Shlaen's script, was called *Babyn Yar: pravda pro trahediiu* (Babyn Yar: The Truth about the Tragedy). It was an emotional work that ended with the words: "At Babyn Yar, over 150,000 Jews were annihilated by the Nazis in the first five days. One hundred and three weeks of Babyn Yar followed."[17]

But the authorities changed their minds. Shlaen was taken off the project and was replaced by the prominent writer Vitalii Korotych, who oversaw a radical revision of the film and included extra scenes. Korotych, who wrote and read the voice-over, also appeared on screen himself. The final product, a 55-minute Russian-language television documentary *Babii Yar: uroki istorii* (Babyn Yar: The Lessons of History), was broadcast on September 29, 1981 on the Soviet Union Channel 1. Production credits for the country's one and only released documentary about Babyn Yar were attributed to Korotych, Georgienko, Shlaen, Anatolii Vashchenko, Khem Solganik, and unnamed "others."[18]

Unlike Georgienko's original version based on Shlaen's script, the new

16 V. R. Nakhmanovych, "Bukovyns'kyi kurin' i masovi rozstrily ievreïv Kyieva voseny 1941 r.," *Ukraïns'kyi istorychnyi zhurnal*, LI, 3 (Kyiv, 2007), p. 90.

17 DVD with copy of the film (donated by Alla Revenko), archive of the author

18 Film 2677, "Babi Yar. Lessons of History," United Holocaust Memorial Museum, RG- 60.4200, available for viewing online at https://collections.ushmm.org/search/catalog/irn1002768 [last accessed June 3, 2021]

film was not about Jews but about the universal evil of mass murder, whereby Babyn Yar was presented as its "most flagrant experiment."[19] Some 200,000 people were buried at the ravine, it was claimed. The film included contemporary narratives by survivors and also footage from the 1940s: Pronicheva testifying at the Kyiv tribunal, and footage filmed at Babyn Yar with sound early in 1944 of Efim Vilkis (misidentified as Vladimir Davydov), who was a survivor of the corpse burnings. Auxiliary Ukrainian policemen were not mentioned.

When Soviet Ukraine's Ministry of Foreign Affairs demanded that an English version be shown in the West and at the United Nations, it became *Babi Yar: Lessons of History*. Korotych also provided the voice-over, but it was at 42 minutes much shorter than the original. It now included a passage about Anatol Kabaida, in 1942 the commander of the Staff of Kyiv's auxiliary police. According to Korotych's commentary: "Today, Zionists are ready to embrace those who yesterday organized pogroms. Today they chew the same gum and [use] the same words. Today we see the merging of all anti-Soviet forces."[20] This was part of the KGB's campaign against contacts between the Jewish and Ukrainian diasporas.

The film was rebroadcast in September 1986. The original version surfaced only in September 1991, one month after Ukraine declared its independence. The showing on Ukrainian television accompanied the first ever official national commemoration of the Babyn Yar massacre.

A full history of the production and its various versions still remains to be written. It is clear, however, that Shlaen had asked the Public Prosecutor to prevent the showing of Korotych's version, but to no avail. According to Shlaen's widow, the art historian Alla Revenko, he was punished for his intransigence with accusations of Zionism, the opening of a criminal case against him, a home search by KGB officers who attempted to plant drugs, and a blacklist. Subsequently, no one offered him any cinema work. In 1992, using previously unused material, Georgienko released another television documentary, in Ukrainian, *Zhinky z vulytsi Babyn Yar* (The Women from Babyn Yar Street), about four non-Jewish women who had seen some of the shootings.

---

19 Film 2677, "Babi Yar. Lessons of History."

20 Film 2677, "Babi Yar. Lessons of History."

### *The Ladies' Tailor*

The one and only Soviet Ukrainian film explicitly intending to reenact the Babyn Yar massacre was called *Damskii portnoi* (*The Ladies' Tailor*). Released in 1990, it is still the best known Russian-language film about the Holocaust. The film was based on the 1980 play, also called *The Ladies' Tailor*, by the Jewish playwright Alexander Borshchagovskiy. The play (staged by the Jewish Drama Ensemble in Moscow for just one week in October 1980) is set in Kyiv on the night before the morning of September 29, 1941, with two flash-forwards about the initial escape, and then arrest, of a Jewish girl, the tailor's granddaughter.

Together with the Jewish Ukrainian director Leonid Horovets/Gorovets, Borshchagovskiy turned the play into a film script. Funding was secured (from the "Progress" Cooperative), but the Kyiv Film Studios refused any involvement with a movie about Jews. Consequently, Horovets found a private producer in Moscow, Fora-Film, which worked without any government interference. Filming took just four months in 1990, including in Kyiv. There is a scene with a Jewish man being shot in the street, but not the main massacre itself. The action centers on the evening before the deportation.

The leading role is performed by Innokentii Smoktunovskii, a famous actor of Belarusan origin, who for his performance earned the "Nika" Prize for best male actor. [see Plate **XLVII**] Smoktunovskii himself contributed to the publicity materials with the words: "Forgive us, brothers and sisters! Forgive us that we remained alive and could not save you!"[21]

The film opens with the text of the 28 September order to the Jews to appear, shown for half a minute, to the disturbing sound of a harmonica, which later the viewer will recognize as stemming from a German walking the streets. Then we see the tailor, Isaac. In Smoktunovskii's performance, he is a strong person: he foresees the bleak future, faces his imminent death calmly, and is warm, welcoming into his home a family (a grandmother, pregnant mother, and a boy) relocated there by the new authorities. Their arrival turns the apartment into a new, strange place.

---

21 Booklet with DVD *Ladies' Tailo*r (Waltham, Mass.: National Center for Jewish Film, n.d.).

On the other hand, Isaac is weak: as he says himself, he cannot resist or fight. Because of his ironic humor, and frequent use of Yiddish, he seems straight out of the mythological *shtetl* of Sholem Aleichem's tales.

Isaac's daughter Sonia is optimistic: she believes the Germans will send the Jews to a happier place. But Isaac's daughter-in-law Ira realistically expects them to be killed. A key scene is the funeral of the son of their neighbors, a Jew who was just shot for trespassing the curfew. Then follows a scene in which Isaac envisions marchers dressed in white.

The film shows the march of the doomed. Because the producers could not find buses to get the extras from the studio to the location, those who arrived came with the metro fully clothed as the characters they were playing and wearing Nazi uniforms. An elderly woman who saw the crew in action came forward to say she had survived the Nazis and was allowed to join the crowd scene.

The march toward the ravine is depicted from the front, as the Jews walk up toward it. We see present-day cars and busy traffic in the background. Horovets deliberately left the contemporary cars in the final cut, because he felt that their presence suggests a relationship to the present. Indeed, the film offers many parallels to the contemporary mass emigration from Ukraine of Soviet Jews, keeping in mind that non-Jewish characters *envy* the Jews who supposedly will emigrate. Ukrainian auxiliary policemen are not shown at all in the film, probably because of the tense situation in Ukraine in 1990.

As customary in Soviet films about Nazi crimes, *The Ladies' Tailor* includes still pictures from the extermination camps. The film also refers to the crimes of Stalinism. Isaac's apartment block custodian, Anton Horbunov, is antisemitic, immoral, and mistreats his wife and his Jewish tenants. But at one stage, he directly addresses the viewer and explains that he was deported in the 1930s for being a so-called kulak. He tells how in exile he became a Gulag guard and was forced to commit crimes. In other words, here Stalin's regime gets part of the blame for his behavior.

All light is overexposed, and the film is shot darkly, whereby the non-Jews almost always, and symbolically, remain in darkness. Horbunov's wife Nastia is a pleasant person, however. She begs Ira to leave her uncircumcised son behind, but to no avail. She then joins the march. Her husband runs after her, shouting: "But she is not a Jew," and is shot dead on the spot.[22]

*The Ladies' Tailor* premiered in Moscow in 1990 one week after the director migrated to Israel. It was reviewed widely but was not shown beyond festivals. Television re-runs made it familiar, however. Outside Russia and Ukraine, it was only on sale in the United States, where the National Center for Jewish Film offered a shortened version on DVD with subtitles. Despite its stereotypical characters and slow pace, no other fiction film in Russian or Ukrainian dealing with Babyn Yar is better known than *The Ladies' Tailor.*

**Ukrainian and German failures**

Two other full-length feature films produced a little over a decade later were failures. Although some praised these films when they appeared, today they have no defenders. Both entitled Babyn Yar, they appeared in Ukraine (2002) and Germany (2003).

*Babii Yar* (2002) is a Russian-language television film directed by the Ukrainian directors Mykola Zasieiev-Rudenko and Oksana Kovaliova and produced by "AV TV" Studio. Zasieiev-Rudenko had walked around with the script for seven years when Vadim Rabinovich, businessman and president of the All-Ukrainian Jewish Congress, put up the funds. Ukraine's first lady Liudmyla Kuchma also seems to have given important assistance. Zasieiev-Rudenko said it was the story of his courtyard, where there used to live a seven-year-old Jewish girl who he lost at Babyn Yar.

The film tells the story of a Jewish survivor played by a star of Soviet cinema, Elina Bystritskaia (born in Kyiv in 1928 from Jewish parents), and one of the German killers. Eleonora Kolmer narrowly survived the Babyn Yar massacre, but lost her parents, sister, and son there. Interspersed with flashbacks from September 1941 (discussed below), a truly unlikely story unfolds. On a specifically shown date, 25 September 2001, Eleonora has arrived in Kyiv, this time as an Israeli diplomat back in her

22 The quotation is from the DVD. My description is based on Gershenson, *The Phantom Holocaust*, 206-222, and Judith Deutsch Kornblatt, "'*Ladies' Tailor*' and the end of Soviet Jewry," *Jewish Social Studies*, V, 3 (Stanford, CA, 1999), pp. 180-195.

native city to commemorate Babyn Yar. Her first shock is seeing the TV Center at Melnikova Street, a "monstrosity on top of human bones," as her voice-over says.[23] At the monument for the murdered children, she meets a German called Erwin Tanz, played by Igor Vasilev. Tanz speaks fluent Russian, and she accepts from him a gift: a drawing that he made of her on the plane to Kyiv. I was shot here, she says, and walks away.

Eleonora reunites with the woman who saved her in 1941, but central to the film is the strange relationship with Tanz, who even lives on the same hotel floor. In their final meeting, on 2 October, Eleonora confronts him with a drawing that she found at a local museum, made by a German of her and her son at Babyn Yar right before the shots ran out. "I curse you," she says.

Director Zasieiev-Rudenko offers the former Nazi a platform to explain and—the German hopes—to defend himself. He has been struggling with himself ever since, and wonders: "Why remember the past?" But once more at the Babyn Yar memorial, Tanz starts hallucinating and, to a voice-over reading the *Einsatzgruppe* report of October 1941, envisions a crowd including small children and his wartime-self drawing near. Now his conscience really hurts and, screaming in anguish, he wants to die. The younger Eleonora appears with her son, of whom he asks forgiveness. He collapses and dies. The next day, on the plane, Eleonora catches the television news: last night, a German citizen called Erwin Tanz died at the Babyn Yar monument from a heart attack. She says to herself: "Death is forgiveness. But I cannot forgive, for my country [Israel] is in mortal danger. We must not allow a new Babyn Yar."[24] Across from her sits a young man with a swastika.

Flashbacks filmed in black and white are scattered throughout the film. Eleonora, as played by Vlada Volianskaia, crawls out of the mass grave (15 seconds) and is sheltered by a nearby girl whose father is a fully uniformed policeman. Later there are a few seconds of Eleonora's friend and sister screaming before being killed, and eight minutes of the massacre in a very artificial setting (seemingly a large photograph of the

23 "Babii Iar," viewed at https://www.youtube.com/watch?v=Qks1TyoWl8E [last accessed June 3, 2021).

24 "Babii Iar."

slopes of Babyn Yar). A uniformed auxiliary policeman is present as the younger Tanz leisurely takes his time to draw a portrait of Eleonora and her son, proclaiming that now he is God, and, finally, shooting the Jews in front of him. The film does not explain why the elder Tanz travels to Kyiv and its story is too implausible overall to enable one to suspend disbelief. Moreover, the camera work and the settings often look unprofessional and there is far too much mediocre and repetitive music, even over important voice-overs.

*Babii Yar*'s first broadcast on Ukrainian television was aired on the Kyiv-based Era channel in the early morning. Israeli television also showed the Russian-language film. Overall, its reception has been highly negative. There also arose ugly situations, which to date have not yet been clarified. For instance, in 2003 the film was suddenly dropped from the main competition at the Cinematic Forum "Vmeste" in Yalta, and then bestowed with a new prize, "For Deep Revelation of One of the Tragic Pages of Humankind during the Second World War."[25]

The only Western full-length film reenactment of Babyn Yar premiered in Germany on 3 July 2003 under the title: *Babij Jar: Das vergessene Verbrechen* (*Babyn Yar: The Forgotten Crime*). Two Americans collaborated on this project: Stephen Glantz wrote the screenplay, and Jeff Kanew was the director. [see Plate **XLVIII**] The main force behind the film, however, was its highly successful producer, Artur Brauner, a Holocaust survivor from Poland who had lost relatives (on his mother's side) at Babyn Yar. Brauner's ambitious aim was to improve upon the films *Schindler's List* and *The Pianist*, which he deemed unrealistic. He believed that Germans and others had "forgotten" Babyn Yar. (To be sure, such as notion was not uncommon in Germany, as confirmed by the subtitle of a documentary about Babyn Yar shown on national German television in January 2012, which was described as a "forgotten massacre.") Braun's goal was nothing less than the creation of a timeless memorial—a "document that will be available a hundred, even two hundred years from now."[26]

25 Interview with Elina Bystritskaia in *Evreiskii obozrevatel'* (Kyiv), no. 6/246, June 2013, online at https://jew-observer.com/lica/ya-vsegda-byla-samodostatochnoj/ [last accessed June 3, 2021].

26 "Presseheft" for "Babij Jar. Das vergessene Verbrechen," archive of the author.

Yet seemingly not a single historian was consulted. How, otherwise, can one explain the many historical errors and Braun's own statement that only one Jew by the name of Anatoly Kuznetsov survived Babyn Yar? Like all the re-enactments preceding it, the film does not show or refer to the great fire in Kyiv that preceded the 29–30 September 1941 massacre of the Jews, and emboldened the Nazis to carry it out at soon and in a single stroke.

The cast was international, but all the actors speak or were overdubbed in German. It was filmed in Belarus with the low budget of 5 million euros, which seemingly forced the producers to insert some images from the low-quality wartime German newsreel. This, in turn, required the entire film to be in sepia.

From the beginning of *Babij Jar*, sometime in 1941, the viewer follows two families who live next to each other, one Ukrainian, one Jewish, and also the commander Paul Blobel (played by the German actor Axel Milberg) and his entourage. If Brauner's aim was realism, he failed. In occupied Kyiv, a Ukrainian woman, Lena Onufriienko (played by Katrin Sass, known from the film *Goodbye Lenin*) suddenly becomes antisemitic and denounces her Jewish neighbors as partisans. But because this denunciation is for the wrong reasons, the Nazis send her to her death at Babyn Yar as well, on the very first day of the massacre. That is a highly unlikely turn of events.

The massacre itself takes up a large part of the film's 108 minutes. The main Jewish characters end up dead in the ravine with their clothes on. The bodies in the ravine show little blood, are quiet, and do not move. As in almost all other reenactments, the auxiliary policemen wear uniforms of the auxiliary police.

The failure of the film, as noted in almost every review, stands out all the more when compared to Brauner's 2008 production, *The Last Train*, about the deportation of Jews from Berlin. That film is of high quality and does not repel the viewer, as does *Babij Jar*, in which all the characters all are stereotypes. For instance, on the very eve of the massacre, Blobel makes a phone call home and ask his wife how his little child is doing.

Often, a bird flies high and a cawing sound is heard; we are supposed to think it is a crow (even though crows cannot glide) and sense all the better the horrors shown. Intermixed in the massacre scene is a flash-forward: a happy scene in which Lena's son Stepan gets married to Franka, the Jewish refugee from western Ukraine. The addition of this "optimistic" scene in between the long scenes of horror is probably the film's greatest flaw.

The film *Babij Jar* left German movie theatres, probably forever, after having drawn 9,418 viewers. It was shown on German television from January 2005 until the outset of 2008. The DVD produced in 2004 has subtitles in English and Dutch, although the film remained virtually unknown outside Germany until 2011, when it began circulating on YouTube. Screenshots often appear online without captions explaining that they show a reenactment.

In 2009, the American Anatoly Fradis, who worked in film in Moscow until his emigration in 1979, purchased the film rights to Anatoly Kuznetsov's book. As announced in *Variety*, Fradis was to coproduce this drama with Barry Lewinson, who would also direct it on a budget of 35 million dollars provided by Russians, Ukrainians, and Poles. The film was to be filmed in Romania and Ukraine, but for reasons not reported—probably a lack of finances—nothing became of the plan.

**The mythological "Death Match"**

There exists various films and documentaries about a so-called death match in Nazi-occupied Kyiv. The story is that soccer players from Kyiv's prewar Dynamo team, now on a team called Start, beat a German team in a match held in August 1942. The German authorities had ordered Start to lose, or else its players would be killed. Indeed, they were sent to the Syrets camp near Babyn Yar and shot. This Soviet myth has been disproved many times. The Start team did play and win ten matches in July and August 1942; but its final game was not against Germans and the reasons for the arrests, and the execution of some of the players half a year later, have remained unclear.

In 1962, one popular Soviet film, *Tretii taim* (*The Third Half*), directed by Evgenii Karelov and based on a script by Alexander Borshchagovskiy, told the soccer match story, but did not depict any shootings. Fifty years later, on May 1, 2012, a two-hour long film called *The Match* by the Russian director Andrei Maliukov was released in Russia; soon followed by a four-part television series that added an hour to the original version. [see Plate **XLIX**] The film was funded by Russian producers and the Russian government, but support from officials in President Viktor Yanukovych's Ukraine had enabled all filming to take place in Ukrainian localities: Kharkiv, Vasylkiv, and a quarry near Kyiv.

Set in June and September 1941 and in May 1942, *The Match* contains a reenactment of the murder of Babyn Yar's "other," non-Jewish victims. This was the first time the theme of Babyn Yar's "other" victims, such as the Roma and Ukrainian nationalist activists, was portrayed on film. For six minutes, we see the ravine being prepared for what a German calls a *rehearsal.* Then psychiatric patients are violently evicted and shot in a specifically dug pit, with the scene done partly in slow motion. Germans with rifles are the main killers, but Ukrainian auxiliaries with blue-and-yellow armbands and weapons of their own assist and seem to enjoy their task. One of them actually shoots to kill.

*The Match* also offers the first depiction of explosions of Soviet mines which preceded the main massacre, and of spontaneous anti-Jewish violence. Shouting "They burned our Kyiv!" auxiliary policemen loot a synagogue and beat Jews. A German arrives on the scene and warns the rabbi that a real pogrom is at hand. Presenting it as good news, he adds that in two days, however, the Germans will "evacuate" the Jews to Germany for work.[27]

Eventually, well-dressed Jews, who despite the presence of auxiliaries are initially in good spirits, walk toward Babyn Yar. They must undress and are beaten (six minutes in total). The shootings themselves are not depicted; there is only the gruesome aftermath—heaps of shoes, jewelry, and naked corpses (two minutes).

The hunt for escaped Jews has some strange aspects. When an informant notices that a Jewish girl lives all alone in a house and receives food there, the Germans are not informed at all. Her father, Mikhail Svirskii (played by Vladimir Nevelskii), wore a kipah before the German invasion; now he walks the streets openly and even plays in soccer matches.

---

27 "Match," part 2 (here, from 14:19), available at https://www.youtube.com/watch?v=BCcAAeQTdZo [last accessed June 3, 2021].

The film's main topic, however, is the death match. As early as September 1941, soccer player Nikolai Ranevich (played by Sergei Bezrukov) is released from a POW camp thanks to the mayor, who was approached by Ranevich's fiancée, Anna (played by Elizaveta Boiarskaia). She gives in to the demand to reward the mayor by marrying him.

Meanwhile, Ranevich, while working at a bread factory, develops a strong soccer team. On the eve of a replay against German players, Eberhardt's associate Brinkmann arrests Ranevich and warns him: he must ensure a victory for Germany, otherwise he, his team, and Anna will be killed. Once Ranevich notices her in the audience of the match, his natural cheerfulness and political maturity return. "Some things are worth dying for," he tells his teammates. All agree enthusiastically, no questions asked, and celebrate wildly when they win. Then follows a message on screen that "After the match, Nikolai and his comrades were allowed to live for seven happy days."[28]

Because of its anachronisms and other flaws, the film does not convince, whether in reenacting Babyn Yar, wartime soccer, or even wartime Kyiv in general. The love story is also far-fetched, and it is studiously neutral about the questionable relationships of its two main women characters, Anna and a nurse who accepts the courtship from Hans, the supervisor of shootings at Babyn Yar. *The Match* is best known, however, for its unmistakable anti-Ukrainian tone. When mayor "Barazii" (as the credits call him, played by the Ukrainian actor Stanislav Boklan) addresses German Commander of Kyiv, Eberhardt, in Ukrainian, an interpreter gruffly orders him to switch to Russian. Contrary to fact, public announcements during the soccer matches are in German and Russian, not Ukrainian. Ukrainian speakers are unsympathetic or worse, except for an elderly man who helps a Jewish girl in hiding, and one of the soccer players. But this Mykola says that he is a proud "Soviet sportsman."[29]

Ukrainian nationalism of any kind is considered marginal and ideologically deeply mistaken. The mayor, appointed by the Organization of

28 "Match," part 4, available at https://www.youtube.com/watch?v=eMahe01GabY [last accessed June 3, 2021].

29 "Match," part 3 (here at 28:24), at https://www.youtube.com/watch?v=t_DGQlIwnhA [last accessed June 3, 2021].

Ukrainian Nationalists, favors another local soccer team, Rukh, which he calls Ukraine's "national team," although no one cheers for it. It is only out of love that he helps Anna to evade the Germans and rescue the Jewish girl.

Another odious Ukrainian is modeled on an actual Kyivan soccer player, Heorhii Shevtsov. He is the leader of the Rukh team, plays dishonestly, drinks too much, and smokes. But worst of all is building custodian Deshchenia (played by the Ukrainian actor Ostap Stupka). Deshchenia dons a yellow-and-blue armband, saying in Ukrainian, "There will be order"[30]; then he helps to murder the psychiatric patients. This antisemite with a "Ukrainian" moustache is not really an adult. Ranevich's moral authority weighs so heavily on him that he does not dare denounce either Ranevich (a Communist and NKVD man), or any member of the Jewish Svirskii family. When Germans arrest him, he screams out in panic. In April 2012 (just weeks before Ukraine would be co-hosting the UEFA European Championship), the Ukrainian State Film Agency blocked the release of *The Match*. Then, in September 2014, it fully banned television broadcasts or sale of the film.

**Reenactment in documentaries**

A detailed analysis of the large number of documentaries from various countries that somehow deal with Babyn Yar has yet to be undertaken. There are, for instance, the US-based History Channel's *Who Destroyed Kiev?*, an episode in its *History's Mysteries* Series (2000), and the German ARD public television channel's *Babij Jar: Das vergessene Massaker* (Babyn Yar: The Forgotten Massacre, 2012). Ukrainian documentaries include Aleksandr Chaika's *Babii Yar* (2004), and an episode directed by Oleksandr Makhonko of the *Velyka viina* (Great War) series (2013). Babyn Yar has also been a prominent part of general documentaries, such as Serhii Bukovskyi's *Spell Your Name* (2006), coproduced by Steven Spielberg and Viktor Pinchuk and distributed widely.

Various documentary film makers have not been deterred by the failed efforts at reenactment of Babyn Yar. On 22 June 2010, the official

30 "Match," part 1 (here at 35:16), at https://www.youtube.com/watch?v=56h4Y-x8xWU [last accessed June 3, 2021].

Day of Sorrow and Commemoration of the Victims of War, Ukraine's television's Channel 1 showed *Kyiv: Pochatok viiny* (*Kyiv: The Start of the War*), a 55-minute film about Soviet and Nazi terror in the city and at Babyn Yar, where the "fascists" shot "over 100,000 adults and children of various nationalities."[31] Consultants were two staff members of the Museum of the History of Kyiv, Dmytro Malakov and Tetiana Yevstafieva. At the end, the actress Rymma Ziubina performs a reading of a Ukrainian translation of Dina Pronicheva's testimony, while a male actor plays an auxiliary policeman with a cap. A British-American documentary, *The Unseen Holocaust* (2013), has a two-minute reenactment of Pronicheva's ordeal. The shooters wear helmets and fire only single shots, from guns or rifles. A female voice-over reads what are claimed to be Pronicheva's words.

That same year, in November, the 27-minute Russian television documentary, *Babii Yar: poslednie svideliti* (*Babyn Yar: The Last Witnesses*) was aired. It was written and directed by Sergei Logovchenko, produced by Maksim Rybakov, and presented and presumably financed by Aleksandr Diukov's Historical Memory Foundation. The project was supported by Ilia Levitas, director of the Memory of Babyn Yar Foundation and president of the Jewish Council of Ukraine. The film, shown on Russian television and immediately placed online as well, is noteworthy because it offers not only interviews with the survivor Raisa Maistrenko and non-Jewish witnesses, but also convincing reenactments by young actors.

Neverthless, *Babyn Yar: The Last Witnesses* is a very flawed product. The voice-over complains about slander against "the Red Army, the partisans, the defense industry, not to mention the Kremlin leadership," the slander being that "the Reich, the Wehrmacht, and the SS" were "innocent victims of Soviet propaganda."[32] Who says this absurdity is not specified, nor can it be. The film also presents Holocaust deniers as highly influential and in urgent need of refutation. Finally, there is an unsurprising but unconvincing link to the present: "In Ukraine, nationalism

---

31 Viewed online from a link that as of 2021 is no longer active.

32 DVD of the film, which is also available for viewing at https://www.youtube.com/watch?v=KfjOWYASSB0 [last accessed June 3, 2021].

has raised its head—nationalism in its most frenzied form." It does not take long for the self-satisfied male voice-over, the constant music, and the flashy cuts to irritate the viewer.

We have found that while the former killing site itself was used to film, for the first time in the world, Jews being led by Germans to their death as a group, the first reenactments explicitly set at Babyn Yar were American productions, unseen in Ukraine at the time of release. The first full-length feature film about Babyn Yar was a Ukrainian product from the period when the country was heading for independence. Unfortunately, other attempts at reenactment made since then have been artistic failures that do all but provide emotional knowledge, or they are marred by an overly politicized context. Thus, there is little cause for satisfaction. The wait is now for the results of work by the German-based acclaimed Ukrainian director Serhii Loznytsia, who for some time has been working on a film about Babyn Yar based on a script of his own.

CHAPTER 11

# Babyn Yar in Sculpture and Painting

*Iryna Klimova*

Every art has its own distinct language. In literature it is the word. In music it is sound. In painting we see the interplay of tones and colors, in the graphic arts we see lines, while sculpture possesses form, a silhouette. The Babyn Yar tragedy is so important that it is extraordinarily difficult to reflect it in words and concrete images. Distinguished painters and sculptors who devoted themselves to this theme possessed a singular aptitude for experiencing human pain. Owing to their own inner strength, they were cognizant of their mission to convey the truth about this horrific tragedy to their contemporaries and descendants.

**Early artistic depictions on the Babyn Yar theme**

Paradoxically, the first art works devoted to Babyn Yar appeared while the tragedy was still unfolding. The artist and ethnographer Yurii Pavlovych, who lived in Ukraine's capital city during the German occupation, made pencil sketches of the ravine every single day. He planned to create an album entitled "Kyiv through the Eyes of an Artist," for which he painstakingly recreated scenes of daily life in the multinational city. Pavlovych also made sketches of the Jewish residents of Kyiv, who on 29 September 1941 went to Babyn Yar alone or in the company of their families. [see Plate **IX**] Of all the artists who were living in Kyiv at this time, Pavlovych was the only one who "noticed" the sad procession of the crowds of Jews heading to their place of execution.[1]

After the city was liberated from the Nazis, Vasyl Ovchynnykov, the monumentalist painter and director of Kyiv's Museum of Western and

1 Lev Drob'iazko, "Trahichnyi veresen' 1941 roku," Forum natsiï, No. 3 (Kyiv, 2003); idem, *Babyn Iar. Shcho? De? Koly?* (Kyiv: Kyi, 2009), pp. 5-6.

Oriental Art, returned from the front. The building in which he had lived before the war lay in ruins. But it was not his destroyed former home but the news of the brutal violence against the Jews of his city that shocked this Kyivite to the core. As Ovchynnykov's daughter later recalled: "He began asking about the fate of his neighbors. It so happened that many of our neighbors were Jewish families. 'The Zaldyses?' 'They went to Babyn Yar.' 'The Knyzhnyks?' 'To Babyn Yar.' '???' 'To Baby Yar, to Babyn Yar…'"[2]

Stunned by the news, Ovchynnykov went to the ravine, where day after day he sketched the hills of Babyn Yar, those mute witnesses of a horrific crime. Chilling pictures of the merciless destruction of so many people formed in the artist's imagination. His work at the ravine sparked the idea to create a requiem series of seven canvases. By the summer of 1947 Ovchynnykov had nearly completed four paintings, each of which was a realistic recreation of the events that took place in Babyn Yar. [see Plate **XXXIII**]

The series began with a canvas depicting a room, through the window of which one can see the back of a German soldier and a street filled with a crowd of people who are heading toward the unknown. Inside the room a weeping mother embraces her daughter in despair. The second canvas depicts elderly people, women, and children walking past the semi-demolished wall of the Jewish Cemetery. People, objects, monuments, stone, and trees bending in the wind—all this is unitary and monolithic. The third canvas depicts the severe lines of a landscape, the autumn sky, and a sense of impending doom felt by the crowd of people who are approaching Babyn Yar from the depths. The fourth painting, entitled *Retribution*, shows an executioner sitting in a trench. He is gripping a machine gun, but his head is lying next to his feet.[3]

Ovchynnykov's body of work included a frieze of a pantheon whose creation was planned in keeping with a resolution handed down on 13 March 1945 by the Council of People's Commissars of the Ukrainian

---

2 Elena Ovchinnikova, "Vasilii Ovchinnikov delal pervye v mire raboty, posviashchennye tragedii Babiego Iara," cited in Mykhailo Hutor, *Zberezhennia pam'iati pro trahediiu v Babynomu Iaru v chasy radians'koï vlady* (Kyiv: Natsional'nyi istoryko-memorial'nyi zapovidnyk "Babyn Iar," 2019), pp. 18-20.

3 D. Fedorovs'kyi, "Bab'iachyi Iar v maisterni khudozhnyka V. Ovchinnikova," *Radians'ke mystetstvo* (Kyiv), 30 July 1947.

SSR and the CC CP(b)U, entitled "About the Construction of a Great Monument to Those Who Perished in Babyn Yar." The government assigned the project to Oleksandr Vlasov, the chief architect of Kyiv, and the sculptor I. Kruglov, who envisioned a three-faceted pyramid of black granite (15 meters at its base), with a bas-relief in the center and a set of stairs leading to a podium repeating the relief of Babyn Yar.[4]

The construction of the monument was initially planned for 1946–1947, and some funds were even found. The "Plans for the Restoration and Development of Kyiv's Urban Economy for 1948–1950" (completed in 1947) in Babyn Yar still mentioned the construction of a park and a "monument to the victims of fascist terror."[5] But the plans went no further. One important reason was the announcement by the Stalinist government of a crackdown on "rootless cosmopolitans," which was clearly antisemitic in nature. One of the indirect victims of this campaign was Ovchynnykov himself, whose canvases from the Babyn Yar series were harshly criticized in May 1949 at the plenum of the Union of Artists of Ukraine for his "distorted images of the Soviet people" (probably because of the Jewish features of the people depicted in his paintings).[6] According to Ovchynnykov's daughter, the series of paintings was destroyed. Three of these works, however, now known as the *Babyn Yar Triptych*, are held in the collections of the National Museum of Art of Ukraine.[7]

**Monumental projects at Babyn Yar, 1965-1966**

In keeping with the Soviet government's policy of "erasing" Jewish memory and "diluting" Jewish identity throughout the 1950s, from time to

4 Tat'iana Evstaf'eva, "Babii Iar: poslevoennaia istoriia mestnosti," in *Babyn Iar: masove ubyvstvo i pam'iat' pro n'oho—Materialy mizhnarodnoï naukovoï konferentsiï* (Kyiv: Ukraïns'kyi tsentr vyvchennia istoriï Holokostu, 2012), pp. 21–31.

5 Tat'iana Evstaf'eva, "Babii Iar vo vtoroi polovine XX v.," in Tat'iana Evstaf'eva and Vitalii Nakhmanovich, eds., *Babii Iar: chelovek, vlast', istoriia—Dokumenty i materialy*, Vol. I (Kyiv: "Vneshtorgizdat Ukrainy," 2004), pp. 187–204.

6 "Vystup holovy Komitetu u spravakh mystetstv URSR M.P. Pashchyna na IV plenumi SKhU (1949) iz krytykoiu robit Z.Sh. Tolkachova 'Okupanty,' 'Maidanek,' 'Khrystos v Maidanek,' 'Tsvety Osventsyma' ta hrafichnoho tsyklu V. Ovchynnykova 'Babyn Iar.'" Cited in Hutor, *Zberezhennia pam'iati*, pp. 16-17.

7 Ovchinnikova, "Vasilii Ovchinnikov," p. 20.

time proposals were put forward to transform Babyn Yar into a place of rest and recreation by building attractions and other facilities. On 23 December 1959 the earlier decision to construct a monument in Babyn Yar was rescinded. As a result of public pressure, the government revisited the idea of erecting a monument on the eve of the 25th anniversary of the tragedy, but it had no intentions of retreating from the "official" treatment of Babyn Yar as the place of execution of "Soviet citizens, not Jews." This was attested by the very title of a resolution issued by the Council of Ministers of the Ukrainian SSR on 5 July 1965, "About Holding a Closed Competition for the Creation of Designs for a Monument in Honor of Soviet Citizens and Captive Soldiers and Officers of the Red Army Who Died at the Hands of the German-Fascist Occupiers during the Occupation of the City of Kyiv."[8]

In 1965–1966 two rounds of the competition were held, during which several dozen preliminary designs were presented. [see Plates **L** and **LI**] Well-known artists, sculptors, and architects took part in the completion, and some submitted two or three designs. For the most part, the participants adhered to the official guidelines of the competition to reflect the "heroism and unshakeable will of the people," "the courage and gallantry of the Soviet people," and "the nationwide grief for thousands of inconspicuous heroes," all of which a priori obscured the Jewish topic and thereby pushed the innocent victims of Babyn Yar into the background. The writer Viktor Nekrasov focused on this circumstance.

> Before me passed symbols and allegories, protesting women, completely realistic, half-naked, muscular men, more uncertain figures, and lines [of people] heading to their execution....I saw stairs, stylobates, mosaics, flags, barbed wire, the imprint of feet....And suddenly everything became clear to me: Places of the biggest tragedies do not require words. Literal symbolism pales before the events themselves; allegory is powerless. I, who came here to bow to the remains of those who perished, do not need to be told how these people died. I know everything. And one

8 Tetiana Ievstaf'ieva, "Do istoriï vstanovlennia pam'iatnykiv u Babynomu Iaru," in *Kyïv i kyiany: materialy shchorichnoï naukovo-praktychnoï konferentsiï*. Vol. I (Kyiv: Kyi, 2001), pp. 20-25.

does not need to shout either. I myself know where and when one should shout. I simply want to come and lay flowers at the mass grave and stand above it silently in solitude.[9]

Only a handful of preliminary designs submitted to the competition focused on the importance of understanding the value of human life and grief for the victims by proposing to depict the tragic deaths of tens of thousands of Jews. One such design was submitted by the architect Yosyf Karakis, who planned a memorial complex that would include a commemorative park laid out in the form of seven symbolic ravines connected by gangways. [see Plate **LII**] The bottom of the ravines was supposed to be covered with red flowers (poppies) or red gravel, as a reminder of the human blood shed there. Karakis envisioned the extant part of Babyn Yar as a symbolic preserve where no human foot might tread.

Three versions were proposed for the design of the central part of the memorial. The first, by the sculptor Yakiv Razhba, featured a monumental statue of the Fatherland with high-relief figures symbolizing heroism, suffering, and death. The second proposed a concrete stela featuring the silhouette of a person, an eternal flame, and a granite mosaic panel on the Babyn Yar theme located along the right side of the ramp on the retaining wall. The third depicted groups of petrified human bodies in the form of a broken stump of a split tree, inside of which would stand a two-story memorial with frescoes portraying scenes of grief and celebration of life painted by Zinovii Tolkachov,[10] a distinguished artist whose works are now regarded as artistic symbols of the Holocaust.[11] [see Plate **LII**] This, however, did not prevent the Stalinist regime from branding all three versions as "profoundly depraved," and Tolkachov himself as the "personification of rootless cosmopolitanism."[12]

---

9 Viktor Nekrasov, "Novye pamiatniki," *Dekorativnoe iskusstvo SSSR*, No. 12 (Moscow, 1966), pp. 23-27.

10 Tatiana Evstafieva, "K istorii ustanovleniia pamiatnika v Bab'em Iaru," *Evreiskii obozrevatel'*, No. 11 (Kyiv, 2002).

11 Halyna Skliarenko, "Zinovii Tolkachov: khudozhnyk i ioho chas," in idem, *Zinovii Tolkachov: tvory z muzeinykh ta pryvatnykh zbirok—Al'bom* (Kyiv: Dukh i Litera, 2005), pp. 6-34.

12 Tolkachov's painting *Taleskotn* (1944) became a symbol of the Shoah among eastern

The design submitted by the architect Avraam Miletskii envisioned the creation of a memorial complex featuring a granite stela inscribed with the words "Babyn Yar" in several languages and a retaining wall with seven artistically shaped ravine spurs. The first one contained a damaged stroller and parasol; the second, a violin fingerboard; the third, a little ball, etc. Miletskii felt the tragedy of Babyn Yar particularly keenly because his grandmother and mother perished there.[13]

Originality, the profundity of the artistic decision-making process, and the philosophical understanding of life and death marked a design entitled *When the World Collapses: Babyn Yar*, submitted by the sculptor Ada Rybachuk and her husband, the architect Volodymyr Melnychenko. [see Plate **LIII**] Using the expressive devices of architecture and sculpture, these young artists tried symbolically to depict human life that is filled with joy and sorrow, but which is interrupted abruptly. The idea for this striking design is elucidated in the writings of the Russian philosopher and art historian Karl Kantor:

> One had to sympathize with those who perished and with those who mourned them so sincerely and so powerfully as Ada [Rybachuk] and Volodia [Melnychenko], so that the Jewish melodies of resignation, suffering, and grief would resound with such purity in their Ukrainian hearts, which are sensitive to the pain of people of all races and nationalities. Fashioning out of great slabs of stone a high wall that surrounds and protects the burial place of those who were shot, the two artists seem to be recreating the washed-out ravine. Here it is once again before us: the Babyn Yar that once was.
>
> Descending the broad steps to the Urn containing the 'ashes' of the dead, you are not simply looking at a monument from the side but re-

---

European Jews. The Taleskotn (*tallit katan* in Hebrew) is a tetragonal cloak with a cut for a head and with long tassels by the corners, worn for the administration of a will according to the Pentateuch's Book of Leviticus. The painting depicts a fence with a barbed wire and a taleskotn unwinding above. It stands within barren, plundered land. The long tassels of a prayer cloak reach to the sky like human hands. The symbology in this tragic work evokes individual thoughts and associations in each viewer. The painting was exhibited for the first time in 2000 as part of the artist's personal exhibition at the Yad Vashem Art Museum in Jerusalem.

13 Evstafieva, "K istorii ustanovleniia pamiatnika v Bab'em Iaru."

> peating the route of those who were once hurled into the bottom of the ravine. The walls fashioned out of stone blocks along which you are walking seem to come to life all at once. This is that same group of Jews who are walking meekly to their death. And you are walking together with them. . . .
>
> The stones comprising the wall move in a peaceful rhythm at first; then the step strays, the rhythm breaks off; the stones begin to split, crumble, and sink. These are the executed people, mowed down by bullets, who are falling.
>
> The stone presses on the soul; in practically a physical way you feel the sharp corners of the stones digging into the body, the head.
>
> You recall Christ's crown of thorns because this wall is like a stone wreath around the forehead of a people chosen for suffering.
>
> Without having even seen the gravestones of Jewish cemeteries, Ada and Volodymyr 'guessed' at them in their design. . . . The imagination does not need prompts.[14]

None of the designs submitted to the competition found favor with the government. The jury's decision was annulled, and the book containing commentaries on the designs was confiscated. Instead, a granite obelisk was erected in the southern part of Babyn Yar in October 1966. Its inscription read: "Here a monument will be erected to Soviet people, victims of the crimes of fascism during the temporary occupation of the city of Kyiv in 1941–1943."[15]

### The Soviet monument at Babyn Yar, 1976

Ten years later, on 2 July 1976, a bronze monument was erected "To the Soviet citizens and captured soldiers and officers of the Soviet army who were shot by the German occupiers in Babyn Yar." Both the Jewish community and the opposition-minded Ukrainian intelligentsia were deeply disenchanted by this. At issue was the fact that the design for this monument had not been submitted to any competition. Moreover, it was

14 A. Rybachuk, A. Mel'nychenko, and V. Mel'nychenko, *"Kogda rushitsia mir...": kniga-rekviiem, kniga- pamiatnik* (Kyiv: Redaktsiino-vydavnyche pidpryiemstvo "Iuhinform," 1991), p. 11.

15 Evstafieva, "K istorii ustanovleniia pamiatnika v Bab'em Iaru."

roundly criticized for aesthetic reasons due to its indistinct contours and silhouettes; its appearance from a distance as if it were an amorphous, accumulated mass that was too small for the purpose of organizing the space; its misplacement in the landscape, etc. [see Plate **LIV**] The point was that the artistic ideas conveyed by the design were completely at odds with the spirit of the tragedy that unfolded in Babyn Yar in September 1941 and therefore were too removed from the real feelings experienced by the descendants of the victims.

The author of this multi-figured bronze monument was the architect Mykhailo Lysenko who was renowned for his heroic-romantic monuments. Lysenko was recognized by his colleagues as an extraordinarily talented individual, although at the same time he was very loyal to the party bosses and the government. Lysenko's collaborators on the design were the sculptors Oleksandr Vitryk and Viktor Sukhenko, and the architects Anatolii Ihnashchenko, Mykola Ivanchenko, and V. N. Ivanchenkov. The group worked under the keen supervision of party officials whose main concern was that the monument be reflective of an appropriate political and ideological spirit. There was no question of the monument portraying any Jewish character. Even the area slated for the memorial was deliberately "neutralized" by the nearly half-kilometer's distance from the real site of the tragedy. Thus, in subsequent decades the monument that the government offered as the official symbol of the Babyn Yar tragedy turned into a symbol of falsehood as well as of the retribution that was meted out to the artists who had sacrificed their talents in the service of ideology.

The convoluted history behind the erection of the 1976 monument remained secret for a long time. It is interesting to learn that in the first version of Lysenko's design the monument showed what looked like a funeral procession. He was forced to abandon this design, however, because it did not promote the idea of "the triumph of life over death." The next version, which formed the basis of succeeding versions, showed the figure of a naked, young woman with her hands tied behind her back with barbed wire, who is breastfeeding the infant child lying on her lap. According to the artist's idea, this composition was supposed to generate a feeling of hatred toward those who humiliate people while at the same time inculcate in the viewer feelings of love and hope.

Nevertheless, this design did not appeal to the project overseers, who relentlessly "advised" Lysenko "to intensify" the idea of resistance and the struggle against fascism. Accordingly, the female figure was placed on a pedestal and the traditional grouping of figures typical of Soviet monuments was added: a worker, a soldier, and a sailor raising clenched fists raised above their heads before being shot. Subsequently, other figures were added. These included: to the right of the trio of figures a young woman balancing between life and death; at the back, a group standing that included a little girl weeping over the body of an old man; and figures of two naked people who are falling at the same time as huge boulders broken off the monument, symbolizing the executed people falling into the ravine.

A site for the monument was found at the heart of the shallow ravine, where one of the collaborating architects, Anatolii Ihnashchenko, proposed that it be suspended in mid-air. At the last moment, virtually at the final stage of the project, the party censors "interpreted" the six spurs of the ravine created by nature as a Star of David that was "deliberately coded" by the authors of the project. The designers were then compelled to come up with another idea: to fill the bottom of Babyn Yar with red smalta [stained opaque glass in the shape of cubes and plates used to create mosaics—trans.] to mimic a bleeding wound in the earth, which would be covered with a 350-meter thorn-covered branching fiber-optical conductor. The situation reached the point that the party overseers forced Lysenko to cover the figure of the naked mother with a Ukrainian blouse. When the monument was finally erected, the designers' names were not indicated. This did not, however, save them from experiencing years of brutal criticism at the hands of their colleagues and the general public.[16]

### Other depictions on the Babyn Yar theme

Despite the enduring political and ideological pressure in the Soviet Union and the very real threats to any attempts to present an unbiased picture of the Babyn Yar tragedy, the theme continued to fascinate many

16 Liudmila Lysenko, "Dve monumental'nye istorii," LiveJournal [Zhivoi Zhurnal], 2 July 2014.

artists. [see Plates **XXXIV** and **XXXV**] Artistic approaches to the Holocaust and Babyn Yar differed, as did their individual destinies. Some artists, ignoring all ideological obstacles, worked on the theme indefatigably and openly; others not only avoided advertising their works, but tried to conceal them.

The career of the Moscow artist Aleksandr Tikhomirov is a clear-cut illustration of this phenomenon. In his youth he fell victim to the government's campaign of persecution during the 1930s that targeted "formalists," with the result that he was forced to abandon "high art." Earning a living at the Moscow Industrial Complex of Decorative Design and Decorative Art, Tikhomirov spent most of his life painting billboard-sized portraits of Soviet leaders. One of his gigantic portraits set a kind of record: a huge (42 m x 22 m) portrait of Lenin decorating the building of the Ministry of Foreign Affairs on Smolensk Square.

In the 1960s, when Babyn Yar began to be discussed publicly, this historical event made such a profound impression on Tikhomirov that he began working secretly on a series of graphic works devoted to this theme. [see Plate **XXXVI**] Twenty years later, after the artist's death, his granddaughter discovered a file in his personal archives filled with these works. One distinct element in Tikhomirov's drawings is the figure of a person: a solitary individual or part of a multi-figure composition, incorporeal or powerful, acutely dynamic or petrified. In portraying the human body and its plasticity and gestures, in deforming forms, and presenting black-and-white contrasts, the artist conveys inhuman pain, suffering, and despair. Tikhomirov's graphic works are also saturated with feelings of grief for those who perished in Babyn Yar.[17]

The talented sculptor Vadym Sydur, a native of Dnipropetrovsk, immersed himself deeply in the theme of the Holocaust and the Babyn Yar tragedy. This artist had absolutely no qualms about being unappreciated, and he felt free to flout the guidelines of Socialist Realism. Nor was he afraid of offending the traditional view of pictorial art depicting the "Soviet people." It is no wonder that Sydur, too, was targeted in the campaign against the "formalists." Later in his career the artist created a style

17 I. Krupnitskaia, *Kompozitsiia na temu Petrushki: zhizn' i tvorchestvo khudozhnika Aleksandra Tikhomirova* (Saint Petersburg: Maier, 2018).

known as Coffin-Art (he was forced to earn a living designing gravestones). Nevertheless, the authorities had no opportunities to compel the artist to stray from his chosen and forever extraordinary, unique, staunchly independent, and uncompromising path.

During Sydur's life his works were never exhibited in public; his admirers could view his creations only in his studio. Some of his most impressive works are *The Wounded Man* (1963), *Despair* (1963), *Monument to Those Who Perished through Violence* (1965), and *Treblinka* (1966). Sydur's sculpture *Babyn Yar* (1965) is one of the most distinguished of his works. [see Plate **XXXV**] The deceptive nihilism of a philosopher and his ironic and critical attitude to the social order did not extend to Sydur's works that explored the themes of war, life, and death. He searched for an answer to the eternal questions: "Who are we?"; "Where do we come from?"; "Where are we going?" The artist did not deny himself the temptation of experimenting with form and of dealing with purely formal quests. In *Babyn Yar* these quests are embodied to a high degree in generalized images and in the depiction of human tragedy, which does away with superfluous realism and pathos. Applying extraordinarily sparing—if one can say such a thing about wood—lapidary" devices, Sydur compels the caring viewer to feel the full measure of the tragic nature of one of the most horrific events of the twentieth century.[18]

In the 1960s and early 1970s a series of graphic works and paintings dedicated to Babyn Yar was created by Yosyp Vaisblat. The life of this Kyiv-born artist, who was born into the family of the chief rabbi of Kyiv and distinguished theologian Nukhim Vaisblat, was difficult. He devoted nearly twenty years to the monotonous work of creating silkscreens of Soviet leaders and establishing Soviet trusts. In early 1951 he was arrested by the NKVD on typically Soviet trumped-up charges. He was accused of being hostile to the Soviet government [and] a convinced nationalist who for a number of years conducted anti-Soviet agitation of a slanderous, nationalist character among his friends. Among other pieces of evidence indicating his anti-Soviet attitude, the investigators singled out the entries recorded in the artist's diary: "1948—an unspoken direc-

18 Mikhail Sidur, *Vadim Sidur: ocherk tvorchestva na fone sobytii zhizni* (Moscow: Moskovskii gosudarstvennyi muzei Vadima Sidura, 2004).

tive"; "1949—Jews are dismissed from work." Vaisblat was imprisoned in the Gulag for ten years. After his rehabilitation following Stalin's death in 1953, he returned to Moscow, where he was finally able to devote himself to his art, including an entire series of works on Babyn Yar. Reflecting on this matter, he wrote in his diary:

> I have to suspend my 'Babyn Yar' theme for a time. Right now I am excited by the inevitable, that which can fill human life. Love. In the finest and varied understanding of this phenomenon. Attraction between the genders, motherly love, human love.
>
> Admittedly, the tragedy of the 'Yar' is undoubtedly directly related to the theme of love. For love is also manifested in tragedy. This excites and interests me very much. This theme is limitless. True, it is infinite in poetry, in music, in literature, and in art. Here is where there is something to work on in order find a solution of the image. This theme should be understood very broadly . . . love-hostility, love-hatred, love triumphing over death, affliction, despair. . . .
>
> It is in this theme that one can find one's personal, very clear image and its embodiment. The image…is not trivial, not sentimental, [it is] epic and all-encompassing. . . .
>
> And I am interested in the theme of death. But once again, not the external aspect but a juxtaposition—you die and everyone and everything remains . . .[19]

Before commencing his main work on the *Babyn Yar* series (1962), Vaisblat produced a large number of studies and sketches. There is no doubt that his paintings were influenced by work in the domain of sculpture. The central painting in Vaisblat's *Babyn Yar* series is characterized by monumental generality. But his small graphic work entitled *Before the Shooting* creates a more powerful, even shocking, impression on the viewer. It shows barrels of rifles aimed at a group of naked, exhausted people whose only protection is a *huppah*, a Jewish wedding canopy, symbolizing the unity of marriage with death. People's helplessness and

19 Cited in Artur Rudzitskii, "Iskat', derzat', myslit'": delo khudozhnika Iosifa Vaisblata (po materialam arkhiva NKVD-KGB)," *The Jewish World of Ukraine* (2019). http://ju.org.ua/en/publicism/323.html

defenselessness before blind, insane, and cruel power are clearly revealed in *Before the Shooting*.[20]

The Kyiv painter Hryhorii Synytsia, who in the 1960s was persecuted by the authorities and forced to relocate to Kryvyi Rih, had narrowly avoided death at Babyn Yar. Hence this topic concerned him all his life. In 1960 he created two variants of the composition *Babyn Yar*. One was in color. [see Plate **XXXVII**] The other, which was smaller and vertically oriented, depicted only two figures—a mother and child. The painting stuns the viewer with its stern asceticism, sense of fatality, and undisguised truth. Synytsia also tackled the topic of Babyn Yar in his frescoes from the late 1960s.[21]

In the late 1970s the Kyiv-born artist Efim Simkin was also drawn to the theme of Babyn Yar, where his relatives perished in September 1941. Simkin had lost an arm in the war, a theme which always played an important role in his art. His paintings *Babyn Yar* (1979) and *Before the Shooting in Babyn Yar* (1980) are filled with dramatic effect and feelings of grief and the pain of loss. [see Plate **XXXVIII**] They convey the artist's ideas about good and evil, mercy and cruelty, and the real value of human life.[22]

As noted above, Vasyl Ovchynnykov never stopped working on the Babyn Yar theme. In 1974 his series, *Occupiers in Kyiv*, a unique sequel to his partially destroyed series *Babyn Yar*, was shown at his solo exhibition at the Museum of Western and Oriental Art (he died nine days before the opening). The central canvas, entitled *One Hour before the Shooting*, depicts a group of women stripped naked before being killed, among whom a young woman, on the verge of death, feeds her infant. Another painting, *The Path of the Condemned*, was recreated from the 1946 series.[23]

In an effort to understand the philosophical problems of evil and suf-

---

20 Ibid.

21 "Muzyka kolioru Hryhoriia Synytsi," *Svitohliad*, No. 2 (Kyiv, 2008), pp. 8–13.

22 V.I. Kostin, comp., *Efim Simkin—Vekhi pamiati—Zhivopis'—al'bom* (Moscow: Sovetskii khudozhnik, 1984); Boris Rubin, "Avtoportret so svechoi," *Gazeta Borisa Rubina*, 18 July 2019. http://www.borisrubin.com/2019/07/

23 Ovchinnikova, "Vasilii Ovchinnikov delal pervye v mire raboty," pp. 19-20.

fering, another artist, Mykhailo Zviahyn, took up the Babyn Yar theme. Zviahyn's father was killed in the war, and during his childhood the artist survived the siege of Leningrad. He began working on sketches in the first half of the 1970s, a time when he was gradually moving away from the realistic manner. Zviahyn's metaphorically rendered painting *Babyn Yar* (1981–85) is iconic. [see Plate **XL**] In it the artist presents a horrific picture of the execution of the human spirit and destruction of human flesh, juxtaposing people with bloodthirsty beasts that embody universal evil. Depicted in orange-red splashes that give rise to a sense of impending catastrophe, vicious, fanged animals resembling fiends from hell devour and torment the unfortunate victims. In the upper part of the foreground a person is hanging from a gallows. As the viewer's gaze moves to the central and lower sections of the painting, one is overwhelmed by a feeling of being submerged in a pit, a grave, a hellish abyss, where people who are still alive are suffering and suffocating. During the Soviet period the fate of both Zviahyn himself and his large-scale (eight square meters) *Babyn Yar* painting was a difficult one. Owing to the "irrelevance" of the theme and the "inadequate" manner of painting, the work was not accepted for exhibition until 1990.[24]

Another distinguished work, *The Wall (Park of Memory)*, created by Ada Rybachuk and Volodymyr Melnychenko, met a tragic fate during the Soviet period. A wall erected at Baikove Cemetery was based on a design that the two artists submitted to the 1965 competition to construct a memorial in Babyn Yar. The design showed that the life of the body is temporary, whereas the spirit is eternal. But their concept encountered fierce opposition from the government with its communist, materialistic ideology and aesthetic standards of Socialist Realism. In 1981 the two artists were forced to destroy the reliefs with their own hands, and only a layer of concrete remained of the wall.[25]

---

24 A. Borovskii, comp., *Mikhail Zviagin: zhivopis'* (Saint Petersburg, 2000).

25 "Samyi sil'nyi pamiatnik zhertvam Bab'ego Iara do sikh por zapechatan betonom," Association of Jewish Organizations and Communities of Ukraine (Vaad), 30 August 2016. http://www.vaadua.org/news/samyy-silnyy-pamyatnik-zhertvam-babego-yara-do-sih-por-zapechatan-betonom

### Depictions of Babyn Yar in independent Ukraine

Essential changes in the memorialization and pictorial representations of the Babyn Yar tragedy emerged only after Ukraine became independent. On 29 September 1991, the fiftieth anniversary of the mass shootings in Kyiv, the government commissioned the construction in Babyn Yar of a monument entitled *Menorah*. [see Plate **LV**] The memorial also featured a paved pathway called "The Road of Grief," stretching from the Menorah Monument to the former office of the Jewish Cemetery. The designer of the Menorah, Yakym Levych, was a native of Kamianets-Podilskyi and one of the most original artists of the Ukrainian underground art movement. His collaborators on the project were the architect Yurii Paskevych, the artist Oleksandr Levych, and the engineer Borys Hiller.

The shape of this memorial to grief is simple and laconic. The reliefs on the branches of the Menorah feature subjects from the history of the Jewish people, whose choice as a symbol was not accidental. The menorah (Hebr. נמוֹהָר , meaning "lampstand") is a golden, seven-branched candelabrum that was placed in the sanctuary of the Tabernacle of Moses during the forty years that the Jews wandered in the desert, and which was moved later to the Temple of Jerusalem, both the First and the Second. This most ancient symbol of Judaism and most widely known national and religious object (alongside the Star of David) is pictured on the emblem of the State of Israel. In January 2001 the Menorah monument was visited by the president of Israel Moshe Katsav. Thanks to his assistance and initiative, a commemorative plaque was installed next to the monument.[26]

During the international film festival, "Babyn Yar: Intolerance," held in Kyiv in September 1991 at the Union of Cinematographers, Ada Rybachuk and Volodymyr Melnychenko presented a number of thematic tapestry applications for decorating halls. Reviews were enthusiastic, but the artists themselves were dissatisfied. They felt that the flat surface of the applications could not convey the depth of their artistic idea, whose realization, they felt, required material that was more "eternal." The epithet eternal suggested a solution: sheep's wool from which was woven the

---

26 Halyna Skliarenko, *Iakym Levych: zhyvopys na perekhresti chasu* (Kyiv: Dukh i Litera, 2002), p.15.

clothing worn by the biblical prophets, as was the shroud of Christ. This led the artists to create a tapestry entitled *When the World Collapses*, a continuation of the Babyn Yar theme. [see Plate **XLIII**]

The couple's work on the tapestry lasted six years, requiring titanic efforts. Rybachuk and Melnychenko hand-wove their tapestry (4.5 m high and 2.5 m wide) into which they introduced their sketches. Professional weavers refused, however, to take on this difficult work. The tapestry is practically monochromatic and features mostly achromatic colors: black and white. The late poet and civic figure Yurii Kaplan characterized this remarkable piece of art in the following way:

> At the center of the composition is a pregnant woman, who was not fated to become a Madonna. Her firstborn is still in the womb, and her belly is dissected, as though shown in an infernal technical drawing. And we meet the gaze with the square, inverted eyes of the infant who will never see the light of day, only the darkness of the Catastrophe. A black nimbus of hair around the head, with each separate hair sticking out, reminds us of a howling question mark. The mother's thin arms instinctively try to protect the child; their unnatural curvature is reminiscent of a flower broken off a Jewish *matzevah* [grave marker]. In general, the tapestry does not feature any specifically Jewish symbols, such as a candelabrum or a Star of David. . . . Huge eyes that seem to have "swum" away from the face in various directions: a graphic equivalent—silver fishes (the most ancient biblical symbol), the eyes on the beautiful face of the Madonna. There are two more pairs of eyes with a look of apprehension, which are unable to absorb the entire horror of what is happening.
>
> The bodies that are plunging into the abyss are curved strangely, and they resemble the Hebrew letters forming the dread name 'Babyn Yar.'[27]

The tapestry, *When the World Collapses*, is a reflection of a universal tragedy. There are certain distinct elements, however, such as the Hebrew letters used in the composition, which are a reminder that Jews were the main victims of the Babyn Yar massacre. In 2002, the tapestry was exhibited in the new building of the Embassy of the Federal Republic of Germany in Kyiv.[28]

27 Iurii Kaplan, "Gobelen placha," *Evreiskii obozrevatel'*, No. 21 [40] (Kyiv, 2002).

28 Ibid.

In the 1990s the well-known artist Isaak Tartakovskii took up the Holocaust theme and created a number of paintings entitled *The Final Route*, *Jews in Captivity*, *Jews and Commissars, Come Out!*, *World Sorrow*, and *Menorah*. The artist also painted portraits of a survivor of Babyn Yar, Yakov Kaper, and a Righteous Among the Nations designee, Olha Rozhchenko, among other individuals. In another painting, *The Tears of Babyn Yar* (1992), Tartakovskii uses the menorah as a symbol of the Jewish people. [see Plate **XLII**] One might think that this use of a commonly accepted symbol might be perceived as a cliché. In this case, however, the menorah is by no means a banal or stereotypical artistic decision because in the hands of Tartakovskii the painting becomes a masterful blend of reality, symbols, and phantasmagoria.[29]

The striking works of the artist, colorist, and academic Stephan-Arpad Madiar are marked by innovation and creative experimentation. The main direction of his scholarly research and artistic quest is focused on correcting, with the help of coloristics, the psychophysiological state of a person in extreme conditions and in everyday life. The artist's diptych *Babyn Yar* is a continuation of his experiments with color. Through the subtle interplay of colors and tones in a nearly realistic landscape, Madiar seems to be opening up a road into the other world. Faces of people peer out from the cleverly interwoven branches of the "Tree of Life," manifesting a new and mysterious sense. The second part of the diptych is meditative and abstract.[30]

The Kyivan landscape artist Hryhorii Minskyi presents a realistic landscape, with the monument "To Those Who Perished in Babyn Yar" in the background, in which color alone elicits sadness, corresponding to the subject matter.[31] In *The Eternal Cry* (alternate title: *Babyn Yar*), the work of the Kyiv artist Hernadii/ Herman Gold, the tense interplay of colors and tones and the dynamic nature of the composition produce a

29 *Isaak Tartakovs'kyi – narodnyi khudozhnyk Ukraïny: zhyttia i tvorchist'* (Kyiv: Sofiia-A, 2008).

30 *Nisaion—Vyprobuvannia—Ordeal: ievreis'ka tema v tvorakh suchasnykh khudozhnykiv Ukraïny* (Kyiv: Mebius-KB, 1994).

31 *Hryhorii Mins'kyi: kataloh* (Kyiv: Kyïvs'ka orhanizatsiia Natsional'noï Spilky khudozhnykiv Ukraïny, 2007).

sense of tragedy. [see Plate **XLIV**] The painting depicts an old man who is carrying the lifeless bodies of two children, emerging from the depths of despair to meet his death.[32]

Women artists introduce a special emotional accent into works devoted to the Babyn Yar theme. *Babyn Yar*, a painting by the artist Olha Petrova deserves special mention. The central element in the composition is the six-pointed Star of David, which, thanks to the intense relationship between tones and colors, conveys dynamism. Without resorting to figurative images, the artist succeeds in conveying the tragic nature of her chosen theme.[33] Another, albeit small work (48 x 54 cm), this one by the artist Tetiana Ilyina and entitled simply *Yar*, is distinctive because it is done in the enameling technique. [see Plate **XLIII**] The expression, tension, and dynamism of the composition elicit confusion and apprehension, yet the decorative nature of the painting in no way detracts from its tragic theme.

Among the most famous artists who have devoted themselves to the theme of the Holocaust is the Kyiv-born painter (now United States citizen) Mykhailo Turovskyi, who created a series of sixty-eight works on the Catastrophe, six of which are devoted to Babyn Yar. [see Plate **XXXIX**] This series of works, which has been exhibited in major European and American museums, was shown for the first time at the National Museum of Pictorial Art of Ukraine in 2001. A marvelous draftsman, Turovskyi has a subtle understanding of the nature of color that he uses masterfully. It is no wonder that French art critics, raised on the Impressionists and Post-Impressionists, are thrilled by his paintings. In addition to the professional qualities displayed by his body of work, Turovskyi's paintings demonstrate the "impatience of the heart" that cannot by supplanted or imitated by any means. His paintings always garner special attention at art exhibitions because of the hyper-realistic depiction of the sufferings of the victims, who are being immolated in the fires of the Holocaust. In several canvases the artistry behind the depiction of human suffering

32 Mykhailo Hutor, "Hernad Hol'd," in his *Babyn Iar: v sertsi strakh, v sertsi bil', v sertsi rozpach* (Kyiv: Natsional'nyi istoryko-memorial'nyi zapovidnyk "Babyn Iar," 2015), pp. 18-20.

33 Ol'ha Petrova, *Maliarstvo, hrafika* (Kyiv: Artek, 1995).

surpasses established and acceptable limits. Although excessive naturalism often creates an impression that is the opposite of the desired effect, Turovskyi's canvasses, nevertheless, rank among the most famous works devoted to the Shoah and Babyn Yar.[34]

Kyiv-born Michael/Mikhail Gleizer, who today lives in the United States, also took up the Babyn Yar theme. In 1980, Gleizer's series of illustrations to the novels of the Lithuanian writer Grigorijus Kanovičius was purchased by the Graphics Department of the Pushkin State Museum of Fine Arts in Moscow. One of the volumes in Kanovičius's trilogy, *Candles in the Wind*, illustrated by Gleizer, was devoted to the Holocaust in Lithuania. As a rule, the artist works within a complex range based on the most subtle interplay of grey-brown and ochre tones and colors. Open, local colors do not appear often in his works; Gleizer explains this by the state of his soul. In the US the artist created a large-scale painting entitled *Babi Yar*, which is composed of nine fragments. This work is devoid of superfluous exaltation and dramatic tension. People disappear in a foggy mist, like grass, like wind, through which they break through to death. As the people disappear, the sky becomes tinged with red. This painting, first exhibited in 1992 at the Chassidic Art Institute in Brooklyn (New York), is one of Gleizer's finest works from his American period.[35]

The Babyn Yar theme is being explored today by budding young artists in Ukraine. Every year the Ukrainian Center for Holocaust Studies holds a nationwide competition devoted to "The History and Lessons of the Holocaust." The work of one participant, a schoolgirl named Olha Novak, works on the emotions through both narrative and clear-cut devices of pictorial art. Contemporary realities (the entrance to a subway) are invaded by shadows from the past, and the sign on the tunnel that reads "Dorohozhychi Subway Station" gives a documentary slant to the drawing. The child phantoms depicted in the drawing are both moving and tragic. To the viewer they are entirely real, but the passersby in the drawing, whose backs face the viewer, cannot see them. A soft, warm light emanates from these children, strangers from the past, who died

34 Irina Klimova, "Vstrechaite – Turovskii," *Evreiskii obozrevatel'*, No. 9 [28] (Kiev, 2002).

35 "Mykhailo Hleizer," in *Nisaion*, pp. 16-17.

tragically in Babyn Yar. Adults living in the present are heading in the direction of an uneasy, leaden blue sky and a dark abyss. This work features diverse color and tone nuances, and the figures of the children are drawn with understated humor. The images, which work on the viewer's mind and emotions, are conspicuous in their authenticity and elicit a sinking feeling of involvement in the events depicted in the drawing.[36]

From this cursory survey of the works produced by artists, sculptors, and monumental painters who in various periods explored the tragic theme of the Babyn Yar massacre, one can see how much these creative individuals have done in responding to the call of their conscience in order to convey the truth about this tragedy to the general public. It is also clear that much more remains to be done to preserve the memory of Babyn Yar and to champion the humanist values that are important to all of mankind.

---

36 "Holokost ochyma ditei Ukraïny," Association of Jewish Organizations and Communities of Ukraine (Vaad), September 2013. http://vaadua.org/news/golokost-ochima-ditey-ukrayini-vistavka

Vasyl Ovchynnykov: *Babyn Yar*, triptych, 1947

Yosef Kozakovskyi: *People Transported for Execution* (Babyn Yar), 1948

Feliks Lemberskyi: *Babi Yar*, 1952

Boris Prorokov: *Near Babi Yar*
(from the series *This Should Not Happen Again!*), 1959.

Vadym Sydur:
*Babyn Yar*, 1966.

Sava Brodsky:
Illustration to Anatoly Kuznetsov's
novel *Babi Yar*, 1966.

Aleksandr Tikhomirov: *Babi Yar*, 1960s.

Hryhorii Synytsia: *Babyn Yar*, 1972

Efim Simkin: *Before the Shootings in Babyn Yar*, 1980.

Mykhailo Turovskyi: *Babyn Yar*, 1980s.

Mykhailo Zviahyn: *Babi Yar*, 1980s.

Ilya Kleiner: *Babi Yar*, 1991.

Isaak Tartakovskii: *The Tears of Babyn Yar*, 1992.

Tetiana Ilyina,
*The Ravine*, 1997.

Ada Rybachuk and Volodymyr Melnychenko
before their tapestry: *When the World Collapses*, 1990s.

Hernadii Gold: *Eternal Call* (Babyn Yar), 2000.

Olha Novak: *Dorohozhychi Subway Station*, 2014.

*The Unvanquished* (Russian: *Nepokorennye*; USSR, 1945), director Mark Donskoi, screenplay by Boris Gorbatov.

*The Ladies' Tailor* (Russian: *Damskii portnoi*; USSR, 1990), director Leonid Gorovets [Horovets], screenplay by Aleksandr Borshchagovskii [Oleksandr Borshchahivskyi].

*Babij Yar*
(Germany and Belarus, 2003),
director Jeff Kanew, screenplay by
Artur Brauner and Stephen Glantz.

*Babi Yar* (Ukraine, 2002), directors Nikolai/Mykola Zasieiev-Rudenko and Oksana Kovaliova, screenplay by Nikolai Zaieiev-Rudenko.

*The Match*
(Russia and Ukraine, 2011),
director Andrei Maliukov,
screenplay by Dmitrii Zverkov
and Igor Sosna.

Competition for the Design of a Babyn Yar monument, 1965

Competition designs at the House of Artists (Kyiv).

Competition designs at the House of Artists (Kyiv).

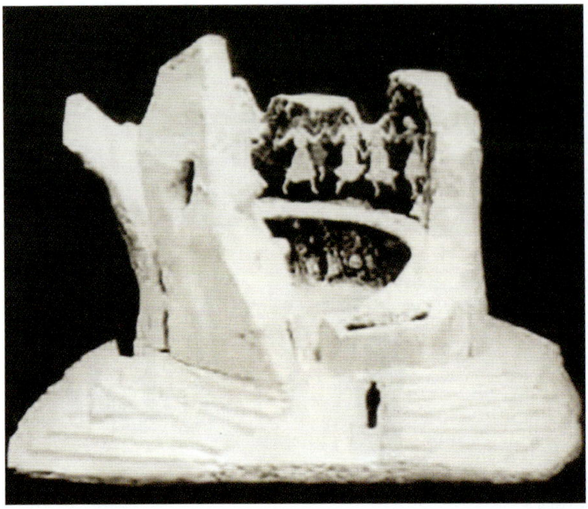

Yosyf Karakis's design

Zinovii Tolkachov's frescoes (for Yosyf Karakis's design).

Ada Rybachuk and Volodymyr Melnychenko's design entitled
*When the World Collapses: Babyn Yar.*

Monument "To the Soviet citizens and captured soldiers and officers of the Soviet Army shot by the German occupiers in Babyn Yar," 1976.

The Menorah monument
dedicated to the memory
of the Jewish victims
shot in Babyn Yar, 1991.

Commemorative marker at the place where the prisoners
of the Syrets concentration camp were shot, 1999.

Commemorative marker dedicated to the *Ostarbeiter* (Eastern Workers), 2005.

Commemorative marker dedicated to the prisoners
of the Syrets concentration camp, 1991.

Commemorative cross in honor of OUN-M members, 1992.

Commemorative crosses erected in honor of German POWs, 1999.

Commemorative cross erected in honor of executed clergymen, 2000.

Monument "To the children shot in Babyn Yar," 2001.

Remnants of the Jewish Cemetery.

Monument to the Soviet Jewish underground fighter Tetiana Markus, 2009

Commemorative marker dedicated to the victims of the 1961 Kurenivka tragedy, 2006.

Commemorative marker dedicated to the exterminated patients of the Ivan Pavlov Psychiatric Hospital, 2003.

Monument to the writer Anatoly Kuznetsov, 2009.

Commemorative stela with the inscription:
“A monument to the victims of the Roma Holocaust” (to be installed 2009/2011).

Television tower built on the site of the ruined Orthodox Brotherhood (Bratske) cemetery.

Former office of the Jewish Cemetery.

Commemorative marker erected at the spot
where on 29 September 1941 the "Road to Death" began, 2011.

CHAPTER 12

# Babyn Yar in Music

*Natalia Semenenko*

Artists play a special role in the social perception of the Babyn Yar tragedy. Feeling the pain of this loss keenly, it is artists who, for the most part, are the first to display courage and take on the responsibility to grasp tragic events of the past. In revealing these events by artistic means, they often anticipate by entire decades the eventual reaction of official state institutions. Sensing with their exposed nerve endings the contradictory and tragic nature of contemporary existence, and with the aid of individual artistic-stylistic devices, artists do not simply recreate a panoramic picture of the world or a certain fragment of history; they also act as a powerful generator of new and timely spiritual meanings.

Music is the universal language of mankind, which can exert a fundamental impact on mass consciousness. An outstanding musical composition is capable of shattering an official code that has been imposed on society, and breaching cultural barriers. And, in penetrating the philosophical depths of human existence, it is capable of preparing collective awareness for radical transformations, thereby responding to the challenges of the age. The sacred memory of the innocent victims of the Holocaust, the largest mass grave of which in Ukrainian lands is Babyn Yar, has been preserved for the coming generations by emblematic musical works written by foreign and Ukrainian composers. Each artist who has touched on this tragic theme has relived, recast, and defined for himself the genre and array of expressive devices in order to create a musical memorial to Babyn Yar. Recognizing music's ability to carry out the functions of a commentary, social pamphlet, and political appeal, various composers have demonstrated solidarity during the creative process to create compositions that are in harmony with his own time.

## The Holocaust in music

The phenomenon of musical representations of the Holocaust began with the cantata, *A Survivor from Warsaw* (*Ein Überlebender aus Warschau*, 1947), composed by the Austrian-Jewish-American composer Arnold Schoenberg. This seven-minute compostion, whose premiere took place in 1948, essentially marked the opening of the world's catalogue of musical works devoted to this vitally important theme.

The cantata was commissioned by the Koussevitzky Music Foundation. Embedded in Schoenberg's composition are documentary sources that, in keeping with the composer's conception, are transformed into the story of a prisoner from the Warsaw ghetto, who somehow survived miraculously. The narrator's account, as the personification of the image of an eyewitness of those horrific events, is performed in English. The recitative clarity of the narrator's part is achieved thanks to the extraordinary psychological veracity of the recreated state of a man who has been condemned to death. The coarse shouts of the sergeant (rendered in German), the officer's commands, and the order to bring the prisoners to the gas chamber harshly interrupt the voice of the narrator, who in the final, tragic moments of his life recalls his relatives who disappeared without a trace.

The arresting, dominant emotion of the entire work is the singing of the ancient Hebrew hymn *Shema Yisroel*,[1] which in its choral rendition becomes a symbol of the Jewish people's spiritual consolidation, even at the dramatic moment of their execution. This biblical poem is recited by Jews both as an everyday prayer and as an entreaty before imminent death. The men's choir sings in ancient Hebrew, and the prayer is strengthened by the penetrating tone of the trombone. With sparse instrumental timbres the composer paints a realistic picture of everyday life in the concentration camp: The trumpet solo recreates the morning wake-up signal, the anxious throbbing of the small drum becomes a

1 The biblical verse *Sh'ma Yisra'eil Adonai Eloheinu Adonai echad* (Hear, Israel, the L-d is our G-d, the L-d is One) reflects most accurately the Jewish symbol of faith: the monotheism of Judaism. For two thousand years Jewish martyrs have gone to their death uttering the words of the Shema. The faithful say this prayer four times a day, and by tradition it is also said prior to a peaceful death.

unique code of the camp atmosphere—of spiritual unease, nervousness, tension, danger, and—finally—a presentiment of death.[2]

After a lengthy interval of nearly two decades, in 1965 the composer Günter Kochan premiered his cantata, *Die Asche von Birkenau*, which was followed a year later by the premier of the collaborative cantata, the *Jüdische Chronik*, an artistic effort spearheaded by the East German composer and conductor Paul Dessau. The impetus for the *Jüdische Chronik* was given by a series of anti-Jewish terrorist acts, particularly the defacement in 1959 of a synagogue that had just been restored in Cologne, West Germany. These distressing events spurred Dessau into writing a five-part cantata, whose text recalls various episodes from the persecution of the Jews during the Holocaust. Joining the musical project on Dessau's invitation were composers from both West Germany (Boris Blacher, Karl Amadeus Hartmann, and Hans Werner Henze) and East Germany (Rudolf Wagner-Régeny and the librettist Jens Gerlach). [3]

**Dmytro Klebanov**

The very first composer to create a musical reading devoted to the unprecedented extermination of Jews in Babyn Yar was the Jewish composer Dmytro Klebanov from Kharkiv, Ukraine. [see Plate **XXI**] In 1945, after returning from evacuation to his native city, the composer learned of the mass destruction of the Jews in Kyiv. Disturbed and shocked to the core by the news, he resolved to commemorate the martyrdom of the innocent victims in music and composed *Symphony No. 1*: *In Memory of the Martyrs of Babyn Yar*. This was truly a heroic act on the composer's part. In a sense, it was a singular act in anticipation of musical works of the highest quality, which were created in the following decades on the way to establishing a panoramic musical interpretation of the Holocaust theme dispersed in time.

---

2 Abby Anderton, "A discourse on Arnold Schoenberg's A Survivor from Warsaw and Dmitiri Shostakovich's Thirteenth Symphony (Babi Yar)" (Bucknell University Music Department, B.A. Honors thesis, 2006).

3 Emi Volodarsky [Amy Lynn Wlodarski], "Muzykal'nye pamiatniki Kholokosta: Klassicheskaia muzyka," *Music and the Holocaust*, 10 July 2021, https://holocaustmusic.ort.org/ru/pamjat-okholokoste/memorials/

Klebanov was a pioneer among Soviet artists in general and in Ukraine in particular. He was someone who had the audacity to proclaim at the top of his voice the tragedy of Babyn Yar through purely symphonic devices (without the use of any texts with concrete subject and thematic reference points), and thus to open people's eyes to this vicious Nazi crime. At the same time, the composer sought to ensure that his musical material corresponded as much as possible both to historical events and to the imagistic richness of the content of his work. Before writing his symphony, Klebanov made a thorough study of all printed sources that were available in Ukraine at the time: recordings of Jewish folk melodies, ancient religious chants (dating to the Old Testament times of King David)), religious hymns, etc. He also sought the advice of the well-known Kharkiv choir conductor and expert on the Jewish musical treasury, Zynovii Zahranychnyi.[4]

The "biography" of Klebanov's symphony, like that of the composer himself, was complicated. The very run-up to its public presentation was a source of considerable stress for Klebanov. Figuratively speaking, the final rehearsal took place in an emotionally charged atmosphere. The Communist party leadership of Soviet Ukraine and the curators of the concert and theater industry (essentially censors) were indignant and genuinely perturbed by the music's "nationalistic sound," in particular because the score was woven out of typical and easily identifiable Jewish folkloric intonations and steeped in distinctively Jewish melodies and rhythms. Symphonic development unfolded on a foundation of the colorful Jewish Freygish scale (altered Phrygian scale). The culmination of the final movement, which includes a part for solo soprano, was reminiscent of the function of the *hazzan* (cantor), the improviser and performer of traditional and new Jewish prayers. The finale immediately elicited in informed listeners associations with the mourning ritual prayer *Kaddish*.[5] The music spoke to everyone in the language of grief. This was

4 Irma Zolotovyts'ka, *Dmytro Klebanov: tvorchyi portret kompozytora* (Kyiv: Muzychna Ukraïna, 1980).

5 The *Kaddish* prayer was written in Aramaic more than two thousand years ago. Several variants are said during every community service. Three of them are also said in memory of the deceased. However, the prayer itself is not about death. Its central theme is the magnification and sanctification of G-d, which is reflected in the opening words: *Yit'gadal v'yit'kadash sh'mei raba* (May His great Name grow exalted and sanctified).

indeed a requiem for the Jews who were murdered in Babyn Yar.[6]

Despite various complications, the Kharkiv premiere of Klebanov's symphony, *In Memory of the Martyrs of Babyn Yar*, took place in 1947. The following year it was performed in Kyiv under the direction of the acclaimed conductor Natan Rakhlin. By 1949, however, at the height of a widespread campaign against so-called cosmopolitanism, Klebanov became the target of ideological pressure. His symphony was condemned as a work "imbued with the spirit of bourgeois nationalism and cosmopolitanism" and that was "replete with biblical motifs and steeped in tragic doom." Although Klebanov as composer and pedagogue was quite famous by this time, he was nonetheless dismissed from his posts as chairman of the Department of Composition at the Kharkiv Conservatory and head of the Kharkiv branch of the Union of Composers of Ukraine. The process of granting him the title of professor was delayed for decades. All performances of the Babyn Yar symphony were banned, and for decades its score lay gathering dust in a drawer, with no prospects that it would ever be performed.

Wide public recognition came to Dmytro Klebanov's symphony only after the composer's death. On 29 September 1990, the day set aside to honor the victims of Babyn Yar, the work was performed by the National Symphony Orchestra of Ukraine under the direction of Ihor Blazhkov, the discoverer and promoter of numerous "forgotten" scores. (The conductor Blazhkov, a friend of the late composer, regarded the revival of the Babyn Yar symphony as his own moral obligation in tribute to the memory of its creator). Shortly afterwards fans of Klebanov's works based in Zhytomyr became acquainted with the symphony, which was performed by the same group of musicians. Eventually, Ukrainian Radio made a recording of the symphony.[7]

Thus, thanks to Dmytro Klebanov, a stable foundation was laid for

---

6 Olena Roshchenko, "Pam'iati muchenykiv Babynoho Iaru: represovana symphonia," *Muzyka*, No. 4 (Kyiv, 2016), pp. 31-33.

7 Marina Sutorikhina, "Kak simfoniia stala Kramol'noi, *Vozrozhdenie* (Jerusalem), September 1990; Tatiana Frumkis, "Trudnosti udesiateriali moiu energiiu . . .," *Evreiskaia gazeta*, 10 January 2011; Olena Roshchenko, "Ukraïns'ka symfoniia pam'iati muchenykiv Babynoho Iaru: dolia avtora ta ioho tvoru," *Kul'tura Ukraïny*, No. 56 (Kharkiv, 2017), pp. 215-224.

future musical commemorations of Babyn Yar, something that various composers developed assiduously over the next several decades. Some of them relied on Klebanov's first efforts. Today, listeners of Klebanov's Babyn Yar symphony are struck by the richness of its musical tapestry, replete with the lush intonations of Jewish folk songs, and by the wealth of motifs from synagogue chants.

### Dmitrii Shostakovich

The Soviet composer Dmitrii Shostakovich was fated to carry out the noble mission of introducing the Babyn Yar theme into the global musical space. [see Plate **XXI**] His *Symphony No. 13* (subtitled *Babi Yar*, in keeping with the title its first movement), is based on a poem by Yevgeny Yevtushenko. Sounding like a warning signal, Shostakovich's work alerted the international cultural community and progressive public to the tragic events that took place in Kyiv in September 1941.

Preparations for the first performance were hindered by numerous obstacles. From the outset there were lengthy, tense negotiations between the composer on one hand, and Soviet government officials, orchestral conductors, and soloists on the other. The search for a solo bass voice was particularly complicated. Shostakovich had his eye on the renowned Ukrainian bass Borys Hmyria, with whom he enjoyed close collegial relations with the composer and who was the foremost performer of many of Shostakovych's vocal chamber works. Unfortunately, Hmyria, who was very much aware of the authorities' prejudiced attitude toward him (because the singer had continued living in Ukraine when it was occupied by the Germans during World War II), was forced to heed the "recommendations" of the party leadership and refrain from taking part in the project. Neither was Shostakovich able to enlist the collaboration of the famous conductor Yevgeny Mravinskii, who had conducted the premiere performances of all his symphonies.[8]

The premiere of *Symphony No. 13* finally took place in Moscow on 18 December 1962, under the direction of Kirill Kondrashin and featuring the bass Vitalii Gromadskii. Music lovers' responses to the work were

8 Sofiia Kkhentova, *Plamia Bab'iego Iara: 13-ia simfoniia D.D. Shostakovicha* (Saint Petersburg, 1997).

ecstatic. "This music contains the entire, immense amplitude of our life, from profound disappointments and tragic conflicts to enlightenment and proud hopes," declared the legendary cellist, conductor, and citizen of the world Mstislav Rostropovich after attending the premiere of Shostakovich's symphony.[9]

The symphony begins with the distant, measured sound of bells, which is layered over the ostinato of stringed instruments in a low register, and gradually acquires power with the sound of brass instruments. The gloomy and sinister tone of the introduction is emphasized by the sound of a wailing wind. The severely restrained voices of the men's choir seem to be reading out the verdict handed down to those who have been condemned to death, and they are reinforced by sorrowful motifs in the low sounds of the bassoon, contrabassoon, and bass clarinet, together creating a generally menacing atmosphere of utter horror and torpor.[10]

Shostakovich's symphony was performed a second time in March 1963, in Minsk. Thereafter the work was unofficially banned. Nevertheless, a record was released in the West, based on a recording made at the Moscow concert and smuggled abroad. Within the Soviet Union itself, the score and a vinyl record appeared only nine years later, but it was another version, featuring changes to the text of the first part. However, several subsequent performances, especially the one that took place in 1966, during the Shostakovich music festival in Leningrad, invariably attracted a negative reaction from the Soviet authorities.

Until the end of Shostakovich's life, *Symphony No. 13* remained a work whose performances the Soviet leaders sought to hinder. But their efforts were in vain. Moreover, the authorities never dared to ban it outright, and the work was preserved in the repertoire of the Gorky and Novosibirsk symphony orchestras and of the Moscow Philharmonic Orchestra (until Kondrashin's emigration). It was performed many times in the finest concert halls throughout the world: in France (conducted by Daniel Barenboim); in Germany (Kurt Masur, Leipzig); and in the United States

9 Cited in R. Blokker and R. Dearling, *The Music of Dmitri Shostakovich: The Symphonies* (London: Tantivy Press, 1979).

10 Karen Kopp, *Form und Gehalt der Symphonien des Dmitrij Schostakowitsch* (Bonn: Vlg. Für Systematische Musikwissenschaft, 1990).

(Kurt Masur, Boston, and from 1988, Mstislav Rostropovich conducting the New York Symphony Orchestra).[11] In Ukraine, *Symphony No. 13* was first performed in 1988 in Kyiv by the State Academic Orchestra, under the direction of Volodymyr Kozhukhar, the Dumka Capella, and the soloist Anatolii Safiullin. Shostakovich's requiem to the innocent victims of Babyn Yar is now part of the treasury of world musical culture.[12]

**Yevhen Stankovych**

An important, contemporary musical work in which the Babyn Yar theme is highlighted monumentally and panoramically and interpreted artistically and aesthetically is by the distinguished Ukrainian composer Yevhen Stankovych. His *Babyn Yar (Kaddish Requiem)*, set to a poem written by the eminent poet Dmytro Pavlychko, correlates with the tragedy through its sound as well as humanitarian and historical content. [see Plate **XXX**]

The writing of this epic, dramatic work was timed to coincide with the fiftieth anniversary of the Babyn Yar tragedy and, as the composer noted, was specially commissioned for the occasion by the Ukrainian government. Stankovych's creative process was faciliated by his prior consultations with the rabbi of the Podil synagogue in Kyiv, who acquainted him with the logic and, most importantly, the texts of the commemorative prayer. Subsequently, the prayer was translated into Ukrainian and provided to Pavlychko so that he could create the versified foundation of the work.[13]

The premiere of this multipart work was held on 23 June 1991 in the Column Hall of the National Philharmonic of Ukraine. It was performed by the country's leading ensembles and soloists: the Symphony Orchestra of the National Philharmonic of Ukraine conducted by Mykola Diadiura; the Dumka Academic Capella conducted by Yevhen Savchuk; the

---

11 Inessa Dvuzhil'na, "pamiat' o bab'iem Iare v zvukakh muzyki," *Chasopys Natsional'noï muzychnoï akademiï imeni P.I. Chaikovs'koho* 1 (26) (Kyiv, 2015), pp. 106-119.

12 Feliks Roziner, "Trinadtsataia Shostakovicha," in Effrem Baukh, ed., *Babii Iar* (Izrael: Bat-Iam, 1981), pp. 99-104.

13 Interview with Ievhen Stankovych, the author's personal archive, 12 April 2015.

soloists Serhii Mahera and Dmytro Popov; and the narrator Oleh Savkin. The performance of *Babyn Yar* by the Dumka Capella and the symphony orchestra conducted by Volodymyr Kozhukhar, which took place at the Babyn Yar site during the ceremony to honor the memory of those who lost their lives there, was unforgettable. In this once ill-omened place, Stankovych's music sounded like a long-awaited *panakhyda* (commemorative church service) for the victims of Nazism.

Notwithstanding such an immense number of performers, consisting of a mixed choir, symphony orchestra, a tenor, bass, and narrator, the composer did not opt for the traditional route of using the verbal structures of the Roman Catholic funeral genre of the requiem mass. Instead, he offered his own secular interpretation of a mass for the dead. While Stankovych's music may elicit certain analogies with Catholic canonical parts of a requiem, running throughout the musical texture of the requiem are intonations of Ukrainian and Oriental songs constructed through the use of contemporary composition devices. The composer called his work a *panakhyda* for the victims of fascism. In a masterful way he synthesized the traditions of writing requiems in various religions and cultures (Jewish, Catholic, Orthodox). The vocal intonations of Ukrainian and Jewish folklore imbue this requiem with particular expressiveness and emotion.

The boundless despair and a heightened, tragic world perception that are embedded in the musical and poetic texts are counterbalanced by a general philosophical interpretation of those horrific events, which instantly raises this work to a world-class level. The author of the versified text, the Ukrainian poet Dmytro Pavlychko, acknowledged that by the time he was invited to create a text for Yevhen Stankovych's *Babyn Yar* he was already very familiar with Jewish themes, having published a poetry cycle entitled *Yevreiski melodii* (Jewish Melodies). The poet regarded his collaboration with the composer as a priority and emphasized that "Ukrainians revealed the great martyrdom of the sons and daughters of Israel."[14]

---

14 Cited in Anna Lunina, "Kadysh-rekviiem 'Babyn Iar' Ievhana Stankovycha: natsional'na trahediia mynuloho kriz' pryzmu suchasnosti," in Ievhen Stankovych, *Babyn Iar [Noty]: kadysh-rekviiem dlia chytsia, solistiv, zmishanoho khoru ta velykoho symfonichnoho orkestru* (Kyiv: Muzychna Ukraïna, 2016), pp. 3-11.

The composition of Stankovych's sprawling, seven-part requiem, featuring a lengthy orchestral introduction, expresses the never-ending, sorrowful gait of a condemned person and the despair and horror experienced by the throngs of people about to be put to death. During its performance this work exerts a genuinely hypnotic effect on listeners, who are left with the impression of being privy to a great mystery. The majestic mosaic of the seven parts—*The Lord of Light*, *Here We Lie*, *Judgment Will Come*, *Bent by the Autumn Wind*, *Gray-Haired Moses*, *Rejoice*, and *Great God*—which move from one into the other, seems to be threaded into a historical chronograph that has been channeled from the distant past to the present day. To listeners it reveals a kaleidoscope of practically realistically sensed gradations of human suffering, despair, sorrow, pain, grief, spiritual protest, and psychological devastation. The realistic nature of the pictures of the mass executions of the victims of Nazism nearly reach the naturalistic limits of pictorial veracity (especially in the orchestral fragments of parts 2 and 5). The idea of the inevitability of divine punishment for this terrible crime against humanity is conveyed with extraordinary expressiveness, creative power, and conviction by the choristers as they chant the words, "Judgment will come," in part 3. And yet several more parts lie ahead, in which the composer, with the aid of the choir and various symphonic devices, creates a worthy musical monument to those who perished in Babyn Yar.

As soon as the *Babyn Yar Kaddish Requiem* was completed, several standard performances took place (both the full version and individual parts), which were timed to coincide with various anniversaries of the tragedy. The performance that took place in Jerusalem on 6 October 2011 at Yad Vashem, Israel's official memorial to the victims of the Holocaust, was, according to the composer, the most symbolic and relevant. The particular atmosphere of the memorial itself inspired the Ukrainian performers to the highest degree of artistic self-devotion. The brilliant cohort of world-class musicians featuring the magnificent Dumka Capella, a recognized representative of Ukraine's age-old national traditions of choral singing; the superb Jerusalem Symphony Orchestra; and one of Ukraine's finest conductors, Volodymyr Sirenko, worked together seamlessly to imbue their performance with a high level of emotion.

The audience, among who were high-ranking government officials and musical figures from Ukraine and Israel, was sincerely moved by the performance, which fostered a sense of psychological unity among the listeners.

During the performance at Yad Vashem, the composer specifically requested that the audience refrain from applauding. Consequently, the multipart vocal and symphonic tapestry was emancipated from the format of established concert standards, thereby emphasizing the sacred and ritual essence of the work. The fact that fifteen years later Stankovych composed a new version of his score, timing it to coincide with another anniversary of Babyn Yar, proves that this theme has taken a firm hold of the composer, who continues to seek and refine new devices for his artistic interpretation of the tragedy.[15]

Anyone listening to Stankovych's *Babyn Yar Kaddish Requiem* cannot fail to note the distinctive effect of interactivity. There is an absolutely realistic sense that the audience is present at the dreadful events that took place in Babyn Yar, with its stupefying scenes of mass murder of innocent victims by the Nazis. When this work is performed in a concert hall, an extremely powerful energy field is created in the audience. It is a kind of psychological state that borders on a genuinely emotional shock similar to the one that occurs while watching documentary film footage or a historical epic about the dramatic conflicts that have occurred throughout history. The intonational and dramatic conception reinforces the general thrust of the work, which calls for reconciliation and tolerance among people. The performance of the text in two languages, Ukrainian and Hebrew, imbues the work with particular artistic conviction.

### Volodymyr Ptushkin

In 1999, the eminent Kharkiv composer and People's Artist of Ukraine Volodymyr Ptushkin, a pupil of Dmytro Klebanov, wrote the *Ukrainian Requiem*. The idea to write such a work was the brainchild of Volodymyr Lukashev, artistic director of the National Philharmonic of Ukraine. Deeply impressed by Krzysztof Penderecki's *Polish Requiem*, Ptushkin

15 Vasyl' Bedzir, "Ievhen Stankovych: 'Meni lehshe, nizh dekomu, bo muzyka-internatsional'na,'" *Uriadovyi kurier* (Kyiv), 14 May 2011.

instantly sensed that an analogous work was lacking in contemporary Ukrainian music.[16]

For the textual basis of his work the composer chose the poems of the well-known dissident poet and Shevchenko Literary Prize laureate Stepan Sapeliak. Ptushkin recently admitted that he was captivated by the particular acuity of Sapeliak's images and symbols as well as by the brilliant sound of the national mentality inherent in his poetry. Ultimately, it was precisely these poetic works that helped the composer create a graceful musical and poetic composition featuring the boldly defined contours of the requiem genre.[17]

The Canadian literary specialist Ariadna Shum accurately described the poet's distinctive voice: "There is great power in the poems of Stepan Sapeliak. They act with that force of content which is offered by form in visual reading, but they have a much stronger impact when they are read out loud. They require a very good reader, who would convey all the nuances of the deep poetical thought in a highly sophisticated form that is powerful in its sincerity."[18] Sapeliak's poetry found just such an accomplished interpreter in the person of the composer Volodymyr Ptushkin, who deeply absorbed the psychological acuity, sincere frankness, and primeval folkloric abundance of Sapeliak's poems. For each poetic phrase the composer found a corresponding musical and intonational counterpart, emphasizing and granting additional power to the impact on the audience of the unique and distinctive poetry:

> Drink, little reapers, and blow the small horn!
> A war from the heavens is coming…
> *The narrator reads:*
> This is Babyn Yar. This day is still burnt by the sun
> And the mourning wall of lamentation …
> And those skeletal tracks rip at the time of the past and unnatural things.
> We remain.

16 Interview with Volodymyr Lukashov, the author's personal archive, 23 April 2015.

17 Interview with Volodymyr Ptushkin, the author's personal archive, 24 August and 30 October 2015.

18 Ariiadna Shum "Poeziia Stepana Sapeliaka," in Stepan Sapeliak, *Bez shabli i Vitchyzny* (Toronto: Ucrainica, 1989), p.11.

That cordage of scars, dreadful echoes.
And the scroll of memory . . .
We remain. And the sky . . . And punishment . . .
And shadows on tar. And . . . do not kill . . . [19]

Every poetic phrase holds within it a powerful store of accumulated, explosive energy that, like a coiled spring, is released swiftly and "fires" into the consciousness of every listener. Sapeliak's poetic voice is a truly unique phenomenon in contemporary Ukrainian literature. His poetry is not marked by traditional rhymes and meters. On the contrary, he directs attention through the singular and unexpected nature of his structure and the whimsical and flexible melodics of his strophe. In its internal workings it can break up into laconic phrases of unequal length that interweave spiritual foundations, seemingly existing outside the verbal form of feeling. It is this intonation of agitated and awakened awareness that by definition cannot have syntactical barriers and clear-cut strophes. This is improvisation that is born spontaneously in the depths of a heart filled with high spirituality and magical power, transcending the limits of the existence of the word itself. Ptushkin was enchanted precisely by this magic and the concentrated energy of Sapeliak's poetry. From the outset it was dear to him and comprehensible, and because of this it was entirely natural for the composer and the poet to embark on a creative collaboration on the Babyn Yar theme as fellow artists and thinkers. The composer became, first and foremost, a retranslator of the poet's eschatological moods.

Ptushkin's central image is that of a "black world." In the listener's imagination the choir's creeping intonations, undulating like snakes and scattered throughout various choral groupings, elicit a bleak picture of physical and spiritual paralysis and hopelessness that has also overwhelmed the surrounding world and the throngs of people who have been condemned to death. The gradual supercharging of the dynamics of choral sonority leads to a maximum splash of drama. The angry shouts

19 Cited in ibid. See also Iryna Verbyts'ka, "*Ukraïns'kyi rekviiem* V. Ptushkina: sproba modeliuvannia zhanry," in *Muzychne i teatral'ne mystetytsvo Ukraïny u dolidzhenniakh moldykh mystetstvoznavtsiv* (Kyïv, 2004), pp. 6-8.

of individual male singers and the accusatory rejoinders of the narrator ring out, until finally the choir, in solid accord, chants the words, "Re-ply wi-th a ho-ly st-ar."

Ptushkin creatively transformed the ancient folkloric genre of lamentation that always accompanied the ritual funeral ceremonies of traditional folklore. In a dramatically justified and subtle fashion, the composer uses the clear and pure timbre of children's voices (choir), which contrasts with the generally gloomy tonality of the music, and emphasizes the tragic nature and atmosphere of the total darkness of the surrounding reality. This part concludes with the ringing of distant bells, against whose background the sorrowful motif is heard again: "And the world is black, black." A sense of the sacred power of poetic thoughts and the penetrating sound of unusual and brilliantly national images from Sapeliak's versified texts are reflected, as though in a mirror, in Ptushkin's music. This is an observation which music critics were quick to point out.

The main principle underpinning the creation of the musical score of Ptushkin's *Ukrainian Requiem* is the memorialization of victims of the twentieth century.To achieve this the composer chose a national foundation of intonational material performed by a mezzo-soprano, baritone, narrator, mixed and children's choirs, and symphony orchestra.

The nine parts of the *Ukrainian Requiem* (*Introduction*; 1. *Prologue*; 2. *The Voice of '33*; 3. *Troparion of Repentance*; 4. *Lamentation*; 5. *Babyn Yar*; 6. *The Guernica of Chornobyl*; 7. *Bells Are Ringing*; 8. *The Voice of Faith*; 9. *Epilogue*) resemble pictures filled with dramatic content devoted to tragic pages in the history of the Ukrainian people in the twentieth century: wars, the Holodomor, Babyn Iar, and Chornobyl. The fifth—central—part of Ptushkin's requiem is *Babyn Yar*. The composer's use of theatrical devices during the performative interpretation of the *Ukrainian Requiem* score and part 5 in particular, became an act of homage to contemporary trends of holding concerts of vocal and symphonic works.[20]

---

20 Iryna Verbyts'ka, "Traktuvannia zhanru rekviiemu u tvorchosti kompozytoriv kharkivs'koï shkoly," in *Problemy vzaiemodiï mystetstva, pedahohiky ta teoriï i praktyky osvity: zb[irnyk] nauk[ovykh] prats'*, No. 13 (Kharkiv: KhDUM im. I.P. Kotliarevs'koho, 2004), pp. 290-298.

The world premiere of the *Ukrainian Requiem* was held on 30 April 2002 in Kharkiv. The Kyiv premiere took place over a year later, on 30 October 2003, as part of the Kyiv Music Fest, featuring the National Philharmonic of Ukraine under the direction of Mykola Diadiura, with the participation of the Khreshchatyk Municipal Chamber Chorus conducted by Larysa Bukhonska, the Skvorushka Children's Choir conducted by People's Artist of Ukraine Volodymyr Lukashev, and the director-producer Iryna Nesterenko. Ptushkin's *Ukrainian Requiem* garnered many positive reactions and recognition from the music community. On 26 April 2007, it was performed to great acclaim in Kyiv by the Chamber Orchestra and choir of the Military Music Center of the Land Forces of Ukraine's Armed Forces, under the direction of two eminent conductors, Oleksandr Shevchuk and Maryna Honcharenko. The concert featured the soloists Roman Strakhov and Myroslava Havryliuk, both winners of international competitions, and the narrator, Volodymyr Baniuk.

**Dmytro Kytsenko**

A qualitatively new page in Ukrainian composers' musical commemorations of Babyn Yar was written in the twenty-first century, when the composer Dmytro Kytsenko created an instrumental work for chamber orchestra and piano. Although his work contains no versified texts referring to the theme, it is entitled *Babyn Yar*. Kytsenko was born in Ukraine, studied music in Kishinev, Moldova, and from 2002 to 2010 he lived and worked in Kyiv. The following year he moved to Canada.

Kytsenko composed his 13-minute work in 2006, during his Kyiv period. The premiere of *Babyn Yar*, which took place that year in Kyiv on 15 November, was performed by the Kyiv Camerata under the direction of Valerii Matiukhin.[21]

Like his predecessors, Kytsenko devoted much time to a detailed study of documented testimonies of the Babyn Yar tragedy and a search for surviving eyewitnesses. This is entirely understandable, inasmuch as the process of delving into such a complex topic, one that was passed over in silence for many decades and which to this day has not been completely

21 Interview with Valerii Matiukhin, the author's personal archive, 26 September 2015.

analyzed, meant that the composer needed to systematize the information acquired not only from printed sources but also from film footage and photographs as well as the invaluable testimonies from eyewitnesses of the tragedy or the relatives of the murdered victims.

Kytsenko's work is distinguished by the extreme laconism of his musical expression. His music is marked by an exemplary economy of intonational devices; there is no place in it for expressiveness, anguish, and naturalistic lamentation. The emotional tone of *Babyn Yar* is noble in its restraint, even somewhat austere. The composer utilizes certain musical symbols and codes based on familiar motifs, which elicit associations that "play" on the general idea of the work and enliven the audience's response.

At the beginning of his composition Kytsenko introduces an epigram in the form of a motif from a Jewish folksong that serves as a kind of guidepost to the work's central idea. Listeners can also detect the magnificent motif from Mozart's *Requiem*, "*Lacrimosa dies illa*", as a symbol of universal sorrow and mourning for the murdered victims. Thus, the presence of the archtypical requiem genre, which is not declared in the title of the work, becomes once again an active device for marking the image-bearing content of Kytsenko's work. In the middle part the composer embeds into the musical texture the melody of an ancient Jewish song of a blind beggar, "I Beg Alms," which is similar to folk lamentations. In the maestro's hands it develops (from one voice in the original song) into a harmonically enriched version. Assigned to the thick, mellow, and dark timbre of the cello, this melody acquires concentrated and dramatic coloration.

For his musical interpretation of the Babyn Yar theme Kytsenko enlists a number of contemporary audiovisual devices. In 2011 millions of Internet users had an opportunity to offer their opinions on the contemporary version of his work, which was accompanied by a video featuring documentary film footage and photographs. The music score thus gained a new, audiovisual, quality and acquired a new range of influence on listeners—and now, viewers. The composer created an artistic intertext that at its heart rests upon the specific features of the screen arts. The introduction into the music score of photographs and film footage maximally strengthens the impression of what is seen and heard at the same time. In such an interpretation, the tragedy of the Jewish people acquires a truly global sound and scale, and the magnitude of its impact increases immeasurably.[22]

Newsreels depict the ruins of buildings left on Khreshchatyk Boulevard after it was mined, a close-up of the text of the Nazis' 28 September 1941 cynical order to the Jewish population of Kyiv, and mountains of bodies piled up by the side of a road. All these images are spiked, as though onto a ramrod, into the penetrating, unhurried sound of violins and altos conveying the desperate groans of masses of people condemned to death. We hear the echoing of a mournful bell, then we see a full-screen shot of barbed wire and, for the purpose of contrast, the naïve, trusting, and defenseless faces of children and the grieving looks of their mothers, who are bent in sorrow over them, unable to protect and save them. Other shots show Nazi soldiers herding people to the Babyn Yar ravine, with body after body falling into it. At this precise moment we hear the single, piercing sound of a violin, which gradually broadens and swells into orchestral sounds. Finally, it fills the entire surrounding space until powerful piano chords—like a volley of cannon fire, like a symbol of blind, pitiless, and destructive power—create an auditory background to pictures displaying piles of clothing and footwear taken from people who have already been shot. And when listeners have no more strength and emotions left after gazing upon these inhuman sufferings, they hear the motif of the *Lacrimosa*, whose sounds, like crystal tears, fall on that evil place where, it seems, woe, fear, and despair have become etched forever on the earth of Babyn Yar. The lonely figure of a woman rooted in her grief, bending over the ravine, over the mass grave, and the meager intonations of stringed instruments seem to hang the air. Time has stopped in order for us to focus our attention on the photographs of the victims who were massacred in Babyn Yar.

The unique concept of this work, the composer's utmost attention to the image-bearing and auditory spheres, the philosophical nature of his

22 G. Kocharova, "Kontseptsii i struktura mul'timediinogo audiovizual'nogo proizvedeniia," in *Muzyka v prostranstve mediakul'tury: sb[ornik] statei po materialam Mezhdunarodnoi nauchno-prakticheskoi konferentsii, 4 aprelia 2014 goda* (Krasnodar, 2014), pp. 294-301..

musical thinking, and the organic interweaving of music and visual elements lead to the conviction that Kytsenko's work has opened up new prospects for composers to embark on a radical contemporization of the format of academic-class musical works that from now on can be aimed at the entire world, as this happened with *Babyn Yar*.

**The art of cinephony**

It would appear that the audiovisual version of Kytsenko's *Babyn Yar* is logically leading future organizers of artistic events connected with the commemorations of the Tragedy to an understanding of the fact that the musical and visual realization of the universal theme of Babyn Yar should take place on a significantly larger scale and, accordingly, that such artistic endeavors should garner greater public recognition. This can happen only with the use of the cinephonic format, as was the case with Shostakovich's *Symphony No. 7*, which was performed during the commemoration of the anniversary of World War II.[23]

Cinephony is a new genre of art combining symphonic orchestral pieces with video. The use of historical newsreel shots is aimed at ensuring the veracity of an author's conception. The immersion into cinephony is achieved when the individual attending a cultural event enters a different psychological state. The viewer/listener becomes a witness and, simultaneously, virtual coparticipant in certain historical conflicts and events. In that way, music and newsreel sequences create a whole artistic complex. The results of scientific research suggest that auditory and visual perceptions penetrate the sole zone of 90-percent resonance. The distinguished American psychologist Rudolph Arnheim has written that the perception of time-based arts, such as music and dance, is mediated by visual thinking that organizes time sequences within a spatial complex. The impression gained from something heard and seen a single time becomes immeasurably more three-dimensional and holographic because, according to the American neuropsychologist Jarrid Levy, the left hemisphere of the brain arranges spatial information in a time sequence, and the right hemisphere—in spatiality.

---

23 Natalia Semenenko, "Pro mystetstvo buty pershym," *Den'* (Kyiv), 1 September 2011

It would appear that there are sufficient arguments for advocating this way of presenting a work of music and, perhaps, a composition comprised of fragments taken from the works of various composers. Essentially, the short duration (thirteen minutes) of Dmytro Kytsenko's composition for string orchestra and piano in its audiovisual version has sparked a new synthesized genre of contemporary music signifying an experimental and fundamentally modern approach to the Babyn Yar theme. It is clear that this theme has not lost its importance and topicality.

**Coda**

The musical works created by the composers discussed in this chapter attest to their artistic insight into past events and their determination to rethink the tragedy of Babyn Yar on the highest energy level. Above all, this process has taken place as a result of the need to make their presence felt and to leave behind their own personal musical commentary. Each of these composers succeeded in choosing an absolutely unique emotional key for recreating the palette of tragic moods, sorrow, and bright sadness as a token of remembrance of the souls that were mercilessly killed at Babyn Yar.

The memory of the innocent, murdered victims of Babyn Yar, a name that has become a sorrowful emblem of a national catastrophe and suffering, remains holy in human consciousness throughout the ages. With the approach of every anniversary of this tragedy, the pain becomes more acute and anger blazes in the hearts of people and the handful of surviving eyewitnesses. And so, for future generations the artistic milestones of collective memory are all the more precious.

Through the universal language of music, composers have built a monumental, solemn arc uniting the tragic past and understanding of the present, and thereby having assured the linear progression of historical events. The images of Babyn Yar are eternal stigmata on the body of Ukraine. It is therefore not surprising that their tragic nature will always appear before the inner vision of composers, who are aware of the supreme mission of artists and art in this land.

## CHAPTER 13

# Babyn Yar: A Place of Memory in Search of a Future

*Vitaliy Nakhmanovych*

On 23 December 2015, during a meeting of the Kyiv municipal state administration, Mayor Vitalii Klychko announced: "Next year is the 75th anniversary of the Babyn Yar tragedy. However, to this day nothing has been done to create a memorial and commemorate the victims. As the mayor of the capital city, I believe it is my mission to build a memorial in honor of the victims of Babyn Yar."[1]

Exactly three months later, on 23 March 2016, the then prime minister of Ukraine Arsenii Yatseniuk, speaking at a government meeting, announced that an Avenue of the Righteous and an Avenue of the Martyrs would be built at Babyn Yar by the 75th anniversary commemoration (29 September 2016). The announcement proclaimed: "It is necessary to switch from discussions that have been taking place for two decades to building these two avenues and commemorating the victims of the Babyn Yar tragedy. This is a sacred matter, and we should do this!"[2]

One can agree with Yatseniuk's statements, especially when one considers how Ukraine prepared for the previous round-number anniversary in the history of Babyn Yar. On 5 July 2011 Ukraine's parliament, the Verkhovna Rada, ratified a resolution entitled "On Marking the 70th Anniversary of the Babyn Yar Tragedy." The resolution proposed following tasks to be authorized by the Cabinet of Ministers of Ukraine: "to

1 "Moia misiia—realizuvaty proekt sporudzhennia muzeiu pam'iaty zhertv Бabynoho Iaru v stolytsi," *Sait Vitaliia Klychka*, 23. XII. 2015, accessed at https//kyiv.klichko.org/10001559

2 Arsenii Iatseniuk, "Do rokovyn trahediï Babynoho Iaru bude sporudzheno Aleiu Pravednykiv ta Aleiu Muchenykiv," *Uriadovyi portal*, 23. III. 2016, accessed at https://www.kmu.gov.ua/news/248912109

grant the Babyn Yar National Historical Memorial Preserve the building located at 44 Melnikova Street, where its directorate and a themed photography exhibition will be established; and to provide funding for the project aimed at developing the Babyn Yar National Historical Memorial Preserve, in which the following elements are to be included—the Spadshchyna/Heritage Scholarly and Educational Center and a monument to the victims of the pogroms."[3]

The expectations of Boris Glazunov, the director of the proposed Memorial Preserve, were more modest. In an interview he said: "I would love to conclude at least two fundamentally important issues by 29 September [2011—V.N.]: overhaul the large monument and build the Avenue of the Righteous.... Today we want to fence in our territory.... We want to restore it to its proper condition, we want to begin building the first museum premises. Of course, we would like a full-fledged museum complex built eventually, so that the names of those who perished in Babyn Yar will be collected and commemorated."[4]

Ukraine's Jewish community also felt that it was necessary to become engaged. The head of the Oversight Council of the Babyn Yar Memorial Foundation made the following announcement:

> On 3 October of the current year [2011—V.N.] Viktor Yanukovych, the president of Ukraine, together with the heads of the Babyn Yar Charitable Foundation, will lay the cornerstone of the memorial complex. In accordance with the approved project, the entire area measuring nearly two hectares will covered by an immense *talles*,[5] and a museum will be located in the middle of it. On four nearby hectares we are planning to plant 32,000 trees; on each of them there will be a tablet indicating the

3 "Pro 70-richehia trahediï Babynoho Iaru: Postanova Verkhovnoï Rady Ukraïny," *Holos Ukraïny* (Kyiv), 16. VII. 2011.

4 "Interv'iu dyrektora Natsional'noho istoryko-memorial'noho zapovidnyka 'Babyn Iar' Hlazunova Borysa Ivanovycha hazeti 'Einykait'," *Babyn Iar. Natsional'nyi istoryko-memorial'nyi zapovidnyk. Ofitsiinyi saït*, 5.V.2011, accessed at http://babyn-yar.gov.ua/%D1%96nterv%E2%80%99yu-direktora-nats%D1%96onalnogo-%D1%96storiko-memor%D1%96alnogo-zapov%D1%96dnika-babin-yar-glazunova-borisa-%D1%96vano]

5 A *talles* is a rectangular, white shawl with black (or blue) stripes along the edges, which married Jewish males use to cover their heads during prayers.

> name of a person who was shot in Babyn Yar. In the center there will be a commemorative tree [planted] in memory of those thousands and thousands of people whose names it has not been possible to identify yet.[6]

It must be mentioned straightaway that not a single element of what was planned five years ago came to fruition. Not even the territory of the National Preserve was fenced in. At the present time there is no telling what will be come of this year's plans. But it would be a mistake to assume that the black abyss of the former ravine, filled with the bones and ashes of thousands of people who were shot there, has been lying for 75 years in the middle of Kyiv, forgotten by all and not marked in any way or commemorated. The exact opposite is true. Babyn Yar, the ravine that witnessed two years of Nazi terror, has physically not existed for half a century. On the site of the Babyn Yar killing field, as well as on the immense territory surrounding it, no less than three dozen monuments and commemorative plaques were erected that more or less mark all possible aspects of the tragic events that took place here during World War II and afterwards.

Nevertheless, today the prime minister of Ukraine and the mayor of Kyiv, as well as many civic activists both in Ukraine and outside its borders believe that the memory of Babyn Yar has still not been commemorated in a worthy way. That being the case, it is pointless to try to convince people that what today exists at Babyn Yar is acceptable. It is much more important to determine why the situation is what it is and to see if the problem can finally be resolved.

**Postwar Babyn Yar as a place of memory**

The Soviet era was marked by a confrontation between the public's need to honor the memory of the Jewish victims of wartime Nazi rule and the actions of the postwar authorities which vacillated between the desire to destroy the ravine and the attempt to impose an artificial memory of anonymous "innocent Soviet civilians" who were liquidated there. The "physical," so to speak, consequence of this, given the obvious incom-

---

6 Cited in V.R. Nakhmanovych, "Babyn Iar: istoriia, suchasnist', maibutnie?," *Ukraïns'kyi istorychnyi zhurnal*', No. 6 (Kyïv, 2011), pp. 107-108.

mensurability of forces, was first and foremost the inundation of Babyn Yar in the 1950s by a deluge of pulp flowing from the Petrovskyi brick plants. The result was the notoriously tragic Kurenivka mudslide of 13 March 1961, when the pulp smashed through the flimsy dam and gushed into the adjacent area, destroying the Krasin streetcar depot and submerging homes. According to official data given at the time, 145 people died, although current research suggests that there were nearly 1,500 fatalities. Thus, even during peace time another tragedy was added to the sad chronicle of Babyn Yar. [see Plates **XVIII** and **XIX**]

In subsequent decades new streets were laid across the filled-in ravine, and the adjacent cemeteries—Jewish, Orthodox Christian, Karaite, and Muslim—were closed, destroyed, and built over to a large degree. The erection in 1976 of a pretentious and tasteless monument "to the Soviet citizens and captive soldiers and officers of the Soviet Army who were shot by the German fascists in Babyn Yar" involved the destruction of four out of seven small ravines that remained at the very summit of Babyn Yar. [see Plate **LIV**] Rumor had it that some important official interpreted the number seven as an allusion to the menorah, the Hebrew seven-branched lampstand.

A brief period in the history of Babyn Yar coincided with a transitional period in the history of Ukraine, the years 1990 and 1991, when Ukraine as a whole experienced environmental rallies, the country's first revolutionary street protests, and the referendum on independence. This period was also characterized by earnest cooperation among all national minority communities, and it was a time when both the nationally oriented Ukrainian public and the old communist government (soon to be transformed into the government of a newly independent Ukraine) sought to achieve harmony throughout society. For Babyn Yar this period was marked by the joint commemoration of Jewish victims by the Jewish and ethnic Ukrainian communities as well as by state leaders, including Leonid Kravchuk, then head of the Verkhovna Rada. Two new monuments were erected at Babyn Yar in 1991: the Menorah Monument dedicated to the memory of the Jewish victims, and a commemorative marker in honor of the prisoners of the Syrets concentration camp.

These two monuments, however, contained the seeds of further topographical falsifications and semantic conflicts. The Menorah Monument was erected on a plot of land that was originally part of St. Cyril's Orthodox Cemetery and after its closure, the Jewish Cemetery. [see Plate **LV**] But this was not the main problem. The point is that its location (on one side of Babyn Yar) was chosen by the screenwriter, publicist, and amateur historian Aleksandr Shlaen. He was a leading figure in the movement to commemorate the Jewish victims of Nazism and head of the Council of the Soviet (later: Republican) "Babyn Yar" Civic Historical and Educational Center. It was Shlaen's research activities that led to the false conclusion about the site of the shootings and the final route taken by the Jews on 29 September 1941—allegedly through the Jewish Cemetery to the ravine behind it. Later, a bronze menorah was erected above the ravine, and a so-called Alleyway of Sorrow leading to it was laid right across the graves of the ruined Jewish Cemetery. (Current plans call for constructing the Avenue of the Martyrs alongside this path).

The memorial to the prisoners of the Syrets concentration camp was installed in Syrets Park, at the corner of Shamrylo and Ryzka streets. [see Plate **LVII**] This was done not because the camp was located there during the war, but because at the time the park was under threat by urban development. Local residents thought they could save the park if it had a monument.

The Menorah Monument clearly appealed to Jewish national and religious tradition both by its very form and the biblical words, written in Ukrainian and Hebrew, which were carved on two adjacent stone slabs: "The voice of thy brother's blood crieth unto me from the ground." By contrast, the inscription on the commemorative marker to the victims of the Syrets concentration camp was classically Soviet in form: "Tens of thousands of Soviet patriots were murdered in this place during the German-fascist occupation, behind the grates of the Syrets camp." That same year, 1991, two new plaques were added to the older 1976 Soviet monument, which repeated, in Russian and Yiddish, the already existing Ukrainian text: "Here in 1941–1945 more than a hundred thousand residents of the city of Kyiv and prisoners of war were shot by the German-fascist aggressors." This "nod" to the Jews, which embellishes the monument to this very day, is absolutely surrealistic because it is still unclear why, of all the languages that were spoken by the ill-starred residents of the city of Kyiv and prisoners of war, Yiddish was chosen.

The era of independence marks another stage in the evolution of Babyn Yar. On the one hand, unprecedented activism has been demonstrated by various civic organizations, informal groups, and local authorities, all of whom have been working toward the goal of commemorating "their own" victims. On the other, the era is characterized by the "policies" of the state, which has distanced itself nearly totally from active participation matters related to Babyn Yar. At the same time, despite the ostensibly official, annual commemorations of the victims of 29 September 1941, the government has in fact pandered to all projects having to do with the commercial, economic, and commemorative development of Babyn Yar and the adjacent cemeteries. The creation of the Babyn Yar National Historical Memorial Preserve has done nothing to change this situation.

**Commemoration and mythologies**

Before trying to systematize the mosaic of commemorative markers and monument-erecting practices pertaining to Babyn Yar and the adjacent area, a brief overview of mythologies connected with the history of World War II and the Holocaust seems in order. Without a doubt, Ukraine's post-Soviet mythologies still predominate in terms of influence. I have chosen the designation post-Soviet mythology, since it differs in fundamental aspects both from classical Soviet and contemporary Russian mythology, although it is unquestionably closely tied to both of them. All these mythologies emphasize the central place of the "Great Patriotic War" as an event that was and remains the justification of the entire history of the Soviet period, as well as the principal motive behind continuing to preserve Soviet values. The difference between the Soviet and all post-Soviet mythologies lies in the treatment and understanding of the Holocaust. Soviet mythology did not simply ignore the Holocaust, its proponents actually banned and punished harshly any attempts by members of the public to honor the memory of its victims.

Antisemitism, as an invariable component of postwar Soviet policies, was not even the main reason behind this. Rather, it was recognition of the exceptionality of the tragedy that befell the Jews during the war which violated the thesis that the Nazi terror was aimed above all against the Slavic peoples, who, indeed, had suffered the greatest losses. Victims were supposed to be divided "fairly" among all the "fraternal peoples of the Soviet Union" in proportion to their population. This approach has attained its logical culmination in contemporary Russia, where the country's highest authorities declared that the Russian Federation suffered the greatest losses during the war, and that it was precisely through the efforts of "Russians" that the war was won. Clearly, this contentious aspect is the natural point of bifurcation, where the Russian and Ukrainian post-Soviet myths of the Great Patriotic War part ways.

Where the events of the Holocaust are concerned, however, the Ukrainian and Russian post-Soviet myths share much in common. Their main theses are the following. From the beginning of the Great Patriotic War, the Soviet Union, as the sole and consistent enemy of "German fascism," waged a liberation mission in all the Nazi-occupied lands. Hence, the Jews who survived the Holocaust owe their lives to the Soviet Union. After all, it was the only state that had a sincere desire to rescue Jews at a time when all the other participants in the war tried, in one way or another, to destroy them or was indifferent to their fate. In the end, it was the Red Army that rescued from death Jews who remained alive in the occupied territory of the former Soviet Union and eastern European countries, especially Poland, where most of the Nazi death camps were based.

It is clear that we are dealing here with an attempt to exploit two features of contemporary Western society: the widespread interest in the Holocaust; and the obsolete, left-wing sympathies of a considerable proportion of intellectuals. In this way a bridge is built to the State of Israel and the Jewish community, which has its own mythology of the Holocaust.

The Jewish historical myth derives from the concept of a victim nation that has suffered unjustified persecution in all periods of history. As regards the Holocaust, this myth consists of the following theses: the Holocaust is the logical result and apogee of centuries-long European (especially Christian) antisemitism; the scale of the Holocaust would have been utterly impossible without mass support on the part non-Jewish population; the scale of the Holocaust in eastern Europe is the result of the "congenital" antisemitism of the local population and nationalist movements. In Ukraine, it is directly connected with the traditions of pogroms from the seventeenth to twentieth centuries that were ultimately fed by the anti-Jewish ideology and practice of the "OUN-UPA" (whatever is meant by this phantom combination).

In a strange way, this Jewish mythology has given a significant boost to modern-day German mythology about the Holocaust. Its emergence is entirely understandable from the standpoint of mass psychology. Clearly, public awareness cannot exist for an extended period of time saddled with a permanent historical-guilt complex. One way of eradicating it is to redistribute blame for the Holocaust, which is occupying an increasingly larger place alongside the official position of acknowledging Germany's responsibility for Nazi crimes. This new concept is based on two methods: (1) pushing into the background the Nazi Reich's leading role in carrying out the Holocaust that took place in the occupied territories; and (2) shifting the main blame for anti-Jewish crimes on Ukrainian, Lithuanian, and other police subunits as well as armed nationalist formations.

From the Ukrainian standpoint it is obvious that the three above-mentioned mythologies coincide in their anti-Ukrainian orientation, inasmuch as they seek to place the main blame for the fate of local Jews on Ukrainians in general and their political and armed formations in particular. In the émigré milieu this led, in the immediate postwar period, to the formation of a Ukrainian myth about the Holocaust. After independence, this myth was accepted by a significant proportion of Ukrainian society and became part of the general mythology encompassing Ukrainian-Jewish relations.

The Ukrainian myth is comprised of the following theses. Throughout history Jews have sided with Ukraine's enslavers (Poland and Russia). Following the Bolshevik coup, Jews became the bulwark of the new regime; they constituted a disproportionately large portion of the Communist party, the soviets, and the punitive apparatuses of Soviet Union and, therefore, carry much of the blame for all the crimes perpetrated by the Soviet regime. In interwar Poland, Jews did not support Ukrainian aspirations, and when the Red Army arrived in 1939, they welcomed the Soviets with joy and offered significant support to the new regime. Antisemitism was never prevalent among Ukrainians. As for the pogroms that took place from the seventeenth to early twentieth centuries, they were a spontaneous response to Jewish abuses. Moreover, most of the pogroms that took place during the Civil War and the Ukrainian liberation struggle were carried out by non-Ukrainian forces. Ukrainian leaders, in particular Symon Petliura, tried their utmost to put a stop to them. The OUN and the UPA (Banderite structures are meant here) were not anti-Jewish organizations and were in no way involved in exterminating the Jews. The local population did its utmost to help save Jews, and the role of the "Ukrainian" police in helping the Nazis carry out their anti-Jewish plans is unjustifiably exaggerated.

In addition to the various myths described above, there is a whole array of mythologies connected with the group history of communities that remain today on the margins of the sociopolitical process in the sphere of historical memory, for example the Roma, Orthodox Christians, etc.

In order to appreciate why the attainment of genuine understanding and cooperation among the various actors in this field remains illusory, it is necessary to realize the fundamental heroic/sacrificial dualism inherent in each of the mythologies described above: "Our" struggle was just and noble, and "our" victims were always the most numerous and most blameless. Given such attitudes, it may be possible to tolerate "other" victims, but under no circumstances can the latter be placed on the same level as "ours." Where "other people's" heroism is concerned, it is often utterly unacceptable to honor it because the goals of those struggles all too often did not coincide with the goals of "our" struggle.

**A mosaic of monuments**

How, then, is this "map of virtual history" reflected in the real map of Babyn Yar? The Soviet legacy is represented above all by the large monument erected as long ago as 1976. The presence on it of plaques inscribed in Ukrainian, Russian, and Yiddish is perceived not in the spirit of contemporary Western tolerance, but of the classic Soviet ideology of "friendship among peoples." [see Plate **LIV**] It is no accident that this monument is still the main object of the official, state commemorations of the victims of Babyn Yar held every year on 29 September, with the exception of a few years when this date has fallen on a Saturday or a Jewish holiday (a bizarre blend of an absolutely Soviet-type ceremony with a concession to the religious traditions of the victim community).

In addition to this monument, Soviet mythology is invoked by the above-mentioned commemorative marker dedicated to the prisoners of the Syrets concentration camp, as well as by another commemorative marker to those same victims, which was installed in 1999 in the courtyard of a building on Grekova Street, where the remains of some prisoners were found at one time. [see Plate **LVI**] The inscription on the Grekova Street market reads: "On this spot during the German-fascist occupation of the city of Kyiv in 1941–1943, prisoners of war, players of the Kyiv Dynamo soccer team, and civilians of Ukraine were shot. May their memory and glory be eternal." Part of this text refers to one of the most widespread Soviet heroic myths, the so-called Death Match.[7] The same subject is commemorated by two other Soviet-era monuments dedicated to the allegedly executed Kyiv soccer players. The first was erected in 1971, near the Dynamo Stadium located in downtown Kyiv, and the second in 1981, near the Start Stadium located on Sholudenko Street, just south of Lukianivka Square. This is the same stadium where, at the beginning of the Nazi occupation of Kyiv in the fall of 1941, a division of the POW camp was located, from which Jews and commissars were transported to Babyn Yar and shot.

The next large-scale urban construction project was launched in 2010 on Olena Teliha Street, on the site of a large filled-in spur of Babyn Yar. In an attempt to stop the development, over the next two years local residents erected two crosses with inscriptions on the street, right next to the building site. The crosses, by dint of the Soviet myth, were supposed to protect this area. It is worth citing the naïve and ungrammatical (Russian-language) texts on the crosses.

The first inscription reads:

7 For details, see above Chapter 10.

> Here is soil bedewed with the blood of martyrs who perished for the Motherland. On this spot in 1941–1943 the German fascists shot our prisoners of war. In January 1942, Odessa sailors, who were driven barefoot in severe frosts, chained hand and foot, were shot. The sailors sang: 'Our proud sailor does not surrender to the enemy, no one desires mercy...' There are living eyewitnesses. May the spilled blood of our people turn into flowers. Memory eternal to the fallen heroes!

The second inscription reads:

> The years 1941–1945 of the Great Patriotic War. Syrets. The 40-meter-deep ravine of Babyn Yar is filled with slain prisoners of war, sailors of the Soviet Army. Three hundred members of soldiers' families were brought, drenched in gasoline, and burned. Prisoners of war were shot, and the blood flowed like a river to the Dnieper River. The people who were shot were brought to this small ravine from Shevchenko Boulevard and from the gallows, from the hands of fascists and nationalists, driven and beaten with cudgels, faster, faster. In January 1941 [sic!], barefoot and naked, they filled the small ravine; each murdered person is a SAINT. Living witnesses, eyewitnesses, erected a cross on this spot. Ferents, Mariia Yakovlevna; Drukarenko, Vladimir Andreevich; Stasiuk, Aleksandr Vladimirovich; the defenders of the Fatherland, a family that saw combat actions: Shkura, Petro, Uliana, Marusia, [and] Halyna Efimovny. Memory eternal to them. Rubchynnik-Shkura, Valentina Vas[ilevna] tends to the crosses.

In addition to the Menorah Monument, Jewish memory is represented directly or in a veiled manner by a number of other commemorative markers. In 2001 a memorial dedicated to the "Children Who Were Shot in Babyn Yar in 1941" appeared next to the Dorohozhychi subway station. [see Plate **LIX**] Although the children's nationality is not indicated, it is obvious that the reference is to Jewish children (Roma children were also killed here, but this is a general flaw in the memory of Babyn Yar and the Nazi terror, which will be discussed later). Ten years later a granite stone was installed at the intersection of Melnikova and Dorohozhytska streets. The inscription reads: "Here began the 'Road to Death,' along which on 29 September 1941 the fascist occupiers drove the Jews to be shot in Babyn Yar." This stone is the starting point of an annual commemorative procession to the Menorah Monument, organized by the Jewish community of Kyiv on the last Sunday before Yom Kippur.[8]

The fusion of Jewish and Soviet mythologies is exemplified by the monument to the Soviet underground member Tetiana Markus, which was erected in 2009 near the summit of Babyn Yar, on the corner of Olena Teliha and Dorohozhytska streets. [see Plate **LX**] The initiator of this project was Ilya Levitas, head of the Jewish Council of Ukraine and the Memory of Babyn Yar Foundation. Funding was provided personally by Leonid Chernovetsky, head of the Kyiv City Council, and Sergei Maksimov, co-president of the Jewish Confederation of Ukraine. Several Jews belonged to the Kyiv underground and were among its leaders, and some of them died tragically. But it was Tetiana Markus who became the stuff of legend.[9] This legend stood Levitas in good stead, as he had always consistently emphasized the need not only to honor Jewish victims, but also to promote Jewish heroism during the war.

Ukrainian memory is recorded not only in commemorative markers but also in toponyms. In 1992, a wooden cross and three granite slabs inscribed with the names of 62 executed people were erected near the Soviet monument. [see Plate **LVII**] The inscription reads: "In 1941–1943 in occupied Kyiv 621 members of the anti-Nazi underground of the Or-

---

8 Yom Kippur, also known as the Day of Atonement, is one of the most important Jewish holidays of the fall season. It is often mistakenly called Judgment Day, even though in Jewish tradition the days of judgment are Rosh Hashanah (New Year) and the following eight days before Yom Kippur. According to a widely circulated myth, this holiday coincided with the first day of the shootings in Babyn Yar, 29 September 1941. In fact, that year Yom Kippur was celebrated on 1 October.

9 Immediately after the liberation of Kyiv, a myth surfaced in official reports of the Soviet underground about a beautiful "princess Markusidze," who had poisoned dozens of German officers in a cafeteria or flirted with them in order to lure them to her residence, where she murdered them. The real life of the young girl, who was the courier and lover of Heorhii Levytskyi (a member of the clandestine municipal party committee), was not quite so enchanting. After taking part in one or two terrorist actions, she was captured while trying to flee Kyiv. She was held in the Security Service and SD prison until someone denounced her as a Jew, after which she was executed.

ganization of Ukrainian Nationalists were killed in the struggle for an independent Ukrainian State, among whom was the poet Olena Teliha. Babyn Yar became their mass grave. Glory to the Heroes!" In 1993 the street named after Demian Korotchenko (a mid-twentieth century leader in Soviet Ukraine), which goes past Babyn Yar, was renamed in honor of Teliha, who was not only a poet but also an active member of the OUN(M), who was executed by the Nazis together with her husband. The question of erecting a monument to Teliha at the site of the cross has been discussed for many years, but the city fathers have not yet been able to raise the necessary funds. In the meantime, mourning ceremonies organized by Ukrainian nationalist organizations are held next to the cross every year on 22 February, the day Teliha was executed.

In 1993, the memory of another distinguished figure of the OUN, Oleh Olzhych, was immortalized when the street that was known as Babyn Yar until the early 1950s and later renamed in honor of the Soviet poet Demian Bednyi was renamed in Olzhych's honor. A commemorative marker was installed on a building located on the corner of Olzhych and Teliha streets. Its inscription reads: "This street was named in honor of the Ukrainian poet, archaeologist, and OUN leader Oleh Olzhych (Kandyba), 1907–1944." Today, as part of the ongoing decommunization process in Ukraine, discussions are taking place about renaming Melnikova Street (which honors the Bolshevik Yuvenalii Melnikov) either in honor of the OUN(M) leader Colonel Andrii Melnyk or the Ukrainian National Republic Brigadier-General Mykola Kapustianskyi, who in emigration was a colonel-general and the head of the OUN(M) Executive.

The Roma people's memory of the Babyn Yar tragedy is still encountering obstacles. An attempt in the late 1990s to erect a monument in the shape of a Roma/Gypsy wagon, funded by charitable donations, was decisively rejected by the Kyiv City Council, claiming that the design of the monument was incompatible with the overall design of the memorial ensemble. The fact that there is no memorial ensemble in Babyn Yar in the first place reveals the spurious nature of the City Council's opposition. Perhaps some public figures who did not wish to mention any other genocide apart from the Jewish one had a hand in this?

This view is, in part, corroborated by the history of the trials and tribulations of a commemorative stela that was unveiled with pomp in 2009 near the Soviet monument. [see Plate **LXII**] Its inscription reads: "A monument to the victims of the Roma Holocaust, will be installed on this spot." A year later the stela was destroyed by unknown perpetrators. A new plaque, but smaller and more unassuming, bears a much more unassertive inscription: "In memory of the Roma who were shot in Babyn Yar." As we can see, this is not about either the Roma Holocaust or any future monument, even though discussions continue, especially about the return to Babyn Yar of the metal Roma wagon that, following its rejection by the Kyiv City Council, found a home in the far western Ukrainian city of Kamianets-Podilskyi. One way or another, the Roma community now has a spot to hold its own annual commemorative ceremonies on 2 August, Roma Genocide Remembrance Day.

Another group of commemorative markers is connected with the history of the extermination of patients at the Pavlov Psychiatric Hospital (now called Kyiv Municipal Clinical Psychoneurological Hospital No. 1). The markers are grouped compactly on a small, central square of this hospital. A large granite slab was installed in 2001. A cross and a Star of David were engraved on it with the following inscription: "In memory of the 751 hospital patients who were killed by the Hitlerite regime in 1941–1942. Memory eternal." In 2003 and 2004, another two commemorative markers were unveiled nearby. One is dedicated to the memory of the murdered patients, [see Plate **LXI**] the other to the hospital employees who managed to save some of the patients in their care. The latter marker is embellished with the trident, the state emblem of Ukraine. All these markers were erected through the efforts of the management and staff of the hospital. In 1998, the Ukrainian Psychiatric Association established specialist prizes named after the hospital's chief physician, Musii Tantsiura, and a medical assistant and head of the medical ward Ananii Mazur, both of whom contributed most to saving their patients.

Members of the Ukrainian Orthodox Church (Moscow Patriarchate) have been consistently and tenaciously creating their own place of memory on a plot of land situated on the grounds of the former St. Cyril Orthodox Cemetery, adjacent to the Menorah Monument. In the late 1990s, five iron cross were erected in memory of several clerics who were murdered by the Nazis. The inscriptions are unpretentious and laconic: "Archimandrite Aleksandr Vyshniakov, shot in 1941"; "A Divine Liturgy was served on this spot in 2000"; "Archpriest Pavlo Ostrianskyi, shot on 6 November 1941"; "Schema-nun Yesfir, shot by the fascists on 6 November 1941"; and "On this spot people were killed in 1941. O Lord, repose their souls." It has not been determined yet whether these people were actually shot here or whether the Menorah, which was already installed at this time, was used for the purpose of orientation.

In 2000, a large wooden cross was installed closer to the Menorah Monument. [see Plate **LVIII**] Underneath it was laid a granite slab inscribed with the following text written in a bizarre mishmash of Ukrainian and Russian: "On this spot on 6 November 1941 the clerics Archimandrite Aleksandr Vyshniakov and Archpriest Pavlo Ostrianskyi were shot for their appeal to defend the Homeland from the fascists." Below it is a fragment from a psalm in Old Church Slavonic: "Precious in the sight of the Lord is the death of His saints."

For a long time these crosses were the sole reminder of the murdered clerics. But in 2012 a tiny wooden chapel was erected on a small square near the crosses, and next to it a stela was installed with the following inscription engraved on a granite tablet: "Memorial chapel to the victims of the genocide and the Holocaust of the Ukrainian and Jewish peoples." However, this naïve attempt, in the spirit of President Viktor Yushchenko, to unite the memory of the genocides of the two peoples is no longer relevant. A year later the tablet was changed with the following text: "Temple-chapel in honor of the clerics who were shot for their appeal to defend the Motherland during the German-fascist occupation of the city of Kyiv, Archimandrite Aleksandr Vyshniakov, Archpriest Pavlo Ostrianskyi, Schema-nun Yesfir, and other innocent citizens of various nationalities who were killed." This Soviet-Orthodox text tallies far more closely with the politics of memory pursued by both President Viktor Yanukovych and his spiritual fathers from the Ukrainian Orthodox Church—Moscow Patriarchate.

Three other groups of commemorative markers are connected with wartime events. The first group is comprised of memorial crosses installed in 1999 on the grounds of the German prisoner-of-war cemetery that was rebuilt with funds provided by the German Embassy.[10] [see Plate **LVIII**] A granite tablet was attached to the central cross, bearing the following inscription in Ukrainian and German: "Here repose prisoners of war, victims of World War II." The second group of commemorative markers includes a monument dedicated to the writer Anatoly Kuznetsov, whose family lived nearby during the war. [see Plate **LXII**] It was installed in 2009 near a house located on the corner of Frunze (now: Kyrylivska) and Petropavlivska streets. Two metal tablets were installed on the building. The inscription on one of the tablets is the text of the order issued to the Jews of Kyiv to assemble on 29 September 1941. The text of the other inscription states: "In order for the past not to repeat itself, find the courage to look it in the eyes: The whole truth is in *Babi Yar: A Document in the Form of a Novel* by the eyewitness of events Anatoly Kuznetsov (1929–1979)." Today this is the only memorial to the memory, so to speak, of Babyn Yar itself.

The most interesting commemorative marker was erected in 2005 by the Kyiv municipal administration, once again near the Soviet monument. [see Plate **LVI**] The front side of the marker features the word *OST* and the following inscription: "Memory for the sake of the future." The reverse side states: "To the world maimed by Nazism." Alongside it is a granite stela inscribed with the following text: "Let us bow down to the memory of 3 million citizens of Ukraine who were forcibly deported during the World War II to Nazi Germany, many of whom were murdered by excessive slave labor, starvation, torture, shot, and burned in crematorium ovens." It is difficult to fathom the connection between the *Ostarbeiter* alluded to in the stela's text and Babyn Yar. Clearly, in the minds of many people, including Kyiv's city leaders, Babyn Yar is associated with all the tragedies of wartime and occupation.

Perhaps our inability to unite for the sake of a cause, even the most noble one, is demonstrated by three commemorative markers dedicated to the victims of the Kurenivka mudslide tragedy that took place in 1961.

10 After Kyiv was liberated, German prisoners of war were held, in keeping with the traditional Soviet practice, in the former Syrets concentration camp until 1946. A cemetery where German POWs were buried was built behind the camp, where the intersection of Ryzka and Shchusieva streets is located today.

The first marker, erected in 1995 on what was then Frunze Street near the Podil (originally Krasin) streetcar depot destroyed during the catastrophe, is dedicated exclusively to the depot workers who were killed. The second marker appeared in 2006 near Olena Teliha Street, in Babyn Yar Park,[11] situated two blocks from the Dorohozhychi subway station. [see Plate **LXI**] It consists of two ornamental granite stelae featuring a commemorative versified inscription on one stela, which is repeated on the other: "Erected on the 45th anniversary of the Kurenivka tragedy on the initiative of and with funding from the 'Party of the Defenders of the Homeland' and Ivan Mykolaiovych Suslov, 13.03.2006." The typeface on both stelae is the same size. No comment necessary, as they say. The third marker is a wooden cross that was erected on Olena Teliha Street, near the staircase leading to the St. Cyril Church. Affixed to the cross is a granite tablet bearing the following inscription: "Erected by the general public of the city of Kyiv in memory of our countrymen who perished during the Kurenivka catastrophe on 13 March 1961." This appears to be the only example of the urban community's self-initiated and selfless commemoration of its countrymen on the territory of Babyn Yar.

### Competing mythologies and yet-to-be realized monuments

The final but still unrealized project in the legacy of Ilya Levitas, the head of the Jewish Council of Ukraine, is the above-mentioned Avenue of the Righteous. In 2011, a small granite stone was installed near the exit of the Dorohozhychi subway station, at the beginning of an avenue of poplar that goes over the riverbed of the filled-in Babyn Yar ravine. Its inscription reads: "The Avenue of the Righteous—Ukrainians who, in risking their lives, rescued Jews during the Great Patriotic War, will be built on this spot."

Oddly enough, from the very outset there was a problem with this undoubtedly noble initiative. The fact is that the honorific "Righteous Among the Nations" is bestowed on non-Jews who saved Jews during the Holocaust. It is awarded only by Yad Vashem, Israel's official memorial to the victims of the Holocaust. The criteria for recognition are quite

11 This is still the official name of the former killing grounds: Babyn Yar Park of the Shevchenko District.

strict, particularly at the stage of approving the decision to bestow this title. For example, the saved individual must still be alive, and the rescuer had to have reached adulthood during the war. During the Soviet period it was forbidden to mention the Holocaust and, hence, the efforts to rescue Jews. Consequently, over time many rescuers and the individuals whom they saved died. Nevertheless, between 1990 and 1 January 2016 the honorific title, "Righteous Among the Nations," was bestowed by Yad Vashem on 2,544 Ukrainian citizens (Ukraine occupies fourth place in the ranking of countries whose citizens saved Jews, following Poland, the Netherlands, and France).

Considering the difficult circumstances of obtaining this recognition, Ilya Levitas, in the name of the Memory of Babyn Yar Foundation that he headed in 1989, began bestowing the honorific "Righteous of Babyn Yar" to people about whom there was information that they had saved Jews in Nazi-occupied Kyiv. A total of 618 people have received this title (150 of them were eventually recognized as "Righteous Among the Nations" by Yad Vashem). The plans called for commemorating these very individuals with the Avenue of the Righteous. But since the criteria for bestowing the honorific "Righteous of Babyn Yar" were not defined and the decision to award it was made strictly on Levitas's decision alone, many scholars and civic figures, even those based in Ukraine, do not recognize this honorific title and have challenged the legitimacy of the official commemoration of these individuals.

As it turned out, however, this was not the only obstacle to completing this project. A considerable number of Jewish activists both in Ukraine and other countries hold the view that it is inappropriate to build an Avenue of the Righteous. During public discussions they have insisted that honoring the Righteous cannot precede the worthy commemoration of the victims (they regard existing memorials, including the Menorah Monument, as inadequate to the scope of the Jewish tragedy). In private conversations they claim that honoring the Righteous will detract attention from those individuals who had a direct role in destroying the Jews or who denounced them to the Germans. The sacrificial model of Jewish memory which they espouse demands that other nations must continuously atone for their involvement in the Holocaust. Even simply acknowledging the existence of numerous rescuers violates the established stereotype, according to which all participants of those events were divided exclusively into executioners, victims, and indifferent bystanders.

In Babyn Yar and alongside the former ravine there are several other commemorative markers. These symbolize entirely different dangers and threaten the site and the memory of the tragic events that took place there.

On 30 September 2001, in the upper reaches of Babyn Yar, near the commemorative cross dedicated to executed members of the OUN, President Leonid Kuchma and the mayor of Kyiv Oleksandr Omelchenko took part in a solemn ceremony to lay a symbolic cornerstone, on which inscriptions were engraved in three languages: Ukrainian, English, and Hebrew. The Ukrainian inscription reads as follows: "This stone was laid on the 60th anniversary of the mass killing of Jews in Babyn Yar to mark the intent to construct on this site the Spadshchyna Community and Cultural Center." The English and Hebrew inscriptions are somewhat different, however: "This cornerstone of the Jewish Heritage Community Center was laid on the 60th anniversary of the Babi Yar massacre." The upper part of the stone features the logo of the American Jewish Joint Distribution Committee and the emblem of Kyiv, a shield depicting the Archangel Michael; the pairing of these images supposedly attests to the close cooperation between the city and the Jewish community in the efforts to carry out the project.

The differences among the three texts indicate that the project initiators were aware of its controversial nature even before it raised heated public debates. It is no wonder that the Ukrainian text (intended for the local population) emphasized that the stone was laid above all on the day of the mass shootings, whereas the two other inscriptions (aimed at sponsors) noted openly that the main goal of the project was the construction of a community center on this site. It must be noted that building a cultural community center in Babyn Yar in no way troubled the sponsors, initiators, and architects.

Amos Avgar, the American Jewish Joint Distribution Committee's Country Director for Central, Western, and Southern Ukraine, put forward two arguments in favor of this decision. The first one was sociopolitical in nature: "The Spadshchyna/Heritage Jewish Community Center," he wrote, "will proclaim a serious Jewish presence in this area."[12] The second reason was ideological: "We will transform the place alongside Babyn Yar into a source for the brilliant revival of community life." "This will not be disrespectful toward the memory of those who were killed nearby, but rather a commemoration of their lives through the revival and glorification of their traditions and culture."[13]

Avgar wrote these words in mid-2002, in the midst of the scandal surrounding the project. For that reason, he tried his utmost to underscore the fact that the center would be built not in Babyn Yar itself but next to it. But six months earlier the authors of the winning design, the Israeli architects Daniela and Ulrik Plesner, were completely frank about their belief in the legitimacy of this construction project. In their view, "the community center should represent the life, death, and rebirth of the Jewish community of Kyiv and Ukraine, whose historic roots are found in Kyiv and which enter the soil of Babyn Yar, over which new life is blossoming among the branches, leaves, and birds, as though not realizing what took place here."[14]

However, this concept proved to be unacceptable, above all, to many ordinary Jewish residents of Kyiv, who began to speak publicly against what they termed sacrilege. It is indicative that Ukrainian and Kyiv-based organizations either openly supported the American project or sought some kind of compromise that would help save face and the sponsors' funding. Since the efforts of the Jewish community proved inadequate to block the project, the opposition was joined by many members of the Ukrainian public at large. They were displeased not only by the attempt to build what was in fact an entertainment center on the victims' bones, but also by the avowed wish to establish Jewish dominance in the physical and memory space of Babyn Yar. Thus, the Spadshchyna project was halted through joint efforts, even though, as we have seen, ten years later

12 Amos Avgar, "Evreiskii obshchinnyi tsentr 'Nasledie': pamiatnaia zapiska," *Khadashot*, No. 5 [91] (2002).

13 Ibid.

14 "Arkhitekturnaia masterskaia Pleznerov: Evreiskii obshchinnyi tsentr 'Nasledie'," in ibid.

some Jewish activists tried to revive it by means of a decision taken by Ukraine's Parliament.

The conflict surrounding the community center provided an impetus for an entire array of falsifications of the topography of Babyn Yar, with which the project supporters tried to legalize the project. Through a stroke of bitter irony, a leading role in this thankless task was played by Ilya Levitas, who by that point had spent many years preserving the memory of this site. The problem emerged several years earlier, when, during the construction of the Dorohozhychi subway station, numerous bodily remains were found in what had been the epicenter of the killing grounds. Levitas then began working with a commission set up by the municipal administration, which "successfully" determined that the massacre site was located fifteen meters more to the right of the building site. Thus, the opening of the new subway station in March 2000 went ahead quietly, without a scandal.

For the Spadshchyna/Heritage Center's needs, Levitas generally "relocated" Babyn Yar, claiming that its starting point was not near Dorohozhychi Street, where the remnants of three small ravines around the large Soviet monument have been preserved and where the community center was supposed to be built, but near today's Melnikova Street, below the subway station. He offered his "expert finding" again in 2006, when the time came to start the construction on Olena Teliha Street (local residents installed the two crosses expressly to counteract his efforts). Then Levitas retracted his long-standing theory that the shootings had taken place in the large spur of Babyn Yar that was transected by this street and where the tower block was supposed to be built.

Regrettably, the conflict around the attempts to build a community institution on the bones of the Babyn Yar victims did not preclude further such attempts. On 3 October 2011 a granite stone was ceremoniously laid in a section of the ruined Jewish Cemetery, which had been converted into a soccer field. [see Plate **LX**] The ceremony was attended by a number of well-known Jewish activists and businessmen, as well as a number of foreign guests. The stone was inscribed with the following text: "On the sad 70$^{th}$ anniversary of the shootings in Babyn Yar, the first stone in the building of the Babyn Yar Memorial and Museum Complex was laid in this place."

This project was launched back in 2006, when a group of Jewish businessmen headed by Vadim Rabinovich, president of the All-Ukrainian Jewish Congress, united to form the Memory of Babyn Yar Foundation,[15] and set about building a museum and a religious and educational complex on the site of an unfinished building that at one time was slated to be part of the Avanhard sports complex.

There are two problems with this memorial complex, as with the Babyn Yar Museum that was designed in 2012 on the personal initiative of the famous Ukrainian architect Larysa Skoryk with the support of the board of the Babyn Yar National Historical Memorial Preserve. First of all, both of these projects are clearly and exclusively "Jewish" even in terms of their architectural motifs (Skoryk's design features a Star of David, while the design proposed by the Babyn Yar Foundation features a *talles*). Both ignore the memory of the other victims who lost their lives in this tragic place. This omission has caused much greater opposition from a segment of the Jewish community than from any non-Jewish one.

Second, the site of the planned location of this complex immediately sparked a public outcry. It must be noted, however, that the non-Jewish community is much less actively involved in this situation than in the Spadshchyna Center, because this time around the issue is about building something not on the site of the mass grave in Babyn Yar but on the grounds of the former Jewish Cemetery. Conventional wisdom would suggest that this is an internal concern of the Jewish community. Moreover, even the nature of the project is not as bold because at issue is the construction of a commemorative institution, not one intended for recreation. Nevertheless, the initiators of the construction project claim that a cemetery never existed in this area, or that even if there had been a cemetery there are no longer any graves on the site.

These projects are inextricably tied to an entire saga that unfolded around the designation of the area and the transfer of the buildings comprising the Babyn Yar National Historical Memorial Preserve. A direc-

15 The very name this new foundation is a perfect illustration of the ways the various Jewish civic organizations compete with each other; it should not be confused with the Memory of Babyn Yar Foundation, founded back in 1989 and headed until recently by the late Ilya Levitas.

tive about its creation was issued by President Viktor Yushchenko on 23 September 2005, on the eve of the next anniversary of the tragedy. But the Cabinet of Ministers, headed by Viktor Yanukovych, approved a resolution about its realistic implementation only much later, on 1 March 2007. One of Yushchenko's final acts as president (24 February 2010) was to grant national status to the preserve. Six months later, on 28 October 2010, the Kyiv City Council finally allocated land to the National Preserve.

The grounds of the National Historical Memorial Preserve are comprised of three separate sections. The first is an area located at the summit of Babyn Yar, around the large Soviet monument (bordered by Dorohozhytska, Teliha, Melnikova, and Oranzhereina streets). The second is an area that is approximately twice as large as the former ravine. It is located behind Melnikova Street and the Dorohozhychi subway station (to the right of Olena Teliha Street). The third is an area comprised of three elements: the former St. Cyril Orthodox Cemetery (where the Menorah Monument, the crosses, and the small chapel dedicated to executed clerics are situated); a tiny section of the Jewish Cemetery restored with funds provided by the Jewish-American community of San Francisco; and the so-called Path of Sorrow leading from the Menorah to Melnikova Street. A considerable portion of the as yet undeveloped grounds of the Jewish and Karaite cemeteries was not included in the Memorial Preserve because it was already spoken for in the grandiose Babyn Yar Memory Foundation project. As regards any existing buildings, year-long efforts have failed to allocate to the Memorial Preserve at least the former office of the Jewish Cemetery, which in the meantime has been privatized by certain "business" speculators.

The logical culmination of the complex developments discussed above came in 2012 with the announcement of a "Plan for Organizing the Territory of the Babyn Yar National Historical Memorial Preserve." The purposely chosen author of this document was the All-Ukrainian Scientific-Methodological and Research Information Center of Architectural Heritage, which, unlike the Kyiv City Planning Institute (Kyivhenplan), for example, had never dealt with this type of question. As a result, the 2012 plan allocated for the place of executions a small plot of land behind the subway station, which is guaranteed to be safe from possible urban development projects.

### A space of memory or non-memory

What might one say in more general terms about the problems that have contributed to the situation outlined above, and what are the possible ways to resolve challenges posed by Babyn Yar as a landscape of memory or "space of non-memory"? The first problem, which continues to spark endless attempts to construct a memorial zone, is essentially an ethical one that is connected with the general attitude to the burial site. It would be incorrect, however, to lay all the blame on the Soviet legacy. Purely materialistic communist ideology did indeed show utter disregard for the graves as real, physical objects. This did not prevent the communists from creating ostentatious necropolises modelled on the Kremlin Wall, where they buried their leaders and heroes. Nevertheless, it was the actual monument, not the remains of a person that was important. This is clearly demonstrated by the disgraceful state of affairs surrounding the remains of hundreds of thousands of Soviet soldiers killed in World War II, which are lying to this day in the forests and swamps of the European part of the former Soviet Union, even though monuments with lists of the names of the fallen stand in every village.

In the history of Babyn Yar this duality in attitude is graphically illustrated by the work of the Kyiv-based architect Oleksandr Vlasov, who was active in the immediate postwar years. He was the author of the first project (unrealized) to build a monument dedicated to the victims of Babyn Yar. He also designed a new, general plan of Kyiv, which, in keeping with prewar plans, entailed laying new streets across the ravine and the adjacent cemeteries, and transforming the territory into a sports/park zone. To a significant degree these projects were eventually carried out, and it was these very projects that caused the Kurenivka mudslide in 1961.

Equally negativistic is the attitude toward graves reflective of contemporary postmodernist values, which generally reject all established traditions. This was clearly demonstrated in the design of the Spadshchyna/Heritage Center, initiated by an American charitable organization. Not only was this body not a Ukrainian one, even the winners of the architectural competition were non-Ukrainians.

The other problem, which occasionally leads to the emergence of new, grandiose memorial or pseudo-memorial projects, is the view that a place of memory must invariably include some kind of ostentatious building. In keeping with this vision, the absence of a monument is assumed to mean the absence of memory as such; hence, the scale of a tragedy should be reflected in the physical size of the memorial. Calling this vision exclusively post-Soviet or post-totalitarian would also be incorrect. The Egyptian pyramids, ancient temples, and Europe's Gothic cathedrals plainly demonstrate the validity of this approach under absolutely differing historical conditions.

These two problems influence the very preservation of memorial space. But no less important are problems connected with its arrangement. The positions held by the main actors are evident, and for all practical purposes they exclude the possibility of productive cooperation. Jews who have always been, objectively speaking, the natural and recognized guardians of the memory of Babyn Yar, consistently seek to "appropriate" Babyn Yar as a physical place of memory. Other groups of "victims' heirs," including Ukrainian nationalists, the Roma people, and the Kyiv community in general demonstrate a fundamental unwillingness to take responsibility for resolving the complex problem of memorial space. The latter do not even profess to take part in this resolution, although they are ready to limit themselves to their own small parcel of land for the commemoration of "their" victims and to demonstrate a minimum of respect for "their" commemorative ceremonies. Under these circumstances, the Ukrainian state, which should take on the function, if not of organizer then at least of dialogue moderator, has completely bowed out of this process, restricting its activities to showing ritual support for any civic initiative and equally ritual participation in commemorative ceremonies.

It would be a mistake to consider this situation as the result of someone's evil intent. The problem lies in the fundamentally different views of the very symbolism of Babyn Yar. The Jewish community and the world beyond Ukraine view Babyn Yar as exclusively a symbol of the Holocaust, whereas for Ukrainian society it is a symbol of many tragedies that took place during the Nazi occupation. For the city of Kyiv, Babyn Yar is also a symbol of the place's whole, lengthy history before and after World War II, which includes the burial of victims of the Holodomor and Soviet terror in the cemeteries adjacent to the ravine,[16] the sacrilegious destruction of the historic necropolis, the Kurenivka tragedy, etc.

The absence in contemporary Ukraine of a shared memory of World War II and the Holocaust argues against the possibility of eradicating this dispute at least on the internal level within the framework of a joint and universally accepted model. This is not to say that such a model would be acceptable to the international Jewish community, which is still an influential participant in all the ongoing disputes surrounding memorialization at Babyn Yar.

It is evident that the solution to this state of affairs should be sought, above all, on the ideological level. The challenge of Babyn Yar demands essentially new approaches that would include such radical steps as the "restoration" of the Holocaust to general world history, its transformation from a unique event into a universal symbol, and, finally, a return to the history of God Himself as a supreme source of human morality. It is equally evident that such a task is much broader than the problem of how to set up even such a distinguished place of memory as Babyn Yar in a worthy manner. The current situation in Ukraine and the rest of the world does not offer hope for a speedy resolution to these global problems. Therefore, it falls to us merely to safeguard Babyn Yar for future generations.

16 In contradiction to existing myths, victims of the Soviet regime were never buried in Babyn Yar. For some time, however, the Lukianivska Orthodox Cemetery was used for burying executed people; a mass grave was dug in Bratske Cemetery, and the bodies of people who had starved to death on the streets of Kyiv were buried there.

# In Lieu of an Afterword

*Paul Robert Magocsi*

The 75th Anniversary of the September 1941 massacre of the Jews of Kyiv prompted a renewed interest in the question of memorialization at Babyn Yar. The first body to act on this matter was the Ukrainian Jewish Encounter (UJE), a non-governmental organization based in Toronto, Canada, whose mission is "to deepen an understanding . . . of Ukrainian-Jewish relations over the centuries with a view to the future."[1] With that in mind, the UJE set out in late 2014 to prepare a major week-long commemorative event to culminate, on 29-30 September 2016, the 75th anniversary of the "Holocaust by Bullets" carried out against Kyiv's Jewry at the ravine of Babyn Yar.

The UJE-sponsored commemoration took place under the patronage of the President of Ukraine (Petro Poroshenko) and the World Jewish Congress in cooperation with a wide range of governmental and non-governmental bodies within and beyond Ukraine. The commemoration included four aspects: education and consciousness raising among youth; a public symposium focusing on the results of a new book, *Babyn Yar: History and Memory*; a commemorative concert at the National Opera in Kyïv; and the presentation of awards to winners of an international competition for a landscape design to transform Babyn Yar into a sacred place of memory for future generations of visitors to the site. The UJE event took place in Kyiv (23-29 September 2016) with the participation of hundreds of students, scholars, public intellectuals, musicians, artists, actors, landscape architects, and visitors from Europe, the Middle East, and North America.[2]

A full year after the UJE began its planning and preparatory work,

1 *UJE-Ukrainian Jewish Encounter* (Missisauga, Ontario, 2012), p. 2.

2 *Program: Babyn Yar/A Commemoration—Kyiv, Ukraine*, September 23-29, 2016.

Ukraine's president, Petro Poroshenko, issued a decree (November 2015) to create a National Organizing Committee whose goal was to propose state sponsored commemorations for the 75th anniversary of the Babyn Yar tragedy. As is the case with many state commemorations in Ukraine, nothing much was done until the seemingly last moment, concretely until mid-summer 2016, a mere two months before the commemorative date. In the end, the belated plans were realized, so that on the night of 29 September 2016, the government of Ukraine, led by President Petro Poroshenko, hosted guests from several countries, in particular Israel, Germany, and the European Council at a grandiose event on the grounds of Babyn Yar.[3]

Clearly, commemorative events were appropriately carried out by both non-governmental and governmental bodies. But what about Babyn Yar itself? Would the ambitious commemorations on the 75th Anniversary lead to a transformation of Babyn Yar into a place worthy of its status as the Auschwitz of the East—the symbol of World War II Europe's Holocaust by Bullets?

At the very same time that the weeklong commemorative events in Kyiv sponsored by the Ukrainian Jewish Encounter (UJE) were taking place, so too were meetings being held that resulted in the formation of the Babyn Yar Holocaust Memorial Center (BYHMC). Its goal was to build at Babyn Yar a Holocaust Museum under the direction of a Supervisory Board headed by the former Soviet dissident and Israeli politician Natan Sharansky and including four figures who were the project's primary source of funding: Mikhail Fridman, German Khan, Pavel Fuks, and Viktor Pinchuk. All five of these figures were born in Soviet Ukraine, and that fact, they argued, gave them the right to create Jewish memorials in their former homeland, now independent Ukraine. In reality, for decades all but one of them lived and worked elsewhere: the politician Sharansky in Israel; the oligarchs Fridman, Khan, and Fuks in Moscow

---

3 *Svidok: prysviacheno 75-m rokovyny trahediï v Babynomu Iaru/Witness: Dedicated to the 75th anniversary of the Babyn Yar tragedy* [Kyïv, 2016]; Tamar Pileggi, "75 years after Babi Yar massacre, Ukraine reexamines its dark history," *The Times of Israel* (Jerusalem?), 3 October 2016; Vladislav Davidzon, "A Babi Yar Memorial, A Tenor of Somber Acknowledgement," *Tablet* (Jerusalem?), 30 September 2016.

and/or London. The leading donor behind the well-funded Babyn Yar Holocaust Memorial Center (BYHMC) was Mikhail Fridman, whose business interests and wealth was, like that of Khan and Fuks, closely tied to Russia and its increasingly autocratic leader Vladimir Putin.[4]

In order to achieve its goals and enhance its prestige on the international scene, the BYHMC created an international scholarly council whose historical consultant was the respected Dutch historian Karel Berkhoff. It also engaged the Moscow-based Russian film director Ilya Khrzhanovskii, known for his promotion of immersive theater and audience role playing—to be sure innovative, yet controversial artistic and performative practices.

While the BYHMC project was undertaking preliminary research and construction planning, Ukraine's Ministry of Culture at the behest of President Poroshenko commissioned the Institute of History of Ukraine at the National Academy of Sciences of Ukraine (NANU) to prepare a proposal for an all-encompassing Babyn Yar National Memorial Preserve. The result was a concept paper submitted in 2018 for a Memorial Museum to Honor the Victims at Babyn Yar, and an expanded version one year later that included as well a proposal to transform the site into a National Historical Preserve in the form of a necropolis to honor those buried there.[5]

Hence, within two years of the 75th Babyn Yar anniversary, there were

---

4 As it turned out later, Fridman admitted to being part of a circle of oligarchs that Putin convenes "every few months." Brendan Hoffman, "Is Ukraine's New Holocaust Museum Also an Instrument of Kremlin Propaganda?" *Time Magazine*, 29 September 2021. The Mafiosi-like Fuks, banned in 2017 from entering the United States, was suspected of supporting Russia's campaign to depict Ukraine as a neo-Nazi state, something for which he claimed was an "assignment" from Putin which he had to carry out in order to stay in business in Russia. Seth Hettena, "Exclusive: Sources Say Oligarch Funded Scheme to Paint Swastikas in Ukraine," *Rolling Stone* (New York), 23 March 2022. After Russia's invasion in February 2022, German Khan was sanctioned and opted to leave London and return to Putin's Moscow where he felt safe. *Bloomberg News*, 8 September 2022.

5 Instytut istoriï Ukraïny, Natsional'noï akademiï nauk Ukraïny: *Kontseptsiia Memorial'noho muzeiu pam'iaty zhertv Babynoho Iaru: proekt 4.04.2018* (Kyiv, 2018) and *Kontseptsiia kompleksnoho rozvytku (memorializatsiï) Babynoho Iaru z rozshyrenniam mezh Natsional'noho istoryko-memorial'noho zapovidnyka 'Babyn Iar' 7.05.2019* (Kyiv 2019).

two proposals about how to transform the site. One was the Babyn Yar Holocaust Memorial Center (BYHMC) put forth by an externally-funded international body; the other was put forth by the Academy of Sciences Institute of the History of Ukraine, through the auspices of Ukraine's Ministry of Culture, for a Babyn Yar National Memorial Preserve. Both projects were ultimately dependent on acceptance by the government of Ukraine as well as the administration of the City of Kyiv which owned the land at Babyn Yar.

Perhaps it is inevitable that if there were two projects there would be a rivalry between them.[6] Indeed, a rivalry did soon develop in which various stake holders took sides: Jewish and Ukrainian community organizations and their spokespersons in Ukraine; Ukraine's government bodies; public intellectuals and the media within and beyond Ukraine; and the Jewish and Ukrainian diasporas.

The rivalry turned acrimonious after the Babyn Yar Holocaust Memorial Center announced the proposed design of their artistic director Ilya Khrzhanovskii. His goal was to create an atmosphere of hyperreality in which the visitor, interacting with various monuments, would experience exceptional thoughts and emotions. Khrzhanovskii's design provoked a barrage of criticism, in particular from Jews within and beyond Ukraine, one of whom wrote for the *Wall Street Journal* an article entitled, "Ukraine's Holocaust Disneyland."[7] So egregious were Krzhanovskii's plans that in April 2020 the BYHMC's academic director Karel Berkhoff publicly resigned, explaining: "I used to sense the project had a moral compass, but that is no longer the case."[8]

Seemingly unphased by the controversy, the BYHMC project contin-

---

6 A useful review of the conflicting positions was provided by Halya Coynash, "Russian oligarch plans for Babyn Yar seem aimed at fueling anti-Semitism in Ukraine, 31 December 2020," Information Portal Human Rights in Ukraine.

7 Vladislav Davidzon, "Ukraine's 'Holocaust Disneyland'," *Wall Street Journal* (New York), 10 July 2020. See also Yohanan Petrovsky-Shtern, "Saviour on the Blood, or Ilya Khrzhanovsky's Babyn Yar Experimental Museum," *Krytyka* (Kyiv), 16 October 2020.

8 Letter of Karel Berkhoff to Natan Sharansky, Chairman of the BYHMC Supervisory Board, dated 3 March 2020, University of Toronto Chair of Ukrainian Studies Archive (hereafter: Toronto Chair Archive).

ued to move forward and to press Ukraine's national government and Kyiv's city authorities for formal access (ownership or a long-term lease) to land and buildings at the Babyn Yar site.[9]

For its part, the Academy of Sciences Institute of the History of Ukraine undertook a comprehensive revision of its proposal. Aside from its own collegium of eighteen authors (headed by the Institute's deputy directory Hennadii Boriak and the noted World War II Holocaust and Jewish history specialists Oleksandr Lysenko, Vitalii Nakhmanovych, and Anatolii Podolskyi), the Institute engaged the services of 43 scholars world-wide to review and propose changes to the document. It was finally released in 2021 under the title: "Concept for the Memorialization of the Babyn Yar National Historical Memorial Preserve."[10] The Historical Institute concept called for the creation of two museums: one devoted specifically to the history of Babyn Yar and to all its victims, the other devoted to the Holocaust not only in Ukraine but also throughout Europe. Central to the proposal was a memorial park, drawing on ideas from the 2016 UJE international landscape design competition that would transform the Babyn Yar killing grounds into a sacred space (necropolis).

President Poroshenko, whose administration had initiated the work of the Institute of History project, also welcomed the initiative of the outside-funded Babyn Yar Holocaust Memorial Center (BYHMC). The National Organizing Committee that he created in 2017 included state functionaries and representatives of both Babyn Yar projects.[11] Cooperation between supporters of the two projects proved impossible, however.

Meanwhile, in the midst of the growing controversy over memorialization at Babyn Yar, the political scene in Ukraine changed radically. The results of the presidential elections in May 2019 brought a new head of state to the country, Volodymyr Zelenskyi, who called for elections to parliament which two months later resulted in a majority victory for his party, Servant

9 Babyn Yar Holocaust Memorial Center, "Statement of the BYHMC Scientific Council, 6 May 2020," copy in the Toronto Chair Archive.

10 *Concept for the Memorialization of the Babyn Yar National Historical Memorial Preserve*, 2$^{nd}$ revised and expanded edition (Kyiv, 2021).

11 "Ukaz prezydenta Ukraïny [P. Poroshenko], No 331/20.X.2017," Toronto Chair Archive.

of the People/Sluha narodu. The new powers in control of Ukraine's presidency and parliament changed the dynamics of the Babyn Yar debate.

That debate revolved around several issues. Should the memorialization focus solely on Jews or on all peoples who perished at Babyn Yar during World War II? Should the focus be solely on the Holocaust period, or on all the tragedies that occurred at Babyn Yar? Should the memorialization be primarily conceived by Jews, or should experts, regardless of their ethnic or religious background, be involved? And perhaps most sensitive of all, should the project be under the control (regardless of funding source) of Ukrainian governmental and scholarly bodies, or under the control of those putting up the funds.[12]

Since the Babyn Yar Holocaust Memorial Center (BYHMC) was being funded primarily by one person (Mikhail Fridman), and since his investments were tied largely to businesses and financial institutions in the Russian Federation, the Babyn Yar memorialization controversy was reduced to a simple dichotomy: the "Russian" project versus the "Ukrainian" project.

The spokespersons for both projects turned to President Zelenskyi and Kyiv mayor Vitalii Klychko for endorsement. Jewish activists in Ukraine were divided on this matter. Several religious and secular organizations supported the Russian project, while others, calling themselves "Ukrainian Jews," expressed support of the Ukrainian project.[13] Speaking on behalf of civil society, no less than 800 intellectuals in Ukraine, fear-

---

12 On the conceptual differences between the Babyn Yar Holocaust Memorial Center and the Institute of History projects, see the results of an international scholarly conference (September 2021): "Mizhnarodna naukova konferentsiia 'Pam'iat' Babynoho Iaru i Holokostu" and the comporative analysis by Vitalii Nakhmanovych, "Kontseptsiia kompleksnoï memorializatsiï Babynoho Iaru ta proekt Memorial'noho tsentru Holokostu 'Babyn Iar': porivnial'nyi analiz," *Ukraïns'kyi istorychnyi zhurnal*, LXV, 6 (Kyiv, 2021), pp. 197-199.

13 See the report by Josef Zisels, co-president of VAAD (Association of Jewish Organizations and Communities of Ukraine), "What is Happening around Babyn Yar Today?, 2.IX.2018"; "Ukraïns'ki ievreï vdruhe zvernulysia do hromadians'koho suspil'stva," in *Dyskusiia*, 24 December 2020; and "Appeal of [160] Ukrainian Jews living in Ukraine, Israel, Canada, the Netherlands, Germany, Poland, Russia, the United States, France, and the Czech Republic to the Civil Society of Ukraine, October 2020," copies in the Toronto Chair Archive.

ing Russian ideological influence over the Babyn Yar memorialization, expressed adamant opposition to the Russian project.[14] The most representative of diaspora organizations took sides, with the World Jewish Congress chairman (Ronald Lauder) seeking to find accommodation with the Russian project, and the World Ukrainian Congress chairman (Paul Grod) pledging support and funding for an alternative Ukrainian project.[15]

What about the new government leadership in Ukraine? To be sure, Russia's invasion of Ukraine on 24 February 2022 became a profound turning point in modern Ukrainian history. In that context, it is necessary to note that there was President Zelenskyi *before* February 24 and President Zelenskyi *after* February 24. Already before the start of the second phase of the war, Zelenskyi accepted the principle that any memorialization at Babyn Yar should be carried out as a joint venture of the state and the private sector. It was never made clear, however, as to how much control either party had over the conceptualization and implementation of any future project. To be sure the BYHMC certainly had enough financing to pay for the entire memorialization.[16] Whether because of conviction or because of practical realism, Zelenskyi, with the encouragement of his closest advisors (in particular the presidential Chief of Staff Andrii Yermak) favored the BYHMC "Russian project." For its part, the Kyiv City Council was opposed to the property demands of

14 Petition addressed to President Zelenskyi, Prime Minister Denys Shmigal, and Mayor of Kyiv Vitalii Klychko: "Zvernennia, 25.V.2020"—English translation in *Krytyka* (Kyiv), https://krytyka.com/en/articles/ukrainian-cultural-and-academic-communitys-appeal-commemoration-babyn-yar. See also the petition of the Ukrainian Catholic University in L'viv: "Zvernennia Ukraïns'koho Katolyts'koho Universitetu shchodo sytuatsiï dovkola memoriializatsiï Babynoho Iaru, 15.VI.2021," copies in the Toronto Chair Archive.

15 "Memorandum of Cooperation Between the Government of Ukraine and the Ukrainian World Congress," signed 10 December 2020; "UWC pledges support [$20M] for National Babyn Yar Memorial Project," Ukrainian World Congress Media Release, 5 August 2021, copies in the Toronto Chair Archive.

16 The BYHMC general director Maxim Yakover reported that by mid-2020 their project had already spent $14 million dollars during the preparatory stage and that the total outlay of expenses would likely be $100 million. Results of the BYHMC board meeting 11 July 2020, Babyn Yar Memory Place website.

the Russian project, but not so Mayor Klychko. Consequently, the Zelenskyi government concluded a memorandum of agreement (July 2021) with BYHMC project.[17]

All the efforts of the Academy of Sciences Historical Institute with the help of the Ukrainian Institute of National Remembrance seemed for naught. After all, the Historical Institute had originally been commissioned to do its work by Zelenskyi's now forgotten and actually disgraced predecessor, Petro Poroshenko (subjected to a government-inspired lawsuit).

The 80th Anniversary of the 1941 massacre prompted a new flurry of activity on the eve of the commemorative date, 29-30 September 2021. The Ukrainian Institute of National Remembrance, whose director Anton Drobovych was an outspoken supporter of the Ukrainian project, organized a solemn commemorative ceremony on the evening of 29 September, the first day on which Jews were shot dead.[18]

Meanwhile, the Russian project had originally planned to complete its Babyn Yar Holocaust Memorial Center by the time of the 80th Anniversary. Although that goal was not achieved, it did manage to erect some "interactive" monuments and to stage in early October a Khrzhanovskii "transformative" performance.[19] Even more significant was the government's decision through its Ministry of Culture taken on the last day of 2021 to lease the only remaining historic building on the grounds of Babyn Yar (the former office/*kontora* of the Jewish Cemetery) to the

17 "Memorandum pro partnerstvo mizh Ministerstvom osvity ta nauky Ukraïny ta 'Blahodiinyi fond Memorial Holokostu Babyn Iar', 15.VI.2021," copy in the Toronto Chair Archive.

18 The National Remembrance Institute, in cooperation with the Academy of Science's Institute of the History of Ukraine and the Ukrainian World Congress, issued for the occasion a handsome guidebook in English and Ukrainian: *Babyn Yar 80 Years—Informational and Reference Material* (Kyïv, 2021).

19 Because of its controversial nature, the "event" provoked extensive coverage in the world press; select examples include: Maria Varenikova and Andrew E. Kramer, "A Tech-Savvy Holocaust Memorial in Ukraine Draws Critics and Crowds," *The New York Times*, 5 October 2021; David L. Stern, "In Ukraine, plans for the world's largest Holocaust memorial complex can't escape modern feuds," *The Washington Post*, 6 October 2021; Liza Rozovsky, "Marina Abramovic Has Healed From her Own Art, Now She's Healing Visitors to Babi Yar," *Haartz* (Jerusalem), 21 October 2021.

Babyn Yar Holocaust Memorial Center, which promised to create an "innovative museum" by 2026 at the latest.[20]

Then came 24 February 2022 and Russia's invasion of Ukraine. Everything changed. The leading financial backers of the Russian project (Fridman, Khan, Fuks) were soon publicly compromised.[21] In such circumstances, one might assume that neither President Zelenskyi's or any subsequent government would allow a project connected in anyway with Russia to operate in Ukraine. And yet, as the Russian-Ukrainian war raged on, President Zelenskyi met in October 2022 with the chairman of the Babyn Yar Holocaust Memorial Center (BYHMC) Natan Sharansky, the chairman of the World Jewish Congress Ron Lauder, former US Senator Joe Liberman, the last of the original five oligarch financial backers Viktor Pinchuk, and one of Ukraine's chief rabbis, Yaakov Dov Bleich.[22] Urged by his closest advisor Andrii Yermak, the president reaffirmed his support for the implementation of the Russian project. He made it clear that "we [the Ukrainian government] have not forgotten and we definitely must realize this [BYHMC Russian] project."[23]

Despite the government's on-going inclination toward the Russian project, the Historical Institute's Ukrainian project remains a viable alternative whenever Ukraine returns to a modicum of peace and stability.[24] Since that is not likely to occur soon, one must—however sadly—repeat the words of Vitalii Nakhmanovych: that "even such a distinguished place of memory as Babyn Yar" has still not been commemorated "in a worthy manner."[25]

---

20 "'Babyn Iar'—prorosiis'komu pryvatnomu tsentru," *Homin Ukraïny* (Toronto), 18.I.2022, p. 12.

21 See above, note 4.

22 https://www.president.gov.ua/news/zaraz-nadzvichajno-vazhlivo-zahishati-lyudyanist-i-posilyuva-78725

23 https://tsn.ua/politika/memorialu-golokostu-babin-yar-zelenskiy-rozpoviv-scho-bude-dali-z-realizaciyeyu-proyektu-2187865.html

24 Belatedly, and at the time as a seemingly symbolic gesture, the "defeated" Ukrainian project was described in a beautifully illustrated large format 32-page brochure released and published by the National Academy of Sciences Institute of the History of Ukraine: *Kontseptsiia memorializatsiï Babynoho Iaru—prospekt* (Kyiv: In-t istoriï Ukraïny NANU, 2022).

25 See above, Chapter 13, p. 416.

# Illustration Sources and Credits

50th anniversary of the Babyn Yar tragedy. Photographs by Shimon Redlich (Private archive).

A. Rybachuk and V. Melnychenko. *Babyn Yar: Knyha-rekviiem, knyha pam'iatnyk*. Kyiv: Ukrinform, 1991.

Art Gallery of the Kyiv Polytechnical Institute (works of Hryhorii Synytsia). http:// boryviter.etnoua.info/novyny/hryhorij-synytsya-halereya-tvoriv/.

*Babi Yar: Chelovek, vlast', istoriia: Dokumenty i materialy*. Vol. 1. Compiled by Tatiana Evstaf'eva and Vitalii Nakhmanovich. Kyiv: Vneshtorgizdat Ukrainy, 2004.

Babyn Yar Civic Committee. http://www.kby.kiev.ua/komitet/ru/reserve/art00082. html.

Center for Research on the History and Culture of East European Jewry, National University of Kyiv-Mohyla Academy. Collection of archival documents, posters, and posters.

Faces of Babi Yar in Felix Lembersky's Art: Presence and Absence. fmwww.bc.edu/SL-V/LemberskyEhrenburgBabiYar2011.pdf.

Gold, Hernadii (Herman), (artist). http://www.liveinternet.ru/users/seniorin/post368317466/.

*Ievreis'ka tematyka v tvorakh khudozhnykiv Kyieva: Zhyvopys, hrafika, skul'ptura, instaliatsiia; Kataloh tvoriv*. N.p., 2001.

*Istoricheskaia topografiia: Khronologiia sobytii*. Kyiv: Vneshtorgizdat Ukrainy, 2004.

Karakis, Iosyf. karakys.narod.ru/index2.html.

Kleiner, Ilya (artist). www.ikleiner.ru/gallery/holocost.

Kozakovskii, Yosef. *Konvoiruemye na kazn' (Babii Iar).* https://knesset.gov.il/birthday/ru/KnessetBuilding2_ru.html. *Kyïv: 1941–1943: Fotoal'bom.* Kyiv: Vydavnytstvo Kyi, 2000.

Nakhmanovich, Rafail. *Vozvrashchenie v sistemu, ili Martirolog meteka.* Kyiv: Feniks, 2013. National Art Museum of Ukraine (collection of paintings).

M. T. Rylsky Institute of Art, Folklore Studies, and Ethnology, National Academy of Sciences of Ukraine (Archive and full-scale sketches of Yurii Pavlovych).

Tartakovskii, Isaak (artist). http://isaak.tartakovsky.kiev.ua.

Tikhomirov, Aleksandr. "Ne predavaia zabveniiu." cultobzor.ru/2013/10/aleksandr-tihomirov/14-227/.

Tkuma Ukrainian Institute for Holocaust Studies. Collection of newspapers, posters, and photographs.

Ukrainian Center for Holocaust Studies. Collection of children's drawings.

Zviagin, Mikhail. "Moe iskusstvo ne dlia slabonervnykh, a dlia mysliashchykh." www.borisrubin.com/2014/03/01.

# INDEX